The New Apostolic Reformation

ALSO BY JOHN WEAVER

*The Failure of Evangelical Mental Health Care:
Treatments That Harm Women, LGBT Persons
and the Mentally Ill* (McFarland, 2015)

*Evangelicals and the Arts in Fiction:
Portrayals of Tension in Non-Evangelical Works
Since 1895* (McFarland, 2013)

The New Apostolic Reformation

History of a Modern Charismatic Movement

JOHN WEAVER

McFarland & Company, Inc., Publishers
Jefferson, North Carolina

LIBRARY OF CONGRESS CATALOGUING-IN-PUBLICATION DATA

Names: Weaver, John, 1980– author.
Title: The new apostolic reformation : history of a modern charismatic movement / John Weaver.
Description: Jefferson, North Carolina : McFarland & Company, Inc., Publishers, 2016. | Includes bibliographical references and index.
Identifiers: LCCN 2016008317 | ISBN 9780786499564 (softcover : acid free paper) ∞
Subjects: LCSH: Church. | Apostolate (Christian theology) | Pentecostalism. | Church renewal.
Classification: LCC BV601.7 .W43 2016 | DDC 270.8/3—dc23
LC record available at http://lccn.loc.gov/2016008317

BRITISH LIBRARY CATALOGUING DATA ARE AVAILABLE

ISBN (print) 978-0-7864-9956-4
ISBN (ebook) 978-1-4766-2421-1

© 2016 John Weaver. All rights reserved

No part of this book may be reproduced or transmitted in any form or by any means, electronic or mechanical, including photocopying or recording, or by any information storage and retrieval system, without permission in writing from the publisher.

Front cover image © 2016 Igor Zhuravlov

Printed in the United States of America

McFarland & Company, Inc., Publishers
 Box 611, Jefferson, North Carolina 28640
 www.mcfarlandpub.com

To William M. Barto, for inspiring my love of history.
You are missed.
To Rachel Weaver, who will always be my favorite sister.
And to David Weaver, in the hope that he will always be
the Last Frankenstein!

Acknowledgments

There are several people I wish to thank for help on this book. First, a big thanks must go out to Bruce Wilson and Rachel Tabachnick, who answered numerous questions over a period of many months. My friend Andrea Davis looked at an early stage of the manuscript and provided valuable comments. As always, thanks must go to Chelsea, Sean, Sarah, and Tanya, who provided the impetus for much of this research. Cindy Kunsman, as always, gave me both great feedback and good inside information on current happenings in the evangelical subculture. My friends Josh Lewis and Mikhail Gofman provided much needed encouragement, as did my former dissertation director Gayle Whittier. I also wish to thank Kathryn Joyce for commissioning an article on the Templeton Foundation toward the tail-end of this project. The article not only provided me with much needed funds for research, but also allowed me to finesse my understanding of the Foundation's relationship with the NAR. Kathryn's critique of my writing was also immensely useful; my style, to put it mildly, has always bordered on "King James verbosity," and Kathryn's suggestions on how to implement more concise arguments were wonderfully instructive. I also wish to thank my entire family for putting up with me over many months of writing and proofreading.

Table of Contents

Acknowledgments	vi
Preface	1
Introduction	5
1. From Parham to Bickle: The Origins of the NAR	19
2. Spiritual Mapping and the NAR	70
3. The Apostolic Networks: A Brief Rundown of a Few of the Major Players	94
4. NAR Economic Ideas: Marketplace Ministers, the Great Wealth Transfer and the Dangerous Economic Eccentricities of the Charismatic Right	144
5. The NAR and Race: When Race Isn't Race (But Is)	170
6. From the Others of the Americas to the Others Overseas: The NAR's Global Campaign for Reconciliation and Identificational Repentance	188
Conclusion: Where Does the NAR Go from Here?	254
List of Abbreviations	259
Glossary	261
Chapter Notes	269
Works Cited	273
Index	301

Preface

This book originated in an odd way. When I entered graduate school in 2006, I was unaware of the New Apostolic Reformation (NAR), despite specializing in evangelical studies. This lack of awareness was typical of many scholars during the period. The few scholars that had heard of this movement dismissed its existence as the product of left-wing paranoia, or alternately as a fringe group whose existence was largely confined to extremists like Becky Fischer, star of the expose *Jesus Camp* (2006). At the time I saw *Jesus Camp*, I dismissed the documentary's participants as a fringe movement.

Fast forward two and a half years. In the fall of 2008, I began blogging about a "deliverance ministry" called Mercy Ministries. Deliverance ministries are exorcism ministries that are ubiquitous throughout much of evangelical culture (particularly among Charismatics and Pentecostals) (see Cuneo 44). Mercy Ministries was among the worst examples of such exorcism practice in the West. As I have documented extensively in my book *The Failure of Evangelical Mental Health Care: Treatments that Harm Women, LGBT Persons, and the Mentally Ill* (2014), Mercy Ministries became notorious for its exorcism of mentally ill, sexually traumatized, and LGBT individuals (Weaver 95); so notorious was this ministry that it was expelled from Australia due to a massive public backlash, in which I played a part. My experience of researching Mercy Ministries eventually led me to the theoretical material undergirding their beliefs, including the exorcism manual *Restoring the Foundations*.

As I began researching for *The Failure of Evangelical Mental Health Care*, my research led me to connect the dots and see that Mercy Ministries was just a small cog in a network of churches, deliverance ministries, and "apostolic networks" that fall under the moniker of the NAR. The NAR is a movement dedicated to the restoration of the so-called fivefold gospel of Ephesians, in which the roles of apostles, and prophets in particular, are restored to the modern evangelical church. Given the movement's Charismatic character, these roles are also accompanied by an increasing emphasis on the "prophetic" (words of knowledge) and on divine healing.

The NAR has promoted projects ranging from Operation Ice Castle, a 20,000-foot climb up Mount Everest to do territorial spiritual warfare against the "Queen of Heaven" demonic entity (Wagner, *Confronting the Queen* 37) to a call by one of its more conservative members, Rick Joyner, for a coup against President Obama ("Rick Joyner Praying for Military Coup Over Obama"). NAR apostle Kimberly Daniels, who was elected to the Jacksonville City Council, has promoted the idea that demonic curses can be transferred to children via trick-or-treating, and more seriously has advanced the anti–Semitic notion that "the Jews own everything." Another apostle in the movement, Jim Ammerman, promoted New World Order conspiracy theories (Daniels; Besen; Tabachnick, "Col. Jim Ammerman"). One of the leading apostles of the movement, Cindy Jacobs, has suggested that the mass deaths of some birds may be linked to the repeal of the military's "Don't Ask, Don't Tell" policy (Mantyla, "Jacobs: Birds Are Dying").[1]

The average reader might be inclined to think that such extremism means that these figures cannot be taken seriously or do not represent the mainstream of a religious movement. Yet in the U.S. alone, if movement leader C. Peter Wagner is to be believed, the movement accounts for at least 8 to 10 million adherents (Wagner, *Churchquake!* 8). The larger Third Wave Pentecostal movement as a whole, of which the NAR is a large part, is estimated to have included over 295 million people worldwide as of 2000 (Synan 404). While not all Third Wavers fall into the new apostolic paradigm, it is undeniable that a large percentage of modern Charismatic churches do fit into that model. Some of the Charismatic movement's most popular preachers, such as Mike Bickle, Bill Johnson and John Arnott, follow New Apostolic teachings (see Chapters 1 and 3 on this) and their views are no less extreme than those I have mentioned above. Indeed, Cindy Jacobs, Kimberly Daniels, and Rick Joyner all represent mainstream thought in the NAR. The NAR, more than any Charismatic or evangelical movement previous to it, is trying to reinsert supernatural agency into all spheres of American life, from politics to healthcare, and it is the movement's quasi-magical theology that makes it a cause for concern.

Even for a former evangelical insider like myself, the beliefs of the NAR were so perplexing that after reading several books by movement authors and consulting the best source then available on the subject, René Holvast's *Spiritual Mapping in the United States and Argentina 1989–2005: A Geography of Fear* (2009), I was at a loss. I needed a tutor, one who could explain to me the inner workings of this new form of "doing" church.

The tutor I found was PRA Associate Fellow Rachel Tabachnick. Over the course of many months and countless phone calls and discussions, Tabachnick helped me navigate the imposing amount of material the NAR had produced. Like Tabachnick, I was stupefied that the mainstream media, while not oblivious to the NAR, did not cover it with any depth. Academia, thanks to a number of Pentecostal and Charismatic-friendly scholars, was speaking of the NAR as a forward thinking, socially progressive movement, an interpretation so contrary to the actual facts-on-the-ground that it eventually led me to distrust contemporary scholarship on the Charismatic movement. As this book will demonstrate, that mistrust is well-founded.

The actual text of this book came together quickly, but it was the byproduct of over a year of research into the Charismatic and Pentecostal movement, spiritual mapping, and Charismatic deliverance practices. It represents, along with Sean McCloud's *American Possessions* (2015), one of the first widely available American critiques of the NAR. McCloud's work centers on, among other things, the NAR's relationship to neoliberalism, a goal not necessarily in contradiction with my own ("Sean McLoud: Associate Professor"). My own approach, in any case, is more concerned with framing the NAR within the larger historical context of the Pentecostal and Charismatic movements. As such, it will represent the first overarching history of the NAR, and after McCloud's work, the second analytic work devoted to exploring NAR ideology.

Almost nothing of any scholarly value has been written on the NAR. Margaret Poloma's and Candy Gunther Brown's scholarship makes frequent reference to new apostolic networks, but as the reader will see, there is every reason to doubt the veracity and objectivity of both of these scholars' analyses. The coverage of the NAR in *The International Dictionary of Pentecostal Charismatic Movements* (2002) is so lackluster that it allowed the NAR's proverbial leader, C. Peter Wagner, to write the entry describing the very movement he did so much to advance (Wagner, "New Apostolic Reformation" 930). This lack of commitment to scholarly integrity unfortunately characterizes almost all contemporary Charismatic scholarship on the NAR, though decent scholarship can still be found about non–NAR related Charismatic and Pentecostal beliefs (Grant Wacker is a good example in this regard).

Nevertheless, there are a few sources of particular value to understanding the NAR. The one absolutely essential source I would argue is the aforementioned *Spiritual Mapping in the United States and Argentina 1989–2005: A Geography of Fear*. Holvast's work stands above all other scholarship on the NAR and Third-Wave Pentecostalism. Although Holvast only treats the NAR in its current form rather briefly, he extensively explores the spiritual mapping ideology that helped give birth to it. For people trying to understand the movement, Holvast's work is indispensable. A few other works are also notable for their quality. Stephen Hunt's scholarship is fairly sound on contemporary Charismatic history and is characterized by a refreshing lack of appeal to supernatural agents as explanatory factors for Charismatic spiritual and historical phenomena, appeals that one still sees *even in modern Charismatic academic historiography*. Roland Howard's *Charismania* (1997) documents important developments in British Charismatic circles in the 1980s and '90s. Many of those developments are important in contextualizing the NAR's appeal in the U.K, and despite Howard's godsploitation-like title, *Charismania* is sympathetic to the religious movement it studies. Marci McDonald's *The Armageddon Factor: The Rise of the Christian Right in Canada* (2010) is by far the smartest piece of investigative reporting on the NAR by any contemporary journalist. It is an important work for understanding the surprisingly prominent role radical Charismatic and Pentecostal theology have played in Canada since the Latter Rain revival of 1948.

This work is heavily reliant on a group of researchers known as Political Research Associates (PRA), of whom Rachel Tabachnick is a part. PRA is a social justice think tank founded by the late Jean Hardisty in 1981, which, among its accomplishments, has a long history of tracking religious right activism (McKenna). Most of the reliable information on the NAR that I found in researching this book, whether written for academia or the mass media, has been either produced by PRA staff or is heavily reliant on PRA research. By contrast, most non–PRA academic scholarship on the Charismatic movement was so tainted that it was unusable. This is not some byproduct of historical chance, but is the direct result of deliberate attempts to "spin" the NAR in as favorable a manner as possible. Every time I fact-checked the scholarship and research of PRA staff like Rachel Tabachnick, Kapya Kaoma or Fred Clarkson, their research was both accurate and meticulously documented. By contrast, gross scholarly distortions characterized much of the Charismatic-friendly scholarship I encountered, with the exception of Jürgen Römer. Thus I rely on the work of Tabachnick and Bruce Wilson of Truth Wins Out, the leading American experts on the NAR, as well as other left wing independent researchers, over academics; there is simply no other way of doing quality research on the NAR, given the state of Pentecostal/Charismatic studies today.

Nor should the readers take my comments here as being motivated out of prejudice towards the Charismatic community. My interactions with the Charismatic/Pentecostal community have been cordial throughout my entire life, and I greatly prefer the Charismatic movement to the Reformed movement that played a formative role in my own intellectual development. A source of concern for me in writing this book has been the pain it will cause my Charismatic friends. But perhaps, through pointing out the problems inherent in the New Apostolic paradigm, the evangelical church can see its way to promoting a truly democratic form of church polity.

Introduction

Because so much of the material I cover in the Preface and Introduction will have to be re-introduced in Chapter 1 and 2, I will settle herein for a fairly simple description of the New Apostolic Reformation, followed by chapter descriptions, a definition of terms, and a section about the state of contemporary scholarship on the Charismatic movement.

The Preface has made the case for why the NAR is an important theological movement. What is particularly important to understand for the context of this book is how potentially powerful the NAR's sway also is over conservative power politics. Between 2008 and 2012, no less than three major political candidates were either directly affiliated with the NAR (Michelle Bachmann and Sarah Palin) or aligned themselves with major new apostolic figures (Rick Perry) (Tabachnick, "Spiritual Warriors").

New Apostolic churches[1] are grouped into what are called "apostolic networks." Evangelical churches in the U.S. have traditionally had democratic leadership structures, either established through congregational vote or via elected deacons or elders (Tabachnick, "Spiritual Warriors"). However, since the 1970s, as Chapters 1 and 2 will establish, those Charismatics and Pentecostals who subscribe to the New Apostolic model have been moving from this democratic model to one in which power is transferred from democratic church institutions to NAR apostles, leaders in the movement who are seen as having special spiritual gifts that make them fit for leadership. These leaders provide what is known as "apostolic covering" for their followers, which is seen as a form of spiritual protection and "cover" against "demonic" attack (Tabachnick, "Spiritual Warriors"). Chapter 1 argues that despite modern Charismatic claims to the contrary, much of the modern apostolic church structure has uncanny similarities with an extreme form of 1970s Christian discipleship known as shepherding, which was widely seen by many evangelicals at the time as being an abusive practice, yet whose true history has largely been erased by Charismatic hagiographers of the shepherding movement.

Within the NAR, apostles and prophets are seen as being chosen by God. This chosenness is often proven through prophecy. Unlike traditional evangelicals, NAR apostles claim to receive "extra-biblical revelation," a fact that has made their movement controversial among cessationist evangelicals who believe the age of miracles has ceased. These NAR claims eventually resulted in a 2013 conference, "Strange Fire," hosted by Reformed pastor John MacArthur; the conference was a cessationist broadside directly at the NAR and garnered widespread attention in the evangelical media (Tabachnick, "Spiritual Warriors"; see also Barnhart). The NAR also promotes the aforementioned "restoration of the fivefold gospel" based off a verse in the New Testament book of Ephesians. This message is predicated on the restoration of the role of church apostles and prophets in the modern age (Tabachnick, "Spiritual Warriors"). Most NAR material sees the restoration of the fivefold gospel as providing the foundation for the restoration of ever more miraculous powers on the part of the church and its adherents. Some quasi-racialist manifestations of this idea will be explored in Chapter 5.

The reasons for, and the extent of, the NAR's success will be documented throughout the rest of the book. One crucial point should be made up front: The networking system that the NAR set up was an extremely adaptable system that could not only work across, but often simply bypass, traditional denominational distinctions. An Apostle or Prophet, for instance, might lead several churches/ministries, all of different denominations, or more likely, given the often non-denominational characteristics of the movement, across churches/ministries of vastly differing theologies. What is more fascinating for secular outsiders is that the NAR based its widely successful growth strategies on a combination of Pentecostal experientialism, focused on demonic combat and healing, with a pragmatic application of the social sciences to the problem of retaining and enlarging church membership rolls. The movement's phenomenally successful application of these concepts will be explored throughout the book, but particularly in Chapter 1.

Chapter 1 begins the story of this book. Here I provide an extensive overview of the history of the Pentecostal/Charismatic movement. I briefly touch on Pentecostal origins, as the debate over whether William James Seymour or Charles Parham is the true founder of Pentecostalism is of some interest to the story of the NAR. I will contend that, for the NAR, at least, Parham is the more influential figure. I will then explore the influence of the Latter Rain revival and the teachings of William Branham on the development of modern Charismatic beliefs. A crucial contention here is that both the Latter

Rain revival and Branham's influence tend to be underplayed by establishment Pentecostal and Charismatic historians, because, as in the case of Parham, neither the Latter Rain revival nor Branham do much to improve the world's image of the Pentecostal movement.

After these sections, I explore the Charismatic Renewal movement and its relationship to shepherding, both of which provide a context for understanding the modern Charismatic movement. Next, I explore what may seem a separate phenomenon—the development of the church growth movement at Fuller Seminary. It would be the church growth movement's fusion with Pentecostal healing and deliverance practices, mainly through the influence of John Wimber and C. Peter Wagner that would propel the apostolic and prophetic movement to prominence in the '80s and '90s. The chapter finally looks at the ministry of Wimber, a crucial figure in the history of Charismatic practice and delves into the controversial group known as the Kansas City Prophets.

Chapter 2 explores the practice of spiritual mapping and continues the narrative of the NAR's history that started in Chapter 1. Utilizing the scholarship of René Holvast, Chapter 2 looks at both spiritual mapping practice and theory. Chapter 3 then looks at a number of the most influential apostolic networks. Particular attention is paid to three of the largest and most easily traceable networks: Revival Alliance, which was birthed out of the Toronto Blessing; the International Coalition of Apostles (ICA); and the Morningstar Network. Stylistic differences between the networks are noted. A major argument in this chapter is that though the apostolic networks aim for similar objectives, each network tends to brand itself in slightly different ways.

Chapter 4 looks at the NAR's economic philosophy, paying particular attention to the concept known as the Great Wealth Transfer in which the world's money is going to be transferred to the people of God (a.k.a. Christians). Other NAR socioeconomic ideas, notably its now famous 7-Mountains campaign of dominionist national takeover and a new and highly evolved form of NAR economic philosophy called transformationalism, will be explored. This chapter will also highlight the relationship between Christian Reconstructionism, a movement steeped in Reformed cessationist Calvinism, and the NAR. Finally, Chapter 4 will explore how certain ideas that are mainstreamed in evangelicalism today—non-NAR derived "transformationalism" and the Business as Missions Paradigm (BAM)—play directly into the economic and political agenda of the NAR, and show considerable evidence of NAR influence.

Chapter 5 takes a look at how the NAR conceptualizes race. Though the NAR is ostensibly dedicated to eradicating racism, it tends to re-racialize theology in truly bizarre ways, most notably through such concepts as "spiritual DNA" and the idea of a "church race" in which racial identity is based not on skin color, nor ethnic identity, but on church membership (for examples, see Hamon, *Prophetic Scriptures* 77).

Chapter 6 provides an overview of the NAR's influence overseas, while critiquing how the NAR's racial views affect its interaction with both Western peoples and people in the developing world. The abuse of indigenous cultures in NAR theology is especially noted, as is the movement's promotion of dangerously ideological provocations in the Middle East. The chapter concludes with a description of six countries on five different continents and how the NAR has affected their cultures, sometimes moderately (as in Australia), but usually profoundly (in the case of Uganda, Canada, and Guatemala).

The conclusion focuses on the continued need for scholarly vigilance in dealing with influence of the NAR. It notes especially the need for a more theologically literate reaction to Charismatic and Pentecostal culture that seeks neither to glorify nor too hastily condemn Pentecostal spiritual practice.

Definitions of Evangelicalism

One of the favored definitions for evangelicalism is advanced by British historian D.W. Bebbington. Bebbington outlines four distinguishing characteristics of evangelical belief: "conversionism, the belief that lives need to be changed; activism, the expression of the gospel in effort; biblicism, a particular regard for the Bible and what may be called crucicentrism, a stress on the sacrifice of Christ on the cross" (Bebbington 2–3). Although Bebbington's work in evangelical studies is valuable, this definition questionably privileges right-wing explanations of evangelical belief. The biblicist element, in particular, does not seem relevant to a modern evangelicalism that is starting to form both conservative and liberal forms of postmodernist scriptural critique that question the traditional evangelical literalist hermeneutic. Bebbington's definition also ignores the significant similarities that historically have existed between traditional evangelicalism and mainline Protestantism.

Similarly, as I have argued in *Evangelicals and the Arts in Fiction* (2013), denominational definitions are a problematic tool for defining evangelicals. Many denominations have both evangelical and mainline wings, ranging from the Mennonites to the Southern Baptists. Also, even groups which are traditionally thought of as mainline denominations have large evangelical wings (see Sweeney 19). Since denominational identities are not fixed, the historical time period in which one is looking at is also important to understanding whether a denomination is evangelical. For instance, the denominational ancestors of the United Churches of Christ would have arguably been considered evangelical during the early nineteenth century, but not today. Fixed denominational definitions of evangelical belief therefore simply do not work (Weaver, *Evangelicals and the Arts in Fiction* 11).

I therefore personally have come to prefer, with a few caveats, the system offered up by Fritz Detwiler. Detwiler divides the religious right into six parts (one of which is Catholicism). The five major divisions of evangelical belief that Detwiler argues for are fundamentalists, Holiness, Pentecostal/charismatic, born-again evangelicals (which in this work are referred to as neo-evangelicals) and Reformed Christians (Detwiler 150–155). Fundamentalism is a theological movement originally characterized by its opposition to theological modernism and evolutionary theory (Marsden 3–4). Holiness Christianity is notable mainly for the primacy it places on the pietistic life as the mark of true Christian behavior (Detwiler 152). Neo-evangelicalism is largely distinguishable from fundamentalism, its spiritual progenitor, by a greater willingness to embrace a diversity of hermeneutical viewpoints concerning Scripture, and by a tendency to try to engage with culture, instead of fight against it.

Reformed Christianity is a theological system that is much too complex to simply and neatly define. However, in popular evangelical usage today, it typically refers to those evangelicals who draw their theological inspiration from the "teachings of John Calvin" (Detwiler 154), or, much more rarely, one of the other early Reformed leaders, such as Guillaume Farel. Opponents of Reformed Christianity often simplify its core doctrines to simply a belief in predestination or the famous, and frequently misused, TULIP designation (Total depravity, Unconditional election, Limited atonement, Irresistible grace, and Perseverance of the saints). However, Reformed beliefs go beyond such simplifications. As Molly Worthen notes, the Reformed tradition focused on "the depravity of humankind, the awesome sovereignty of God, and the Christian mandate to transform earthly society according to God's command" (Worthen, *Apostles of Reason* Loc 276). Central to most modern Reformed thought (outside of now mainline Reformed denominations), is a strong belief in the value of pastoral care, a firm belief in the value of church discipline, and a preoccupation with correct ecclesiology. Although the story of the NAR is mainly the story of Charismatic and Pentecostal beliefs, one should not ignore the Reformed movement's interactions with Charismatic Christianity. Although longtime critics of Charismatic Christianity, certain elements of Reformed Christianity have been willing to make tactical alliances with Charismatics and Pentecostals in recent years.

The Emergent church, not much referenced herein, is a liberal body of evangelicals distinguished from other left-wing evangelicals mainly by a devotion to a postmodernist, usually non-literalist reading of scripture (Weaver, *Evangelicals and the Arts in Fiction* 193–194). Another ill-defined group of evangelicals, the seeker-sensitive church movement, has no set denominational affiliation, but concentrates mainly on gaining new followers and creating massive megachurches. As a general rule, if seeker-sensitive churches do have a denominational or theological leaning, it is to the Word of Faith movement (Prosperity Gospel), which has its roots in Charismatic teaching, or to the Third Wave Charismatic movement, whose most influential contemporary figure is C. Peter Wagner.

The one significant difference between this work's definition of evangelicalism and the one presented in *Evangelicals and the Arts in Fiction* is that it contends the difference between Charismatic and Pentecostal belief (two theological systems characterized by a devotion to the "gifts of the spirit") is much larger than most scholars have previously realized. In popular evangelical *lingua franca*, churches are often labeled Charismatic as a means of denoting them from what many see as the more extreme Pentecostal brand of Christianity. In fact, if one looks into the history of the Charismatic movement as it has developed over the last fifty years, the opposite image emerges. While the initial impetus towards Charismatic belief arose in mainline Protestantism during the 1960s and was therefore seen by some as a liberal alternative to the then disreputable mainstream Pentecostal churches, the Charismatic Renewal became increasingly hardline over the course of its existence. When the Renewal eventually hit non-mainline churches—that is mainstream evangelicalism—it would morph into what is commonly called the Third Wave of Pentecostalism. This wave, in turn, would evolve into the NAR, which would bypass traditional Pentecostal denominational hierarchies in favor of a top down system of almost dictatorial control on the part of certain "apostolic" leaders.

A plethora of terminology is used to describe the Pentecostal and Charismatic movement. The difference between Charismatics and Pentecostals is important to understand, but the problem is the difference is often irrelevant to the actual spiritual and political practice of the two groups. In addition, there is a huge overlap between classical (traditional denominationally based) Pentecostalism and the Charismatic movement, particularly in many Third Wave Charismatic churches. Nor is the scholarship on Pentecostal and Charismatic terminology very helpful. Much of the scholarship on Third Wave Pentecostals for instance, emphasizes the Third Wave movement's rather restrained character. C. Peter Wagner, for instance, has characterized the movement's "acceptance of tongues" as "low-key" and has said the movement avoids "divisiveness at almost any cost" (Wagner, "Third Wave" 1141). Yet anyone with any knowledge of the contemporary Charismatic movement knows that the most radical theology coming out of the movement today either originated in the Third Wave or was adopted by the Third Wave from First Wave (classic Pentecostal) and Second Wave (Charismatic Renewal) Charismatics.

Far from being apolitical, the Third Wave represents a far more aggressively political, even theocratic, form of Charismatic practice than ever dreamed about by classical Pentecostals. One of the major contentions of this work, particularly in Chapter 1, is that classical Pentecostals have received an inexcusable level of blame on the part of non–Charismatic/Pentecostal evangelicals, non-classical Pentecostal Charismatics and secular critics alike for theologically and politically aberrant doctrines that are mainly a byproduct of more modern and extremist forms of Pentecostal and Charismatic belief than that practiced by classical Pentecostals.

There is no good way to refer to Pentecostal belief as a whole. The use of the term Charismatic/Pentecostal is too unwieldy, and while Margaret Poloma's abbreviation of that to C/P in *Main Street Mystics* (Poloma, *Main Street Mystics* passim) is serviceable, I have found that its usage tends to jar the reading of a text. I therefore have typically used the term Charismatic to refer to the movement as a whole, Pentecostal to refer specifically to classical and denominational Pentecostalism, and Charismatic Renewal to refer to the second wave of the Charismatic movement. When needed, I have also used the term Third Wave Charismatic, the rubric under which the majority of NAR adherents would fall.

A Note on Charismatic Terminology

Before proceeding to Chapter 1, I should introduce some broadly used terms within the Charismatic movement that are useful to understanding the movement as a whole. I also provide a glossary at the back that the reader can flip back to for information on these terms as well.

Glossolalia, better known by most people as "speaking in tongues," is a "religious phenomenon of making sounds that constitute or resemble a language not known to the speaker" (Splitter 670). While current linguistic analysis suggests that glossolalia is not in any meaningful sense a language (Samarin 127–128), glossolalia is a religious phenomenon of immense spiritual importance to many Charismatics, one that this work has no intention of belittling.

Deliverance is defined in this text as a form of Charismatic exorcism. James Collins, one of the two leading experts on deliverance ministry within the evangelical movement, distinguishes between exorcism, which is more of a *"sacramental* rite" (italics in original) aimed primarily at those who are possessed, whereas deliverance is a "less formal" process aimed at those who suffer from "demonization" as opposed to possession (Collins 4). This requires a little elaboration. Demonization is a term, widely used among deliverance proponents, which argues that while a Christian cannot be demonically possessed or owned, they can be demonically oppressed or inhabited (Collins 4). This distinction was popularized by two early Charismatic leaders of enormous importance, Derek Prince and Don Basham. It is vitally important to understand this distinction because it was what allowed deliverance ministries—that is Protestant exorcism ministries—to flourish in evangelicalism (see Cuneo 92–93). While true Christians could not be possessed by Satan in this system, they could be tormented or afflicted by him, including sometimes having their physical bodies or minds inhabited by demonic forces. The popularity of deliverance ministries after the birth of the Charismatic Renewal in the 1960s played a large part in the growth and eventual widespread influence of the NAR.

Another term commonly used among Charismatics and of major importance to understanding the movement's theology is generational curses. Generational curses, referred to sometimes as "intergenerational evil" or "congenital demonism" (see Cuneo 149), are curses/demons that are passed down the family line and inherited from ancestors, in a form of transmission that is almost pseudo-genetic. The ideological assumptions that are foundational for the idea of generational curses also are foundational in the idea of strategic level spiritual warfare (SLSW) and spiritual mapping that are described in Chapter 2. It is vitally important to understand that for many Charismatics, demonic inhabitation is tied to issues of heritage and lineage, in ways that may seem bizarre or quasi-racialist to non–Charismatics.

René Holvast argues that spiritual warfare is the "concept of a dualistic war between good and evil. It may also refer to a movement among Evangelicals with a special interest in one or a few of the many forms of expression of this concept" (Holvast 6). While technically spiritual warfare is a concern of all evangelical Christians, the doctrine is much more emphasized in Pentecostal and Charismatic circles than elsewhere. Within these circles, the belief that demons are literally battling Christians (or sometimes angels) is common, as the rest of this book will demonstrate. Strategic level spiritual warfare aims to "effect power encounters" that will essentially disempower territorial demonic spirits which hold possession over certain "social groups or geographical locations with which they are identified" (Collins 103). In short, it's spiritual warfare against demonic entities within a certain specific social group or geographical region.

Finally brief mention should be made of a group that will not appear much in this text: the Word of Faith (WOF) movement, or the prosperity gospel. The preferred term for this movement among Charismatics, though seldom used, is "Positive confession" theology. Strictly speaking, WOF represents simply one form of the prosperity gospel, though in practice it is by far the most widely disseminated today; this work uses the acronym WOF as a shorthand for the prosperity movement writ large (see Bowler loc 1240 on the varying usages of the term Word of Faith). The WOF movement teaches that followers can receive "physical healing, inner healing, freedom from demon oppression, and prosperity, in response to the 'word of faith'" (Synan 358). WOF teaching has been controversial in evangelical circles as a kind of get-rich-quick scheme, a "name it and claim it" theology, as some evangelicals call it (Synan 358–359). While there is some overlap between WOF teaching and the NAR, it is both beyond the scope of this book to trace that overlap and perhaps misleading to make too large a link between these two strains of Charismatic practice. While I am skeptical of the claims of WOF teachers, I am also mindful of Candy Gunther Brown's assertion that much of the health and wealth gospel has a particular appeal "for the poor and disenfranchised worldwide" (Brown, "Introduction" 17). While this work is not supportive of Brown's scholarship regarding the Charismatic movement, she is right to caution against a too-ready stereotyping of WOF adherents, a stereotyping that has too often taken on a classist and racist character in the estimation of this work.

A Note on Scholarship

This work seeks for painstaking accuracy in its account of the NAR. But the reader must understand that deciphering truth from fiction in the historical record concerning the NAR is a difficult process. First, not only is much of that record first person accounts by highly partisan supporters of the NAR, but also often is by equally partisan critics of the movement. This means that particularly with both the scholarship and first person accounts of Charismatic belief written by movement insiders or sympathizers, it is hard to tell what is factually accurate.

The worst examples of this scholarly trend are a number of scholars associated with the Templeton Foundation. Particularly noteworthy in this regard is the Flame of Love project, which received its support from a "grant award to the department of sociology at the University of Akron and the Institute for Research on Unlimited Love (IRUL) funded by the John Templeton Foundation" (Lee and Yong, "Preface" ix). The grant for this project totaled some

$2,326,362 ("The Flame of Love: Scientific Research on the Experience and Expression of Godly Love in the Pentecostal Tradition" Grant ID: 12490). Among the co-directors of the project and arguably its most key figure is Margaret Poloma ("Co-Directors"). Poloma is often portrayed as one of the leading sociologists examining Charismatic belief. What is less commonly emphasized is that Poloma (like a large number of scholars working in Pentecostal studies today) is herself Charismatic. Poloma's pastors, Jeff and Beth Metzger, were involved in the Toronto Blessing (Poloma, *Main Street Mystics* 11). Poloma has herself received praise from C. Peter Wagner, who has called her one of the "greatest born again kingdom minded sociologists that we have" (Wilson, "C. Peter Wagner Claims").

Poloma's scholarship is intimately tied to the NAR, despite her attempts to obfuscate this fact. In her Templeton-funded study *The Heart of Religion: Spiritual Empowerment, Benevolence and the Experience of God's Love* (2013), co-written by Matthew T. Lee and Stephen Post, Poloma characterized herself as shocked by an interviewee's acceptance of the politics of Lou Engle (specifically Engle's desire to shut down abortion clinics) which the book claims Poloma said was "not very loving from my position" (Lee, Poloma and Post 212). Yet Poloma's own *Main Street Mystics* (2003) spends a considerable amount of time promoting Engle's ministry, along with his ally and apostle Ché Ahn (Poloma, *Main Street Mystics* 173–181, 186–187). Ahn's ministry was birthed out of the Toronto Blessing by Poloma's own admission (Poloma, *Main Street Mystics* 173–181) and Poloma herself was an important player in the drama surrounding the Toronto Blessing, so much so that John Arnott, the man who had initiated the revival at Toronto, asked Poloma to intercede on his behalf with John Wimber, then leader of the Vineyard movement, which Poloma promptly did. Poloma ended up writing a four-page statement to Wimber noting her assessment of the revival, which she was afraid would be hurt by a breach between Wimber and Arnott (Poloma, *Main Street Mystics* 243). Given Wagner's regard for Poloma and Poloma's repeated involvement in the NAR, it is highly unlikely that Poloma's testimony about her "surprise" at New Apostolic beliefs has any validity.

The concept of Godly love, which is the centerpiece of the Flame of Love project, is the study within Christianity (later supposedly to be expanded to Islam and Judaism), of its "'Great Commandment' to love God and love neighbor as self" (Lee, Poloma and Post, "Introduction" 6). According to Poloma and company, this concept is "premised on the existence of 'exemplars' of Godly love—people who have lived out the Great Commandment to an unusual degree and have been recognized by their community for their benevolent acts" (Lee, Poloma and Post 7). What makes this point significant is how many of these exemplars are participants in the NAR. One of the chief exemplars is Ché Ahn ("Ché and Sue Ahn"), whose Call ministry while proclaiming its condemnation of the Ugandan "death for gays" bill, openly praised the bill while actually in Uganda (Kron). And Ahn is far from alone in his questionable choice of ways of expressing "Godly love." A similar case can be made about the various members of the Revival Alliance who make up elements of the study. No less than 5 of the 6 ministries associated with this important apostolic ("Revival Alliance"; "Exemplar biosketches") network have one or both of their leaders (all couples) listed as godly exemplars, including Ahn and his wife.

Then there is the research of Candy Gunther Brown. A Templeton-funded study that Brown conducted reported marvelous results of what she is called "proximal intercessory prayer" (Brown et al., "Study of the Therapeutic Effects of Proximal Intercessory Prayer" 864). Brown complained that previous studies of intercessory prayer had been poorly conducted, especially because one of the groups studied originated in the Unity Church, a group that differs significantly in theology from Pentecostalism (Brown et al., "Study of the Therapeutic Effects of Proximal Intercessory Prayer" 865; see also "John Templeteon Spiritually Rich"). However, rather than pick the subjects for her study at random, they were chosen directly out of a charismatic meeting being led by Iris Ministries and Global Awakening (Brown et al., "Study of the Therapeutic Effects of Proximal Intercessory Prayer" 865; Tabachnick, "Christian Right Antigay"). The latter group is led by Randy and DeAnne Clark; Randy Clark is an exemplar for the Flame of Love project, which funded the study (Brown et al., "Study of the Therapeutic Effects of Proximal Intercessory Prayer" 865; Poloma, *Great Commandment* 154). Even more troubling is the fact that Stephen Mory, one of the co-authors of the study, has himself been asked to be a public speaker at Randy Clark "ministry settings" that occurred before the study took place ("Instructors: Stephen Mory").

The study had no control group and was not double-blind (Brown et al., "Study of the Therapeutic Effects of Proximal Intercessory Prayer" 867). Its sample size was only 24 people (Brown et al., "Study of the Therapeutic Effects of Proximal Intercessory Prayer" 864). Brown and her fellow researchers suggest that future studies might have possible control groups that include "subjects receiving 'sham' PIP or Therapeutic Touch" (Brown et al., "Study of the Therapeutic Effects of Proximal Intercessory Prayer" 868). How one can possibly define what is sham prayer and real prayer, let alone differentiate between the two, is a question Brown apparently does not ask. Brown suggests that

> future study seems warranted to assess whether PIP may be a useful adjunct to standard medical care for certain patients with auditory and/or visual impairments, especially in contexts where access to conventional treatment is limited. The implications

are potentially vast given World Health Organization estimates that 278 million people, 80% of whom live in developing countries, have moderate to profound hearing loss in both ears, and 314 million people are visually impaired, 87% of whom live in developing countries, and only a tiny fraction of these populations currently receive any treatment [Brown et al., "Study of the Therapeutic Effects of Proximal Intercessory Prayer" 868].

Thus, Brown wants to use faith healing as an adjunct to "standard medical care" in the developing world, because without such care these individuals will continue to suffer from hearing and visual impairment. Indeed, so enamored was Brown with the concept of faith healing that she cooperated with Global Awakening, one of the apostolic networks involved in this study, in the formation of the Global Medical Research Institute (GMRI), an organization devoted to medically verifying healings (Clark 167–168).

When it comes to Pentecostal and Charismatic historians themselves, I found such historians constantly invoking the Holy Spirit as a historical phenomenon. For instance, take the relatively reputable Vinson Synan's description of the Azusa Street revival: "When someone would receive an anointing for a message, they would stand and preach. If they were acting out of the flesh they were soon convicted and sat back down. The power of God would flow through the room at different times knocking people down in ones, twos, and sometimes by the hundreds" (Synan 57). Yet how does Synan possibly know whether it is the power of God moving through that room? Such unskeptical language characterizes his whole approach to historiography, which essentially amounts to little more than cheerleading. Similarly, take historian S. David Moore's *The Shepherding Movement: Controversy and Charismatic Ecclesiology* (2003) whose acknowledgement section proclaims: "Words are inadequate to express my thanks to the Lord Jesus, who met me so many times and guided me in this project" (Moore acknowledgements). One could argue, of course, that such "Thank you Jesus" acknowledgement sections are ubiquitous in conservative Christian scholarship and do not necessarily imply scholastic bias. The problem is, the topic Moore writes about is a movement he was a former part of (Moore 8), and his approach to that movement, much like his approach to Christ, is based on faith, not argumentation. As I note in Chapter 1, Moore ignores a mountain of evidence that indicates a considerably more negative critique of shepherding than that presented in his book and his research often relies on the testimony of the Fort Lauderdale Five—that is the five leaders of the shepherding movement—when such testimony should be seriously questioned. Simply put, little research on Charismatic belief is trustworthy, as too often it is written by partisans of the movement.

As for the movement's critics, few have been scholars and many early works by critical academics on Charismatic religious practice were unenlightened, tending to myopically focus on WOF teachers and faith healing. Very little of the "popular" Christian critical literature finds its way into this book at all, other than a nodding reference to Charismatic pastor's Bill Randles's criticism of "spiritual elitism" in Chapter 1 and a passing reference to Steven Lambert's critiques of shepherding. In Randles's case I merely have adopted a concept, and in Lambert's case, I simply use his testimony to reinforce more reliable material. But I should note that while I do not find Randles or Lambert "reliable," that is the view I have of virtually every other Charismatic or ex–Charismatic source on the NAR, barring Jürgen Römer (and to a lesser degree, Nigel Scotland).

Some non–Charismatic evangelicals have written worthwhile histories or critiques of aspects of the Charismatic movement. Of these, outside of Holvast's excellent work, the best is Kenneth Horton's "The Vineyard Movement and Eschatology: An Interpretation" (1999). Horton's work remains one of the most objective and dispassionate accounts I was able to find on the history of the Vineyard and its relationship to Mike Bickle's Kansas City Fellowship (KCF), both movements which are of keen interest in the study of the NAR. Yet for every work of careful scholarship like this by non–Charismatic evangelicals, there are three or four tedious and bigoted accounts of Charismatic religion, usually by authors with no academic training. John MacArthur, for instance, has made a living off such attacks ever since the publication of his book *Charismatic Chaos* (1993).

Most of my documentation, therefore, comes from primary source materials, scholarly material from movement insiders, the few decent academic works on the NAR and from independent researchers like Bruce Wilson and Rachel Tabachnick. With Wilson and Tabachnick's work, I have primarily relied on their writing for "professional" sources—news agencies, Truth Wins Out, PRA and its publications, *The Huffington Post*, *Alternet*, etc.—and have in almost all instances avoided utilizing their extensive documenting of the NAR on the site *Talk to Action*. In my estimation, *Talk to Action* is far more reliable than any of these aforementioned sources, but such are the constraints of academic practice. The frequent references to Kyle Mantyla and Brian Tashman refer mainly to videos concerning the NAR that they saved on the People for the American Way-sponsored website Right Wing Watch, all of which I watched to ensure they were transcribed accurately (which they were). In a couple of cases, I also utilize theoretical insights from Mantyla and Tashman as well, which is the main reason why I have cited the videos through Right Wing Watch itself, rather than through their Youtube links (when available). In the case of all the independent scholars and non–Charismatic reporters and academics I utilized,

I have every reason to believe their accounts of the NAR are not only accurate, but considerably more accurate than the mainstream coverage of Charismatic history currently being offered by scholars like Margaret Poloma and Candy Gunther Brown.

Finally there is one last note I should make on sourcing. I have used the gay news web site *Box Turtle Bulletin* extensively in Chapter 6, for which I make no apology. The persecution of LGBT people does not receive nearly the amount of attention it should in the mainstream press, and *Box Turtle Bulletin* frequently reports on issues that the mainstream press refuses to cover. I refuse to either reward lazy reporting by the mainstream press or "punish" alternative gay news outlets like *Box Turtle Bulletin* or *Gay City News*, simply because the latter two organizations are unable to find straight publications willing to utilize their work. Although I do not rely greatly on either of these sources, their work has been important in documenting evangelical anti-gay efforts in Uganda and their reporting on that country deserves greater media attention.

1

From Parham to Bickle
The Origins of the NAR

To understand the history of the NAR, one must look at how Pentecostalism, and later the Charismatic Renewal, has developed over the course of the last century. The next two chapters are not meant to be an exhaustive history of the entire Pentecostal and Charismatic movement. However, certain themes need to be drawn out of Pentecostal and Charismatic history that will be important to understanding the NAR's development. In particular, one can only understand why so many denominational Pentecostals, evangelicals, and ex-evangelicals have expressed concern about the NAR if one looks into the history of the Pentecostal movement, particularly the idea of the "Latter Rain." It is to that history we now turn.

Pentecostal Origins

Pentecostalism arose at the turn of the 20th century, but its origins preceded it in a number of 19th century religious movements. Pentecostals inherited from Wesleyian theology the concept of a "'second blessing' subsequent to salvation" (Synan 2). According to this concept, sometimes referred to as "entire sanctification" or "perfect love," an individual would undergo an experience of immense spiritual power that cleansed them spiritually (Synan 2). The second blessing idea had a major impact on Pentecostalism, through its transmission from Wesleyian theology to the Holiness movement, largely via Holiness leader Phoebe Palmer (Allan Anderson 26).

One concept that arose out of the Holiness movement that would become crucial in understanding how the NAR developed was the idea of the "latter rain" (Anderson 27). The concept originated in a revival in 1857–1858, and was originally used to denote a worldwide revival—the "latter rain"—that would occur just prior to the return of Christ (27). Crucially, the Holiness movement linked this idea of the latter rain to the "'second blessing' experience of sanctification with a worldwide revival" (Anderson 27). In later formulations of the Latter Rain doctrine, while the emphasis on sanctification was retained, there was also attached to the idea a strong concept of spiritual elitism, whereby those who received the newest blessing of the Holy Spirit became the new spiritual elite of the Pentecostal movement.[1]

From Edward Irving's Catholic Apostolic Church (no relationship to Catholicism), Pentecostalism obtained the idea of "a restoration of the gifts of the Spirit in the modern church" (Synan 2). Significantly, Irving's church experienced tongues and prophecies as an element of their religious experience, but ultimately Irving was not successful in his attempt at a "restoration" of the New Testament church (2). Irving's church not only believed in the gifts of the Holy Spirit and the restoration of "charismata" but also argued that "the apostolic office had been restored for the end times" (24). Although Irving himself never took on the rank of apostle (Synan 24), the idea of a return of the apostolic gifts persisted into the twentieth century, and would end up being a crucial concept the NAR used to legitimate movement leadership.

The third major originating factor within Charismatic belief was the Keswick movement. The Keswick movement shifted the emphasis in Pentecostal theology away from "cleansing" of the Spirit, to the "anointing by the Spirit" (Synan 29). The Keswick movement was influenced by important Reformed thinkers of the late 19th century (see Synan 28). This ended up meaning that Pentecostalism, while maintaining an identity largely shaped by Arminian ideology, also proved itself amenable to accepting some ideas associated with the Reformed movement. For the NAR, this would have a marked effect on how the movement perceived eschatological issues.

Perhaps the most influential healer for the later history of Pentecostalism was the ex–Baptist pastor Frank Sandford. Sandford strongly emphasized among other things, "'spiritual warfare' (intercessory prayer) and a belief in Anglo-Israelism, the theory that the White-Anglo-Saxon Protestant nations ... were descended from the 'lost tribes' of Israel" (Anderson 33). Sandford's ideas provided a "formative influence" on Charles Parham (34), arguably the founder of modern Pentecostalism, and through Parham's influence, much of the racialized theology of Anglo-Israelism would, as we will see, creep into later Pentecostal and Charismatic movements, though not in the way one might expect.

The Origins Debate

Two significant issues about Pentecostal origins cause controversy. The first is the issue of Reformed influences on the movement, which this work concurs with Edith Lynn Waldvogel in acknowledging as a real and not imagined phenomena (see Goff 9 on Waldvogel's opinion on Reformed influence). The second debate is over who is the "true" founder of the Pentecostal movement: William Seymour or Charles Parham. This debate is heavily political, because Seymour, as an African American, represents the Pentecostal ideal of leadership, while Parham's life story hints at a darker vision of Pentecostal origins. According to Douglas J. Nelson, Seymour is virtually the "unqualified founder of a heroic religious movement [Pentecostalism]" (Goff 10). For Nelson, it was the "interracial worship" exhibited during the earlier part of the Azusa Street Revival, led by Seymour, that was the truly revolutionary Pentecost experience (Goff 10). James R. Goff, Parham's biographer, is skeptical of this reading, arguing that "Nelson's thesis suffers from an inability to support such a redefinition of Pentecostalism given the admitted brief tenure of interracial worship and the subsequent failure of Pentecostals to prevent racial church segregation" (Goff 10). Despite the understandable desire on the part of Charismatics to valorize Seymour at the expense of Parham, especially given the huge acknowledged influence Seymour did have over the Pentecostal movement, when dealing with the history of Pentecostalism in the decades after the 1948 Latter Rain Revival, the Parham thesis better explains how the Pentecostal movement developed (especially among white churches).

Parham's biography is largely unimportant to this work, but it should be noted that in 1900, Parham fell under the sway of Frank Sandford (Anderson 33). Parham came to accept Sandford's ideas, including Anglo-Israelism and Sandford's promotion of "the possibility of foreign tongues given by the Spirit to facilitate world evangelization" (Anderson 33–34). At his Bethel Gospel School, Parham gave some of his students the assignment to look through the Book of Acts for "'some evidence' of the baptism with the Spirit" (Anderson 34). Parham argued that these students had not yet received the "full outpouring of a second Pentecost." Initiating a form of revivalism that was later copied by the 1948 Latter Rain revival, Parham convinced his students that they needed to undergo fasting and intense prayer in order to receive the gifts of the Spirit (Anderson 34). By the time Parham returned from his trip, the students contended that "the biblical evidence of Spirit baptism was speaking in tongues" (Anderson 34). After an all-night vigil, on January 1, 1901, Agnes Ozman, one of Parham's students, asked him "to lay hands on her to receive the gift of the Spirit" (34). Ozman then began speaking in tongues.

Pentecostals and Charismatics differed from cessationists in believing that tongues, prophecy, healings, miracles, and other such unusual spiritual phenomena had not ceased after the early church (McGee 784). In the eyes of classical Pentecostals, what had happened was that tongues-speaking, while disappearing during the apostolic age, could be recovered in the modern period. Early Pentecostals believed they had "rediscovered and reinstated the doctrine due to the end times 'outpouring' of the Spirit as foretold in Joel 2:28–29" (McGee 784). What Parham did for Pentecostalism was link Spirit Baptism with tongues.

Parham significantly also argued that only "Spirit-baptized believers" would be raptured. This belief was later rejected by mainstream Pentecostals (and also Charismatics), but as G.B. McGee points out, this latter teaching still is significant in that it "highlighted a basic issue that has challenged Pentecostal theologians through the years: the unique difference of the Spirit's work in a Christian who speaks in tongues from one who does not" (McGee 786). While such spiritual elitism is hardly confinable to the Pentecostal movement, the Pentecostal tradition has had a tendency to conceptualize itself in spiritually elitist terms.

The modern NAR often feeds on this kind of thinking, encouraging people to join "Joel's Army," or the "Forerunners," or any host of different terms for what is basically the same thing: a new spiritual elite distinct from mainstream Christians. The invocation of Joel 2:28–29 is crucially important for understanding the particular form of apocalypticism practiced by the NAR. Following in the tradition of both the initial Pentecostal revivals and the 1948 Latter Rain Revival, the supporters of the NAR would come to see themselves, through these verses, as an especially prophetic people, gifted with dreams, visions, and other abilities that distinguished them from the spiritually "normal."

McGee also points to another crucial factor in Parham's theology that would become quite important to understanding both the 1948 Latter Rain Revival and the current NAR: Parham's "restorationist hermeneutic" (McGee 786). Restorationism in some ways is identical to the concept of primitivism. The basic belief system that motivates it is that

> something went very wrong very early in the history of the Christian church, so that the simple and biblical teaching and practice of the apostles was gradually corrupted through the addition of pagan ceremonies.... The other side of the equation is the belief that the restoration of the church ... began with the Protestant Reformation of the 16th century and proceeded in successive waves up to the present in preparation for the return of Christ to the earth [Ware 1019].

Here again, the biblical motif from the prophet Joel that was used is that of "the latter rain" (Joel 2:23). It was this Latter Rain ideology that would give shape to Pentecostalism's view of both history and eschatology and would in many ways distinguish the movement considerably from more fundamentalist conceptualizations of millennialism. In early Pentecostalism, the most "definitive articulation" of this idea was given by D. Wesley Myland in his book *The Latter Rain Covenant and Pentecostal Power* (1910) (Ware 1019). This idea contended that

> the history of the church was analogous to the rainfall patterns in Palestine. The first Christian Pentecost describe in Acts 2 with the descent of the Holy Spirit typified the "early rain" of Palestine's agricultural season, followed by the long dry period of Christianity's corruption during the Middle Ages. The Pentecostal revival of the early 20th century was therefore indicative of the latter rain, causing a ripening of the crop of humanity just before the harvest, or end of divine dealings with humanity [Ware 1019].

The restorationist impulse of this Latter Rain eschatology separated it distinctly from the eschatological pronouncements of fundamentalists in some important ways, which ultimately would make the ideology ultimately far more dangerous to non–Charismatics than the premillennial dispensationalism of fundamentalists. Premillennial dispensationalism, in its basic formulation, is largely a theology of despair. Dispensationalists have never had much hope about their ability to change the world. Contrary to popular belief, traditional premillennial dispensationalists do not look forward to the End Times, for a number of reasons. Many for instance, secretly fear they will not be raptured, whether or not they are saved. This fear is compounded by the fact that many traditionalist dispensationalist churches do not believe in a pre-tribulation rapture (where believers are raptured before the Tribulation period), but a mid-tribulation or post-tribulation rapture, in which the church will undergo extensive persecution and many will forsake their faith to take on the mark of the beast, assuring themselves of eternal damnation. For these reasons, and also because many traditional premillennial dispensationalists fear what will happen to "unsaved" relatives during the End Times, the movement is particularly prone to historical pessimism. In traditional dispensational historiography, except for the flurry of hope that characterized the Reformation, the church is heading steadily towards despair.

By contrast, the restorationist tradition within Pentecostalism, as interpreted by Parham and later Pentecostals, interprets church history in more hopeful terms (see Ware on this 1020). For restorationists, the church is progressing from generation to generation, each generation building on the last. Whereas traditional dispensationalists tend to see the End Times as something to dread, Pentecostal restorationists came to see it as something to look forward to, a proving ground for God's elite. Those saints, unlike in dispensationalism, were better than previous generations, and could use their will to alter events in the world. Many concerned Charismatics today believe that this Restorationist concept is what is badly slanting current Charismatic practice. For instance, Pentecostal pastor Bill Randles argues that if one buys into restorationism, it sets one up "for the evolutionary church concept, a deluding, intoxicating idea that makes the current expression of the church feel that she is the ultimate center of God's purposes, over and above all previous expressions of the church" (Randles 39). Randles's point is a valuable one. Because restorationists view history in quasi-Lamarckian terms, there is a tendency among them to believe they can affect historical change in a way unavailable to non-restorationists.

In practical terms, this means that restorationists, since they are inclined to anticipate the End Times, lack the kind of cultural break on fanaticism that the more pessimistic visions of dispensationalism provide. Moreover, Restorationists, at least in the Charismatic movement, often see themselves as intensely involved in perfecting the world in anticipation of Christ's return. Therefore there are fewer breaks on social activism within Charismatic and Pentecostal circles than in fundamentalist ones. Since the primary direction of Charismatic and Pentecostal political ideology remains profoundly conservative, this means there are fewer barriers between secular conservative activists and potential Charismatic constituents than there would be among more fundamentalist and pietistic evangelicals, who often eschewed politics well into the era of the Moral Majority and the new religious right.

Divisions over issues related to tongues eventually became numerous because of doubts about how important Parham's idea of "initial evidence" was for the movement as a whole; Pentecostals, even in Parham's time expressed concern at "making tongues a litmus test" for spirit baptism (see Anderson 193; McGee 788). This issue became particularly important after the emergence of the Third Wave Charismatic movement. Third Wave churches often started off evangelical and many times remained "unrelated or no longer related to the Pentecostals or charismatic renewals" even as they emphasized Spirit Baptism and the gifts of the Spirit. Because of their often non-denominational and even distinctly non-"classical Pentecostal" allegiances, the Third Wave movement often put much less emphasis on tongues, seeing them as "optional or even absent or unnecessary" (Synan 396). Much of the success of Third-Wave churches, which became the breeding ground for the NAR, lay in their ability to look normal even as their own theology deviated into more politically extremist rhetoric than the supposedly more dangerous classical Pentecostals.

Parham had one other effect on Pentecostalism that was extremely important to the history of the NAR; he "infused British-Israelism [Anglo-Israelism] into the premillennial evangelical sects that were emerging out of Midwestern Methodism" (Barkun 21). In its origins, British-Israelism was, for its time, philo-Semitic (see Barkun, *Religion* 11). In America, this philo-Semitism morphed into an extremely anti–Semitic ideology, and became a formative influence on the racist Christian Identity movement (see Barkun passim, but especially ix-x). Parham, operating at a time when Anglo-Israelism had not devolved into Christian Identity, adopted Zionist ideas in the late 1890s, even going so far as decrying anti–Semitism in Russia. Parham's defense of the Jewish people was specifically based in Anglo-Israelite ideology. According to Parham, the United States was responsible for helping Jews out because Americans, having a "predominance of English blood ... were themselves descendants of the chosen tribes" (Goff 101). Parham's racial theory argued that there were three separate groups of "Israelites" who went their separate ways to "India, Japan and Western Europe" and developed sophisticated cultures in all these areas. In Western Europe, these Jews became the Angles and Saxons. For Parham, this belief led him to draw a "clear dichotomy of chosen peoples versus the ungodly" (Goff 102). The Jews were responsible for the various spiritual peoples of the world, including Anglo-Saxons, Germans, Danes, Swedes, Hindus,[2] and the Japanese. Gentiles represented the largely "formalistic" peoples of the world: French, Spanish, Italian, Greek, Russian, and Turks. The heathen were blacks, Native Americans, Malays, and Mongolians. These apparently represented the most ungodly group to Parham (Goff 102).Parham's racial views, coupled with the influence of Anglo-Israelism, led him to develop a highly esoteric view of human origins, in which he argued for a gradual process of creation, largely in line with evolutionary development.

Parham's racialized theology ended up having profound influences on Pentecostal identity. In particular, the idea of a spiritually elite race that Parham promoted (see Goff 103–104) would spring up time and time again within Pentecostal theology, under a variety of different names. In the late 1940s, under the influence of the 1948 Latter Rain revival, this elite would be known as the Manifest Sons of a God, a term that even today is still in use among certain elements of the NAR (see Riss 95–96 on origins of term). In the eighties, the term "Joel's Army" was much favored, though the massive blowback that that term created has led to its abandonment. Similarly Mike Bickle's modern concept of Forerunners and Lou Engle's development of the heavily racialized rhetoric surrounding "Nazarite DNA" resemble Parham's form of British-Israelism. Besides the 1948 Latter Rain revival, much of the reason for the continued viability of the idea of a spiritually racial elite derives from the massive influence of healing revivalist William Branham, who conceptualized the world in virtually identical terms with Parham. Branham's source of influence may also possibly have been Daniel Parker, a 19th century preacher who argued that there was a primal division between the elect and the non-elect contained in the "seedlines" of Eve. Those who were descended from the "serpent seedline" were incapable of being saved, so evangelizing them was fruitless. Branham would end up developing a similar—indeed almost identical—view of the serpent's seed (Barkun, *Religion and the Racist Right* 121–122). For critics of the movement, it is this strange mixture of multicultural Charismatic belief with its intrinsically racialized theology that makes the movement so prone to both spiritual elitism and culturally triumphalism.

Moreover, there is an important reason why Pentecostalism has evolved in its current authoritarian direction and it is every bit as paradoxical as Pentecostalism's multicultural racialized ideology. This is the profound desire on the part of Pentecostals and modern Charismatics to avoid denominationalism and factionalism. The early Pentecostal movement sought to "sweep away what they considered mere human constructions, such as denominational hierarchies. The Pentecostals wanted to replace these structures with divinely inspired governance based upon the Bible" (Synan 54). Similarly, the early Pentecostal church sought to erase the lines separating "clergy and congregation" (Synan 55). Early Pentecostals scorned "anything that smacked of hierarchy in favor of the rule of the Holy Spirit, the rights of the congregation, and individual liberty of conscience" (Robins 39). What ultimately would morph this anti-ecclesiasticism into a rigid theocratic authoritarianism was the combination of Pentecostal experientialism with a widespread yet somewhat peculiar reading of Ephesians 4:8–11, with its emphasis on the fivefold gifts of apostle, prophet, evangelist, pastor and teacher.

Pentecostalism's experiential and anti-intellectual approach to theology meant that church doctrines were often not judged on the basis of either their reasonableness nor on their affinity to creedal statements, but instead were adopted piecemeal, with the personal charisma of the new doctrine's promulgator being more important to the doctrine's acceptance than any rational argumentation. What morphed the movement's experiential ideology in a distinctly authoritarian direction would be the Latter Rain revival's and the shepherding movement's promotion of the restoration of the roles of apostle and prophet as tools for advancing spiritual hierarchalism, a hierchalism at odds with classical Pentecostalism's anti-authoritarianism. To understand why this peculiar evolution occurred, we must skip over several decades and turn to the Latter Rain Revival of 1948 and the related Healing Revival, whose main early champion, William Branham, would play an essential role in the development of this new authoritarianism.

The Latter Rain Movement: Manifest Sons and the Beginning of the New Pentecostal Authoritarianism

The 1948 Latter Rain movement originated in North Battleford, Saskatchewan, Canada, on February 12th and 13th of that year (Riss 11). Richard Riss, himself an admirer of Latter Rain theology (see Riss 9), argues that the revival meetings of healing evangelist William Branham, particularly in Vancouver, British Columbia, profoundly influenced the emergence of the Latter Rain revival. It should be noted, however, that contrary to assertions made by some non–Latter Rain critics of the movement, Branham was not the originator nor leader of the Latter Rain revival. Rather, the Latter Rain revival and the Healing Revival that Branham did so much to pioneer were in reality "parallel developments" within evangelicalism during this period (Riss 11). As Riss points out, "both movements occurred within the milieu of Pentecostalism, both were rejected by most major Pentecostal denominations, and both played a part in influencing the development of the Charismatic movement [here referring to the Charismatic Renewal] of the 1960s and 1970s" (Riss 11).

Tom Craig Darrand and Anson Shupe's study of the Latter Rain movement, *Metaphors of Social Control in a Pentecostal Sect* (1983) contends that the Latter Rain movement was the byproduct of a conflict between George Hawtin, the president of Bethel Bible Institute in Saskatoon, and the elected Pentecostal Assemblies committee that had been given the duty of overseeing the school (Darrand and Shupe 34). According to Darrand and Shupe, both Hawtin's "maverick expenditure of money for new buildings and his lack of qualifications to implement the educational plans on which he had already embarked provoked the Committee's request for George Hawtin's resignation" (36). Hawtin subsequently resigned, taking seventy students with him, who became the first students of the Sharon Bible School, an independent Bible School located in North Battleford. Hawtin and his colleague Percy Hunt also were helped by the support of Hawtin's younger brother Ern and his brother-in law Milford Kirkpatrick, who joined the North Battleford ministry (Darrand and Shupe 36–37).

At the time, Pentecostals were anticipating changes in their movement. The movement had suffered the loss of three major early leaders in 1944 (Smith Wigglesworth, Charles Price and Aimee Semple McPherson) (Darrand and Shupe 37). Cold war anxiety also fed intensely into the movement. Both Franklin Hall, whose fasting rhetoric provided much of the initial impetus for the Latter Rain revival, and George Warnock, whose book *Feast of the Tabernacles*

(1951) became the revival's manifesto, showed themselves to be interested in the idea of nuclear power—and sometimes nuclear warfare (Hall, *Atomic Power with God* 1, 11–12; Warnock 8, 78). In this climate, Branham's healing campaigns caused profound excitement among the North Battleford group (Darrand and Shupe 38). This led the group to adopt the fasting practices of Franklin Hall in anticipation of revival (Darrand and Shupe 39).

Ern Hawtin ended up giving a prophecy that great things were going to be done for God. Hawtin claimed that he "felt led ... to lay hands on one of the students because he thought he wanted to 'receive the baptism' of the Holy Spirit" (Shupe and Darrand 39). Hawtin prophesied that the gifts of the Spirit were to be restored to the church. Crucial for the Latter Rain was the idea that these gifts were to be restored by the "laying on of the hands of the presbytery" (40). The movement was evidently influenced by Branham's apparent power to "heal" through "vibrations on his hand," as well as Branham's legendary powers of discerning spiritual and physical afflictions by "words of knowledge" (Shupe and Darrand 41; see also C. Douglas Weaver 166). The reason this idea of laying on of hands was so significant to the future history of Pentecostalism, was Hawtin's claim to "have received further divine authority to 'impart' all spiritual gifts to ready believers" (Shupe and Darrand 41).

Latter Rain ideology was, from the beginning, prone to authoritarianism (Shupe and Darrand 45). Shupe and Darrand, speaking of a then modern Latter Rain church which largely followed the original teachings of the 1948 revival, argue that the Latter Rain movement conceived of church structure largely in terms of a "theocratic chain of command" (Shupe and Darrand 67). In a process that would be copied by the shepherding movement in the 1970s, authority was seen as invested in the leadership of the movement through the power of the trinity itself. It then descended from what the movement called "five ascension-gift ministries," now more commonly known as the "fivefold ministry" of "apostle, prophet, evangelist, pastor and teacher," borrowed from Ephesians 4:8–11 (see Darrand and Shupe 67). These leaders were seen as "divinely appointed representatives with the greatest God-given authority and consequently the greatest access to and knowledge of God" (Darrand and Shupe 67). Below the five-fold ministry were elders, deacons, and finally the laity who engaged in "congregational ministries" (67). The movement's recognition of present-day apostles, prophets, evangelists and teachers was vitally important to the spread of Latter Rain, and later NAR theology, and more importantly set the tone of authoritarianism that characterized the Latter Rain, the shepherding movement and eventually the NAR.

The strong hierarchicalism of the 1948 Latter Rain revival is ironic when one considers how strongly the movement reacted against what it saw as the controlling nature of classical Pentecostal denominations in running church life. Indeed, the Latter Rain helped spawn hundreds of churches that were almost always "independent and autonomous" (Riss, "Latter Rain Movement" 832). What distinguished the Latter Rain revival from previous manifestations of Latter Rain thinking was the greater degree of control invested in the apostolic role, as well as the greater acceptance of spiritually elitist ideology, here exemplified by the Latter Rain's adoption of the idea of "Manifest Sons of God" theology.

In traditional denominational churches, authority was invested primarily in the denomination, and then delegated by the denomination to individual leaders, usually pastors or elders, within the denomination. Although classical Pentecostalism had accepted the idea of modern day apostles and prophets (see Riss "Latter Rain Movement" 832), in practice the movement had quickly conceded to the pull of denominationalism and church hierarchy based on shared creedal commitments. The Latter Rain movement, by contrast, sought to invest power in powerful Charismatic figures whose leadership was "inspired directly by God" (Darrand and Shupe 65). Because their power was seen as deriving directly from God, rather than creedal commitments, the leaders of the Latter Rain, like the shepherds of the Charismatic Renewal and the apostles of the NAR, would be invested with enormous authority by their followers, authority not typically delegated to church leaders within traditional denominational structures. In classical Pentecostal denominations, by contrast, believers were encouraged to check the pronouncements of their leaders against the denomination's creed, as well as against their own conscience.

More significantly, the democratic nature of these classical Pentecostal denominations, whose ecclesiology typically veered to a presbytery or democratic system of church governance, became increasingly marginalized in later Restorationist movements that adopted Latter Rain ideology, including the NAR, but especially the shepherding movement. The shepherding movement, for instance, did not perceive itself as "an ecclesiastical structure; rather it was an organic network based on relationship and true spiritual authority" (Moore 79). Similarly, the NAR's vision of church governance argues that apostolic networks are not led by "a group but by an individual apostle." In this formulation, it is this "divinely appointed apostle, as opposed to a board or presbytery, a democratic vote or institution who was seen bearing responsibility for making decisions and guiding adherents" (Holvast 158–159). The advantage of such a system for rapid church growth was obvious. Skilled apostles could make decisions quickly, effectively, and without worrying about having to deal with red-tape or bureaucratized denominational structures. In a religious free market, such a system ends up rewarding church growth strategies that emphasize innovation and creativity. Those churches incapable of adapting quickly enough to changing social conditions died out. The pragmatism of the Latter Rain movement's shepherding and NAR descendants allowed them to more quickly employ new ideas concerning worship, music, and church structure than other evangelicals (for NAR pragmatism, see Holvast 28, 273). These organizational advantages, coupled with the already existing predisposition of many 20th century Christians—American and non–American alike—to adopt increasingly emotive worship practices, gave the shepherding adherents of the Charismatic Renewal and the apostles of the NAR an insurmountable advantage over traditional denominations.

The downside to this church structure, however, was considerable, because its commitment to apostolic authority led to a de-emphasizing of democratic church structure in favor of top-down pastor/laity or apostle/laity hierarchicalism. Even in traditional non-denominational, non–Charismatic evangelical churches, abuses in the church were typically limited by the fact that these churches often had strong boards of deacons and/or elders that prevented abuses. Moreover, in these churches, as in denominational Pentecostal churches, leaders, while specially gifted by God, were not invested with literal divine authority, much less special spiritual gifts delegated to them by irreproachable apostles. In practice, too, despite the heavy degree of prophetic ideology within many non–Charismatic evangelical churches, traditional evangelicals remained quite skeptical of claims by modern-day prophets to accurately predict the future. Indeed, some of the more perceptive critics of Latter Rain ideology and its inheritors were motivated at in part by traditional evangelical concerns about the misuse of prophetic gifts in manipulating church laity (see on this score, Beverly's criticisms of the Kansas City Prophets, Beverly 121–133). Latter Rain theology, not having these breaks on it, quickly degenerated into increasingly bizarre forms of prophetic excess.

Perhaps the most extreme idea to come out of the Latter Rain was the Manifest Sons of God. Christian academic Rene Holvast defines the Manifest Sons idea as a "belief in a new kind of Christian elite who wield special spiritual power in order to subdue the earth and who will actually conquer the earth in the end times" (Holvast 164). The powers of this new elite people were elaborated in their most extreme form in George Warnock's *Feast of the Tabernacles.* Warnock saw this End Times people—which it must be remembered, the Latter Rain movement saw itself as being potentially a part of—as a super-race of human beings with abilities that far surpassed the fantasies of science fiction. According to Warnock,

> There will not be a country on earth that will be closed to this Gospel of the Kingdom. It will be just as simple to proclaim the Truth in Communist Russia as

anywhere else on earth. The authorities will send the police to arrest this strange personage that is so boldly preaching Christ, and working the works of God, and he will have disappeared; for he shall have been caught away in the Spirit like Philip the evangelist.... They may rush upon him with sword or bayonet, and their weapon will be blunted as truly as if they had charged an armored tank; for no weapon that is formed against him shall prosper. They might fire a shot, and the bullet will glance off his brow, as it would from a heavy plate of steel.... They shall seek to prevent the Gospel from being proclaimed over the air; and yet even without the aid of radio or transmitter the voice of the overcomer shall be heard in the streets or in the homes, as it penetrates the atmosphere at God's command and in God's place.... And "nothing shall be impossible" unto the man who believes! The most powerful atom or hydrogen bombs ever invented shall be perfectly harmless to the man who is hid away in the secret place of the Most High [Warnock 78].

Warnock literally believed Latter Rain saints would be able to survive nuclear warfare through faith alone. They would have superhuman defensive powers unavailable to the uninitiated and would be able to communicate the Latter Rain message through superhuman methods that resemble some of the parapsychological powers that New Thought and New Age philosophy claim for their adherents. The Latter Rain movement also foresaw a time when it would be able to tear down Soviet power, literally through the power of spiritual faith.

Nor were these the only unusual powers available to the Manifest Sons of God. According to an excerpt quoted in Richard Riss's history of the Latter Rain movement, there was a growth of belief within the Latter Rain, particularly at the Northwest Bible Institute in Edmonton, that there would be an "elect" who "would receive 'redemptive bodies' here and now and that any person who died had not been able to appropriate the 'redemption body' and was therefore not one of the 'overcomers.' In the final analysis, to be an 'overcomer' meant affiliation with the Sharon Group [of Latter Rain adherents]'" (Jaenen 89; Riss 96). Riss's contention is supported by the more careful discussion of Latter Rain doctrine found in Michael Moriarty's critique of the Latter Rain. According to Moriarty, Latter Rain supporters believed they would be able to reach an immortal state, which "some referred to as 'godhood,' which would be attained by those overcomers who received higher revelations and continuous spiritual experiences" (Moriarty 325). While Moriarty does not realize how much residue there is of Manifest Sons doctrine still operative in Pentecostalism (see Moriarty 325), he fully admits that these ideas have clearly influenced important contemporary Charismatics like Bill Hamon and Earl Paulk (Moriarty 325).

Moriarty also speculates that the "little gods" idea found among some WOF teachers may have at least been partly influenced by Latter Rain ideology. According to Paulk, "just as dogs have puppies and cats have kittens, so God has little gods," those little Gods being human beings (Paulk, *Satan Unmasked* 96; Moriarty 106–108). While it is unclear how much Latter Rain thinking influenced WOF thought, still less how much the WOF movement is tied or not tied to NAR thinking (some WOF leaders have close ties, while others do not), Moriarty's point is still a valid one. Within Latter Rain and WOF theology there is a strong component of theosis, but without the breaks on the theosis-derived egoism that the Eastern Orthodox church, for instance, provides. Within the Latter Rain and WOF formulations of theosis, the idea of becoming like God is taken so literally that it skews the believer's perceptions of what they are capable of doing in this world. While an Eastern Orthodox believer might say that they want to become more like God; a Latter Rain believer would be more inclined to want to become *like God*. The degree of relative humility observed towards the human condition is crucial to understanding why Latter Rain believers and their Charismatic descendants went to greater doctrinal extremes than those exhibited by Eastern Orthodoxy. Even some normally unreliable Pentecostal historians have claimed to be concerned by the doctrinal excesses of Manifest Sons doctrine. Vinson Synan, for instance, notes that the "the teaching that an end-time group of 'super apostles' known as the 'manifested sons' would usher in the end times…" was a "troubling problem" with the Latter Rain Revival (Synan, *An Eyewitness Remembers the Century of the Holy Spirit* 35). Similarly, Bill Jackson's hagiographic (and highly unreliable) history of the Vineyard movement admits that there are dangerous elements within Manifest Sons doctrine, including the ability to overcome death, and the ability to move at will "from country to country and from city to city." Indeed, according to Jackson, some of the Latter Rain teachings he has encountered concerning the Latter Rain include the ability for believers to change their physical forms, speak any language, and restore themselves to their "pre-fallen state" (Jackson 185–186).

It is important to note that in addition to promoting the Manifest Sons theology, the Latter Rain movement also linked this idea to the concept of "latter rain." The fivefold ministry of "apostle, prophet, evangelist, pastor and teacher" became linked in Latter Rain theology with the "latter rain" prophesied in Joel 2:28 (see Robins 80). This linking of fivefold ministry with the idea of a Latter Rain, would, when coupled to the concept of an elite end time band of missionaries, elite Christians, and/or an army of God, would lead to the most extreme forms of end time apocalypticism in the history of the contemporary Charismatic movement, particularly the "Joel's Army" teaching of the '80s and '90s that was promoted by Kansas City Fellowship (KCF) and even, for a time, the Vineyard movement (Horton 115–116).

The Latter Rain revival eventually lost steam, but it had a huge influence on subsequent Charismatic movements that cannot be overemphasized. A number of churches and Institutes ended up carrying on Latter Rain teachings, notably the Elim Bible Institute of Lima (originally Hornell), New York, as well as the Bethseda Missionary Temple in Detroit (Riss, "Latter Rain Movement" 832–833). Elim influenced a number of major evangelical leaders, including Randall Terry, the founder of Operation Rescue, who graduated from Elim (McBride 158), and most significantly provided employment for Bob Mumford, one of the founders of the shepherding movement, during the mid–1960s. According to David S. Moore's hagiographic history of shepherding, it was "at Elim that Mumford felt a profound call to minister transdenominationally after hearing Pentecostal ecumenist David du Plessis speak at the college" (Moore 38). Considering how heavily the shepherding movement also emphasized the fivefold ministry idea, it would not be surprising if Mumford inherited some Latter Rain concepts from his time at Elim. In any case, he is by far not the only link between the Latter Rain movement and later Charismatics. *Logos-Journal*, a major Charismatic journal during the Charismatic Renewal, was edited by Joseph Mattson-Boze, a player in the Latter Rain Revival who also served as a contributing editor to the major shepherding periodical, *New Wine*, for a while (Riss 141).[3] Ern Baxter, one of the five major leaders of the shepherding movement ("The Fort Lauderdale Five") during the 1970s, had George Warnock for a secretary for two or three years preceding the 1948 Latter Rain movement (Riss 141). Significantly, Baxter was also a member of Branham's revival teams for seven years, starting in 1949 (C. Douglas Weaver 47; Moore 36). Eventually, according to Baxter (as interpreted through Moore), he left Branham's ministry because he was "concerned over imbalances he observed" (Moore 36). While this statement is likely true—some of Branham's most fanatic supporters soured on his teachings as they became increasingly aberrant in the late fifties and early 1960s (see C. Douglas Weaver 96–98 on this score)—the fact remains that these twin influences likely influenced Baxter's shepherding theology in significant ways. In addition, James Lee Beall, son of Latter Rain leader, M.D. Beall seems to have had some influence on the shepherding movement (see Moore 206 for Beall's writings on shepherding). M.D. Beall had been an important leader in the Latter Rain movement almost from its inception (Riss, "Later Rain Movement" 832–833).

As Riss points out, various Latter Rain beliefs would end up entering the Charismatic Renewal, "including spiritual singing and dancing, praise, the foundational ministries of Ephesians 4:11, the laying on of hands, tabernacle teaching, the feast of Tabernacles and the foundational truths of Hebrews 6:1–2. In addition, elements of various eschatological views of the Latter Rain movement were adopted by many Charismatics throughout the world" (Riss 141–142).

Significantly, one of the leaders whose eschatology the Latter Rain influenced was Eldon Purvis (Riss 142): it was Purvis's Holy Spirit Teaching Mission (HSTM) which founded *New Wine*, the shepherding movement's major magazine and press organ (Moore 26–27), which helped spread shepherding doctrine worldwide. Indeed, purported scandals surrounding Purvis's administration of HSTM were largely responsible for the birth of shepherding doctrine itself (see Moore 28–30).[4]

The most nakedly Latter Rain doctrines—specifically those derived from Manifest Sons theology—would go underground, but return with a vengeance in the 1980s, thanks to Mike Bickle's KCF and its embrace of prophet Paul Cain. While the NAR has at least openly distanced itself from Manifest Sons teachings, the movement still embraces much of Latter Rain philosophy, both through the influence of C. Peter Wagner, the movement's chief leader, who embraced Latter Rain teachings in 1999 (Holvast 164), as well as well as prominent NAR apostle Bill Hamon, a major NAR apostle who was heavily influenced by the Latter Rain and who in turn deeply influenced Wagner.[5] In Hamon's work, in particular, we will see Manifest Sons theology largely borrowed wholesale, with little modification, from its original base in the Latter Rain. But key to the spread of Latter Rain theology was the Healing Revival, particularly the teachings of William Branham. It is to the Healing Revival and fifties Pentecostalism that we now turn.

William Branham, the Healing Revival and Full Gospel Business Men's Fellowship International (FGBMFI)

William Branham (1909–1965) started the Healing Revival that swept the Pentecostal church after World War II (D.J. Wilson 440). Branham's status among the Pentecostals of his day was legendary. According to Branham, throughout his life he was "guided by an angel who first appeared to him in a secret cave in 1946" (D.J. Wilson 440). Many Pentecostals were impressed by the uncanny talents and "words of knowledge" uttered by Branham. Walter J. Hollenweger, for instance, a revered Pentecostal historian, interpreted for Branham at a meeting and stated that he was unaware of any cases in which Branham's words of knowledge were in error (D.J. Wilson 440).[6] Throughout the late 1940s and early 1950s Branham held Healing Revival meetings around the world. In 1950, Branham held campaigns throughout Scandanavia. A few years later he was in Africa. Subsequently he would make a trip to India and another trip to Europe. At the height of his popularity, Branham was able to fill to capacity the greatest stadiums and meetings halls in the world. In the late 1950s, however, Branham's career slumped, as it experienced "financial difficulties" (Collins 27). Branham alienated himself from mainstream Pentecostals by increasingly bizarre doctrinal innovations he introduced into his ministry after the late 1950s (Collins 27). Branham had always been something of an outsider within mainstream Pentecostalism because of his association with the group of Pentecostals known as "Jesus Only" or "Oneness" Pentecostals (Collins 25). By the end of his career, Branham came to see "trinitarianism and denominationalism as diabolic" and also started attacking women in deeply misogynistic ways (Collins 27).

In spite of this Branham always maintained a high reputation among his fellow Pentecostals. Part of this popularity stemmed from the total sincerity of Branham's efforts. There was more than an incipient amount of class critique, for instance, in Branham's condemnation of the increasing prosperity of his fellow Pentecostals (see Collins 27). Branham bitterly denounced the educated and came to feel that it was "the common people, characterized by their lack of education" who were the best Christians (C. Douglas Weaver 113). Indeed, many of the perceived heretical doctrines that Branham introduced into his theology were directly predicated on this hostility towards the rich. In addition, people thought Branham possessed great moral integrity. As D.J. Wilson points out: "In contrast to the caricature of the image-minded evangelist, he [Branham] lived moderately, dressed modestly and boasted of his youthful poverty. This endeared him to the throngs who idolized him. He was self-conscious about his lack of education, but the simplicity of his messages had worldwide appeal" (D.J. Wilson 440–441). It must be remembered that in the fifties many Pentecostals were preoccupied with the public perception of their belief-systems. The Healing Revival was viewed quite negatively by secular contemporaries, seen most notably in the 1960 adaptation of *Elmer Gantry*, which is arguably as much a refutation of Pentecostal healing revivalism as extremist fundamentalism. Branham, by defying secular stereotypes of healing revivalism, helped to raise the social capital of the healing revivalists, even as he himself hailed from a profoundly impoverished heritage.

The doctrinal innovations that Branham began introducing into his ministry in the late 1950s and early 1960s were seen as deeply heterodox. Foremost of these doctrines was the now notorious "serpent seed" idea. According to Branham's version of that idea,[7] Branham believed that two seedlines had descended from Eve. According to the doctrine, the serpent in the garden had sex with Eve in the garden, producing Cain and the descendants of Cain's bloodline. Cain's bloodline, according to Branham, was filled with the "intelligent" and "educated" and were also "builders and scientists." For Branham, these were bad things. The godly strain was represented by Abel's "godly seed" and was continued through the "progeny of Seth like Noah, Abraham, Isaac, Jacob, David, and Jesus Christ. Modern possessors of this godly seed were those Christians who accepted a supernatural gospel" (Weaver 124). For Branham, the idea of a Godly seed took on a rigid predestinarian character drawn from Branham's Calvinist roots. The predestined believer, for Branham had a special "predestinated Germ" and therefore his soul was "that gene that come from God" (Branham qtd. in C. Douglas Weaver 123).[8] As Weaver points out, what this ideology essentially boiled down to was a form of literal Christian genoism, where salvation was determined by "simple genetics" (C. Douglas Weaver 123).

Branham's ideology was similar to Latter Rain ideas in its support of a spiritual elite who bore some supernatural talent that put them above the human norm. What's more, Branham coupled his racial idea with the idea of "a super Church; a super Race" that would be so much like Jesus that "they will be in His very image, in the order to be united with him. They will be One. They will be the very manifestation of the Word of the Living God" (Branham, "Spoken Word is the Original Seed #2"; Moriarty 55). This idea of a super Church, of ecclesiological structure being represented in racial terms, was most graphically illustrated within the NAR by the church-race concept of Bill Hamon. Hamon sees Branham as a figure with an "'Elijah-type' anointing" (Hamon, *Eternal Church* loc 2203) and as a prophetic figure (Moriarty 56). The idea of a divinely mandated ecclesiological structure would become a common one in the NAR. What separated these movements from previous Protestant manifestations of primitivist impulses was the degree to which they sought to bypass traditional denominational structures and concentrate on the idea of the "body of Christ" as an organic whole. While both the shepherding movement and the NAR were perfectly willing to work within denominations, they were also willing to control adherents from outside the denominational structures in which those adherents resided.

This was, in a sense, all in keeping with Branham's thinking, as he, much like the Latter Rain movement's leadership, abhorred denominationalism. Indeed Branham saw denominationalism as the means by which the "image of the beast" (Protestantism) would unite and succumb to Catholicism ("the beast") (Weaver 115). Consequently, Branham believed that confederations of churches were warning signs of the "mark of the Beast" (Weaver 115–116). For Branham, much as for the Latter Rain movement and the NAR, the key to effective Christian witness was to avoid the factionalism Pentecostals saw as inherent in denominationalism. While neither the Latter Rain revival nor the NAR would go the extremes of anti-denominationalism favored by Branham, both movements' leadership saw the benefits for themselves in bypassing traditional denominational structures in favor of direct trans-denominational control of believers by apostles and prophets.

Branham's influence over subsequent Pentecostals and Charismatics was enormous. Even today the movement has not been able to play down the importance he played in shaping Pentecostalism. According to James Collins, Branham "worked closely" with the FGBMFI leader Demos Shakarian during the height of his early revivals (Collins 27). Indeed, Branham was the keynote speaker at a number of FGBMFI meetings during the initial years of that ministry, and was instrumental in the creation of several chapters of the organization (Tallman 199–200). In turn the FGBMFI also at times supported Branham. His last major overseas tour was sponsored by Miner Arganbright, a prominent leader within the FGBMFI (Weaver 51–52). *Voice*, the FGBMFI's official periodical, promoted Branham throughout the 1950s and 1960s through "numerous glowing reports of Branham's extensive meetings with the businessmen's organization" (C. Douglas Weaver 180). The FGBMFI, which played a crucial role in kick-starting the Charismatic Renewal, in many ways shared Branham's skepticism about the benefits of denominationalism, though to a more moderate degree. The FGBMFI was aimed at church laity, allowing laity to translate the message of the Healing Revival to the more refined environment of a "hotel ballroom or a restaurant." Yet, in significant ways, the message was the same. People spoke of their healings or the deliverances that they had undergone. The FGBMFI also played a large role in the promotion of the "faith teachers" (Zeigler 653; see also Harrel Jr. 148). It is plausible that some of the doctrinal innovations pursued by the WOF movement might have had their origins in interactions with Branham's teachings, whose influence over both the WOF and modern deliverance movements was considerable.

It is impossible to assess the degree to which Demos Shakarian, the founder of FGBMFI, borrowed from Branham and the Latter Rain movement. The leading chronicler of the FGBMFI, Matthew Tallman, points out that there are tantalizing connections between the development of the FGMBFI and the Latter Rain movement. A number of significant players in the formation of the Latter Rain movement, including T.L. Osborn, Jack Coe, A.A. Allen, and David DuPlessis also were instrumental in the formation and growth of the FGMBFI as well (Tallman 188–189). Demos Shakarian also invited Carlton Spencer, the then-president of Elim Bible Institute to a "convention in Washington in 1953," which as Riss points out, highlights the "Latter Rain influence upon the early development of the Charismatic Renewal" (Riss 140). Tallman points out that the perception of the Latter Rain movement that "older Pentecostal denominations had become formalized and spiritually hardened resonated with the ecclesiological and pneumatological hermeneutic of Shakarian" (Tallman 190).

What is clear is that Shakarian's particular ecclesiological commitments were able to mesh with Latter Rain and Branhamite doctrine in surprising ways. The 1948 Latter Rain movement and Branham were so devoted to antidenominationalism that neither Branham's followers nor the Latter Rain's were able to prosper long term. Shakarian's ecclesiology, by contrast was not antidenominational because he thought all denominations were evil, but because Shakarian's heritage as an Armenian Christian allowed him to see the truth of Christianity as working in many different Christian traditions; this perception has long been characteristic of Armenian Christianity (Tallman 55–57). Thus, the emphasis on finding Christian truth outside of a denominational context likely resonated with the ecumenical spirit of Shakarian's theology (see Tallman 56). Shakarian might very well have seen the Latter Rain as making common cause with the FGBMFI against the denominational structures of classical Pentecostalism, which tended to eschew lay leadership in favor of pastoral and denominational authority (see Harrell Jr. 147 on the denominational Pentecostal leadership's view of FGMBFI).

What the FGBMFI and independent Charismatic churches did is help authoritarian leaders bypass traditional churches' commitment to maintaining doctrinal and ecclesiological orthodoxy, including commitments to abiding by such concepts as church bylaws and legal procedures, in favor of the top-down leadership approach that the shepherding movement and NAR would come to prefer. Moreover, the FGBMFI also played a crucial role in furthering the careers of the independent revivalists of the fifties, many of whose ideas would end up influencing later Charismatic practice. The fellowship "offered a much-needed source of funds and business leadership, as well as a way to circumvent the jealous regulation of church officials. Nearly all the evangelists became unofficial promoters of new chapters during their campaigns" (Harrel Jr. 148). Again, while it is questionable whether it was the intention of the FGBMFI to deliberately promote doctrinal innovation within healing revivalism, by bypassing denominational leadership, the FGBMFI ended up creating a much freer market for doctrinal innovation than had already existed in Pentecostalism's unusually open religious free market. By taking the denominational breaks off of healing revivalists' tendency for doctrinal unorthodoxy, the FGMBFI created an environment in which virtually any doctrinal innovation could be accepted by the Charismatic church.

One should note one final part of Branham's ministry which would have an important effect on future Charismatic practice. Branham was an important promoter of the idea of "transgenerational demon possession" (Collins 30).

This idea (today's generational curses) would become an important element of NAR theology, as it would influence their concept of SLSW and the movement's understanding of certain people groups or territories as being fundamentally cursed. Though Branham was not the only "innovator" in deliverance ministry, the sheer scope of his influence meant that many of the ideas he promoted about deliverance would end up receiving a wide adoption (Collins 30), despite his doctrinal heterodoxy. In the process the Pentecostal movement would evolve in directions no one anticipated, dangerous directions that at this time threaten to destabilize not just fellow Pentecostal churches, or even fellow Christian denominations, but entire nation-states. But to understand how this evolution took place, we must delve further into Pentecostal history, looking into the Charismatic Renewal, the shepherding movement it birthed, and the church growth movement with which it intertwined.

The Charismatic Renewal: Charismatic Practice Gone Awry

By the early sixties, many independent Pentecostals did not share denominational Pentecostals "scruples against fraternizing with mainliners and Catholics" (Robins 91). In addition, influenced perhaps by David Du Plessis, many of those seeking Pentecostal revitalization urged those in mainline churches to "work for renewal within their own denominations rather than join an openly Pentecostal body" (Robins 91). Mainstream evangelical organizations like the National Association of Evangelicals (NAE) brought Pentecostal leaders into fellowship with other evangelicals, a union that would end up contributing directly to the formation of the NAR through the influence of Third Wave movement leaders like John Wimber, C. Peter Wagner, and Charles Kraft (Robins 91). By the late 1950s, the mainline denominations possessed a number of Charismatics-in-training who would go on to become major leaders in the Charismatic Renewal, including Agnes Sanford, John Osteen and Pat Robertson (Robins 91).

The immediate cause of the Charismatic Renewal, in most tellings, is the charismatic experience of Episcopalian pastor Dennis Bennett at St. Mark's Episcopal Church in Van Nuys, California, which occurred in 1960. Bennett, after speaking in tongues, was criticized by his congregation and bishop, which both wanted him to resign. Bennett's actions, occurring as they did in the staid environs of the Episcopalian church, led to a media frenzy, one that ended up creating what is now called the Charismatic Renewal (also known as Neo-Pentecostalism) (Synan 149–151). The Charismatic Renewal differed from classical Pentecostalism in some significant ways. Generally, members of the Charismatic Renewal had a higher opinion of historic Christian traditions than either denominational or independent Pentecostals (Robins Jr. 94). In addition, Charismatic leaders tended to be more conversant with theological dialogue than their Pentecostal peers, and as a consequence many of the most sophisticated theologians within the wider Pentecostal/Charismatic movement came out of the Charismatic Renewal (Robins Jr. 92, 94). The neo-Pentecostals of the Charismatic Renewal were also characterized by the fact that they tended to be less emotional than traditional Pentecostals and often implemented their use of the gifts of the Spirit in more private settings than did classical Pentecostals. In addition, many came from the ranks of the educated clergy and lay professionals (Synan 154), which in all likelihood exacerbated the already tense situation between less affluent classical Pentecostal traditions and the Renewal movement.

Over the course of the 1960s, the Charismatic Renewal gave birth to many organizations, retreat centers and publications. More significantly, a "flourishing network of leaders" emerged within mainline denominations to provide direction to the Charismatic Renewal. Some of these leaders, such as Larry Christenson[9] would merely become popular in the shepherding movement; others, such as Don Basham (Disciples of Christ) and Charles Simpson (Southern Baptist) would prove to be major leaders within shepherding circles. The Renewal movement proved to be enormously controversial, causing major rifts within mainstream Protestantism. Almost all Protestant denominations conducted some form of study on the Renewal, but only a few fundamentalist groups ended up resisting it with any degree of consistency (see R.G. Robins 92). Most of the denominations who undertook a study of Charismatic Renewal neither welcomed it "with enthusiasm" nor rejected it as "inauthentic" (Hocken 483). Cautious openness was the rule (Hocken 483). By the early 1970s, one saw a plethora of Charismatic literature being published, much of it from new Pentecostal-Charismatic publishing houses like Logos International, others of it from more traditional publishers like Fleming H. Revell (Hocken 483). A number of Charismatic books became best-sellers, including Don Basham's demon-busting expose *Deliver Us from Evil* (1972), which would become a major text in the deliverance movement. New works on healing by authors like Francis MacNutt, Michael Scanlan, and Ruth Carter Stapleton, were also prominent (Hocken 483–484). Charismatics became quickly skilled in the use of mass media.

One aspect that characterized the Charismatic Renewal, particularly its nondenominational contingent was its "restorationist emphasis," including a focus on fivefold ministries. Major Pentecostal denominations tended to view this restorationist emphasis as "dangerous and deviant." However, because of the increasing percentage of non-denominational churches involved in the Charismatic Renewal there was a much wider acceptance of the fivefold ministries, especially the ministries of apostle and prophet (Hocken 516).

At this time as well, Charismatic churches began experimenting with "the cell system" idea. This strategy was first tried on a large scale at David Yonggi Cho's Yoido Full Gospel Church in Seoul, South Korea (Hocken 502). Under Cho's system, churches were divided into "homogenous cells" composed of up to 5 or 10 families (Brouwer, Gifford and Rose 117). Basing itself on the homogenous unit principle popularized by Donald McGavran (Brouwer, Gifford and Rose 43–44, 117–118), Cho divided his church up by common "orientations or occupations" (Brouwer, Gifford and Rose 117). Cho's system was constructed in a pyramidal fashion, with "neighborhood leads, subpastors, and pastors under his authority, but with sufficient lateral openness through the 'cell system' that they do not necessarily threaten bureaucratic stagnation at a certain size" (Brouwer, Gifford and Rose 121). Cho's church, in part because of this sophisticated but highly controlling church growth strategy, became the biggest church in the world (see Allan Anderson 1 on the size of Cho's church). What is significant to note is that the shepherding movement in some ways pioneered this cell church model even before the model became popular in Korea (Moore 4). In addition, both shepherding and Cho's cell church theory shared with each other a common idea of a militarized church structure, with each shepherd-led church, much like Yoido Full Gospel, being led by a "lay pastor" who "was submitted to another pastor in a kind of chain of command with a senior or presiding pastor overseeing a local church network of pastoral leaders. Each presiding congregational pastor was in turn submitted to one of the five teachers or his designate" (Moore 2). It would be this hierarchical structure which would lead the shepherding movement to become one of the most successful yet scandal-ridden movements within Charismatic history.

The Shepherding Movement

The shepherding movement, also known as "discipling" or "covenanting," was a movement that swept throughout the Charismatic community in the 1970s (Cuneo 121). The leadership of the movement felt that the Charismatic Renewal was in danger of losing its moorings because it was not adequately grounded in "the requirements of the faith" (Cuneo 122). In order to tighten control of the Renewal, the leadership of the shepherding movement (in particular the Fort Lauderdale Five, consisting of Ern Baxter, Charles Simpson, Bob Mumford, Derek Prince, and Don Basham) began setting themselves up "as a kind of infallible leadership caste" (Cuneo 122). The shepherds argued that their power came direct from the Holy Spirit, and that that power allowed them to "define strict lines of authority for charismatic prayer groups across the country. And they also claimed that individual charismatics were required to submit themselves, totally and unflinchingly, to the authority of specially designated elders or 'shepherds' from their local communities" (Cuneo 122).

By the early 1970s, Christian Growth Ministries, the flagship ministry of shepherding, had managed to create an "extensive network of rigidly authoritarian prayer groups throughout the Protestant wing of the renewal" (Cuneo 122). The movement spread into the Catholic wing of the Renewal as well, leading to the creation of "covenant communities." Critics of these communities, much like critics of the shepherding movement within Protestantism, complained that the covenant communities were little more than "petty fiefdoms" run by authoritarians who brooked no dissent from their followers (Cuneo 123).

Cuneo wisely cautions readers not to believe every story about shepherding, as some were undoubtedly exaggerated. But as he points out, there is also "little question" that a "good many" of the shepherding communities "were committed to a kind of spiritual engineering, trying to transform ordinary charismatics into entirely new and submissive children of God" (Cuneo 123). As he points out, there is also a high probability that deliverance practices were used coercively against those people who were deemed insufficiently submissive by their shepherds (Cuneo 123).

Horror stories about the shepherding movement are ubiquitous throughout evangelicalism. I encountered some of them while researching for my second book, even though I was not looking for them. It is therefore disappointing that the leading historian of the shepherding movement, S. David Moore, pays the movement's critics hardly any attention. Moore claims that

> there were, no doubt, serious abuses of spiritual authority among the Shepherding movement's practitioners. I knew that going into my research…. I discovered that some of the issues attracting critics' charges, which initially seemed so black and white became grey when I interviewed all sides. The defenses given for the movement's many casualties also proved inadequate. Still, I found no evidence that the Shepherding movement's principal leaders led a conspiracy to take over the Charismatic Renewal or had evil designs to exploit and dominate their followers. Quite the opposite was the case. The research suggested that the movement's five leaders were well-intentioned and well-motivated [Moore vii-viii].

Moore's statement is disingenuous. It may very well be true that the Fort Lauderdale Five's immediate goal was not the takeover of the Charismatic Renewal.

That may be too conspiratorial a reading of their actions. However, it cannot be denied that once the movement began aggregating power, the majority of its leadership, especially those in the mid-level between the "sheep" and the "Fort Lauderdale Five" seemed quite reluctant to relinquish that power, even when charges of abuse were so rampant as to virtually assure that there were serious structural problems in the way the shepherding movement viewed ecclesiastical authority. And it is, of course, entirely possible for the leadership of a movement to have good intentions and its membership still be abusive, even assuming the Fort Lauderdale Five's intentions were pure. As Sara Diamond, a more reliable secular source on shepherding reports, by the mid-1970s, "scores of 'sheep' were reporting to the larger Christian community that the rigorous demands of the shepherds were depriving them of all independent decision-making powers" (Diamond, *Spiritual Warfare* 116). Even a relatively pro–Charismatic scholar like Nigel Scotland, while admitting benefits of shepherding, has documented extensive abuses of shepherding practices in British Charismatic circles, ranging from a "pressurized regime of fear" that was so oppressive it caused a woman to lose her baby, to leaders intruding "into every area of their [the shepherd's disciples] private lives, their homes, [and] their finances" and to a woman being issued ultimatums to marry a certain man or face dire spiritual consequences (Scotland, *Charismatics and the New Millennium* 112, 122–123). Similarly, *The Discipling Dilemma* (1988; edited by Flavil R. Yeakley, Jr.), a relatively even-handed critique of shepherding, pointed out the numerous emotional problems that were reported with shepherding (Don Vinzant 158–167) and provided extensive documentation of various sources critical of shepherding (Don Vinzant 158–167). Some of the accounts mentioned in both Diamond and Yeakley Jr. went to print, yet they merit only brief mentions in Moore's book, which relies to a large extent on the shepherds' own testimony and on movement-produced primary source material, without seriously taking account of the many critics of the movement.

Yet Diamond was able to find such evidence relatively easy (for Diamond's take on shepherding, see *Spiritual Warfare* 111–122). According to Diamond, members of the shepherding movement were "not allowed to date, much less marry, without shepherds' permission. Some former members of shepherding churches describe having to bring their checkbook registers to 'cell group' meetings in order to prove that they were donating ten percent, called a 'tithe,' of their monthly income to the organization" (Diamond, *Spiritual Warfare* 116). So authoritarian was the shepherding movement that, despite its enormous influence, Pat Robertson banned the promotion of its materials on the 700 Club (Diamond 117). Though Robertson was likely partly motivated by a desire to defend his ecclesiological turf area, there's little doubt that he was also concerned about the direction shepherding was leading the Charismatic Renewal. Other prominent Charismatic leaders, including the well-respected Chuck Smith, condemned shepherding teaching as abhorrent (Moore 113, 155).

Diamond points out that by the late 1980s, the Cult Awareness Network (which was then still an anti-cult organization) had reported an

> upsurge in cases of individuals suffering profound psychological trauma at the hands of authoritarian shepherding church leaders.... In contrast to a cult like the Unification Church, which has a single hierarchical chain of command, the "cell group" structure adopted by independent "charismatic" churches offers room for more bosses and more underlings. Without the oversight measures found in the by-laws of denominational churches, the free-wheeling shepherding churches provide abusive leaders plenty of leeway with little institutional recourse for victimized "disciples" [Diamond 118].

One is, of course, free to disagree with CAN's interpretation of shepherding practice; CAN's own anti-cult record was not by any means ubiquitously clean itself. But besides the fact that Diamond herself is traditionally seen as a careful researcher by at least secular evangelical studies scholars, the plain fact remains that Diamond's narrative of shepherding concurs with that offered up by many individuals who sympathize with Charismatics. Michael Moriarty points out that shepherds often had power over their disciples to "such an extent that decisions such as employment, vacation time, appointments with professionals ... marriage, and even how often a husband and wife could have sex could not be made without the shepherd's approval" (Moriarty 76). Similarly, in a less reliable source, the author of the shepherding memoir/critique, *Charismatic Captivation* (2003), Pastor Steven Lambert, writes that "typically, submitted members must obtain the approval of their group-gurus regarding virtually all domestic matters and matters of romance, such as who members date and marry; health and insurance matters, employment and career matters, and most of all, regarding the details of members' personal finances, which requires their leaders' approval for practically every significant expenditure" (Lambert, *Charismatic Captivation* loc 150). Thus, Charismatics, former Charismatics, and secular critics all see problematic aspects with shepherding practice, aspects that seem to somehow elude the movement's main chronicler.

Diamond's central contention about shepherding practice is similar to the one I made about Latter Rain teachings: Because shepherding lacked the kind of denominational oversight one would see in denominational churches, which were bound by church by-laws, shepherding allowed for what Diamond calls a "free-wheeling" style that left little recourse for people victimized by practices they deemed to be abusive (Diamond 117–118). Authoritarianism could therefore run amok. The problems for Diamond with shepherding are inherent in the structure of the system shepherding set up; they are not ancillary issues, but intrinsic as to why the movement degenerated so quickly from its original goals.

Moriarty speculates that another reason that shepherding practice went awry was the concept of "covering" that became prominent during the 1970s (and remains so to this day). The concept of covering held that for shepherding to be successfully implemented, each member of the church needed to be protected and directed by someone having a "covering over them." What this meant was that "'a church member must have any important decision, and sometimes less important ones, 'covered' or approved by their house-group leader, elder or pastor" (Barrs 369). The idea behind this was that being covered from above "protected those below, who were understood to be weaker and more vulnerable and subject to demonic influence and poor decision making" (Moriarty 76). Moriarty contends that it was this concept of covering that often served as the justification for the shepherds' over-involvement in their "sheep's" lives (Morarity 76–78).

Crucial to note, in any case, is that whatever the degree of abuses there were in shepherding—and even Moore is forced to concede that there were abuses (Moore vii-viii)—there were clearly aspects of shepherding that were seen as valuable by the NAR. Even Moore realizes these connections. As he points out, C. Peter Wagner's idea of networked churches serving under apostolic leaders may have its origins in shepherding. Similarly the NAR concept of organizing relationally rather than through formal organizational structures is an idea that quite likely had its origins in shepherding practice (Moore 188–189). Shepherding based itself on organic networking that, while working within denominational settings, would in its NAR form, at least, transcend these denominational hierarchies (see Moore 80), directly "poaching" from denominational Charismatics.

The shepherding movement's adoption of both the concept of covering and of cell churches also survived long enough to be adopted by the NAR. The idea of covering, originally was ideally seen as a form of protection for more vulnerable members in the church hierarchy, but was later used by NAR leaders as a tool to prevent potentially damaging breaks within the structure of the NAR's "reformation"; this was most graphically seen in the Lakeland Revival, where the apostles used an extensive apostolic covering as a more earthly form of cover from the extreme doctrines of Todd Bentley, the major revivalist at Lakeland.[10] The NAR has found the concept of covering useful because of its nature as a form of quasi spin-control for the Charismatic movement. The issue is no longer solely dictatorialness, though that remains, but of making sure the Charismatic church is more self-conscious of its media-image.

The shepherding movement, like the Latter Rain movement, believed in the importance of the fivefold ministries, and placed a similar emphasis on the role of the apostles (see Moore 72 on shepherding movement's use of fivefold ministries). Crucial to this idea was the concept of "personal pastoral care" where each person was being mentored or disciple by someone higher up the church hierarchy (Moore 74). According to Moore, "contrary to charges of critics, the shepherd-sheep relationship never carried any soteriological dimension. The movement's leaders never questioned that salvation and entry into the universal invisible Church was through anything but faith in Christ" (Moore 74). Again, Diamond's account of shepherding is at variance with Moore's, as Diamond interviewed an ex-survivor of one of Mumford's churches who was taught that one could lose salvation if one disobeyed the shepherd's authority (Diamond 118).

In any case, in Moore's rendering of this "personal pastoral care," the motivation for such action is to make sure the individual's spiritual covering is correctly in place. According to Moore, the shepherd also assumes responsibility for the sheep in return for the sheep's obedience (see Moore 74). A more skeptical reading of such care would accentuate the potential advantages that could accrue to dishonest shepherds. While this work concurs with Moore that such an intent may not have motivated the Fort Lauderdale Five, their unwillingness to halt or reshape their movement after its perceived abuses had become too widely known to ignore made them complicit in the abuses that happened afterwards.

Diamond did not see the shepherding movement as ever truly a dead movement. Indeed, she points out that Don Basham's and Bob Mumford's return to CBN—and therefore the respectability of mainstream Charismatic practice—occurred right at the height of the 1980s PTL scandal, which Basham pointedly, if implicitly, argued would not have happened if Jim Bakker had not been under a shepherd (Diamond 119). Still, Moore's dating of the movement as largely having ended its unified existence with the shutting of the shepherding movement's flagship magazine *New Wine* seems in hindsight to be correct (see Moore 169 on the ending of the shepherding movement). By the time *New Wine* closed its doors, shepherding had done its job in paving the way for the NAR. Degrees of authoritarianism that before had been largely confined to independent Charismatic or Pentecostal churches were now finding their way into denominational structures that had fought decades to keep them out. Even the staunchest opponents of NAR theology within Charismatic circles would be hard-pressed to hold their own against the NAR. And as major a movement as the Latter Rain was, it is certainly doubtful whether it could have affected C. Peter Wagner's vision of church leadership without the memory of shepherding to spur his movement on. Therefore, while shepherding as a form of authoritarian church control was itself a failure, it paved the way for the NAR to eventually successfully market discipling, ecclesiological, and doctrinal innovations that had previously been considered too radical for the Pentecostal mainstream or even the Charismatic Renewal to accept. In the process, the NAR would totally reinvent how church was "done" in America. But to understand this critical issue, we must turn finally to the church growth movement, which would fatally unite itself with the Charismatic movement and provide it with both its greatest leader, C. Peter Wagner, and two of its major doctrinal influences, John Wimber and Charles Kraft. From the 1970s onwards, these men would reshape Charismatic Christianity.

The Church Growth Movement

The church growth movement started with Donald McGavran. McGavran's vision of church growth originated with his missionary work in the mid–20th century. McGavran was interested in maximizing church growth in the developing world. He was perplexed as to why some churches grew while others decayed and died out. Like many Christians of the time,[11] McGavran theorized that "conversions are most numerous if done in 'people movements,' by collective decisions and actions of a group" (Holvast 18). Rather than concentrating on conversion at the individual level, he was concerned with conversion at the social level. This was not a social gospel idea, however, as McGavran saw such ideas as antithetical to Christianity (Burkhalter 156–157; see Terry 149). Nor, for that matter, did McGavran's policy of conversion resemble the kind favored by some missiologists in his time, in which the conversion of elite leaders was seen as a prelude to conversion of entire populations (see McGavran, *Understanding Church Growth* 281). Instead, McGavran's missiology built from the bottom up.

A crucial concept within church growth practice was the idea of the "homogenous group" principle. C. Peter Wagner, who would become the most important leader in the NAR, defined a homogenous group as simply a "group of people who consider each other to be our kind of people. They have many areas of mutual interest. They share the same culture. They socialize freely" (Wagner, *Your Church Can Grow* 110; Terry 91–92). McGavran's vision of homogenous units was somewhat more specific in denoting that units could differ linguistically, ethically, economically, or educationally and therefore be organized around any of these patterns (Terry 92). Wagner and McGavran came to believe that people were more likely to become Christians if they did not have to cross "racial, linguistic or class barriers" (Wagner, *Wrestling* 108–109). Wagner's point was not to create a white-only segregationist church; rather both McGavran's and Wagner's concern was simply pragmatic. This monocultural idea of church was meant to create not merely homogenous units, but a model for church growth that could be shifted from culture to culture without any major need for variation. Thus the model had to be succinct and intensely pragmatic.

Another crucial element of church growth ideology, one that also tended to separate the movement's ideology from that of mainstream evangelical missiology during the '60s and '70s dealt with the movement's methodology. Wagner noted

> that while classical theologians share the same starting point with church growth thinkers, the absolute authority of the Bible, church growth opts for different methods of interpreting that Biblical material. While classical theology relies almost exclusively on philosophy and the philosophical method, church growth opts to use the social sciences and the social science method as a means of interpreting the Scripture in regards to the missiological agenda [Terry 70].

The conviction that the social sciences, particularly anthropology (Holvast 19, 23, 29, 213), were as central to the growth of the church as theology was perhaps the most crucial theoretical insight of the church growth movement, and greatly affected how both neo-evangelical church growth supporters and their descendants in the Charismatic NAR movement viewed how people should "do" church. A few comments should be made here on the most crucial aspects of this new way of doing church. Most critically, as René Holvast points out in reference to the structural-functionalist anthropology of Charles Kraft (who was a leading proponent of both the church growth movement and the NAR), there was an intensely pragmatic bent to church growth ideology (see Holvast 19, 226). As Holvast points out, church growth envisioned missiology as a "set of manageable and pragmatic principles in which theology made use of models of social sciences" (Holvast 19). The church growth model, therefore, tried to apply the scientific method to the goal of expanding Christianity.

One could debate the scientific veracity of the movement's ideology; Jonathan Terry III, for instance, expresses skepticism at the viability of the homogenous unit as a scientific concept, given the lack of true social science grounding found in McGavran's writing (Terry 153). What is harder to debate is that for better or for worse, the methodology the church growth movement developed due to this commitment to the social science method proved superior to the non-scientific ideology of traditional missiology. In other words, even bad science and pseudo-science worked better than traditional missiologies that denied the value of the social science method.

Crucial to McGavran's and later Wagner's disagreement with traditional missiology was a distinction McGavran made between what he saw as the traditional "search principle" of missiology and the "harvest principle." Although the search principle is a complex idea, it boils down to the idea that missionary work was based more on the act of evangelizing rather than the result—the product that is—of evangelization (see Terry 74, who phrases things somewhat differently). Search theology, for McGavran, "denied that results had anything to do with mission" (Terry 75). As a result, as a missiological principle, it was not outward looking enough or aggressive enough in its approach to reaching "unreached" people groups. McGavran also did not agree with the increasing "social" emphasis in missiological circles, which he blamed on the search principle. He felt that programs of social uplift or improvement were not as important as direct evangelization efforts (Terry 76–77).

McGavran, therefore, while not discounting the search principle, preferred the harvest principle, a theology of missions which "puts the emphasis on results rather than simply effort" (Terry 77). As church growth ideology became streamlined over the years, more and more every issue was judged by how it would affect the expansion or contraction of Christian missions. One concern that seems implicit in both Terry's and Holvast's work, is that such a radical focus on pragmatism inevitably affected the ethical presuppositions of the organizations pushing church growth and its later formulations, such as spiritual mapping and the NAR (this is particularly clear in Terry's work). With numbers being the prime concern, issues of social justice and theological orthodoxy both took a back seat. This paradoxical rejection of both the primarily left wing theology of the various social justice theological systems (particularly liberation theology), along with the simultaneous pushback against the more orthodox theologies of missions favored by traditional evangelicals is largely responsible for the church growth movement's fusion with much of the Charismatic Renewal. Though church growth ideology would eventually win over even mainline Protestants (Terry 174) and many mainstream evangelicals, the movement's strongest base continues to remain within the Charismatic tradition, which has most effectively utilized its insights.

The Growth and Institutionalization of the Church Growth Movement

By 1960, McGavran had established an institute with "the purpose of training missionaries and conducting research on the growth of churches." This eventually evolved into the School of World Mission, headquartered at Fuller Theological Seminary (Holvast 23–24). While the foreign missions-oriented nature of early church growth thought is important to understanding the movement's growth, the movement soon was seen as having far wider applications than just foreign missions. In the fall of 1972, a group of interested students met to discuss the subject of church growth. This class became "significant because it marked the first systematic application of Church Growth to American Christianity." With the success of this class and other marketing efforts to Americans, McGavran and Wagner were able to promote the viability of church growth within the American context (Cook 1).

Crucial to the success of church growth in the American context would be C. Peter Wagner (1930–) (Wagner, *Wrestling* 1), who would become the most important leader within the NAR. Wagner's background in some ways made him an unusual candidate to lead either the church growth movement or the NAR. By Wagner's own admission, before accepting a position with McGavran's School of World Mission (SWM), he had serious doubts about the direction Fuller Seminary was heading. The school was also more liberal theologically than Wagner or his wife Doris were then comfortable with. As cessationists who had aligned themselves with some fairly conservative theological positions (on the Wagners' early cessationism, see Wagner, *Wrestling*, 43), the Wagners were concerned with what they saw as the liberalization of Fuller Seminary, particularly its position on biblical inerrancy. Wagner also felt some concern about the faculty the SWM was hiring, such as McGavran, Charles Kraft and fellow SWM faculty Ralph Winter and Alan Tippett, since these men were all affiliated with denominations belonging to the World Council of Churches (Wagner, *Wrestling* 82), commonly perceived as theologically liberal. Wagner was initially repelled by McGavran's scientific approach to church growth, which he felt was the theology of an evangelical "quack" (see Cook 64–65). On a missionary furlough in 1967, Wagner decided to check out McGavran to see what exactly he was teaching and radically changed his opinion in favor of McGavran's church growth ideology (Cook 65). While there may have been some ulterior motives for Wagner adopting church growth ideology, it cannot be denied that he remained devoted to the principles underlying that ideology for the rest of his life.

In 1971, McGavran retired from his position as the "founding dean" of SWM and Wagner, who had already served several times as a visiting lecturer at SWM, now stepped in as an associate professor of Church Growth and Latin American Studies (Cook 66). Wagner was more fanatically committed to American church growth than McGavran,[12] and quickly tried to develop methods of expanding and enhancing church participation and membership in the

States (Cook 66–67). Wagner was crucial in changing the direction of the Doctoral of Ministry (D. Min) program at Fuller, adding an "in ministry model to its curriculum" (Cook 69). This new D. Min program shifted "focus from professional competence toward the growth and development of the local church. It was student and church-oriented, thus reflecting Fuller Seminary's move toward more practical and relational concerns" (Cook 70). Thus the D. Min program at Fuller, which along with Westminster Seminary remained one of the two most respected intellectual "think tanks" of evangelicalism, became a breeding ground for ministers who would replicate the church growth model on a much larger scale than was available to just Fuller Seminary. And like the leaders of the church growth movement, the D. Min's program's philosophy was heavily oriented in a pragmatic, results-first direction.

Equally important for the growth of the church growth movement was Wagner's assignment to be the "Executive Director of the Fuller Evangelistic Association" (Cook 71). At the time, the Association was constrained largely to the "distribution of between fifty and sixty thousand dollars annually to various mission projects from the Charles Fuller trust" (Cook 71–72). Wagner turned the organization into a sort of church growth consultation agency, and envisioned a time in which the organization could provide practical support for church growth questions and problems throughout the country (Cook 72). Therefore Wagner developed the Department of Church Growth of the Fuller Evangelistic Association. It would be this organization that led to Wagner's alliance with John Wimber (Cook 72). Before we explore that alliance in detail, however, we must look at the anthropology of Charles Kraft, which provided the foundation for the spiritual mapping movement that would help to popularize the NAR in the 1990s, and which, along with McGavran's church growth principles, helped provide the intellectual bedrock for the foundational thinkers within the NAR.

Kraft's anthropological ideas were initially influenced by the anthropology of Eugene A. Nida, the secretary of Bible translations of the American Bible Society (ABS). In the 1950s, Nida, allied with a number of other evangelicals, tried to fuse anthropology with missions theory and Bible translation. Missionary anthropology itself started as a sub-discipline within applied anthropology, inspired by major publications in the 1960s by both Nida and Kenneth Pike. Kraft specifically positioned himself within this particular anthropological school and as Holvast points out, he only rarely referred to anthropological texts beyond the early 1980s. Kraft's goal was intensely pragmatic and virtually identical to McGavran's: To use social science—here, anthropology—to further "Evangelical missionary practice" (Holvast 29).

Kraft's orienting principle for anthropology was how he understood culture.

For Kraft, a culture had a "behavioural level" and a "'deep worldview level.'" Worldview was defined as "basic assumptions, values, and allegiances" and "was basic to all aspects of culture; religion was a surface level phenomenon" (Holvast 29–30). For Kraft, it was "worldview that provides the structure that influences behavior. Conversion to the Christian faith involves some changes in the deep worldview level assumptions, values and allegiances" (Holvast 30). There were a number of implications for this idea. For instance, in the spiritual mapping movement of the 1990s, Kraft, along with other spiritual mapping proponents, used these principles to argue that Christians needed to break free of Enlightenment rationalism if they were to effectively minister to those populations of the world who did not think in "rationalistic" terms.

Borrowing from fellow evangelical anthropologist Paul Hiebert (who hardly approved of Kraft's use of his ideas), the spiritual mapping movement argued for the principle of the "Excluded Middle," first popularized in Hiebert's 1982 essay "The Flaw of the Excluded Middle." Hiebert contended that Western Christians typically perceived a two-tiered world. There was a ground-level which human beings could observe, consisting (for instance) of nature and humans, and then there was the level of God in heaven. But, Hiebert argued, there was also an excluded middle zone in "which there are invisible spirits who are also actively involved in the human sphere" (Holvast 32). Foundational to Kraft's beliefs, which would influence both the spiritual mapping movement and the NAR, was that when Western Christians failed to perceive this excluded middle, they failed to perceive all of reality; as a result, if the biblical worldview was to be brought to all peoples, Western Christians must reject the legacy of Enlightenment rationalism for a return to a more truly biblical worldview that embraced the existence of this Excluded Middle and sought to combat those evil forces which often dwelt within it (Holvast 32–33).

Crucial to Kraft's missionary anthropology was the concept of power encounters. This idea, first pioneered by anthropologist Alan Tippett, argued that the primary means of effecting spiritual transformation over an evangelized group was to prove to that group the effectiveness of the transmitting religious ideology's God (Christ) over the recipient movement's gods. Frequently the tools used for these power encounters were often healing ceremonies or exorcisms (Holvast 21). Power encounters became a huge part of John Wimber's ministry as well, which given Wimber's wild popularity, and the dispersion of his Vineyard movement's philosophy through heterodox Vineyard-inspired theological movements like the Toronto Blessing, would in combination with Kraft's vision of power encounters, spread this idea worldwide (see Zichterman 177 on Wimber's vision of power encounters). Kraft perceived power encounters as a more effective evangelistic tool than rational persuasion, using the example of Jesus's acts of exorcism as support of this line of reasoning (Holvast 33).

From a secular standpoint, Kraft's and his allies' anthropology was "oriented toward structural functionalism" (Holvast 30). Structural functionalism was rooted in the organismic analogies of Émile Durkheim, who conceptualized society in organismic terms. Just as biological organisms had both structure and function, so too did societies. As Paul Erickson and Liam Murphy point out, "according to the organismic analogy, the scientific study of societies should include social morphology and social physiology" (Erickson and Murphy 100). Significantly, and damningly for the NAR's self-understanding, structural-functionalism's outlook was "synchronic, meaning ahistorical, rather than diachronic, or concerned with change through time" (Erickson and Murphy 100). Thus, though Kraft and his allies saw the movement as operating within the bounds of the social sciences, the movement generally did not try to interpret its own anthropology, let alone the field of anthropology itself, in historical terms, seeing its anthropological values as transcendental.

Structural functionalism saw social structure as the "matrix or enclosing form of society, while social function was the role that individual parts of society played in maintaining the structural whole" (Erickson and Murphy 101). If a society properly functioned, its social structure maintained itself in equilibrium, or, to use the organismic analogy, "structural health." Deriving their philosophy from Durkheimian thought, British anthropologists in the structural functional school (who were the founders of the movement) saw society as "harmonious and stable," unlike cultural evolutionists, who viewed culture as "prone to change, or Marxists, who saw it as conflicted" (Erickson and Murphy 101). What is crucial to understand for interpreting the development of the NAR was that structural functionalism served two essential purposes for Kraft. One of these purposes is pointed out by Holvast and that is that it justified the essential pragmatism of the church growth movement, a pragmatism largely inherited by the spiritual mapping movement that shaped the NAR's evolution in the 1990s (Holvast 30–31). In Kraft's telling of structural functionalism, culture was "never fully integrated and consistent but in a state of constant change. The all-determining factor in change was the worldview (also called 'religion'): cultures went through a process of constant change of revaluation, re-interpretation, and development of new behavior" (Holvast 31). This provided the justification, according to Holvast, for legitimizing mission anthropologically, because in the view of Kraft and his allies, mission was just one of many factors influencing cultural change; a change that was for the movement inevitable in any case (Holvast 31).

There is a second factor that, in some ways paradoxically influenced the adoption of Kraft's missionary anthropology among both church growth supporters and the spiritual mapping movement: this factor is the need to introduce socially dynamic processes into the church while maintaining social stability. If we think about this through the lens of Cometian positivism, an important influence on anthropology, this division exemplifies the division within social science between what Comte labeled "social dynamics," which searched for generalizations about social change, and social statics, which looked for generalizations about social stability (Erickson and Murphy 42). For Comte, living in the wake of the French Revolution, the Revolution had too heavily favored "dynamic change" and therefore needed to have its most excessive elements "tempered with social statics" (Erickson and Murphy 42). As movements, the church growth movement, spiritual mapping, and the NAR all required major changes to church structures, theologies, and even worship styles. Kraft and Wagner, both of whom started out in mainstream evangelicalism before finding their way into the Third Wave Charismatic movement, were social conservatives and though theological innovators, risk averse when it came to making social changes that affected the basic power structure of the wider society. They therefore needed an ideological system that could introduce the new dynamic innovations being offered by the church growth movement with a minimum of social upheaval.

Evangelicalism, as a belief system, does not tend to favor "social dynamic" theories, like the ones espoused by Kraft and Wagner. The Charismatic movement, where Kraft and Wagner ended up, was much more ideally suited for such dynamism, but the trick was to make the system's ecclesiological and missional structures socially dynamic, while making sure that its views on economics and social justice leaned more in a social statics direction. Obviously, the Charismatic movement is in many ways not necessarily an ideal candidate for this kind of attempt to maintain cultural homeostasis because both its restorationist beliefs and its experiential bias can easily lead to a lack of control of the movement by its leadership.

What the NAR's leadership did so brilliantly was to progressively introduce new spiritual technologies (to borrow a term from Holvast), which were often merely reformulated forms of past spiritual technologies, to reinforce the power of the movement's leadership. These technologies—which I would define either, as in Holvast, "diagnostic tools" or "disciplines" (Holvast 197) or, alternately, certain major innovations in ecclesiology or church structure—served dual functions. First, the spiritual promise these tactics heralded helped to keep old movement stalwarts motivated and gain new adherents; secondly, these tactics simultaneously often allowed the apostles and prophets of the NAR to repeatedly introduce, through these technologies, instant and far-reaching theological and ecclesiological change that would be impossible for the movement to implement as a whole were it not for the movement's belief in both the authority of the apostles and the promise of the spiritual technologies they sought to impart. Thus, the existence of both an authoritarian hierarchy and a flexible and innovative "command and control" element at the heart of the NAR's ecclesiology made it very hard for the movement's opponents to adapt to or even simply challenge NAR presuppositions. The inevitable response to these challenges, from NAR adherents, was that other groups of Christians represented "old wineskins" which were incapable of adapting quickly enough to the radical new gospel being offered up within each successive evolution of NAR theology.

One other aspect of Kraft's anthropology greatly influenced later NAR thinking: his theory of translation. Kraft's theory of translation was based on the idea of "cultural dynamic equivalence" (Holvast 31). Kraft, clearly borrowing from earlier evangelical translation theorists like Eugene Nida and William Smalley (see Smalley, no pagination on dynamic equivalence theory, especially as used by Nida), distinguished between what he called literalistic or "formal correspondence" models of translation and dynamically equivalent ones. According to Kraft's theory of translation, the focus within the cultural dynamic school was on "surface-level linguistic forms through which the message is conveyed" and therefore was more concerned with rendering a translation that is as close to the original as possible (Kraft, *Christianity in Culture* 264). The alternative to this model, which formed the virtual basis of Kraft's entire missiology and much of his ecclesiology, was the idea of "dynamic equivalence." Within dynamic equivalent translations, the translation would be, according to Kraft, "so true to both the message of the source documents and the normal ways of expressing such a message in the receptor language that the hearers/readers can, by employing their own interpretational reflexes, derive the proper meanings" (Kraft, *Christianity in Culture* 269). Thus, a dynamically equivalent linguistic translation, from, say America, could in theory as effectively communicate the spiritual truths expressed in non–English translations of the Bible as it could in English translations. What was crucial to this translation process was the skill of the translator and his ability to effectively communicate between differing linguistic systems.

What was revolutionary about Kraft's anthropology was that he applied this theory of dynamic equivalence to various structures of Christian life, not just linguistics. Kraft crucially argued for a process of "transculturating" or "transculturation," a term which was "intended to signify with respect to culture what the term 'translate' signifies with respect to language" (Kraft, *Christianity in Culture* 280). Kraft, from the beginning saw the potential of this concept.

For instance, in *Christianity in Culture* (1979), he points out that one of the crucial flaws to effective transculturation within Western churches was their over-reliance on "monologue preaching." Kraft pointed out that this fault was a damning one for the church because there were many forms of communicating the Christian message that might be more effective in many instances than the traditional church format of monologue preaching favored by more traditional denominational groups; Kraft pointed to the use of drama, storytelling, and musical presentation in particular as powerful mechanisms for inducing conversion, if churches were willing to rethink how they structured their liturgical and leadership elements (see Kraft 281).

Two elements of this transculturation idea became particularly important in how the NAR later structured itself. The first was Kraft's assumptions about theology. As in linguistic translation, Kraft argued for a dynamically equivalent theology that would reproduce "in contemporary cultural contexts ... the theologizing process that Paul and the other scriptural authors exemplify" (Kraft, *Christianity in Culture* 291). This entails primarily adopting, as Kraft says Christ and Paul adopted, the "linguistic cultural and situational frames of reference of their hearers" (Kraft 299–300). Obviously this idea is not without merit; any "missional" religious movement must learn to adapt its message to changing cultural and environmental situations, hopefully with sensitivity. However, Kraft's vision of theology highly emphasized pragmatic considerations over the ethics of making Christian truth claims. As the eighties rolled on, Kraft's disdain for theology as a mechanism of Christian conversion became increasingly shared by Wagner and thereby colored NAR thought. When Wagner, started his own school, for instance, he designed it so that all its courses were electives, with no required curriculum. As a result, students were not forced to take courses like epistemology (a field Wagner disdained), that they saw as irrelevant to their future church careers (Wagner, *Wrestling Alligators* 36). Wagner faulted traditional seminaries for being concerned 80 percent with "theory" and 20 percent with "practice." Wagner inverted these percentages. He criticized traditional seminary publications for their "long and detailed footnotes," their frequent use of "German, Latin, Greek, and Hebrew" and their reliance on library research; the approach he preferred favored articles and books written in a "popular style," "peppered with anecdotes," that were reliant on "field research" (Wagner, *Churchquake!* 226). Wagner was therefore quite self-consciously building a movement that disdained academic research and theological debate. Theology was seen as being second in importance to missions. This allowed Wagner the luxury of not having to justify his theological positions to his followers because the expectation was that they would not be concerned with theology, but missional issues. An educated church laity was definitely not desired by the NAR.

But it is in ecclesiology that Kraft made his most significant contributions to the NAR. Kraft proposed not simply dynamic equivalent translation at the linguistic and theological level, but at the level of the church as well. As Kraft writes, "as with theologizing, translation, revelation, and all other products of Christianity, however, it is crucial that each new generation and culture experience the process of producing in its own cultural forms an appropriate church vehicle for the transmission of God's meanings" (Kraft, *Christianity in Culture* 315). Kraft condemned formal correspondence model churches because they too slavishly modeled themselves after the foreign churches that founded them (318). He argued instead for a church that would take Christian dominion over indigenous forms and then adapt and use them in their furtherance of Christian ends, ideally without sacrificing either the cultural integrity of the host society nor the truth-claims made by evangelical Christianity (Kraft, *Christianity in Culture* 321; Kraft, *Anthropology and Christian Witness* 377). The implications for ministries adapting church growth to the United States were obvious. What was important in the modern Western context was to adopt the forms of the church—particularly dress and musical style—to the newly emerging indigenous youth culture of the United States (the part of the culture that could further church growth the quickest), while at the same time ensuring that the essential structure of the church (its doctrinal and socioeconomic conservatism) remained unaltered. Thus the development of both spiritual mapping and the NAR can be seen as essentially continuances of the church growth movement's desire for missional innovation, only applied on American soil.

Before moving on to John Wimber's influence on the evangelical movement and his disastrous interaction with both C. Peter Wagner and the Kansas City Prophets, brief mention should be made of Lausanne I. This was a meeting held in Lausanne, Switzerland in 1974 under the provenance of the Billy Graham Association. It convened as an International Congress on World Evangelization (Cook 76). The Lausanne movement took as its goal the "evangelization of the world by the year 2000. More important, McGavran, Wagner and other church growth proponents were able to influence Lausanne to adopt church-growth language, stating that the best way to evangelize the world was not one 'person at a time, but one people at a time'" (Cook 76). The adoption of church growth ideology by Lausanne I not only made the spread of church growth ideology easier, but also paved the way for the acceptance of spiritual mapping ideas and the consequential influence of the NAR after the convening of Lausanne II In 1990 (see Holvast 4, 25–27, 57). But to understand the reason why spiritual mapping was able to develop in such a mainstream part of the evangelical movement as the Lausanne Committee for World Evangelization (LCWE), we must turn to the life of John Wimber and his interactions with the Kansas City Prophets. It would be this interaction that would serve as the birthing point for the contemporary Charismatic movement. And contrary to popular belief, these new Charismatics would be anything but Pentecostal-lite. Instead, they re-invigorated Latter Rain theology, virtually undiluted, for a new generation. The Charismatic movement would never be the same again.

John Wimber: Signs and Wonders

John Wimber was born in the American Midwest in 1934. Wimber was a musician who began a career as a writer for the group the Righteous Brothers. In 1962, Wimber and his wife separated, but their marriage was "saved," they believed, when Wimber "turned to God for help" (C.P. Wagner, "John Wimber" 1199–1200; Beverly 38). By the early 1970s, Wimber had attained the position of co-pastor at an evangelically-aligned Quaker Church in California (Beverly 38).

In the mid 1970s, C. Peter Wagner realized that the Department of Church Growth of the Fuller Evangelistic Association needed an experienced leader. Wimber's Charismatic personality, combined with the staggering growth of his church in the 1970s, gained Wagner's attention. Wimber, therefore, became Director of the Department for Church Growth in 1975. Wimber's position led him to travel across the United States as a consultant, teacher, and troubleshooter concerning church growth (Cook 72–73). Much like Kraft and Wagner, Wimber was primarily concerned with "pragmatic research" in order to maximize each church's growth potential (Cook 73). Besides the considerable work Wimber did in promoting church growth ideology, he had another important effect, which was to pull Wagner into the orbit of the Charismatic Third Wave.

Wagner, according to his own account, was a cessationist in the early part of his career (Wagner, *Wrestling* 115). He did not believe that the spiritual gifts were for the modern era. However, he experimented with tongues as early as the mid–1960s (Wagner, *Wrestling* 116). By the late 1960s, Wagner was surreptitiously attending some Pentecostal services to see what was going on in the Pentecostal world. When Wagner returned to the United States, he wrote the book *Look Out! The Pentecostals Are Coming* (1973). In the book Wagner used church growth principles to explain the growth of Pentecostalism in Latin America (Cook 88–89, Wagner, *Wrestling* 120–121). Thus, when Wagner met John Wimber, the two men formed a "symbiotic relationship" which caused both men's theology to drift into the Third-Wave and Neo-Charismatic camp.

In 1982, Wimber began teaching the first MC510 course ("Signs, Wonders, and Church Growth") at Fuller Seminary and simultaneously took on the leadership of the Vineyard movement, a group—though not really a denomination—of Charismatics that was committed to spreading the Charismatic message (Wagner, *Wrestling* 124). While Wagner was ostensibly the teacher of record in the class, in point of fact Wimber was the main motivating force behind the class and the reason for its success. As Cook points out, a main distinguishing feature of the class was what happened after the class was done, when Wimber conducted impromptu healing sessions. Many students claimed to have been healed through Wimber's healing practice, enhancing his fame and reputation (Cook 96). The course became nationally famous (Wagner, *Wrestling* 128). MC 510 was eventually removed from Fuller's curriculum because of the controversy generated by the course. However, elements of Wimber's healing theology would continue to play a major role at Fuller for the next two decades, thanks to persistent lobbying by Wagner and Kraft to ensure that the legacy of Wimber's power evangelism was not forgotten (Wagner, *Wrestling* 149–150). According to Wagner, Wimber and he parted company over disagreements on spiritual warfare in the early 1990s (Wagner, *Wrestling* 189–190), but by then their influence on each other was so pervasive that even this cordial split could not prevent the two men from continuing to theologically borrow from the similar veins of church growth theology from which they drew.

Wimber's form of Charismatic belief was marked by three particular central ideas: power evangelism, a particular emphasis on prophetic ministry, and an allegiance to the kingdom theology of George Eldon Ladd (which was also primarily an eschatological concept and not to be confused with kingdom now theology). Of these three doctrines, power evangelism is particularly important to understanding Wimber's worldview. Wimber defined power evangelism as evangelism that demonstrates "God's power through signs and wonders" (Wimber 46; see also Zichterman 177). This evangelism involved power encounters that were in principle much the same as the concept of power encounter promoted by Charles Kraft, in which the Christian showed in practical terms the "superiority" of the Christian God over "false" god figures (Zichterman 177). Wimber contrasted power evangelism with what he termed program evangelism, which attempted to reach the mind via naturalistic or rationalistic means (Zichterman 177; Wimber, *Power Evangelism* 56). Programmatic evangelism lacked in its experiential aspect, and therefore, while useful, needed the accompaniment of a more non-rationalistic approach to evangelism (see Wimber 56). Like Kraft, Wimber had come to believe that the Western worldview blinded people from the spiritual truth that the world was not a closed system and did not work solely through logical systems or processes. There therefore was room for extraordinary spiritual gifts, miracles, and wonders that the Western church had not previously believed to be obtainable to the uninitiated (Zichterman 178, 180). Wimber also emphasized healing as an important tool of church growth and tried to systemize its practice into something of a science (see Zichterman 192). Prayers for healing became a "predominant characteristic" of the Vineyard message (Zichterman 193).

Kingdom theology was the second major element of Wimber's theological system. Kingdom theology was predicated on a "now, not yet" eschatology, based on the writings of George Eldon Ladd (Horton 6). Wimber's theology was based upon the desire for a "present realization of kingdom power, assuming that whatever was described in the apostolic church had been prescribed for today's church" (Horton 59). Wimber's theology followed Ladd in proclaiming that God's kingdom "had come in the person of Jesus, invading the present evil age so that we live in the 'presence of the future'" (Horton 71). This theology therefore had both a present and a future component to it, which is perhaps why Wimber eventually felt drawn to the Latter Rain–derived theology of Mike Bickle's KCF.

Ladd's theology, much like kingdom now theology, had an earthly component to it. However, unlike kingdom now theology, which has often been accused of being prone to being overly concerned with dominating this world, as well as the next, Ladd's theology had a distinctly otherworldly component as well. Ladd's theology held that "every aspect of the kingdom must be derived from the character and action of God" (Horton 67). This led to a constant, but ultimately symphonic, tension between the "nature of God's present activity," which is seen as evidence of the kingdom in the here and now and the "redemptive manifestations" of God's rule at the "end of the age" (Horton 67). Significantly, Ladd did not believe that the church was the kingdom of God, but merely that the kingdom of God, through dynamic interaction with Christ, could create the church through people responding in belief to the message of Christ (Horton 70). Thus, within kingdom theology one could see both the motivation for Wimber's acceptance of the Latter Rain–derived message of the Kansas City Prophets and his eventual rejection of that same message. Both kingdom theology and Latter Rain revivalism sought to inject elements of hopefulness into the pessimistic eschatological pronouncements of fundamentalists. Both movements could see the End Times as an era as much to be aspired to as rejected. But because Wimber's theology was rooted in Ladd's eschatological system, there were breaks on Vineyard movement fanaticism, since victory could be achieved in this world, as well as at the end of the time. It is probable that these two rival visions of Vineyard eschatology—the solely futurist view of the Latter Rain and the present-futurist syncretic fusion that was favored by Wimber in his early years, may have influenced the numerous Charismatic churches who derived their theology from Wimber to more readily gravitate to the NAR's dominionist theology (Wagner, *Dominion!* 59–60, 63), which promoted a similar syncretic mixing of present and future oriented eschatological systems. While one should not accuse Ladd's kingdom theology of having inspired kingdom now theology, it is clear that Ladd's eschatology partly paved the way for the more this-worldly oriented direction that Vineyard-inspired Charismatic churches took with the collapse of the premillennialists' stranglehold over evangelicalism in the 1980s and 1990s. And much of that path would be paved by Mike Bickle and the Kansas City Prophets, the final element that would set off the fire that is the NAR.

Bickle, the Kansas City Prophets and the Return of the Latter Rain: From KCF to the Toronto Blessing

The story of Mike Bickle begins in June 1982. According to Bickle, a man named Augustine Alcala, who said he heard the voice of God, prophesied in front of Bickle's congregation. Bickle, impressed by what he saw as the accuracy of these predictions, came to accept Augustine's spiritual guidance. While in Cairo, Egypt, in 1982, Bickle claims to have heard a voice telling him: "I am inviting you to be part of a work that will reach to the ends of the earth" (Pytches 61).[13] Bickle felt "called" to open a church in Kansas City, Kansas City Fellowship (KCF). Within seven years, the church had grown from virtually nothing to over 3,000 members, spread over six congregations (Dagar 128, Jackson 192).

In 1982, a prophet (apparently Augustine Alcalca, though unnamed in the influential Gruen report), delivered to Bickle a 4 point vision: (1) A number of young people would be involved in his movement; (2) There would be a "full manifestation of the gifts of the Holy Spirit"; (3) Bickle would be confronted by a false prophet; and 4) People would rally against Bickle's movement (Gruen 54).[14] According to Ernie Gruen, this prophet (again, presumably Augustine, though unnamed in the Gruen report), was involved in several other "prophetic events" at KCF and spoke in front of the fellowship in 1983 (Gruen 54). This prophet's work was seen as foundational to KCF's ministry during the eighties, though he was later disavowed (Gruen 54–55).

According to Gruen, Bickle saw himself as ordained to start a movement. Bob Scott, Bickle's associate, also spoke on the concept of a "new order" of

Christian believers in December 1982 (Gruen 55). In 1983, Bickle would meet the prophet Bob Jones (not to be confused with the famous separatist fundamentalist Bob Jones family), who confirmed the prophecy Augustine had given over him (Jackson 194–195). Jones had grown up in a sharecropping family in rural Arkansas in the 1930s. Jones served time as a Marine in the Korean War and later ran an illegal liquor store (Jackson 195). Jones, like many Charismatics, underwent a dramatic conversion experience sometime in the mid-1970s and began exhibiting the "charisms" shortly thereafter (Pytches, *Some Say It Thundered* 74–75). Shortly thereafter, Jones felt called to "prophesy against abortion" (Pytches 75), followed by a call to prophesy against homosexuality. The latter event, according to Jones, led a demon to appear and tell him that it would kill him if he continued to prophesy against abortion and homosexuality (Pytches 75).

According to Jackson, Bickle was initially mistrustful of Jones, but accepted his prophetic gifts when Jones predicted that scientists would discover a previously unknown comet. Shortly thereafter, such a comet was discovered, according to Bickle's account (Jackson 197). Jones thus became an integral part of Bickle's ministry. In the mid 1980s, Bickle's prophetic influence Augustine also mentioned to him another prophet, Paul Cain. In April 1987, Bickle, along with some of his "prophetic ministers," encountered Paul Cain at a conference in Birmingham, Alabama. The men attested to being powerfully moved by Cain's teachings, which resulted in Cain visiting KCF the following month and beginning a long-term relationship with KCF (Jackson 199). Cain was seen as having specially gifted powers, including—in one case—the ability to cause electrical problems (Horton 114). He was also seen by many observers as a genuine person, perhaps with real prophetic gifts (see Beverly 129–133).

Why were Jones and Cain so controversial? Mainly because of both men's promotion of an extreme variation of Latter Rain theology based—yet again—on Joel 2: Joel's Army ideology. Jones's sermon Visions and Revelations, 1988, provides perhaps the most graphic and extreme depiction of this end-times army, from which I now quote extensively:

> I went and I seen the Lord, and it was like He was looking at little yellow things—little round yellow things like a spirit of God itself. And there were billions of them. And it was like Him and all the angels were looking through these and every once in awhile, they'd say, "Hey, here's an end-time one, get it down here on the end. Here's another good one."
> I said, "What are you doing?"
> He said, "Oh, we're collecting those who are foreknown and predestinated for the end-times, for you see, they'll be the best of all the seed that's ever been. And we're looking through the seeds and this'll be your grandkids. This will be the end generation that is foreknown and predestinated to inherit all things. And these will be like

grandchildren to you—even those that you minister to won't be this generation; their children will be....

Although their parents will reign over them [the last generation] and be the leaders of the last-day church, their children will possess the Spirit without measure. For they are the best of all the generations that have ever been upon the face of the earth. And the best of all generations are those elected seeds that will glorify Christ in the last days...."

That's the purpose so that Jesus in the last days has the seeds that will glorify Him above any generation that has ever been upon the face of the earth. They will move into things of the supernatural that no one has ever moved in before. Every miracle, sign and wonder that has ever been in the Bible, they'll move in consistently.... They themselves will be that generation that's raised up to put death itself underneath their feet and to glorify Christ in every way [Jones, "Visions and Revelations—Mike Bickle with Bob Jones" (1)].[15]

A number of significant elements can be deduced from this prophecy. First, Jones was playing with ideas similar to Manifest Sons theology. The idea of an End Times generation of enormous spiritual powers and gifts was largely merely rehashed Latter Rain theology. The element of predestinarian thinking present within this vision may have resulted from the growing influence of Paul Cain on KCF, since Cain had interacted with Branham while serving as a healing revivalist in the 1950s (Beverly 131, Jackson 182). Both Beverly and Jackson caution against reading too much in to the association between these two men, since Cain claimed to have rejected Branham's doctrinal deviations (Beverly 131). Yet to take such a position requires an extraordinary degree of naiveté. While Branham may have had some qualms about the Latter Rain (Weaver 142), it is clear that the Latter Rain revival was clearly influenced by much of his teaching (Riss 11). It would therefore be surprising if some of Branham's more heterodox concepts did not influence other healing revivalists like Paul Cain, even if they outwardly rejected Latter Rain theology.

Indeed, the focus on elect "seeds" sounds all too uncomfortably like the "serpent seed" doctrine of Branham transposed to a modern era. What is especially notable is that God is deliberately selecting only the best seeds for the end times, thus reinforcing Randles's charge of spiritual evolutionism within Latter Rain–derived theologies (for Randles's view of spiritual evolutionism, see Randles 39–40). The idea that God would personally select an End Times elite is enormously empowering to those convinced of such a prophecy's accuracy. What becomes problematic with that idea is that, like Branham's theology, it is predicated on the assumption that those who do not fit into this elite are somehow a group of spiritual inferiors. Furthermore, the militant rhetoric Bickle espoused through the Joel's Army (and later, the Forerunner) paradigm, while not necessarily designed to engender violence, is compatible with physical violence when it furthers the missions objectives of Bickle's ministry (The documentary *God Loves Uganda*, for instance, shows how such rhetoric helped further the promotion of anti-gay legislation in Uganda).

Nor can Jones's statements in this vision be seen as somehow extrinsic to the ministry of Mike Bickle or KCF/IHOP. As James Beverly points out, Jones argued that the end-times church would be 10,000 times greater "than the church of the book of Acts. Furthermore Jones and Paul Cain were teaching that Kansas City was going to be headquarters for a group of super-Christians who would form 'Joel's Army' and prepare for the final end-time harvest of souls" (Beverly 123). Cain, almost identically to Jones, preached that in the end times there'd be a "Great army of spirit-led, spirit-endowed people" which no "demon, no man-system, no enemy will stop, nor hinder them, or resist them" (Paul Cain Teachings Track 9 "Joel's Army"). Thus, for Cain, not only was this End Time's army powerful, it was literally invincible. Indeed, Cain referred to this army as the "Man Child" (Paul Cain Teachings Track 9 "Joel's Army"), a term that has long been associated with Manifest Sons teachings. Even Bill Jackson's hagiographic rendering of the Vineyard movement, *The Quest for the Radical Middle* (1999), acknowledges not only that Cain taught of a powerful End Time's army ("Joel's Army in training"), but that that teaching was also promoted by Vineyard leader Jack Deere (Jackson 199).

Paul Cain taught a doctrine virtually identical to that of Joel's Army, which was the concept of the "new breed" (Horton 113–114). This doctrine, once he encountered KCF, became associated with that ministry. In the late 1980s, both the ideas of the new breed and Joel's Army would find a much wider audience through their adoption by John Wimber and the Vineyard Christian Fellowship (VCF). By the late 1980s Wimber was facing professional burn-out and both personal and professional problems (Horton 94). In late 1988, Bickle began to exhort Wimber to take up the "full responsibility of leader" in the Vineyard movement. But it was Paul Cain who really got Wimber's attention, by, allegedly predicting an earthquake on the day of his arrival in Anaheim to visit Wimber. When an earthquake did in fact happen on that day, Wimber began accepting Cain's counsel regarding what Wimber saw as problems with his "spiritual sons" within the Vineyard movement (Horton 94–95). As a result of this event, Wimber invited Paul Cain to speak at a Vineyard conference about spiritual warfare in February of 1989. Cain then gave a "Prophecy for the Vineyard" that would shape the Vineyard's ideology for much of the next two years (Horton 95). Cain argued that Wimber was divinely chosen by God to use his "leadership in a remarkable way" and that Wimber was "the right leader for the 'Last Days' ministry" (Horton 96). At this conference, Cain repeatedly emphasized that Wimber, along with Bickle and emerging Charismatic hero James Robison were the leaders of the "new breed." Cain also denounced any of those who opposed God's visitation on Wimber and the Vineyard movement, saying that they would undergo "God's condemnation" (Horton 97). Cain's sermons specifically referenced the importance of five-fold ministry and portrayed Wimber in apostolic terms (Horton 96), while at the same time promising the Vineyard movement miraculous gifts of the spirit, including the ability to heal people with AIDS (Horton 97).

This last promise was particularly significant because the Vineyard had always placed a strong emphasis on healing, and Wimber's ministry was partly built on the reputation he had gained as a powerful promoter of healing ministry. Although there had always been a fusion of the prophetic and healing ministries within the Vineyard movement, Cain made this syncretic fusion particularly notable. After February 1989, Cain, along with the Vineyard leaders, sought to pursue a modern Latter Rain revival; Horton argues that they tried to replace the extremes of the Healing Revivals with a somewhat more modest approach, and for the less doctrinally innovative members of the Vineyard this may actually have been the case (Horton 115). As Horton himself points out, however, this newly invigorated form of Latter Rain teaching was strikingly similar to what came out of the Healing Revivals (115). In particular, the Vineyard would, after Cain's emergence into the movement, emphasize the union of the "new breed" teaching with the fivefold ministries of apostles, prophets, pastors, teachers, and evangelists, all in anticipation of a "climactic revival" that would occur during the End Times (Horton 115–116). Again this was virtually identical to the kind of teaching promoted by the original Latter Rain revival and bore significant similarities to the shepherding movement as well.

One significant point in Wimber's theology of prophecy—one that would put him at odds with traditional premillennial dispensationalists from both the fundamentalist and Pentecostal camps—was that prophets could be imperfect and sometimes fallible (Horton 117–118). Prophecies therefore had to be tested through a variety of criteria, such as the "spiritual fruits" that they bore and taking prophecies down in writing (Horton 118). Wimber's vision of a theologically respectable form of prophetic ministry proved unsustainable, however, because of Charismatic pastor Ernie Gruen's 1990 publication of *Documentation of the Aberrant Practices and Teachings of Kansas City Fellowship* (Grace Ministries) (Horton 118–119). In this manual, which is almost indispensable to understanding both the history of KCF and the doctrinal disputes that resulted from its teachings, Gruen, as Horton puts it, focused on both "ethical compromises and theological differences" that KCF promoted that distinguished them from other Charismatic churches (Horton 119). Gruen was particularly scandalized by the way in which prophecy was carelessly used at KCF, often to unfortunate ends for people who were moved by these inaccurate prophecies (Horton 119).

Gruen called for a council of leaders to intervene in the situation. John Wimber, doubtlessly fearful of the negative attention such a council would bring, decided to intervene. Gruen wrote John Wimber, repeating the substance of his allegations while acknowledging three minor factual errors in his report (see Horton 120). Gruen withdrew from the process of ministerial correction in 1990, leaving it to Wimber (121). But as Horton points out, where Gruen had seen "deception, fabrication, or moral compromise," Wimber merely saw "exaggeration, inaccuracy and misunderstanding" (Horton 121). Wimber admitted Bickle's KCF into the Vineyard in May 1990. While publicly acknowledging that there were accountability issues with the prophecies being given, the Vineyard was at the same time still aggressively promoting the Joel's Army concept and specifically tying it to the Vineyard, as one element of that army (Horton 122–124). In the Vineyard's formulation of Joel's Army, as preached by Jack Deere, the instrument of God's End Times judgment "will be a totally unique army which Deere associated with the 144,000 witnesses of Revelation, Chapter 7. Those who reject God's revelation will writhe in pain. According to Deere, the issue in this judgment will be one's response to the invincible End-Time Army that will preach the Gospel with unparalleled signs and wonders" (Horton 124). Deere believed Christians at the Vineyard were being called to be part of that End Times Army (Horton 125). As Horton points out, there was a positive side to Deere's message, since it emphasized themes of humility and emotional intimacy that were lacking in the bellicose pronouncements of the KCF. But overall, Horton argues that Deere's message, like KCF's version of Joel's Army teaching, was spiritually elitist, with Deere even associating those Christians opposed to his message with the dead bones mentioned in Ezekiel 37, a passage much invoked against backslidden Christians (see Horton 126).

By the early 1990s, Wimber started to have doubts about his association with the prophetic movement (Beverly 133). This was due largely to a failed prophecy for revival in Britain that Paul Cain gave in August of 1989. When revival did not come, John Mumford of the London Vineyard was scandalized (Horton 126). When Cain made a subsequent prophecy to overcome the negative reaction towards his first one, predicting "tokens of revival" in Britain in October 1990, this revival too failed to occur (Horton 126–127). In mid-1991, therefore, Wimber ceased his collaboration with Paul Cain (129).

Why, then, were the Kansas City Prophets so significant? They were for a number of very important reasons. First, Bickle's KCF would later turn into the International House of Prayer (IHOP) an apostolic network which is now a very powerful force in its own right,[16] despite having eventually departed from the Vineyard in 1996 (Jackson 338). Secondly, because KCF stayed under the Vineyard's banner for so long, it "cross-pollinated" doctrinally with a number of Vineyard churches. This became important in the effect the Kansas City Prophets had on the Charismatic revival known as the Toronto Blessing.

As Jürgen Römer points out, this tie to the Toronto Blessing is hardly surprising, given the semi-official status KCF had within the Vineyard movement (Römer 26). The Toronto Blessing was led by John Arnott, pastor of Toronto Airport Christian Fellowship (TACF) and birthed at the Toronto Airport Vineyard (TAV)[17] (Römer 3) in January 1994. People began exhibiting strong physical reactions, such as holy laughter, shaking, etc. (Römer 3). In 1993, reporting that they were "spiritually 'dry,'" the Arnotts traveled to Argentina and attended meetings with Argentinan revivalists (Poloma, "Toronto Blessing" 1150). Simultaneously, Randy Clark was attending the revival meetings of Rodney-Howard Browne, which were inspiring Charismatics worldwide (Poloma "Toronto Blessing" 1150). Arnott, hearing about Clark, invited him to evangelize at TAV (Poloma, "Toronto Blessing" 1150). Suddenly, the holy laughter phenomena—uncontrollable extended bouts of laughter lasting far longer than most people would consider normal—emerged (Diamond, *Not By Politics Alone* 209). By the end of 1994, 75,000 thousand believers had travelled to Toronto to experience this new spiritual "outpouring" (Diamond 209). As the revival progressed a variety of spiritual "manifestations" were seen. For instance, some of the people "touched" by the Toronto Blessing did "Jesus laps" in which they run around the church during church services. Others made "chopping and swinging motions." What really scandalized evangelical churches at the time were the animal noises made by people at Blessing revivals. Beverly describes people having "roared like lions or barked like dogs.... I also heard one man making noises like a cow. Others have reported people oinking like pigs and crowing like roosters. These animal noises have created the most disgust among some critics" (Beverly 69). Almost as controversial was the practice of getting "drunk in the Spirit" (Beverly 69). Such phenomena excited the derision of many people. While this work aims not to dismiss the personal meaningfulness of such phenomena, it is important to understand how controversial the Blessing was. John Wimber had initially seen some benefit in the revival in Toronto (Horton 138), but became increasingly concerned with what he saw as the potential of the Toronto Blessing to distract the Vineyard movement from evangelism, his primary passion (Horton 138). Nevertheless, a number of the Vineyard churches promoted teachings associated with the Blessing throughout 1994, without opposition from Wimber (Horton 161). The Vineyard leadership became so concerned, however, with the more extreme manifestations of Pentecostal spiritual gifts—namely spiritual drunkenness and animal noises—that they expelled TAVF from the Vineyard in December of 1995 (Horton 164–165).

The links between KCF and the outpouring in Toronto were extensive. The magazine *Spread the Fire* promoted a prophecy by Paul Cain given to John and Carol Arnott. Cain promoted the idea for the Arnotts, under his prophetic mantle, that "'The Lord had initiated the Toronto Blessing, not man'" (qtd. in Römer 26–27). Both Jack Deere's and Mike Bickle's books were recommended on the TACF website (Römer 27). Marc Dupont, an important figure in the Blessing, considered Bob Jones as well to be a prophet of God (Römer 26–27). Arnott has recommended one of Bickle's works written in defense of the Toronto Blessing and Paul Cain has spoken at conferences that were held at TACF (Römer 27). Randy Clark, the second most influential figure at the Toronto Blessing claimed to James Beverly that Paul Cain had prophesied the Toronto Blessing (Beverly 143). Margaret Poloma also speculates that while the majority of the AVC had always been against the more radically prophetic ministries promoted by KCF, a significant minority among "newer members of the AVC" had gravitated to the KCF view of the prophetic (Poloma, *Main Street Mystics* 151). Poloma disingenuously keeps the exact content of the prophetic ministries of the Kansas City Prophets vague, despite the fact that their vision of the prophetic was so extreme that it eventually caught even the concerned attention of the Southern Poverty Law Center (SPLC) (Sanchez).

What Poloma manages to obfuscate even further is the tactical alliances made at the Toronto Blessing that would serve to further the interests of the NAR, particularly the Revival Alliance apostolic network, second only to the International Council of Apostles (ICA) (the network C. Peter Wagner led to 2010. See "About ICAL") in global influence.[18] Ché Ahn, the male member of one of the six apostolic leadership "couples," that presides over the Revival Alliance (his particular ministry is Harvest International Ministries, which is a network of 5,500 churches in 35 nations. See Ahn, *When Heaven Came Down*, backcover), directly credits the Toronto Blessing with restoring "the office of the apostle with the birth of many apostolic networks"; he includes among these John and Carol Arnott's Partners in Harvest, Bill Johnson's Global Legacy, Heidi and Rolland Baker's Iris Ministries, and his own Harvest International Ministry (Ahn, *When Heaven Came Down* 121). All three of these ministries represent one of the six major apostolic networks within the wider (and influential) Revival Alliance network. Randy and DeAnn Clark's Global Awakening is also a member of the Revival Alliance, and we have already seen Clark's close interaction with the Toronto Blessing, as well as the influence KCF had on him ("Revival Alliance"). Thus of the six apostolic couples involved in Revival Alliance, five of them have extensive links with the Toronto Blessing. What's more, some of these groups ending up establishing close ties with Mike Bickle once the furor over the Kansas City Prophets was a distant memory. Lou Engle—famous for his appearance in the documentary *Jesus Camp* (2006)—was part of the leadership team of IHOP in the late 2000s ("Lou Engle"). Engle's chief apostle is Ché Ahn (see Engle, *Digging the Wells*, Backcover), who views Engle with sufficient favor to call him a "covenant brother" (Ahn, *When Heaven Comes Down* 121). James Goll, a Kansas City prophet (Poloma 180), provided several crucial prophecies for Ahn during the 1990s (Poloma 180), and later co-wrote the book *The Call of the Elijah Revolution* (2008) with Lou Engle. Thus, through the Revival Alliance, some of the most radical Latter Rain teachings would make their way into the NAR. And for millions of Charismatics worldwide, their lives would never be the same again.

Conclusion

As the Kansas City Prophets, the Vineyard, and the Vineyard's offshoots evolved over the course of the 1990s, a parallel development took place that eventually encompassed many of these churches and brought them into what became the NAR. This was the practice known as spiritual mapping. Birthed through the influence of Charles Kraft and C. Peter Wagner, spiritual mapping became the theological midwife for the birth of the NAR. Understanding NAR ideology is impossible without exploring this movement. In it we will find ideas that may seem far stranger even than the prophetic announcements of the Kansas City Prophets. But spiritual mapping would for a time virtually dominate all Charismatic discourse and even today many of its basic presuppositions remain foundational to an understanding of the NAR. It can only be hoped that this discourse does not become a permanent fixture on the Charismatic landscape.

2

Spiritual Mapping and the NAR

The formation of the practice of spiritual mapping, which would prove to be the means by which the NAR would organize itself, can be traced to two crucial locations: Fuller Seminary and Argentina. The anthropological principles of Charles Kraft provided the motivating impulses for spiritual mapping, while fellow Fuller professor C. Peter Wagner would provide much of the organizational and practical direction for the movement (see Holvast 28–34 on Kraft's influence, and Holvast, passim on Wagner's even greater influence). According to Wagner, Argentina would serve as a "principal laboratory in which some of us are testing the theories of strategic-level spiritual warfare" (Wagner, *Warfare Prayer* 156). The practice of SLSW—that is, combatting demonic spirits that were seen as controlling geographical territories—became the central tenet of the spiritual mapping movement (Wagner, *Warfare Prayer* 19).

An early figure in the movement was Ed Silvoso. Silvoso was a student at Fuller Seminary who specialized in the study of church growth (Wagner, *Warfare Prayer* 29). Silvoso admits to having been greatly influenced by such missiologists as Donald McGavran, Ralph Winter, Arthur Glasser, Alan Tippet, and Peter Wagner. He calls his experiences with these men the "most exhilarating spiritual-intellectual experience of my entire life" (Silvoso, *That None Should Perish* 28). Yet Silvoso claims to have had some points of difference with Wagner, mainly on the strategy for evangelization in Latin America. Silvoso therefore decided to make an effort to "evangelize an entire city" by combining church growth principles with the mass evangelism principles he had learned from his brother-in-law, the world famous evangelist Luis Palau (Silvoso, *That None Should Perish* 28–30). The degree of ideological difference between Silvoso and Wagner is, however, at best questionable; as we will see, the independence of Argentine spiritual mapping from American influence is a debatable point.[1]

2. Spiritual Mapping and the NAR   71

In 1976, Silvoso, along with Luis Palau, implemented Silvoso's evangelism campaign, which they dubbed Plan Rosario, aimed at the city of Rosario, Argentina (Wagner, *Warfare Prayer* 29). Wagner and Silvoso would see the plan as having achieved great results (Wagner, *Warfare Prayer* 29; Holvast 53–54). In 1978, John Dawson, who would become one of the major early theorists promoting spiritual mapping, took a team of Youth with a Mission (YWAM) evangelists to Córdoba, Argentina. According to Dawson's account, he felt an intense feeling of evil spiritual dominion over the area. After Dawson dealt with these spirits, he claimed to have achieved improved results in his evangelistic efforts. Dawson would later chronicle these events in his book *Taking Our Cities for God* (1989). As a result, Córdoba would become a "point of reference" in many spiritual mapping and evangelism campaigns during the late 1980s and early 1990s (Holvast 54).

In 1980, Silvoso founded Harvest Evangelism or Evangelismo de Cosecha, which would later serve as a major disseminator of NAR doctrine in its own right (see Silvoso, *That None Should Perish* 34 on foundation of Harvest). In 1982, the evangelist Carlos Annacondia conducted a mass public crusade in Argentina that became the benchmark for revivalism in the area; Wagner admitted to being greatly impressed by Annacondia's efforts (Wagner, *Warfare Prayer* 25). Particularly impressive to Wagner –was Annacondia's emphasis on fighting with spiritual "principalities and powers" (Wagner, *Warfare Prayer* 26). Also notable was Pablo Bottari, whose ministry later influenced the Revival Alliance's promotion of the sozo method of deliverance (McMichael and McMichael 94–95, Clark 91). Bottari's teachings were used to promote "ground-level" (individual) deliverance at these meetings (Wagner, *Warfare Prayer* 27).[2]

In the early 1980s, Argentine pastor Eduardo Lorenzo became interested in the practice of spiritual warfare after he came "face-to-face with a demonized woman" (Wagner, *Warfare Prayer* 27). As a result, Lorenzo sponsored spiritual warfare seminars at his church, led by Christian psychiatrist John White and spiritual warfare expert Ed Murphy (Wagner, *Warfare Prayer* 27). Murphy's presence at these seminars was especially significant; he was one of the most erudite proponents of spiritual warfare in the United States, and an early leader in the spiritual mapping movement till he gradually disengaged from it.[3]

By 1985, Silvoso had developed an effective organization which included a skilled church growth team focusing on church planting, a newsletter, and his own television studio. His Cosecha organization was asked to train lay leaders. The rapid growth of the Argentine church began to gain a good deal of American attention (Holvast 55). Wagner visited Argentina that year and met with Omar Cabrera, one of Argentina's foremost evangelical leaders. According to Wagner, his interest in territorial spirits was greatly influenced by Cabrera's practice of "identifying and binding the territorial spirits controlling cities" (Wagner, *Warfare Prayer* 13).

What became the key element of Wagner and Silvoso's plan for Argentina, however, was Plan Resistencia. The plan was started in 1989 by Ed Silvoso. Silvoso's goal was to conduct "significant, measurable evangelism" that combined church growth techniques and spiritual warfare practice (Wagner, *Warfare Prayer* 30). Resistencia was chosen because of its relatively low number of evangelical Christians (the movement estimated only 1.5 percent of the population were "believers"), which Silvoso believed would make it an "excellent testing ground for our principles" (Silvoso, *That None Should Perish* 42). It was this plan that laid the groundwork for the spiritual mapping practice of the 1990s.

The closest thing one can deduce to a formal starting point for this movement was the Lausanne II congress of 1989 (Holvast 57–58). The Lausanne movement was by no means uniformly conservative, and an element of its membership, particularly among its Latin American contingent, pushed for a moderate position on social issues. This had caused particular attention at the Lausanne I meeting in 1974, where there was "evidence to suggest that powerful voices within North American evangelicalism were unhappy with the discussions [about social justice] after Lausanne and felt compelled to push the movement into a safer route" (Filho 122). Among these reactionaries was Wagner, who argued that the Lausanne movement should concentrate solely on evangelization, and shy away from the social gospel (Filho 121).

The tension within the Lausanne movement is important to understand for two reasons. First, Wagner would later renounce his lack of engagement in social issues in his book *Dominion!* (Wagner, *Dominion!* 51). That move, however, was problematic, since Wagner's model of social engagement was not the truly alternative evangelical social theology offered by men like René Padilla and Samuel Escobar, but instead a thinly modified form of dominionism (a form of theocratic thinking prevalent among many Charismatics) (see Wagner, *Dominon!* 59–60 on his switch to dominionism). The second reason this tension is important is because it became a significant point of disagreement between Argentine evangelicals and their North American counterparts over the existence of the AD 2000 and Beyond Campaign, one of the principal vehicles for spiritual mapping used in the developing world.

The AD 2000 and Beyond Campaign was the formal delivery system for spiritual mapping practice worldwide, though spiritual mapping was not its only function. The goal of AD 2000 was drawn from a question asked in the Manila Manifesto: "Now the year has 2000 has become for many a challenging milestone. Can we commit ourselves to evangelize the world during the last decade of this millennium?" ("Manila Manifesto"; Filho 200). A significant group of people, including important evangelical leaders, decided in a meeting following the plenary session on AD 2000 that a formal group needed to be established to "carry forward the AD 2000 vision" (Filho 200). Yet significant voices of dissent emerged, particularly from Samuel Escobar. Escobar faulted AD 2000 for what he called a "managerial missiology" that was characterized by an extreme commitment to pragmatism and that was influenced strongly by "the American functionalist social sciences," that he saw as socially and theologically deficient compared to the message of the Christian Scriptures (Filho 203–204). Spiritual mapping and its structural functionalism clearly was being targeted here, and not without good reason.

Spiritual mapping promised success and social transformation, yet as René Holvast points out, it is quite questionable whether it ever achieved that goal in Argentina (Holvast 145–147). As Holvast points out, spiritual mapping "never developed into a full-fledged movement in Argentina" (Holvast 60). Instead, the movement was replaced by the anointing movement, which focused mainly on the laying on of hands (significantly a practice also promoted by the Latter Rain), but that was not primarily centered on strategic level spiritual warfare (see Holvast 60). And as Holvast points out, despite the promotion of the Argentine spiritual mapping movement as a sort of spontaneous outpouring of the Holy Spirit, its origins were largely American. Eduardo Lorenzo was ignorant of spiritual warfare practice till his encounters with White and Murphy. Dawson was an American. Silvoso studied extensively in America, including at Fuller, and was greatly influenced by Fuller missiologists. Fellow Argentine evangelical Pablo Deiros, another significant figure in the movement (see Holvast 65), was also educated by Americans and explicitly identified spiritual mapping as originating in America. Though Deiros could not pinpoint for certain who originated the movement, he indicates that he thinks it was likely Silvoso in cooperation with Wagner who brought the movement to Argentina (Holvast 64). Similarly, looking at the American adherents of the movement also points to the non–American origins of spiritual mapping: Wagner was influenced by Cabrera, it is true, but Cabrera rejects the interpretation of his ministry that Wagner put on it. And as Holvast points out, according to the Wagners' own recollections, almost no one previous to Plan Resistencia knew about spiritual mapping, but already Ana Méndez (a significant Mexican figure in the movement) and Cindy Jacobs were informed about it. This too seems to point to the likely American origins of the movement (Holvast 64–65).

Argentina's role for the spiritual mapping movement would largely be one of "mythological validation," according to Holvast, giving a kind of divine validation of the movement's spiritual practices (Holvast 67). Argentina would become the "success story" by which the movement would promote its unique form of evangelical ideology. The treatment of the Argentines as "godly exemplars" of the superiority of spiritual mapping ideology would be copied over the years, particularly in George Otis's *Transformations* movies, whose questionable promotion of Cali, Colombia, Guatemala, Uganda, and Kenya as evangelical success stories of social transformation would be disseminated for several decades.

All this was immaterial to Kraft and Wagner. They had their new methodology for church growth, their new mechanism for spreading Charismatic spiritual gifts (the "charisms") worldwide. And it would be this methodology that would allow the movement to develop the networks and leadership structures that now make it so powerful. But to understand how the movement became so successful, we must first examine its ideology.

Spiritual Mapping Methodology: The Devil in the Details

According to Wagner, previous to Lausanne II in Manila, territorial spirits had been a minor concern of evangelicals, even Pentecostals and Charismatics (Wagner, *Warfare Prayer* 45). At Lausanne II, a number of evangelical leaders spoke on the need for "strategic-level spiritual intercession," including Edgardo Silvoso, Tom White, and Wagner himself (Wagner, *Warfare Prayer* 45). Wagner therefore gathered a nucleus of leaders together to discuss the need for strategic level spiritual warfare. Many of the individuals at this meeting were or became heavy hitters in the NAR, including John Dawson, Cindy Jacobs, Edgardo Silvoso, and Charles Kraft (Wagner, *Warfare Prayer* 45).

The basic idea behind SLSW is deceptively simple. Basically, SLSW is a form of deliverance (exorcism) conducted against not simply individuals—though individuals are also exorcised in the process—but against geographical territories and people groups (Collins 103). There are three different levels of SLSW. The first level is ground level spiritual warfare (also known as ground level deliverance). George Otis, Jr., defines this as "Ministry activity that is associated with individual bondage and or demonization" (Otis Jr., *Informed Intercession* 251). In short, this form of deliverance occurs at the level of the individual, and is the kind of exorcism one might see being performed by popular NAR deliverance ministries like the Sozo ministries of Bethel Church in Redding, California, or Nancy Alcorn's Mercy Ministries, operating out of Nashville. Frequently, as I have detailed in my book *The Failure of Evangelical Mental Health Care*, such practices are directed against the mentally ill, including individuals suffering from serious mental health issues like bipolar disorder (see De Silva and Libescher "Sozo Q +A" Session 9, Weaver 83).

2. Spiritual Mapping and the NAR

The second form of spiritual warfare in the spiritual mapping paradigm is "occult level spiritual warfare" (or occult level deliverance). Otis Jr. defines this as "a term that pertains to intercessory confrontations with demonic forces operating through Satanism, witchcraft, shamanism, esoteric philosophies ... and any number of similar occult vehicles" (Otis Jr. 253). While both the spiritual mapping movement's proponents and critics have tended to focus on ground-level deliverance and SLSW as the major components of the philosophy, this does not mean that secular critics should ignore occult-level spiritual warfare, for this practice has potentially serious consequences. This is because the spiritual mapping movement's definition of "occult" is incredibly broad. Thus, the movement promotes the destruction of other cultures religious artifacts because of the fear these artifacts might be demonized. Native American artifacts have frequently been the target of such retribution (Rosenberg, "America's Own Taliban"; Rosenberg, "Rick Perry's Prayer-Rally Politics"). *Transformations IV*, a crucial video made by the NAR, shows the burning of Fijian native art as well (Otis Jr. *Let the Sea Resound*).[4]

Such actions have huge negative consequences. The labeling of rival religions and cultures as demonic has the potential to exacerbate ethnic and religious tensions, especially given the massive influence the NAR currently exhibits worldwide. The wanton destruction of other cultures' treasured religious artifacts, while interpreted by the NAR as an act of spiritual enrichment and evangelization, is often seen by these cultures as a form of imperialism, one with devastating consequences to their own cultural stability. In regions where there is great religious diversity these practices may be especially dangerous to implement.

The third level of spiritual warfare in spiritual mapping, built on the other two levels, is SLSW. SLSW is a "term that pertains to intercessory confrontations with demonic power concentrated over given cities, cultures, and peoples" (Otis Jr., *Informed Intercession* 257). Note that the spiritual mapping methodology developed by Wagner and company, though the most common form of SLSW, is not the only form. Clinton Arnold, for instance, differs notably from some of the extremes shown by other SLSW promoters (see Collins 104–105).[5] Crucial to understanding the need for this kind of spiritual warfare is the concept of spiritual territoriality. In the thinking of the spiritual mapping movement demonic and spiritual powers are "uniquely linked to specific cultures and geography" (Otis Jr. 257). Thus a territory or a people group is considered to be under demonic influence—in Charismatic parlance, "demonized" or demonically oppressed—and that demonic influence must be lifted if that people group or territory is to be fully blessed by God.

There are a number of strategies for implementing spiritual mapping, the most detailed of which is that offered by George Otis, Jr., in his *Informed Intercession* (1999). Before outlining these methodologies, however, the mention of one particularly crucial idea in spiritual mapping should be mentioned: Identificational repentance. Identificational repentance is "a two-stage intercessory action that involves: 1) an acknowledgment that one's affinity group (clan, city, nation, or organization) has been guilty of specific corporate sin before God and man, and 2) a prayerful petition that God will use personal repudiation of this sin as a redemptive beachhead from which to move into the larger community" (Otis Jr. 251). Identificational repentance therefore is a kind of rite of racial or cultural "reconciliation" in the minds of the NAR, but a rite that has a very specific aim, namely the exorcising of other cultures' demons. The colonial culture apologizes for their sins against the aggrieved party, and in return the aggrieved party agrees to divorce itself from its demonic entanglements. For instance, with Native Americans, this often occurs through reconciliation with NAR "designated 'representatives'" for entire tribal groups (Rosenberg, "Rick Perry's Prayer-Rally Politics").

When listening to NAR rhetoric, it is absolutely essential to realize that when the movement talks about racial reconciliation, the term has different meanings from what non–Charismatics might imagine. Here one will usually find explicit rejection of ideas like affirmative action, reparations for slavery, or even serious engagement with the West's responsibility for genocide. In many ways the NAR is racially idealistic, and as we will see in Chapter 5, the NAR has managed to appeal to a wide number of people groups specifically because its ideology is seen as not simply transcending the rhetoric of race, but transforming that rhetoric into categories heretofore unimagined by progressive racial politics. While this new form of racial identity—an idea of race based not in ethnicity or skin color, but one's allegiance to the church—may in the end allow the movement to form a truly progressive racial ideology, it's more likely result is to re-inscribe old racist values, only transferring those values from the old racial categories into new prescribed racial undesirables— the racial other Wiccans, New Agers, Buddhists, Muslims, Jews, Hindus, and other religious groups that have been transformed by NAR rhetoric into the new racial others.

How does the ideology of spiritual mapping work in practice? Otis Jr.'s method of spiritual mapping was the most detailed and thought out, so it is a good place to start. As Holvast points out, Otis Jr. "aimed at coherent and customized data acquisition, analytical standards and report layouts" (Holvast 118). Otis Jr. believed that there were five factors to transforming communities: "Persevering leadership…. Fervent, united prayer…. Social reconciliation…. Public power encounters … [and] diagnostic research/spiritual mapping"

(Otis Jr. 56). Community transformation also had three stages to it. The first phase was the establishment of "spiritual beachheads," in which believers entered into "united prayer." This was followed by a stage of "spiritual breakthrough" in which churches grew rapidly. The third stage a community went through was called "spiritual transformation," in which communities were supposed to benefit from "dramatic socio-political renewal." A fourth stage that Otis Jr. felt was implicit in this progressive form of community transformation was what he termed "spiritual maintenance." Spiritual maintenance was the phase in which "liberated communities" sought to "turn their attention to the business of preserving hard-won victories." Otis Jr. is quite clear about the explicitly political ramifications of this form of community transformation; he tells his readers that "born-again politicians, journalists, businessmen and educators" have a duty to perpetuate "Kingdom values through the institutions they serve" with the ultimate goal of making spiritual transformation a "permanent condition" (Otis Jr., *Informed Intercession* 57–58).

Otis Jr.'s interweaving of Charismatic theology and evangelical power politics is truly brilliant. Indeed, an uninformed reader looking at *Informed Intercession* would be tempted to say the book is not political at all, though in fact politics is evident through every page. One of Otis Jr.'s suggested forms of community transformation is the deceptively simple practice of creating prayerwalking profiles (Otis Jr., *Informed Intercession* 100–101). Prayerwalking is the practice of "on-site, street level intercession. Prayers offered by participants are in response to immediate observations and researched targets" (Otis Jr. 254). What this means usually is a group of evangelical Christians gathering together and walking around a certain targeted area, praying for the area or about the problems within the area. Prayerwalking profiles are the spiritual profiles of certain geographical areas, and thus serve as the basis for spiritual mapping in Otis's system (and in many other spiritual mapping systems).

What makes Otis Jr.'s system brilliant is both how he markets this form of intercession and the information he encourages his supporters to collect. According to Otis Jr., the "best profiles are usually produced by local churches and ministries based in or near the target area." Though he does not ask his audience to standardize their practice, he suggests that they usually include "some treatment of local history, social bondages, and spiritual competition. They also present a brief overview of current problems facing the body of Christ (e.g., apathy, persecution, or disunity)" (Otis Jr. 100–101). What Otis Jr. does so brilliantly—and what other, largely intellectually inferior, proponents of spiritual mapping copied—is to develop an organizational structure for the spiritual mapping movement that was intrinsically self-perpetuating. The movement's main theological innovation—spiritual mapping—was inherently designed not only to gain the movement new adherents, but to effectively network the movement's adherents into larger organizational structures. In addition, the practice of the spiritual mapping effectively gave the movement its own spiritual "intelligence service." Non-NAR commentators have often treated the movement as some faddish evangelical innovation with little practical consequence. In fact, the spiritual mapping movement was a brilliant organizational innovation. It allowed the movement to get free intelligence from its adherents, to effectively network through "user-friendly" organizational structures, and to do all this through a form of evangelism that many Charismatics at the time apparently found "fun." One cannot help but note the evident glee in spiritual mapping literature. The movement, for Charismatics, was enjoyable, and it was that sense of spiritual pleasure, compounded with the movement's organizational innovations, that made it such an effective tool for forming the apostolic networks that would later turn into the NAR.

Indeed, the organizational innovations that Otis Jr. introduced hardly end there. Otis Jr. also suggests that adherents construct timelines and physical maps of areas. For instance, a map could include the locations of such spiritually "deceptive" buildings as Buddhist temples, Mormon stakes, Islamic mosques, strip clubs, and adult bookstores (Otis Jr. 147). Thus, the spiritual mapping movement got free access to intelligence on rival religious and social movements that allowed the movement to effectively plot both religious *and political* strategy. Otis Jr. even discusses prayerwalking as a kind of observational patrol, and weighs the pros and cons of spiritually mapping different areas (Otis Jr. 175, 177). Most importantly, Otis Jr. encourages fellow Charismatics to do hard research on local problems, including looking at dissertations, newspapers, magazines, public records, websites, and broadcast documentaries (Otis Jr. 188–189).

Otis Jr.'s Sentinel Group, which was one of the main disseminators of his particular brand of spiritual mapping, used a number of innovative techniques to spread the practice of spiritual mapping. For instance, the Sentinel Group set up an online forum which was used to exchange information and strategies, as well as providing a communal environment for spiritual mappers to bond in (Holvast 118). Sentinel also provided "Special Explorer Reports" which gave members reports "regularly on prayer and community transformation all over the world" (119). In addition the Sentinel group set up a number of Transformation Networks, also known as Transnets, under the headship of the International Fellowship of Transformation Partners (IFTP). The movement divided the world into 30 "regional transnets," each of which had its own transformation network and its own Transformation Center, the latter of which served as a "local grassroots connection" for those engaged in the process of spiritual mapping (Holvast 119).

Other spiritual mapping methods were also used. Silvoso's Harvest Evangelism formed its own Apostolic Transformation Network (ATN), which sought to change not simply geographical areas, but entire nations (ultimately the goal of Otis Jr. as well). Silvoso, tied to the myth of Plan Resistencia, promoted Resistencia's "success" as a reason for modeling future community transformation on that model. Silvoso's model, best characterized by his books *Transformation: Change the Marketplace and You Change the World* (2007) and *Anointed for Business* (2002), focused primarily on politicians and businessmen (Silvoso, *Transformation* passim; Silvoso, *Anointed for Business* passim; Holvast 119). As Silvoso's form of spiritual mapping—what I have termed here transformationalism—is covered extensively in Chapters 3 and 4, I will not cover it here. Suffice it to say, Silvoso's ideas ultimately found support from other NAR apostles, as his model led more quickly to greater political and financial power while simultaneously almost effortlessly—and falsely—promoting the NAR as the bastion of a new form of progressive politics.

Meanwhile, Wagner was promoting himself primarily directly through the AD 2000 Campaign's United Prayer Track which was under the auspices of Wagner's Global Harvest Ministries. Wagner promoted the idea of what was called the 10/40 Window, and after 2000, the 40/70 Window (Holvast 119). The 10/40 Window was a missiology concept coined by AD 2000 and Beyond movement leader Luis Bush, based on the research of David Barrett. According to Bush, statistics showed that 95 percent of the planet's "unreached peoples" existed within the "latitudes of 10 degrees and 40 degrees north." The goal of reaching these people by the year 2000 became the organizing principle of the AD 2000 Movement (Wagner, *Wrestling* 168). The 40/70 Window that would take the 10/40 Window's place included mainly Europe and central Asia and was characterized by the demonic control of "the Queen of Heaven," whom Wagner classified as a high-ranking demon (Holvast 152). As Holvast points out, Wagner's spiritual mapping methods were relatively basic. He proposed two steps: gathering relevant information and then acting on that information. Wagner focused primarily on research methods and therefore did not include the practical organizational advice in his spiritual mapping material that one would find in Otis Jr. (Holvast 119–120). While Wagner would prove to be a skilled administrative hand in the NAR, rising to the very top of its leadership structure, he left most of the pragmatic aspects of developing spiritual mapping to others.

A fourth method of spiritual mapping was used by Cindy Jacobs's organization, Generals of Intercession (later known as Generals International) which acted as a kind of intercessory "army" for the movement, mobilizing "prayer warriors." Jacobs's organization also emphasized from an early date the importance of the apostolic and prophetic elements of the movement (Holvast 120). A fifth model was provided by Dutch Sheets, whose organization the National Governmental Prayer Alliance (NGPA) served as a "'clearing house for information,'" for intercessors to pray for the U.S. government. The goals of the NGPA were explicitly political and nationalistic, and showed "alignment with patriotic historical notions" which clearly aligned the movement with the Christian Right (Holvast 120–121). In recent years, Jacobs's organization has been moving in a similar direction to Sheets's. Finally, there was Kraft's Deep Healing Ministries. I have covered Kraft's form of inner healing elsewhere, but what is important to note in the context of the spiritual mapping movement is that Kraft's Deep Healing Ministries used spiritual mapping as one of the "components" of exorcism. Kraft, in short, applied spiritual mapping to "pastoral care" (Holvast 121).

Spiritual Mapping and the Theory of Cultural Trauma

Although almost all of the ideology of the spiritual mapping movement was broadly consistent with Third Wave Charismatic thinking and the "Wagnerian" strain of church growth thought, there is a particular facet of spiritual mapping ideology that bears mentioning because of the unique ways in which the movement developed it: Its theory of historical trauma. The prime "traumatologists" in the movement were George Otis, Jr., and John Dawson, two of the movement's foremost innovators. Otis Jr. would provide the spiritual mapping movement with a unique vision of human history in his *The Twilight Labyrinth* (1997), a book that effectively gives a spiritual mapping reading of most of human history (particularly our species prehistory) in a few hundred pages. Dawson Jr.'s earlier work *Healing America's Wounds* (1994) would approach trauma in a more politicized and Eurocentric manner, even as it was used for the goal of advancing racial reconciliation. These works proved significant, as they provided a foundational historiographical viewpoint from which later NAR ideology would develop. Otis Jr.'s historiography is central to understanding not only his theory of trauma, but also his conceptualization of spiritual mapping. According to Otis Jr., for humanists ancient history holds little interest. Humanists as "shapers of the future ... are impressed not with means but with ends; with what will be, not what has been" (Otis Jr., *Twilight Labyrinth* 89). Therefore, for Otis Jr., humanists' reasoning is simple: The front part of human history—the past—is a bad place to start looking for historical answers. For the humanist, the eyes of humanity should be constantly facing the future. Otis Jr. sees this futurist orientation as a major flaw in humanist thinking, as technological and social innovations in human history have as often led to such moral injustices as "interactive pornography, saline abortions, and biological weapons" as to real meaningful social change (Otis Jr. 89). Otis Jr. argues that human history is "morally entropic"—that is, that barring the power of "godly wisdom," human beings get worse over time, not better (Otis Jr., *Twilight Labyrinth* 89).

In a sense, Otis Jr.'s ideology seems at odds with prevailing convictions within the Charismatic world, which tends to have a very high view of human beings. In particular, the restorationist vein of Latter Rain revivalism does not necessarily fit in well with the idea of a morally entropic universe. But only in a sense. What is important to understand within the Charismatic view of history—as we will especially see with the most prominent eschatological expert within the movement, Bill Hamon—is that history is progressive, but only for the godly. Indeed, history after the Reformation goes in two directions. There are a progressive number of "improved" revival movements over time among the Christian faithful (see Hamon, *Prophetic Scriptures Yet to Be Fulfilled*, 123–127, on this), and a progressive moral deadening of the society of "unbelievers" which ultimately can only lead to spiritual conflict, unless averted by the transformationalist message promoted by first the spiritual mapping movement and then the NAR.

Otis Jr.'s view of history is rooted in a very esoteric and quite peculiar view of prehistoric human trauma. For Otis Jr., ancient humanity, cast out of the garden, instilled "tribal myths into the minds of succeeding generations" (Otis Jr., *Twilight Labyrinth* 110). Shamans and clan leaders used "primitive virtual reality displays ... sound effects (drums and chanting) ... and disorientation (dark labyrinthine passages and mind altering substances)" to lead humanity into spiritual darkness (Otis Jr. 110). This prehistoric human trauma was furthered by the development of Goddess cults and the increasing proliferation of urban communities (the latter are seen as being greater demonic strongholds than rural areas by NAR supporters, including by Otis Jr.) (Otis Jr. 113, 118).

Otis Jr. argues that the confusing of languages at Babel represented a crucial historical event. According to Otis Jr.'s reading of the Babel myth, God's actions at Babel involved "a profound rewiring of their [humanity's] cerebral cortices." Because this instant absorption of new tongues bypassed traditional learning mechanisms, human beings were left without an "awareness of internal change." Therefore, seeing that they could no longer communicate with their neighbors, the various tribes descended from the Babelites assumed that their neighbors were bewitched. After Babel fell and humanity spread across the

Earth, human beings began to mythologize the past, with two particular forms of myth—the golden age and Ancient Wisdom—predominating (Otis Jr. 134–135).

What united these tribes' experiences, however, was an "important common denominator," which each had experienced: collective trauma (Otis Jr. 136). Otis Jr. posits that were five forms of collective trauma in the past, trauma that Satan sometimes caused or simply took advantage of: "Intimidating natural barriers…. Climactic and natural disasters…. Disease and pestilence…. Famine and environmental ruin…. Wars and raids" (Otis Jr. 136). Satan used these collective traumas as a form of deception by which he could get primitive peoples to engage in "long-term quid pro quo pacts" (Otis Jr. 136). According to this reading of history, the deal between these primitive peoples and Satan was simple. Human beings received "immediate trauma relief" as well as the knowledge and power of demonic entities in return for pledging their allegiance to demonic agents of Satan (Otis Jr. 136). It was these agreements, made in humanity's pre-history, that allowed Satan to establish demonic "territorial strongholds" that remained in place to this day (Otis Jr. 149).

What is one to make of such a theory of history? Obviously, we are dealing with a form of spiritualized historiography that lacks any historical basis. But Otis Jr.'s vision of human history is still revealing. For the NAR, history before Christ is a history of wounding and pain. History is viewed in terms that are at once first-century, and based in the diabolic, and modern, and based in the psychotherapeutic. The NAR manages to fuse these two ideas so effortlessly because it gives people an outlet for blaming vexing social, political, and personal problems on an external agent, thus releasing the individual from the necessity of acting towards affecting meaningful sociopolitical or personal change. The excuse, whether at the ground level of psychic "wounds" or at the territorial or national level of economic and political ones, is the same: The demons are responsible, not us. And in both cases, the solution is also the same: A return to God.

This psychotherapeutic concept of national grief is exemplified by the concept of "soul ties," an idea promoted by many contemporary Charismatics, which argues that, for instance, when an "injustice or serious sin has been committed, such as child sexual abuse," unforgiveness results and thus a demon is invited into the child's life, thus connecting the abuse victim demonically to his or her abuser (Doris Wagner "Forgiving the Unforgivable," *How to Minister Freedom* 99). John Dawson's *Healing America's Wounds* promotes this concept in particularly disturbing terms, when Dawson connects the trauma of soul ties created by incest to national wounding. Dawson writes:

> Take, for example, father/daughter incest. The little girl is in no way responsible for her father's depraved actions, yet she is given a terrible wound to her soul and spirit.

> Anybody with a counseling ministry knows that this is a circumstance that tormenting spirits use to advantage. It's not fair, but then nothing satanic is fair.... Now think of the implications for a nation. The human story is full of atrocities committed in the name of religious factions, ideologies, races and the nation-state itself. And of course, Satan's greatest empowerment comes when some moral outrage is committed by those who invoke the name of Jesus [Dawson 54–55].

For Dawson, therefore historical trauma is mediated through the lens of psychotherapeutic discourse. One understands the suffering of Third World populations through relating their problems to American angst over sexual abuse. And just as little boys and girls can only be healed of their abuse if they forgive their abusers, so too in NAR ideology can the racially oppressed only be healed if they forgive their oppressors. Ironically, however, Dawson also condemns psychotherapeutic discourse, complaining that "while personal guilt is daily minimized by the gurus of psychobabble, corporate guilt has never been more popular as a concept. Redress of grievance is one of the great rationales of our day, often given as the justification for government programs, laws, curriculum changes, and what the black author, Shelby Steeles [sic], calls 'grievance identities'" (Dawson 187). In Dawson's reading of American history,[6] what haunts American culture is the inability to perform genuine acts of reconciliation. Dawson condemns what he calls "cheap reconciliation"; acts of forgiveness that "overemphasize the significance of solemn assemblies and other formal acts of confession" (Dawson 165). Yet increasingly such acts have come to characterize NAR apostles, particularly the transparently hypocritical Alice Patterson, the granddaughter of a former Klansman, who now promotes herself as a champion of the oppressed and "racial healing" even as she uses her bully pulpit on the Christian right to rip into LGBT people (Daily Mail Reporter, "It Could Come Back").

One can argue that such actions were not Dawson's intention. The problem is such a supposition ignores the fact that Dawson's *Healing America's Wounds* is as full of white racial coding as it is of a reconciliatory message. Dawson, for instance, supports the idea that "ethnic leaders" promote a culture of victimization as a "source of power and moral superiority" (Dawson 123). Dawson's critique of America's culture of victimization, besides being tone-deaf to the suffering of American minorities, elides the fact that there are significant reasons for American racial minorities to continue to hold such grievances.

And this ultimately is the problem with Dawson's view of history. Dawson transmutes massive historical traumas into the cheap acts of grief one sees on Oprah. The lack of sincerity in the apologies of the Christian right for its historical sins is best highlighted by the fact that the movement continues to oppose policies that would likely benefit disadvantaged economic and racial minorities. Instead NAR apostles continue to sell out the people the movement claims to protect.

The NAR's view of history is paradoxical, at once both restorationist and optimistic, yet also nostalgic. This tension can be seen by briefly comparing two important, more recent NAR works: James W. Goll and Lou Engle's *The Call of the Elijah Revolution* (2008) and Bill Hamon's *Prophetic Scriptures Yet to Be Fulfilled* (2010). Goll and Engle's text, though like Hamon's quite optimistic, is ultimately tinged with a degree of melancholy. Dutch Sheets, writing in the book's forward, warns that "America today is in the grip of the spirit of Baal. This spirit permeates our culture and is the dominant worldview that drives virtually every segment of our society, especially moral issues, social issues, politics, the news media, public education and the entertainment industry" (Sheets in Goll and Engle 15). Goll and Engle, too, warn that America is suffering from a "spiritual pollution" caused by the "shedding of innocent blood" namely "44 million innocent unborns" through abortion (Goll and Engle 31). For all three men, each a major leader in the NAR, God is certainly capable of judging America (Goll and Engle 33).

But Goll and Engle's message and therefore their view of history is ultimately redemptive (Goll and Engle 33, 212). The two authors encourage their readers to reject a "humanistic" view of history in which "nothing can be known with certainty" for what they call "providential history." In this reading of history, the focus is "not on randomness in nature but on intelligent creative design…. Therefore, everything from nature to law to art to politics has design and order" (Goll and Engle 212). History for Goll and Engle is ultimately teleological in orientation. It has a cause and it has a purpose. Similarly, America itself has a purpose as well and was brought about for a "divine reason" (Goll and Engle 212). History belongs to Christianity, specifically American Christianity, which has promoted "the greatest evangelistic and missionary enterprise in the history of the world" (212). What seems to be an unintended corollary belief of this providential view of history is that those who oppose this providential reading are cast as enemies of history and progress. Indeed, Goll and Engle complain that humanism and rationalism rob American young people of "their Godly heritage" (Goll and Engle 212). Because the historiographical traditions of these two rivaling philosophical systems are so different—one religious, eschatological and teleological, the other primarily non-religious, biologically evolutionary and non-teleological—there seems little hope of these two systems successfully dialoguing with each other or coming to a historical accord about the future of American culture. The triumphalism of this religious vision—too often matched by similar forms of secular triumphalism promoted by New Atheists—makes future conflicts over "culture war" issues inevitable, so long as these two movements continue to prove unwilling to question their own prevailing historical assumptions. But while secular histories of the West have tended to be self-correcting, the restorationist outlook of the NAR, with its emphasis on continuous spiritual evolution, will likely breed ever-increasing forms of spiritual elitism directed against its secular opponents.

Hamon's historiography is optimistic. Since I deal extensively with Hamon's view of the church, race, and history in Chapter 5, I note it only briefly here. Hamon, better than anyone, articulates a foundational philosophical element of NAR historiography: its ecclesiocentrism. According to Hamon's reading of history, from "God's perspective and purpose, world history … revolves around His Church; in fact the Church is the center of all of God's interest and activities on earth. Thus the Church, and only the Church, is the key to and explanation of history. Therefore, history is only the handmaiden of the Church, and the nations of the world are but puppets manipulated by God for the purpose of His Church…. Creation has no other aim; history has no other goal" (Hamon, *Prophetic Scriptures* 85–86). Thus, Hamon agrees with Goll and Engle's reading of history as providential and teleological, but further adds to this reading the idea that history is ultimately at the service of the "Church." Because history is thus so limited, ultimately any force opposed to the Church is opposed to history. Similarly, any force operating against the clear direction of history—which for Hamon is restorationist and spiritually evolutionist—is ultimately opposing the Church. Such a philosophy of history is convenient for a movement as historically and sociologically pragmatic as the NAR, as it allows the movement to justify any oppressive action under the guise that such actions are willed by transcendent, immutable historical forces that cannot be contradicted without defying the will of God. Also, if one restorationist movement proves too unpopular, it can be replaced with another "brand" of restorationist belief, just as shepherding was replaced by the Kansas City Prophets' prophetic revolution, and as the NAR replaced the prophetic revolution with an apostolic one. As we will see, such pragmatism—which characterized the anthropology of Charles Kraft and the church growth movement—would find a welcome place in the NAR.

The Structuring of the NAR

The New Apostolic Reformation may or may not have consciously willed itself into being, but the movement's current structure was already implicit during the very formation of AD 2000 and Beyond. Luis Bush, the international director of AD 2000 and Beyond, designed the Movement around "13 semi-autonomous tracks." The tracks would each be led by a chairperson who even Wagner admits was pretty much a "figurehead." The real leader of each track, however, would be its coordinator, who was the "de facto leader of the track" (Wagner, *Wrestling* 168–169). Bush appointed track chairpersons and coordinators, made sure people were completing assignments, and connected the various groups together. Wagner praised Bush for his ability to delegate authority while allowing the track coordinators the freedom to develop the structure of their particular tracks as they saw fit. Wagner characterizes the AD 2000 tracks as not being run by "committees or boards" but by "apostolic coordinators" (Wagner, *Wrestling* 169). While Wagner does not explicitly state so, it is hard not to get the impression that it was his experience with Bush's form of networking that eventually influenced his adoption of the New Apostolic model.

Wagner took control of the United Prayer Track (UPT) in 1991, under which he also controlled the Spiritual Warfare Network (SWN). Later on Otis's Spiritual Mapping Track would also be incorporated into Wagner's UPT track. (Wagner, *Wrestling* 170–171). The combination of so many offices of responsibility gave Wagner, already an influential evangelical leader, incredible power to promote his particular iteration of Charismatic ideology. To facilitate his leadership of the UPT, Wagner and his wife established Global Harvest Ministries in Pasadena towards the end of 1991 (Wagner, *Wrestling* 176; Holvast 98–99).

At the Pasadena Post-Lausanne II Consultation on Cosmic-Level Spiritual Warfare, the term spiritual mapping was not yet in use. It was at this meeting that the SWN was first formulated. By 1997, the SWN "would split into national networks under an international umbrella organization." Academic Tye Yau Siew would see the Pasadena meeting as foundational towards the establishment of the characteristic "informal and flexible networks" of the spiritual mapping movement (Holvast 95–96; see also Siew 17–18). Publications started promoting spiritual mapping (Holvast 95) and the practice quickly became widespread throughout the evangelical movement.

In 1990, Otis formed his Sentinel Group, which would be the organization that most directly promoted spiritual mapping practice in the U.S. (see Holvast 98). Around the same time Wagner was teaching his controversial Signs and Wonders course at Fuller Seminary while also implementing new course ideas that used elements of spiritual mapping. Future prominent leaders in the NAR, including Cindy Jacobs, Chuck Pierce and the Wagners themselves were traveling regularly to Argentina by the early 1990s to learn from and/or aid the Argentine revival (Holvast 98).

By 1993, the prayer Campaign Praying through the Window I was in full swing (Wagner, *Confronting the Powers* 29). This campaign for worldwide prayer would be repeated three successive times, in 1995, 1997, and 1999 (Holvast 101). In June 1993, the Sentinel Group conducted the first public conference on spiritual mapping, which then allowed the movement to engage in "regional consultations" in 1994 (Holvast 101–102). In October of 1993, Wagner invited 300 leaders to the First SWN International Meeting, also called the "Gideon's Army" meeting (Wagner, *Wrestling Alligators* 194; Holvast 102). The meeting's makeup was multiracial and was seen by Wagner as an important step in developing the networking process that SWN had set up (Wagner, *Wrestling* 195).

A crucial meeting was held on February 20, 1994, the United States SWN Founders Circle Meeting (6th SWN), which was meant "to evaluate the consultation in Seoul" (Holvast 103). Movement leadership decided at the meeting that the various networks were now to be organized "along regional, national and continental lines" (Holvast 103). In the United States, networks were established on a state-by-state basis, one per state, with a coordinator in each state. The SWN was then given the incredibly awkward name of the United States Spiritual Warfare Network Founders Meeting (USSWNFM) (Holvast 103).

By 1995, AD 2000 and Beyond had reached a crossroads. The movement organized what was called the Global Consultation on World Evangelization II in Seoul (GCOWE 95). GCOWE II recommitted the AD 2000 campaign to reaching "all unreached peoples by the year 2000" and was meant as a massive attempt to organize grass roots support for the movement with more than 4,000 participants. Again, there was a preponderance of non–Western delegates and spiritual mapping figured prominently in several plenary discussions though the GCOWE 95 Declaration did not mention spiritual mapping explicitly (Holvast 104).

At this point, however, Wagner's attention began to waver from the spiritual mapping movement, if spiritual mapping had ever been more than a convenient theological ploy for him. In 1996, Wagner organized the National Symposium of the Postdenominational Church, held at Fuller Theological Seminary. Wagner and 500 other evangelical leaders addressed what they saw as "new paradigms" of church organization, communication, evangelism, prayer, and interaction with supernatural powers (Holvast 106). From 1996 on, Wagner's focus became increasingly the NAR, and his fascination with spiritual mapping as a practice gradually faded away (Holvast 105–106, 110).

According to Holvast, the lack of attention Wagner paid spiritual mapping after this date reflected a general decline in interest about spiritual mapping, a decline that accelerated by the early 2000s and eventually led to the disintegration of the spiritual mapping movement as an independent movement and its incorporation into other ministries and fields of activity, including the NAR and the prophetic movement (which is largely part of the NAR as well now) (Holvast 148). Here Holvast—practically always the best source on the apostolic movement out there—is perplexing. Holvast argues that GHM, Wagner's ministry, suffered major setbacks between 2000 and 2005. Yet at the same time, Holvast lists no less than 5 major ministries that Wagner and GHM helped form in this period, including the country's foremost apostolic network, the International Coalition of Apostles (ICA); the New Apostolic Roundtable, a prominent gathering of apostles; the Apostolic Council for Prophetic Elders (ACPE), another influential apostolic organization, and the Apostolic Roundtable for Deliverance Ministries (ARDM), an organization composed of apostles who specialize in "personal exorcism" (Holvast 159–160). What is clear now, but may not have been to Holvast, writing in 2009, was that far from receding, Wagner's organization was quickly becoming a power player in Charismatic circles, and that the organizational innovations that the NAR was introducing were both revolutionizing the movement and causing a great deal of controversy. It is to these organizational innovations that we now turn.

The Apostles and the Prophets: Why Apostolic Networks Work

So what exactly were the innovations that Wagner and his fellow apostles were introducing into the Charismatic movement? Primarily, the innovation was one that actually was not an innovation at all. NAR churches, according to Wagner, were characterized by differences from mainstream evangelical churches in leadership. Whereas "the locus for trust" for leadership in traditional evangelical churches was centered in groups, within NAR churches the center of power was in individuals (Wagner, "New Apostolic Reformation" 930). Wagner criticized traditional churches for seeing pastors as employees; in the new apostolic model, individual apostles, rather than "presbyteries or annual conferences or cabinets or districts or conventions" provided the "vision-casting" for the church's mission (Wagner, "New Apostolic Reformation" 930). One could pardon the suspicious denominational Pentecostal *canaille* for seeing Wagner's NAR as just a reformulation of shepherding doctrine, for there was in principle little different in Wagner's ideas from those that had been advanced earlier by the Fort Lauderdale Five. The *canaille* protested, but in vain, because within a decade the NAR had infiltrated even many of their churches.

Indeed, it is important to note that Wagner's formulation of the New Apostolic paradigm was more the description of a term for a pre-existing entity, rather than the creation of a new movement out of whole-cloth. The latter assumption tends to color far too much writing on the NAR. Wagner himself did not claim to have created the NAR, nor did he see it as solely a recent invention. Rather, Wagner argued that the NAR was "an extraordinary work of God at the close of the twentieth century, which is to a significant extent, changing the shape of Protestant Christianity around the world.... Particularly in the 1990s, but with roots going back for almost a century, new forms and operational procedures began to emerge in areas such as local church government, interchurch relationships ... leadership selection and training, the role of supernatural power, worship and other aspects of church life" (Wagner, *Churchquake!* 5). While of course there is a good deal of *ex post facto* reasoning here, Wagner's assertion is still largely accurate. In the United Kingdom, for instance, apostolic networks emerged as early as the 1970s (see Kay 20). Also, despite Bill Hamon's argument that the restoration of the office of apostle occurred in the 1990s, there is a fair amount of evidence that Hamon's theology had been trending in the new apostolic direction for a long time. Indeed, Hamon's *Eternal Church* (2003) sees the New Apostolic movement's origins trending back several decades, and he himself claims to have promoted New Apostolic thinking as early as the 1980s (Hamon, *Eternal Church* loc 2707, Kay 20). Wagner therefore was not creating a phenomena, he was *describing it*. Moreover, he was also *branding it.*

This is an important point to understand because a Wagner-centric reading of the NAR, always a temptation to any critic of the movement, neglects the fact that quite a few apostolic networks originated independently of Wagner, and many of them predated Wagner's involvement in the Charismatic movement by several decades. Nor is agreement with Wagner a necessary prerogative for labeling a church New Apostolic. The New Apostolic Reformation is a description of an *organizational philosophy and a theological and political ideology*, one that Wagner certainly played a large part in advancing. It is not, however, an organization, much less a denominational structure. Indeed, the primary strength of the NAR is precisely that it is neither of those things, but rather a flexible alliance of closely-affiliated apostolic networks. Thus different networks brand themselves in different manners. While the underlying ideology and organizational philosophy is in almost all cases identical, movement members are relatively unconcerned about what apostle or group of apostles is seen as running the movement. What matters, in the movement's eyes, is the structure and the thought system behind the movement, not the people doing the structuring. While Wagner, Kraft, Wimber, and Otis Jr. have been disproportionately influential on the movement, they are not in any real sense the movement's founders, but rather simply some of its major early proponents.

Similarly, one should not look for a foundational moment for the NAR. The NAR is not a nation state, it does not have a constitution, a bill of rights, or even any widely-accepted defining creedal statements. To therefore ex post-facto declare that C. Peter Wagner, or alternately John Wimber, created the movement is to misunderstand the NAR entirely. The movement's formation was organic, an evolution out of pre-existing theological systems. It was therefore not in any real sense tied to any specific event, and thus it is ideologically much like other organically created philosophical movements—for instance, conservatism—that have no clear foundational date for their origination.

Where then was the innovational thinking behind the NAR, if the movement's organizational structure and ideology were not the products of one person's or even several people's genius? Bill Hamon, who despite his extremism and folksy speaking style, is one of the movement's most effective thinkers, sees the essential strength of the new apostolic idea in the phenomena of networking. Hamon conceptualizes the networking as being "multilevel and worldwide." Networks could be national or international and would be modeled around Internet networks as various denominations, ministries, separate networks, camps, fellowships, etc., all linked together in alliances that could be as loose or tight as any of these movements wanted (see Hamon, *Apostles and Prophets* 15–17). These apostolic networks, like the shepherding networks that had preceded them, were translocal. Also like the shepherding networks, new apostolic networks are based on relational alliances, primarily between individuals. This allows the movement to concentrate power in a few individuals while effectively freeing itself from the legal and bureaucratic burdens imposed by denominational structures. Again, this characteristic almost exactly mirrored shepherding practice as well (Wagner, *Churchquake!* 127). Hamon's model of apostleship involves the "gradual restoration of the biblical offices of evangelist, pastor, teacher, and finally in the 1980s, the office of prophet and, in the 1990s, that of apostle" (Holvast 159; see also Hamon, *Apostles and Prophets* 53). The idea here is that the fivefold ministries needed to be restored (Holvast 159). Again, however, this was recycled Latter Rain and shepherding doctrine.

However, while the similarities between the NAR apostolic structure and Latter Rain and shepherding leadership structures are striking, there were a few crucial differences that allowed the NAR to more effectively manage its adherents than its predecessors. First, of course, was simply the greater advances made in technology since the Latter Rain revival and the Charismatic Renewal of the sixties and seventies. The use of computer technology, particularly Internet access, through organizations like the Sentinel Group and the Elijah List, gave the movement unifying loci from which to organize itself. The improved organizational strategies that developed out of the networking models of

2. Spiritual Mapping and the NAR   91

Hamon and Wagner and the spiritual mapping ideology promoted by AD 2000 and Beyond also greatly aided the organizational efficiency of the movement. Wagner also correctly asserts that new apostolic churches benefitted from aligning themselves "unapologetically ... to contemporary culture as the major determinant for the style of music they use" (Wagner, *Churchquake!* 158). As the evangelical movement became increasingly oriented towards Charismatics and youth, both markets which preferred newer and edgier music styles, NAR churches benefitted from adapting to this change, while more traditional evangelical churches lost out, unable to compete in the new religious free market

Moreover, if one reads both shepherding and NAR literature, it is quite clear that the latter movement was much more effective in decentralizing its power base and thereby providing the kind of organizational flexibility that could produce a sustainable leadership model for a religious movement. While the NAR, like the shepherding movement, places power in the hands of a relatively few individuals, it does not limit its visible core power base to a mere five people, as the Fort Lauderdale Five fatally did. Thus the movement appears to insiders more transparently democratic than the shepherding movement or its ancestors in the Latter Rain, an important point for those burned by the excesses of the Charismatic Renewal.

Apostolic networks, like the translocal organizations that formed the shepherding movement, had considerable organizational advantages over traditional denominational structures. Since apostolic networks were organized relationally, the network's reach could extend through multiple denominations, even denominations with warring theological positions. Moreover, because these networks lacked the bureaucracy of the denominations, the apostles could react quickly and decisively in making doctrinal or organizational decisions (see Wagner, *Apostles Today* 92). While this gave apostolic networks a relatively authoritarian air, it also made these networks infinitely more adaptive than denominational structures that were bound by legal and creedal obligations. And since the basic creedal commitments of the NAR, beyond an allegiance to conservative evangelical theology, were minimal (see Wagner, *Churchquake!* 66–67), the movement was able to dispense with issues of ecclesiological and theological debate that troubled more doctrinally-oriented churches. For the NAR, the important unifying element of the movement was not its theology but its praxis; in other words, the organizational structure of the NAR came to become its defining feature more than its theological commitments (see Wagner, *Churchquake!* 36). As was so typical of the movements Wagner and Kraft had involved themselves in, a sociological pragmatism oriented towards political, rather than creedal, conservatism, was a defining feature of the NAR. And it was the NAR's obsessive focus on church growth at any price that would ultimately so frighten the movement's opponents, both within and outside of the evangelical movement.

Before closing this chapter, brief mention should be made of the role of prophets within the NAR. While there is agreement within the movement that apostles are usually different from prophets (Eberle, *Complete Wineskin* 25), Harold Eberle, an early NAR thinker, clearly elevates the apostles to a greater role than the prophets. According to Eberle, "apostles are different from prophets, though they all have specific tasks. Prophets have limited messages or purposes and the power of prophets is in their words. Apostles are sent forth to establish and build up groups of believers in all areas of the believers' lives" (25). Therefore, for Eberle, the prophet's role is mainly as an orator and exhorter, whereas apostles provide the organizational and leadership structure for New Apostolic churches. Eberle, writing in 1993 when concepts like apostleship were somewhat in flux, may also have been concerned that prophets would again overstep their bounds as had happened in the case of the Kansas City Prophets.

John Eckhardt, an important early thinker on New Apostolic issues, emphasized the importance of developing a "prophetic lifestyle" (Eckhardt 1). Eckhardt emphasizes the importance of every Christian believer operating in the "prophetic realm" (2). Therefore, Eckhardt tends to emphasize the value of prophesy as a means of inculcating the values of one prophetic generation into the next (4); in short, Eckhardt's promotion of prophetic culture is meant as a sort of radicalization training for learning prophetic powers. Eckhardt condemned the "old covenant mindset" that characterized cessationist and non-prophetic churches, in which prophets met with "rejection, persecution, and exile" (Eckhardt 51). For Eckhardt the prophet's role is to "perfect believers" through confronting the "works of the devil" and by building up "the body of Christ" (Eckhardt 58–59). However, in practice Eckhardt's prophetic philosophy is long on generalities and short on organizational specifics.

And this characteristic of Eckhardt's ministry seems broadly consistent with how the NAR now conceptualizes the role of the prophetic in general. Prophets are still greatly valued, but the line between apostles and prophets is often a narrow one. Some NAR leaders openly embrace multiple roles, including powerful figures like Bill Hamon (Hamon, *Apostles, Prophets*, backcover blurb). What is important to understand is that if the prophet is not claiming the role of the apostle, his main duty today is typically to buffer up the apostles. Prophets are able to do this effectively because Charismatics put a dramatic amount of emotional investment into the prophets' prescience. While this kind of control invites abuse, it also gives the prophets enormous motivating power to inspire obedience to, and love for, the apostles.

Conclusion

The NAR entered the 21st century as a socially cohered collection of apostolic networks that were growing quickly into a major religious movement. In the next chapter, we will trace the development of the NAR over the last decade, primarily through the examination of a number of apostolic networks: the ICA, Morningstar Ministries, Revival Alliance, and the IHOP movement. In the process we will see how the NAR emerged from its obscure beginnings to elevate one of its own to the position of vice-presidential candidate, and to where it now feels it is at the point it can dictate national policies within both the Western and developed world.

3

The Apostolic Networks
A Brief Rundown of a Few of the Major Players

By 1997, the beginnings of the modern New Apostolic network structure were beginning to coalesce in ways previous networks could only dream of. In January of that year, the Spiritual Warfare Network's U.S. branch was reorganized as the United States Spiritual Warfare Prayer Network (USSPN). Within five years, the USSPN would organize 14 "task forces" for interacting with ethnic minorities and would appoint 50 coordinators (one for each state) (Holvast 106). A year earlier, Global Harvest Ministries and the United Prayer Track (UPT) had successfully moved to Colorado Springs to help set up the World Prayer Center (WPC), which would serve as a focal point for the movement for several years (Holvast 106).

At the same time, Ted Haggard, future president of the National Association of Evangelicals (NAE), operating with Wagner's blessing, launched what is surely one of the weirdest spiritual outreach campaigns in evangelical history: Operation Queen's Palace. This was a large "public prayer campaign," started in 1997, that continued until near the end of 1999. The campaign targeted what it saw as one of the chief demonic beings within the 10/40 window, known by the movement as the "Queen of Heaven." More recent manifestations of this idea have identified the queen of heaven as the Virgin Mary when she is worshipped as the Mother of God (Holvast 106–107).

One of Wagner's chief prayer warriors, Ana Méndez, discovered that "a major stronghold of darkness over the whole 10/40 Window was located on the highest of high places, Mt. Everest in the Himalaya Mountains" (Wagner, *Confronting the Queen of Heaven* 36). Therefore, with Wagner's blessing, Rony Chavez organized a team of twenty-six intercessors to assault the Queen of Heaven on Mt. Everest. This campaign was codenamed "Operation Ice Castle."

Méndez's team climbed 20,000 feet up Mt. Everest to do spiritual intercessory battle with the Queen of Heaven (Wagner, *Confronting* 36–37). Wagner glorified this act of anti-demonic alpine warfare in his book *Confronting the Queen of Heaven*, published in 1998.

Meanwhile the apostolic networks that had begun organizing out of Toronto also were making some of their first significant dents in public consciousness. On September 2, 2000, Ché Ahn and Lou Engle, two important members of what would become the Revival Alliance apostolic network, organized the Call D.C., a movement aimed at mobilizing young people "to maintain a 40-day fast with prayer for our nation that would lead up to the elections" (Ahn and Engle 18–19). Ahn credited this effort with ultimately assuring the "final victory for President Bush" after the "bizarre circumstances" of his election (Ahn and Engle 19). The Call soon became an international youth campaign ("Profiles on the Right"). Its most noted and controversial activity would be Lou Engle's very public alliance of the Call with conservative Ugandan Christians in 2010, when Uganda was considering enacting a death penalty for homosexuals (Kron, *God Loves Uganda*).

The NAR's apostolic networks would gain increasing visibility over the course of the 2000s. The first public exposure most Americans had to the NAR was in 2006 with the release of the documentary *Jesus Camp*. *Jesus Camp* showed the practices of a Christian youth camp run by Becky Fischer, a follower of Apostle Ché Ahn (Tabachnick, "The Religious Right's Plot"). The documentary included a dramatic sermon by Lou Engle in which he gets dozens of children to shout in unison, "Righteous judges, righteous judges!" as they waved around miniature fetuses and prayed for the life of the "unborn" and the reclamation of the courts of America by evangelical Christians. However, *Jesus Camp* did little to raise awareness about the NAR, for several reasons. First, though current and former NAR leaders were included in the documentary, such as Lou Engle and Ted Haggard, they were not identified as part of the NAR's leadership, but evangelicalism more generally. Secondly, much of the counter-reaction to *Jesus Camp* focused on what reviewers perceived as its unfair description of evangelical Christianity (see "Jesus Camp: Review" and Overstreet for evangelical reactions to the film). Many evangelicals felt that *Jesus Camp*, by overly-generalizing about all evangelical religion, minimized the differences between the religious education depicted in the film and more mainstream evangelical religious education. While there is probably a certain level of truth to this belief, what many evangelicals failed to understand was the increasing prominence of the NAR within evangelicalism itself. In any case, the documentary failed to raise consciousness about the existence of the NAR.

In 2008, however, it was more difficult not to pay attention to the NAR, because one of its adherents happened to be nominated as the Republican candidate for vice president of the United States: Sarah Palin. This became glaringly evident after a video leaked of Palin being prayed over by Kenyan witch-hunter Thomas Muthee, whose ministry had been glorified in George Otis Jr.'s *Transformations* videos as a model of spiritual mapping. Palin also was part of a spiritual warfare prayer network. Palin's connections to Muthee were hardly incidental. They were indeed a central part of her worldview (Bruce Wilson, "Sarah Palin Linked"). By 2008, Palin was working with the organization Carry the Cure on suicide-prevention in Alaska. However, Carry the Cure's parent "ministry" was Northwind Global Ministries, a group that promoted some of the most extreme elements within the NAR, including Todd Bentley, the leader of the Lakeland Revival. But the NAR again failed to gain the attention it deserved from academics or the media (Bruce Wilson, "Sarah Palin Linked"). Nor did Todd Bentley's Lakeland Revival put the NAR on the map, even after a large subsection of the most influential apostles (including practically the entire Revival Alliance network's top brass, C. Peter Wagner, and Rick Joyner) participated in the Revival (see McMullen on Bentley).

However, when the NAR yet again flexed its might in the run-up to the 2012 election, a few Americans finally began to take notice. This flexing of might came through a prayer rally organized for Perry by Engle's the Call ministry and the International House of Prayer (IHOP), the modern iteration of Mike Bickle's KCF (Tabachnick, "The Evangelicals Engaged"). The event was endorsed by a wide array of apostles, including John Benefiel, Cindy Jacobs, Bickle, and C. Peter Wagner (Rosenberg, "Rick Perry's Prayer-Rally Politics"). Because of Engle's by then infamous reputation and the increasing concerns voiced by secular and evangelical critics alike about the practices of both IHOP and the Call specifically and the NAR generally, controversy became unavoidable for the apostles (controversy also fueled by the huge number of apostles who were in attendance that were not officially linked with IHOP or the Call) (Tabachnick, "Dominionism, Theocracy"). NPR picked up the story of the NAR, as did Rachel Maddow on MSNBC (Lennard). Yet, while the movement was finally on the national press radar, both the American left and the principled elements of establishment conservatism failed entirely to understand the organizational innovations and strategic alliances that the NAR had constructed, both of which made the movement a threat to American democratic pluralism.

This chapter traces the development of a few of the major apostolic networks. A brief mention, however, should be made of what has been variously called the "Seven Mountains Campaign," "The 7-M Mandate" or "The Seven Gates" (here after referred to as the Seven Mountains campaign). Like the

Transformations films of George Otis, which were used so successfully in the late nineties to market proto-NAR ideology, the Seven Mountains campaign was in effect a form of NAR branding—or re-branding if you will—that utilized the language of dominionism in the furtherance of the movement's larger goals of sociopolitical and economic transformation. Although the seven mountains idea was widely adopted throughout the movement, the two prime articulators of it were Lance Wallnau and Johnny Enlow. According to Wallnau, the idea started in a conversation he had with Loren Cunningham, the founder of Youth with a Mission (YWAM), in which Cunningham shared a message from God that had been imparted to both Cunningham and Bill Bright. According to this message, there were "seven molders of culture or seven world kingdoms and he who could take those kingdoms could take the harvest of nations" (Bruce Wilson, "Lance Wallnau Explains"). Wallnau claims the seven mountains are religion, family, education, government, media, art (which included entertainment), and business (which included economics). The person who occupied the top of these mountains therefore shaped the "agenda that forms nations" (Bruce Wilson, "Lance Wallnau Explains").

The critical ideological innovation of the seven mountains movement was that it argued that Christians as a whole had spent so much time on the church mountain—that is in religious and evangelistic activity—that it had forsaken Christians' responsibility "to the rest of the world we are called to influence" (Bruce Wilson, "Lance Wallnau Explains"). Wallnau contended that the evangelical church had put so much emphasis on the "quantitative call of the gospel"—evangelism—that it had forsaken the gospel's "qualitative" emphases, which was to "transform nations" (Bruce Wilson, "Lance Wallnau Explains"). Enlow's book *The Seven Mountain Prophecy* (2008) provided a formal articulation of these principles while cloaking them in semi-prophetic terms. Wallnau, a skilled theorist and a gifted public speaker, was the perfect face to launch the movement; both Enlow and Wallanu showed enormous skill at articulating what was essentially rehashed Christian Reconstructionist rhetoric in the more modern terminology of dominionism.

Make no mistake, what the Seven Mountains movement promoted was dominionism, that is, a largely theocratic vision of American societal transformation. C. Peter Wagner, behind the movement from the start, articulated the movement's goal as "social transformation," which could only come through apostles having the "God-given authority to influence and take charge of a certain segment of society on behalf of the Kingdom of God" (Wagner, *Dominion* 148). That the movement's goal was explicitly theocratic can be seen by Wagner's comments on the best methods of achieving social transformation: "The practical theology that best builds a foundation under social transformation is dominion theology, sometimes called 'Kingdom Now.' Its history can be traced back through R.J. Rushdoony and Abraham Kuyper to John Calvin" (Wagner, *Dominion* 59). Kingdom now theology is typically seen as the Pentecostal form of Reconstructionist thought, though as we will see in Chapter 4, dominionist ideology within Pentecostal and Charismatic circles predates Earl Paulk's promotion of kingdom now ideas by several decades. Instead the movement's own theocratic ideas partly derive from the Manifest Sons doctrine of the Latter Rain movement, and partly from the notoriously theocratic writings of Reformed theologian Rousas Rushdoony, who famously called for the death penalty for homosexuals and disobedient children (W. Martin 353–354; Olson). That Wagner was willing to still invoke Rushdoony as late as 2008 is a telling commentary on the radicalness of the NAR. Nor was Wagner alone in singing the praises of Reconstructionist thinkers. Cindy Jacobs used Rousas Rushdoony's *Institutes for Biblical Law* (1973) as one of her prime research tools for her work *The Reformation Manifesto* (2008) (Jacobs 216).

The Seven Mountains movement has been popular for several years, though the increasing public attention Talk to Action and other progressive websites have put on the movement makes it likely that it will eventually rebrand itself at some point—much as Latter Rain revivalism had rebranded itself at multiple points in its history. It is important to understand that when one talks about the various different transformational campaigns within the NAR—George Otis's brand of transformationalism, Silvoso's form of transformationalism, the Seven Mountains campaign, or the kind of intercessory activism promoted by Mike Bickle's IHOP group of churches—we are not really talking about separate ideologies, but different brands of the same ideology. Each brand is directed at a different target consumer. For instance, Bickle's intercessory activism tends to appeal to the more marginal end of the Charismatic movement: the grunts, if you will. The Seven Mountains movement is a middlebrow approach, while both Otis and Silvoso are likely to appeal more to the intellectual elite of the movement, given their remarkable ability to encapsulate conservative economic and political theory in liberal-sounding rhetoric.

Each leader's philosophy, much like the apostolic networks that they lead, has a kind of individual appeal, and therefore they are collectively able to unite constituencies that might otherwise be kept apart in the evangelical world. Only by understanding how a few of the major networks work can we get a clue to the scope and breadth of NAR influence. Be forewarned, however, that the networks described here represent the tip of the iceberg, nor does this book claim to more than scratch the surface of the apostolic networks it in fact does describe. The NAR's influence by now is so wide and pervasive that it will take a much more concerted study on the part of scholars to truly understand the scope of the movement and its threat to democratic principles.

The Revival Alliance: Toronto Redux

In early 1996, according to Margaret Poloma, shortly after Toronto Airport Vineyard (TAV) had had its relationship severed with the AVC, the Arnotts were approached by a group of pastors influenced by the Blessing who wanted the Arnotts' spiritual covering. A few of these were new church plants; others were "existing churches looking for affiliation with others of like revival mind" (Poloma 182). As of spring 2002, their organization, Partners in Harvest (PIH) encompassed 94 churches/ministers who actively identified with PIH and another 248 who represented Friends in Harvest (FIH) and were somewhat more loosely connected with PIH. According to Poloma, the network unified itself through a number of activities, such as "Family Days," which were gatherings held prior to renewal conferences. Crucial to the Arnotts' organizational schema was an emphasis on "an organizational structure that promotes personal relationships" (Poloma 183). Again, this was a typical move on the part of NAR-aligned churches. According to Poloma's reading of the Arnotts' ministry, which here seems fairly accurate, PIH was primarily concerned with keeping "the coals of renewal burning"—in other words, keeping the revivalistic fruits of the Blessing alive. Therefore, the Arnotts' ministry focused on such Charismatic gifts as "holistic healing" and also sought to empower the next generation of leaders and evangelists (see Poloma 183).

The Arnotts' ministry, at least in its more open pronouncements, sought to espouse an idea of congregational independence from the leadership structure (Partners in Harvest, "Who Is PIH" 2). However, within individual apostolic churches, the Arnotts advised that leadership follow an elder or apostolic based leadership structure rather than a democratic one, emphasizing the common theme of relational networking led by powerfully Charismatic authority figures that characterized new apostolic networks as a whole (Partners in Harvest, "Who Is PIH" 7).

The Arnotts wanted to duplicate the success of the Blessing on a national and international level. One of Partners in Harvest's stated purposes was "to encourage, bless, serve, equip, train and counsel Partners in Harvest member congregations and pastors, and to be available to do the same for the broader Body of Christ" (Partners in Harvest, "Who Is PIH" 8). The Arnotts' way of doing this was by promoting the cultivation of relationships through what they called "Foursomes," which were "very small groups of pastors who work at becoming friends, meeting often to play and pray together." The Arnotts hoped that these groups would provide transparency and accountability to the wider movement—in other words serving a covering role for members and allies of PIH (Partners in Harvest, "Who Is PIH" 8).

Each member of Revival Alliance operates within the "axis of its own relational network" which all partially overlap with that of other relational networks (Brown, *Testing Prayer* 40). The Arnotts established their vision of Toronto as a hub of revival by planting 11 campuses within the Toronto area and by establishing church plants in Raleigh, London, England, Oslo, Norway, Reykjavik, Iceland, and Montréal. By 2009 TACF, formally renamed itself Catch the Fire Toronto, to reflect its now global vision (Brown, *Testing Prayer* 40). As Candy Gunther Brown points out, in a certain sense this move can be seen as a "key moment in transformation of a relational network into a denomination," a move that the Charismatic movement has characteristically been afraid of making, fearing what has been called by scholars of Charismatic culture the "routinization of charisma." Nevertheless, PIH seeks to serve some of the same functions as a denomination, without succumbing to the bureaucratizing and institutionalizing tendencies that the NAR sees as inherent within the denominational model of church governance. By 2009, PIH had established a covering relationship over more than 200 Western churches, but had achieved incredible growth in developing nations, leading some 7000 churches in the developing world (almost all of which seem to have entered via Revival Alliance ally Iris Ministries) (Brown 40–41).

It is difficult to establish the exact influence of PIH, but it is likely exceptional, given the popularity of the Toronto Blessing among the more radical elements of the NAR—and indeed Charismatic culture in general. Its influence on the Revival Alliance network as a whole was threefold. First, Toronto served as the birthplace of the movement and thus has a certain honorary position among Revival Alliance members. Ché Ahn has acknowledged the importance of Toronto in restoring the "office of the apostle with the birth of many apostolic networks, including John and Carol Arnott's Partners in Harvest, Rick Joyner's Morningstar, Bill Johnson's Global Legacy, Heid and Rolland Baker's Iris Ministries and our church's own Harvest International Ministry" (Ahn, *When Heaven Comes Down* 121). With the exception of Morningstar, all these apostolic networks became part of the Revival Alliance. Secondly, PIH is a major supporter of Heidi and Rolland Baker's Iris Ministries, an apostolic network centered primarily in Africa, but with some subsidiaries in the U.S., that serves as one of the more aggressively evangelistic arms of the NAR. Heidi Baker described the relationship between Iris and PIH as a "family link" (Brown 43). This is not surprising considering that Iris Ministries has planted 400 PIH churches in Malawi alone, with a combined membership of 25,000 people (Morrison). PIH has described itself as "partnering together" with Iris in Africa, and Iris's hagiographer Donald Kantel has described the Arnott's TAVF as providing a "large amount" of financial support to Iris (Kantel 153–154; Partners in Harvest, "Who Is PIH" 2). Finally, the Arnotts' ministry has been at the forefront of promoting some of the more extreme healing techniques pioneered by recent Charismatic deliverance practitioners. In particular, the *Restoring the Foundations* (RTF) deliverance model was birthed at TAVF (Brown, *Testing Prayer* 38); this model would provoke a national scandal in Australia when it was discovered that its exorcism based model of mental health treatment was being used to try to cure the mentally ill of their demonic attachments.[1] Although the method's founders, Chester and Betsy Kylstra, would be under the formal apostolic headship of NAR apostle Bill Hamon, their connections to the Arnotts was close. The Arnotts' website Catch the Fire, lists the Kylstras as "Our Friends" in a very select list of ministerial allies that includes not only the Kylstras but most of their allies within the Revival Alliance ("Our Friends").

Georgian Banov and his ministry Global Celebration is in many ways the lightweight among the six Revival Alliance ministries. Banov's ministry oversees 35 churches in Bulgaria, and they travel worldwide holding revivalistic events. The Banovs are particularly involved in converting the Gypsies of Eastern Europe and have expressed concern about Southeast Africa and Central America as well (Brown 42). Georgian Banov started off life living under the Communist Bulgarian regime. He eventually immigrated to the West (Global Celebration, "Biography"), where he became a member of the Christian rock group Silverwind. Among Banov's recent concerns have been "evangelistic outreaches among the poor" and the founding of a "school of the Supernatural" where his followers will be able to learn how to work signs and wonders (Leclaire). While Banov's membership in Revival Alliance clearly marks him as political he has remained relatively below the political radar. This is not to say, however, that he has been uninvolved in U.S politics. Quite the contrary. In 2010, Banov led a major "targeted prayer effort" whose goal was to sway the East Coast vote to a more Christianized form of leadership. Banov and his prayer warriors specifically linked this campaign to the Seven Mountains strategy of dominionist cultural politics as well (Mantyla, "Prayer Warriors Descending"). Banov has played at least a small part in promoting the economic ideas of Bill Johnson's Bethel church, particularly its opposition to the demonic spirits of Mammon and poverty. Though Johnson's idea of the spirit of poverty encompasses more than just material wealth—for Johnson, one can also be spiritually poor as well—it is significant that Banov and Johnson sought to promulgate Johnson's economic philosophy, grounded as much of it is in seven mountains dominionism (see Stephen K. De Silva 95, 99)—at the height of the economic recession (Global Celebration, "Georgian Banov & Bill Johnson").

Iris Ministries (which recently changed its name to Iris Global) is the most evangelistically-centered of the six major apostolic networks within Revival Alliance. Rolland and Heidi Baker started Iris Ministries in 1980 as a non-denominational mission in 1980, focusing on evangelism and church planting (Kantel 127). Heidi Baker, the more public face of the ministry, was converted to a radical form of Charismatic Christianity while on a Choctaw reservation (128). The Bakers spent 12 years in Asia, six of which involved leading Christian "dance-drama crusades" that converted thousands (Kantel 128). From 1992 to 1995 they pursued doctoral work in Britain before moving to Mozambique (Kantel 129). It was at this point that the canonization of Heidi Baker as future evangelical saint began.

This is not meant to be a facetious statement. Heidi Baker self-valorization as a hero figure for the modern era—her constant references to herself as "little ole me" as a sign of her humility—have turned her into a figure of nearly religious veneration by evangelical young people. Perhaps the most notorious example of this trend was a *Christianity Today* feature story on Baker entitled "Miracles in Mozambique: How Mama Heidi Reaches the Abandoned" (Stafford). *Christianity Today* promoted the idea that there were "credible reports that Heidi Baker heals the deaf and raises the dead" and insisted that one thing was certain: "She loves the poor like no other in this forgotten corner of the planet" (Stafford). Candy Gunther Brown commented on Baker that "'Heidi is a hero to young women,' so much so that scholars joke about 'Heidiolatry'" (Stafford) and then herself contributes to this valorization, stating, "For Heidi and Rolland, miracles and concern for the poor are meant to go together.... In their view, you can't separate the two. Power and love are wings, and you need both to fly" (Stafford). Brown's promotion of Iris Ministries was in fact a major element of her scholarship and an important element in the growing valorization of Iris Ministries as a whole. The numerous flaws of Brown's research in this area have already been noted; what is important to understand here is that Brown and Poloma's use of both deeply flawed sociological models and even more flawed healing studies have been utilized to further the beatification of Heidi Baker as healer-saint extraordinaire.

The promotion of Iris Ministries as a place of signs-and-wonders and the lack of emphasis on its NAR links is of a piece with the general Charismatic mood about Heidi Baker today. This emphasis on sign and wonders became particularly evident in Iris Ministries' efforts after the ministry allied itself with Surpresa Sithole in 1996 (on this alliance, see Kantel 153). Sithole, a Mozambican church planter, brought 90 churches under the Bakers' leadership (Kantel

139–140). By the time Kantel's dissertation was published in 2007 Iris was promoting the idea that Sithole had the spiritual gift of xenolalia—that is not only the gift of speaking in heavenly tongues, but the gift of speaking earthly languages of which one has no knowledge (Kantel 140).

Iris currently cares for some 4800 children and has planted more than 7000 churches as of 2007, primarily in Mozambique, South Africa, Malawi, Tanzania and the Congo. Another 5000 children are receiving foster care in the homes of Iris pastors (Kantel 13, 25–26). In 2001, Marc Dupont, a prominent supporter of the Toronto Blessing, went to Mozambique and prophesied that "renewal"—in other words, the spirit of revivalism—had passed from Toronto to Mozambique. He prophesied that it would again return to Toronto, and from there would spread throughout the world (Kantel 126–127). This is in many ways more than a causal prophecy, but reflected a growing Charismatic conviction—which has only been strengthened over the last decade—that the center of Christian power is moving from the West to the "Global South" and that Christian missiology and spiritual practice needs to reflect this fact. This does not mean that the movement in any way embraces a culturally relativistic vision; although the NAR is certainly more multicultural than, say, fundamentalism, it is by no means as racially progressive as it claims. What it does mean is that the movement is increasingly trying to figure out how to contextualize its faith to appeal to African and Latin American audiences. Because of the phenomenal success of the Bakers' ministry, and the generally positive view many Africans have of NAR teachings, Iris Ministries is seen by many NAR-leaning Charismatics as the forefront of a new missionary paradigm.

By 2004, the Bakers had announced a plan to inaugurate a 10-week "Holy Given International Missions School" in Pemba, Mozambique. The Missions School was to be a kind of evangelistic boot camp according to Kantel (Kantel 161–162). By 2005, the Bakers also had five Bible schools in operation in Mozambique (Kantel 162). More ominously, the ministry had planted more than 350 churches in former Muslim villages, which Rolland Baker claimed had caused Muslims a good deal of concern (Kantel 162–163). What is clear now is that Iris Ministries, regardless of the good or evil it does in Africa, has served as a major marketing tool for the NAR, a tool by which the movement has been able to convince non–NAR adherents that the movement's mission is primarily peaceful and progressive. The fact that the actual truth of Baker's healing efforts does not necessarily bear this assertion out does not phase NAR leadership. Pragmatism, as always, ultimately rules the movement's self-perception.

Ché Ahn's Harvest International Ministry (HIM), an offshoot of his Harvest Rock Church, represents perhaps the most important of the apostolic networks within the Revival Alliance. HIM is largely the vision of both Ahn and his chief supporter and cheerleader Lou Engle. When Ahn first met Engle in the early '80s, Engle was "mowing lawns for a living." However, Ahn was greatly impressed by Engle's intercessory abilities, and so when Ahn decided to plant a church in Los Angeles, he recruited Engle to join him as part of his church-planting team (Ahn and Engle 13). Ahn's desire to plant a church came because of a dream he had in 1982, in which an "African-American appeared to me ... and spoke these words: 'The Lord wants you to come to Los Angeles and establish a church, for their will be a great harvest'" (Ahn, *Into the Fire* 27). Six months later, in early 1983, Larry Tomczak, cofounder of People of Destiny International (PDI) asked Ahn to plant a church (Ahn, *Into the Fire* 21).

Understanding the significance of PDI to the history of not simply HIM, but the NAR as a whole, is critical. PDI started off as a shepherding ministry (Diamond 120). An issue of the shepherding magazine *New Wine* contains references to major PDI leaders speaking at shepherding conferences and shepherding historian S. David Moore confirms that there was at least an informal alliance between the shepherding leaders and PDI (New Wine, "June 1977" 10–11; Moore 164). PDI leader Larry Tomczak would play a role in the formation of the Coalition on Revival (COR), which would attempt to implement Reconstructionist-lite values on a national and local level (Grimstead, "A Manifesto" 16; "National COR Steering Committee"; Detwiler 136–137). Significantly, a number of COR's foundational documents, which played an important part in developing Christian right organizational structures in the eighties and nineties, invoked shepherding principles, including the promotion of binding legal contracts between parishioners and their churches that in practice guaranteed that parishioners would be the losers in the case of church discipline (see Kiley and Doane, "Christian Worldview of Discipleship," particularly pages 8–9, as well as Demar and Doner, "Christian Worldview of Government" 13, the latter of which is quite explicit on the need for church contracts).

Yet PDI, which had started off Charismatic, eventually morphed into a form of hyper-extremist Calvinism. In its Calvinist form, Sovereign Grace Ministries (SGM), the organization would count among its allies some of the most powerful members of the Calvinist right, including Albert Mohler, head of the Southern Baptist Theological Seminary (SBTS) and David Powlison, a significant figure in the powerful biblical counseling movement (Charlton, "Evangelical Church Accused"; John Weaver, *Failure* 154, 156). Yet by 2013, the ministry was in danger of imploding—and taking a large percentage of the contemporary Calvinist leadership with it—due to accusations of a massive sexual abuse cover up at the ministry (Charlton, "Evangelical Church Accused"). While a class action lawsuit against the ministry was dismissed on legal technicalities (mainly dealing with the statute of limitations) (Charlton, "Sovereign Grace Sexual Abuse Lawsuit"), what evidence is currently public about the case seems greatly to weigh in the alleged victims' favor. What is significant to understand in the context of the NAR is that for many of the victims of SGM and for critics outside the movement entirely, the abuses at SGM seemed directly traceable to the lingering influence of shepherding (John Weaver, *Failure* 112). Thus, even though Ahn would eventually divorce himself from PDI doctrine and leadership, the influence of PDI views of shepherding can clearly be seen in Ahn's gravitating to Wagner's new apostolic model of church governance.

Ahn claims to have met the man of his prophetic dream in 1992. In 1993, longstanding problems between Ahn and PDI finally came to a head (Poloma 177). Cindy Jacobs, one of the chief prophetesses of the NAR, called Ahn in 1993 and told him that it would be the hardest year of his life. Ahn resigned as pastor of his church in 1993, but did not leave until 1994, severing his alliance with PDI (Poloma 177). After visiting an Anaheim Vineyard Conference, Ahn experienced the phenomenon of holy laughter. In April 1994, Ahn founded Harvest Rock Church. In October of that year, Ahn and Engle visited TACF for their first experience of a "Catch the Fire" Conference. Ahn asked Arnott if he would visit his church in Pasadena to speak. Arnott's appearance at the church led to the church gaining the reputation as a renewal "hot spot," the American version of Toronto. HRC was then aided by its merger with Rick Wright's Glendale Vineyard Church. HRC was briefly a member of the Vineyard but resigned from the AVC right after TAVF was ousted from the Vineyard in December 1995 (Poloma 180). Two other churches soon joined HRC, with Ahn coming to be seen as the leader with the apostolic anointing (Poloma 180–181).

Poloma sees HIM as differing from PIH in its emphasis on "world missions." As we have seen, the Arnotts have a close relationship with Iris Ministries, making that a rather dubious distinction for Poloma to make (but perhaps a justifiable one at the time she was writing *Main Street Mystics* [2003]) (Poloma 183–184). Poloma has also pointed out the relationship between Ché Ahn and C. Peter Wagner, who served as Ahn's professor at Fuller Seminary (where Ahn received a degree in World Missions) (Poloma, "A Reconfiguration of Pentecostalism" 109). As of the late 1990s HIM was apparently still interested in evangelizing Asia and Africa, the proverbial heart of the 10/40 window, and expressed a commitment to using its apostolic anointing to train potential candidates for the missions field. Also, much like TACF (and later Bill Johnson's Bethel church), which had developed its own schools, HIM opened Harvest International School, which offered majors in church planting and missions (Poloma, "Reviving Pentecostalism").

By 2002, Ahn and Engle's The Call was garnering increased attention in the evangelical movement. By The Call's own estimate, anywhere from 85,000 to 100,000 individuals attended its CALL NYC meeting, which promoted both worship and "spiritual warfare" in the heart of New York City (Poloma, *Main Street Mystics* 186). These meetings had been preceded by meetings in Boston in September 2001 and the Philippines in November 2001. Even Poloma notes that though The Call "denies being political, its expression in the United States reflects the religio-political agenda of the religious right in the so-called religious culture wars" (Poloma 186–187). By 2003, it was estimated that The Call had drawn more than 750,000 members to its meetings in South Korea, the Philippines, England, and four U.S. cities (Lobdell). By 2011, when Candy Gunther Brown was correlating information for *Testing Prayer* (2012), HIM had 6,500 churches in 40 countries under its umbrella (Brown 42). Even more significant was Ché Ahn's assumption of the chancellorship of the Wagner Leadership Institute in 2010 ("About Ché Ahn"). This move effectively passed the baton from Wagner to Ahn as the leader of the educational arm of the NAR, giving Ahn enormous influence over the development of future apostolic leaders.

This move was also in many ways an ominous one. Wagner himself is hardly a progressive force in evangelical power politics, but he also is adept at realizing how far he can safely extend his apostolic philosophy. Ahn, like many members of the Revival Alliance, is far more radical, lacking the intellectual sophistication that characterized the NAR's early leadership—particularly Wagner, Silvoso, Otis Jr., and Kraft. Furthermore, many of the Revival Alliance apostles are no longer as intellectually bound by the rationalistic politics that characterize their Reformed allies as Wagner and many other early Third Wave Charismatics were.

Nor do Ahn or Engle's comments on contemporary events inspire much trust in his commitment to productive cultural discourse. Ahn has compared the fight to outlaw gay marriage with abolitionism, even invoking abolitionist William Wilberforce (Tashman, "Ahn: America Needs"). Engle, in the prelude to the Call Detroit in 2011 blamed Detroit's problems on the "rising tide of the Islamic movement." Other Engle pronouncements online contended that "Muslim proclamations for 1400 years have been fueling the demonic realm" (Caron). Because Michigan is home to a large and vibrant Islamic community, local imams were naturally concerned at these pronouncements, but though Engle's Call tempered their message after the public outcry against their literal demonization of Muslims, there is little doubt that the NAR continues to remain virulently Islamophobic in an era when such cultural prejudice can easily incite violence.

Randy Clark, nearly as influential as Ahn, met John Wimber in 1984, and according to Clark's Global Awakening Ministries Wimber prophesied over him, telling him that he would be a "prince in the Kingdom of God" ("About Us: Global Awakening"). Ten years later, Clark helped spur on the Toronto Blessing (Poloma, *Main Street Mystics* 152). Global Awakening, according to its website was "birthed by Randy Clark in January 1994 as a result of God using him to bring the fire of revival to the Toronto Airport Christian fellowship." Global Awakening serves as a major promoter of Norwegian pastor Leif Hetland. Hetland runs a ministry aimed at converting Muslims to Christianity and has served as a staff member on the Global School of Supernatural Ministry (GSSM), one of the two major academic ventures of Global Awakening ("Global School of Supernatural Ministry"; "About Us: Global Awakening History"). Another of Clark's PR campaigns has been promoting the ministry of Pastor Henry Madava, an apostolic leader in Kiev, Ukraine who has supposedly converted over 300,000 people ("About Us: Global Awakening").

Global Awakening claims to have had the most success in Brazil. Between 1999 and 2004 the ministry claimed to have seen 100,000 healings occur in that country, including the healings of blindness, deafness, paralysis, and the healing of those with terminal conditions. Thousands of others, according to the ministry, have been converted and the ministry brags openly that Clark now speaks in some of "the largest soccer stadiums in the nation [Brazil]" ("About Us: Global Awakening").

Candy Gunther Brown treats Clark's revivalistic method as if it were something new. She comments that Clark seeks to "combine Billy Graham's interdenominational networking and follow-up through local churches with the supernaturalist approaches of Latin Americans" (Brown, *Global Pentecostal and Charismatic Healing* 354). In fact, however, while Clark did borrow from Annacondia and Bottari's deliverance methodologies, these methodologies hardly grew in a vacuum. Much of Clark's interdenominationalism can be traced to longstanding NAR anti-denominational prejudices. And while deliverance was clearly practiced by Bottari, Brown's claim that somehow Latin Americans are more fanatic in their practice of it than North Americans, whose sense of "decorum" ends up making them misunderstand Latin American deliverance practice, simply does not mesh with the fact that the best research on the Argentine revival (Holvast's work), has deeply questioned this narrative of the spiritual mapping movement's—and by extension the NAR's—evolution (see Brown, *Testing Prayer* 55).

What is even more damningly absent from Brown's analysis of Global Awakening is any sustained critique of the deliverance material Clark's ministry has promoted. *Restoring the Foundations* (2001), for instance, which was used as a healing model at Clark's Healing Center (Brown, *Testing Prayer* 37–38), is one of the most extreme deliverance models extant. Its taxonomical listing of demonic groupings covers four huge pages and encompasses hundreds of individual entries (Kylstra and Kylstra 397–400). The Kylstras also promoted the existence of succubi and skepticism demons, the latter of which typically appear whenever someone doubts the existence of demons (Kylstra and Kylstra 227, 399). In addition, *Restoring the Foundations* quotes from a wide variety of questionable sources, most notably the theophostic prayer ministry (TPM) of Ed Smith (Klystra and Kylstra 235–236). Smith's mental healing method, promoted by Poloma (Garzon and Poloma and passim), is infamous among evangelicals and has been criticized in journalistic exposes (Fletcher passim) and in articles by professional Christian psychologists (see Entwistle, "Shedding Light on Theophostic Prayer Ministry" both 1 and 2). Meanwhile the Spokane Healing Room model used by Clark derives from Bethel Church, which as we will see, promotes questionable deliverance practices as well (Brown, *Testing Prayer* 38). While it is difficult to prove, it is likely that Clark's Healing Center, given its usage of both RTF and the Spokane model, as well as Clark's alliance with Bill Johnson's Bethel Church, likely utilized the sozo model of faith healing for mental health issues. This is problematic because sozo healing promotes such pseudoscientific ideas and therapeutic paradigms as the healing of mental illnesses through touching specific areas of the brain (McMichael and McMichael 43), and what looks like the deliberate inducement of DID symptoms (dissociative identity disorder) in "shabar" healing ceremonies (De Silva and Libescher, "Sozo Q +A" Session 9; De Silva and Liebscher, "Session 8" audio).

    In addition, the Christian Healing Certification Program (CHCP) that Clark has recently set up also seems to have major problems associated with it, even if one accepts for a minute that faith healing is possible (the presupposition behind the program). For instance, the 2nd and 3rd stage of the deliverance track of the CHCP includes video teachings by Peter Horrobin (Christian Healing Certification Program, "Deliverance Ministry 2" and "Deliverance Ministry 3"), a Charismatic who was one of the prime early promoters of the idea of demonic soul ties created through sexual abuse (see Collins 91, Horrobin 159–160, 385–386). The fourth track features the teachings of Neil Anderson, who has promoted the existence of satanic ritual abuse (Anderson, *The Bondage Breaker* 207–209) and was a major influence on Mercy Ministries counseling model (Christian Healing Certification Program, "Deliverance Ministry 4"). The Inner Healing track features teachings from John and Loren Sandford, whose combination of Freudian ideology and deliverance is only marginally more reasonable than the bizarre forms of deliverance offered by Horrobin (Christian Healing and Certification Program, "Inner Healing and

Soul Care 1 Course Syllabus"). Brown's work deals extensively with Charismatic thinking and healing practice. That she was unaware of the teachings of these individuals is unlikely. One must ask then why she withheld such obviously important information about Global Awakening and the kind of healing ministry it is connected to, when that information was readily available.

Global Awakening material promotes the idea that homosexuality is caused by demonic manifestations (Tabachnick, "Max Myers and the Global School"). The network is most recently notable for its failed attempt to covertly insert a theocracy-supporting NAR leader as a Democratic candidate for governor of Pennsylvania (Tabachnick, "Max Myers and the Global School"). Therefore whatever form of healing Global Awakening ultimately provides, that healing is ultimately viewed through a deeply theocratic lens, one progressive Americans ignore at their peril.

Bill Johnson, the last member of the Revival Alliance, and increasingly one of its most important spokesman (second only to Ché Ahn in influence, and easily first in popularity), initially met Randy Clark in St. Louis in 1997. Clark agreed to visit Johnson's church, which was a member of the Assemblies of God. Johnson claims to have been powerfully moved by the experience, and by the subsequent friendship he developed with Clark (Brown, *Testing Prayer* 41). After "becoming increasingly aligned with Toronto inspired networks," Johnson and his church left the Assemblies of God denomination in 2006. Bethel's International wing has attempted to network with national leaders in Brazil, Mexico, Nicaragua, Croatia, Kenya, and Norway. It sponsors Schools of Supernatural Ministry and Mission Training, based apparently on its U.S. School of Supernatural Ministry, and has created children's homes and leadership teams in the developing world. In Africa, Bethel's most significant work is its alliance with Heroes of the Nation, a nonprofit devoted to "providing food and shelter" for children as well as "raising a generation of revivalists." As in so much of NAR culture, charity ultimately serves explicitly political goals (Brown, *Testing Prayer* 42).

Bethel began its School of Supernatural Ministry in 1998, shortly after Johnson's meeting with Clark. At the time it had only 36 students. By 2010, the ministry had some 1200 students in attendance, 250 of them international (Lepinski 31–32). In 1999, Bethel also launched a very influential youth ministry called Jesus Culture. Jesus Culture conferences were frequently sold out, thanks mainly to their simultaneous emphasis on intense revivalism and cutting edge worship music. According to Lepinski, Jesus Culture conferences have contributed to Bethel's ever constant need to expand the number of church services it offers each week (Lepinski 32). Jesus Culture motivates its members mainly through rhetoric that drinks from the same trough as the Call and

Mike Bickle's Forerunner ministry, but with a slightly more moderate emphasis. The coming generation, in Jesus Culture, is seen as a "different kind of tribe made up of young, motivated revivalists passionately pursuing Christ's call and mission" (Casciotta). Jesus Culture promotes the idea that the new generation is a "new breed of revivalist" (Liebscher, *Jesus Culture* 27), who is "willing to lay it all down so the Lord can rise up with them" (52). According to Liebscher, this new breed of revivalist "is going to be unstoppable. They will be so confident in who they are and so passionate about bringing heaven to earth that nothing else will matter. They will believe that nothing is impossible and adhere to the words of Jesus 'all things are possible to him who believes'.... This is an 'all things are possible' generation" (52). Liebscher also tells Jesus Culture followers that they are "called to take over the world. You are part of a revolution." Liebscher warns that the overthrow he is talking about is not explicitly political; however, given the close alliances the Revival Alliance has made with the promulgators of seven mountains dominionism it is questionable how sincerely one should take such pronouncements (Liebscher, *Jesus Culture* 56).

Johnson's ministry focuses heavily on the young and benefits from two factors: his personal charisma and his ministry's focus on the arts and entertainment. Why exactly Johnson is so popular among young Charismatics is hard to determine. He is certainly not the best public speaker in the NAR and definitely not the most "doctrinally sound" in the evangelical sense of theological orthodoxy. But it's undeniable that for many Charismatic and neo-evangelical young people, Johnson's ministry is the definition of hip.

In any case, more important to Bethel's success than Johnson is its emphasis on entertainment and the arts. According to Lepinski, Johnson's "focus on experiencing God through the musical worship parts of the service was largely shaped by his father. In the 1970s Johnson's father, who started Bethel Church, asked congregants to leave the church as a result of their unwillingness to sing contemporary choruses. These individuals held to the strong belief that only hymns were appropriate" (Lepinski 43). Johnson partly modeled his ministry approach after his father and seeks to give congregants a "tangible experience with God" (Lepinski 43). Often this occurs through Bethel's adoption of a supernaturalist rhetoric that borders on New Age mysticism.

Bethel's "regular inclusion of the arts" as a method to reaching out to "postmoderns" is one of its most unique and fascinating features. Bethel incorporates drama, dance, music, and vocal solos, as well as various forms of paintings, into its worship (Lepinski 56). Bethel's chief teacher on the arts Therese Dedmon, promotes the idea of Christians becoming the "forerunners of music, arts and entertainment that draw people into His [God's] Presence" (Dedmon 46). The idea of forerunners in NAR rhetoric—particularly in the ministry of

Mike Bickle—has largely come to serve as theological code among movement leaders for the kind of "Joel's Army"-like radicalism that characterized KCF in the 1980s. Dedmon thus encourages an application of Forerunner theology to the arts. Dedmon's own theory of the arts—which is relatively sophisticated—emphasizes the importance of community to "transform every sphere of society" (Dedmon 55). Visions and dreams—which represent a significant part of artistic inspiration in Dedmon's schema—are "cultivated in the soil of a revivalist community where they can benefit others and be birthed at the right time for the appropriate season" (Dedmon 56). Thus art, much as in the Reformed-oriented art theory of Francis Schaeffer, has a socially transformative role. For the revivalist oriented culture of Bethel, the arts serve as an evangelizing tool that allows the movement to communicate across cultural barriers that might otherwise prove formidable (see Dedmon 25).

Perhaps the most unique part of Dedmon's teachings is her emphasis on supernatural art forms. She believes in supernatural forms of "dance, drama, art, face painting ... and body art" (70). This style of supernatural art often involves asking the Holy Spirit what He wants the individual artist to create (70). Dedmon offers a huge number of practical suggestions as to how to encourage supernatural art forms within the church, the majority of which are beyond the purview of this study. By far the wildest idea she suggests is what can only be described as a prophetic art crit session, in which the ministry sets up a room where congregants can "bring their artwork in to be critiqued by accomplished artists with a prophetic viewpoint. There was always a line for these critiques because there has really been no place where creative people can go to work in their craft as well as hear encouragement through prophetic ministry" (Dedmon 130). While Dedmon's ideas may seem strange to non–NAR aesthetes, they represent major and sophisticated theological innovations on the part of Charismatics. Dedmon's ministry indicates how successfully the Revival Alliance has been at translating seven mountains ideology into areas the secular world would not think the NAR would be capable of reaching.

Danny Silk's *Culture of Honor* (2009) provides the closest thing to an overview of the total mission philosophy of Bethel Church. A key element of Bethel's self-perception is that it promotes the idea that it is developing a "supernatural culture" characterized by the "conviction that Jesus modeled the Christian life for us" (Silk 29). Silk puts a fairly significant emphasis on fivefold ministry (Silk 53–56), possibly because Bethel, as a former Assembly of God church, likely still contains some dissenters to that Latter-Rain tinged doctrine. Silk teaches—and this is clearly influenced by similar teachings promoted by Bill Johnson in *When Heaven Invades Earth* (2003) and elsewhere[2]—that the

Christian church must develop a "wealth mindset" if it is to see Heaven come to earth and remain there.

This wealth mindset, according to Silk, is characterized by terms like "abundance, freedom and choices" which are all descriptives for "a condition of the soul that we must master if we want a revival culture" (Silk 120). While there is more than a passing similarity here between WOF doctrine and the heavenly economy teachings that Bethel promulgates, Bethel's vision is more concerned with the more ethereal elements of the mind-over-matter wealth gospel. A wealth mindset for Bethel teachers, while often leading to financial results, is not solely about prosperity, as in the WOF movement, but also encompasses a fundamental condition of the soul itself.

Silk promotes a view of social class influenced by Dr. Ruby Payne, which focuses heavily on how each class has a different worldview that influences the way that particular class relates to wealth and the world around them (Silk 127–128). Silk then applies idea at both a natural and supernatural level. He believes that when Christians "see their destiny in God through a poverty class view, they live a natural, not a supernatural, life, and find themselves trapped in natural problems with no hope of heavenly intervention. They learn to blame God as the One who has the power to do something about their desperate situation but chooses to do nothing. As they experience a powerless gospel, they create a theology to sanction that experience, a theology where Heaven is a lot like Earth" (Silk 135). The middle class, by contrast, feels it has more power to change its destiny, but also has a tendency to try to over-manipulate its environment, to the detriment of others (Silk 136–137). The wealthy, are generous, because they have a "mindset of abundance" and a sense of "noblesse oblige" (Silk 137). It is this wealthy mindset that in spiritual terms is what Silk wants to encourage, because it allows participants in the NAR to see the kind of social vision envisioned by the apostles and prophets (Silk 137). The wealthy are also skilled at creating the kind of relational networks that promote the development of unlimited resources. The gathering of these resources is seen by Silk as not an end in itself, but as a means of investing in "things that really matter—people, cultural legacies, beauty" (143). Thus, while Bethel ministers to the poor, its heart is ultimately geared to a "wealth mindset," because it is that mindset that is seen by Silk and other ministry members as providing the cultural tools for social transformation.

The other aspect of the health and wealth gospel—the health part—is even more prominent in Bethel's teachings. Bethel's most famous health initiative is their sozo healing practice, a radical new form of healing and deliverance (Weaver, *Failure* 75). The current practice of sozo began sometime around 1997 (McMichael and McMichael 1, Reese 15). The practice was brought to

America by Randy Clark (McMichael and McMichael 1). This model was based on healing practices developed in Argentina (McMichael and McMichael 1). Pablo Bottari, a leading deliverance supporter in Argentina, developed a model of "prayer for deliverance" called the four doors (McMichael and McMichael 1). These four doors were "sexual sin, occult, fear and hatred" (McMichael and McMichael 1). After this, the McMichaels say, "Dawna" (presumably Dana De Silva, who is the biggest player in the expanding sozo market) and a friend "attended a seminar taught by a brain scientist, Aiko Horman, where other tools were acquired: the wall, divine editing, and how to cure post-truamatic stress" (McMichael and McMichael 1). According to prominent sozo promoter Andy Reese, "thousands have found increasing peace and freedom, and experienced the freshnes of encounters with a loving, living God" (Reese 25–26, Weaver 76).

Although the more public spokesmen for sozo deny that the program is meant to treat serious emotional problems such as mental illness (Reese 29), such an assertion is hard to reconcile with the material of more secretive productions of the sozo movement, which promote the deliverance of individuals behaviors ranging from "anorexia or bulimia" to "emotional disturbances or long-term unbalanced emotions" (McMichael and McMichael 13).

The sozo model borrows heavily from inner healing stalwarts like John and Paula Sanford and Leanne Payne, as well as Charles Kraft. As I have outlined in my book *The Failure of Evangelical Mental Health Care*, most of these individuals have at best questionable therapeutic practices (Weaver 62–86 passim, 203–204). The full details of the sozo model are beyond the scope of this study, and have in any case been detailed in my aforementioned work. A couple elements of the sozo ministry should be noted however. First, many of the practices the ministry uses are fairly clearly guided imagery and thus of questionable therapeutic benefit, given that sozo healing practices are ideally meant to bring emotional healing (Weaver 80–81). The phenomena of "presenting Jesus," which is utilized by sozo healers, invites Jesus into memories in order to heal them, a common practice among inner healers, and one that is open to abuse (Weaver 65, 76). One of the most bizarre practices in sozo healing, divine editing, involves touching a specific part of the brain stem "where it meets the neck" (McMichael and McMichael 43). It is believed that this area of the brain, the reticular formation, stores everything we have done since we were conceived, and when the facilitator breaks through, lies people hold to are broken (McMichael and McMichael 81). Thus, the divine editing process literally promotes the idea of healing memories through the direct application of prayer to a specific area of the brain (McMichael and McMichael 82).

Besides also involving extensive deliverance practice (see Weaver 82–83), the sozo methodology also has one other element, *shabar* healing. As Teresa

Lebscher, a prominent leader in the sozo "movement" describes it, "shabar is a ministry to what we call fragmented people" (De Silva and Liebscher, "Session 8" audio). This ministry is aimed at "those that have a dissociative degree in their life." As I have argued elsewhere, the whole process of shabar healing often suspiciously resembles the process of therapeutically creating dissociative identity disorder (DID) in order to treat it (Weaver 83, De Silva and Liebscher, "Session 8"). Yet this practice has spread like wildfire since its introduction into the sozo model.

The results of sozo practice can be disastrous. The Healing Rooms ministries that are promoted by the McMichaels and run by Cal Pierce feature testimonies of healing from illnesses that range from cancer to depression, paranoia, bipolar and even AIDS ("Healing Room Testimonies"). Though the ministry does not directly claim on these Web pages to be responsible for these healings, this is the obvious implication, particularly since the healings almost always reference a local healing room. Even if it is somehow ethically justifiable to claim one can alleviate mental health problems through inner healing and deliverance, it is unethical to promote the idea that one can heal maladies like cancer and AIDS through faith healing. Even though Pierce's ministry wishes to work concurrently with the medical establishment (Cal Pierce, *Healing in the Kingdom* 121–122), its promotion of the sozo methodology within its healing rooms is at best extremely dubious. Worse, these healing rooms' widespread nature (there were at least 1,300 Healing Rooms worldwide as of 2010, in 52 countries) (Gaines) means that potentially millions of people are being told that their physical or mental healing is as much, perhaps even more, a result of divine intervention than biological intervention. And we do know that sozo has potentially dangerous effects. There has been one rather notorious example of Bethel's faith healing ministry allegedly almost causing a death when two students at Bethel waited to call for help for an injured man because they thought they could raise him from the dead. The man alleges that he is a paraplegic as a result; while his lawsuit against the two students was eventually dismissed, the basic fact that his friends spent several hours trying to use Bethel-inspired faith healing practices on him rather than call for a doctor is not in dispute (Weaver 84–85, 284).

Why, then, promote sozo? Well, one reason may be that Bethel Church sells its DVD curriculm to churches for upwards of $7,000 (Robertson). And of course, there is usually a charge for sozo "services." Sozo sessions of two to three hours typically cost $75 ("Sozo Overview"; "FAQ Sozo: Questions and Answers"). Whether or not Bethel church seeks to directly profit from the practice, it is clear, given the widespread popularity of sozo nationwide that sozo healing keeps more than a few deliverance supporters gainfully, even wealthily, employed. Sozo is big business. And it looks like it is here to stay (Weaver 85).

The Revival Alliance is not the only apostolic network in existence. In the next section, we will deal with the International Coalition of Apostles, a network even larger and broader than the Revival Alliance. It is the ICA and its leadership that have defined the mainstream of apostolic ministry for the last decade and a half and although the leadership of the NAR seems to be gradually switching to the Revival Alliance, one would be foolhardy to underestimate the sheer breadth of the ICA network, which still dwarfs any other apostolic network in existence. It is to the ICA we now turn.

International Coalition of Apostles: Apostolic Networking, Old School

Mapping out the entire ICA network, let alone its history, is impossible. The network is vast, with numerous apostolic ministries under its umbrella, many of which themselves are incredibly large. But one can suggest the scope and breadth of ICA power by looking at a few of its chief members and outreach efforts.

C. Peter Wagner dates the founding of the ICA to an informal meeting of several apostles in Singapore in 1999. Among those present at the meeting were Ed Silvoso, the architect of Plan Resistencia in Argentina, and John Kelly, an important NAR figure who would eventually become the leader of the ICA after Wagner stepped down (Wagner, *Wrestling* 215). One of the crucial elements that made Wagner's networking idea work so well was his conceptualization of apostolic networks as operating both vertically and horizontally. Vertical apostles' chief characteristic was "that they are at the head of an ongoing organization of some type" whose leadership role has been rewarded them because of their relational abilities, not because they have climbed a corporate ladder (that at least is how Wagner promoted this idea) (Wagner, *Apostles Today* 90). Horizontal apostleship, by contrast was not primarily concerned with providing the "spiritual covering" that characterized vertical relationships; instead horizontal apostles' "anointing" was to bring "together peers of one kind or another to accomplish certain purposes better than they could separately." The concept of relational networking still held here, but here the networking was among equals. Horizontal apostleship allowed the movement to organize different parts of the apostolic movement into a coherent whole, many of them (though by no means all) under the ICA banner. The ICA became perhaps the definitive model, along with the Revival Alliance, of this blend of horizontal and vertical leadership.

Wagner's structural innovation here was brilliant. It allowed the ICA to have leadership that had tremendous authority, authority that was not centralized in any bureaucratic institution, but that was instead invested in the charisma of the individual apostles within the ICA. This lack of centralization played a crucial role in the ICA outflanking the progressive left and remaining under its radar for so long. The left was used to thinking of the Christian right in terms of big, easily identifiable church or parachurch organizations—Focus on the Family or the Christian Coalition, for instance. But the ICA hid the extent of its real power, because so many of its networks remained under the radar of media attention. Thus, even when ICA apostles were caught saying outrageous or controversial things—for instance ICA apostle Kimberly Daniels condemnations of Islam while serving on the Jacksonville, Florida City Council (see Steve Patterson; Hurst; Lyons)—few in the local or national press managed to figure out that Daniels was aligned with the NAR. Furthermore, these moves also allowed the NAR to outflank the outmoded organizational models that characterized traditional evangelical denominational structures as well.

The model the ICA set for the NAR was also, as one researcher has put it to me, "not copyrighted" but meant to be duplicated. In other words, anyone could set up apostolic networks. If these networks became sufficiently powerful, the ICA could either admit them into their own network or ally with them as co-belligerents. Nor was Wagner particularly concerned with formally taking more and more ministries under the leadership of the ICA. Therefore, many apostolic networks could exist totally outside the organizational grid of the ICA, but nevertheless have close affinities with the movement, including sometimes enjoying covering, and therefore spiritual leadership, by apostles from multiple apostolic networks. Traditional apostolic governance in Christianity—that practiced by Anglicans, Roman Catholics, and to a lesser extent the Eastern Orthodox Church—is primarily hierarchical, while the traditions coming out of Reformed and Wesleyan thinking are usually democratic or, in the case of elder-led churches, representative. The model that Wagner utilized for the ICA was a revolutionary way of reconceptualizing church organization, because networks were now both vertical and horizontal, with networks overlapping each other. Moreover, unlike other parachurch organizations, which typically are forced to respect denominational boundaries, ICA apostleship allowed the apostles to have an apostolic covering over churches from multiple denominations as well.

Under Wagner's leadership therefore, were a number of institutions in horizontal relationship under his guidance.[3] The Apostolic Council for Educational Accountability (ACEA) and The Wagner Leadership Institute (WLI)[4] were two of Wagner's major efforts. Wagner traced his reasoning for originating these educational initiatives to his experience in world missions. He felt that the dominant model of theological education in the U.S. was "pre-service," where people were theologically educated before they entered the missions field. There were a number of reasons why Wagner thought this was a bad idea. One of his primary objections to this practice was that he thought it was ineffective in the developing world, where the people pastoring often already had families and had not had the opportunity to graduate from ministerial or seminary training. Wagner therefore preferred the ideas of his mentor Donald McGavran, who focused on "in service" methodology. McGavran's idea of the ideal student was someone "who had accumulated significant cross-cultural missionary experience, validated by fluency in a second language" (Wagner, *Wrestling* 248).

Wagner also had existing biases against seminary education, biases he has stated in earlier works. Wagner saw traditional seminaries as being too engaged with theory and not enough with practice (Wagner, *Churchquake!* 225). He decried traditional seminaries for their focus on library research, philosophy, and their commitment to scholars publishing in academic journals. By contrast, the seminarians within NAR churches, for Wagner, should try to "simplify complex theological issues," base their approach primarily on "field research" and aim for "popular magazines" (Wagner, *Churchquake!* 225–226). Wagner's point here was in part to promote populism over intellectualism. But at a deeper level Wagner was merely reflecting the pragmatist, social science bias of the church growth movement. In Wagner's estimation, the reliance on theory and theologizing in seminaries had many of the same flaws that many contemporary humanities majors critique cultural theory for; namely, that church theory (like cultural theory) ignores real world experience and places too much reliance on intellectualization as a successful motivator for social change.

Wagner also criticized the idea of "critical thinking" as it was commonly understood in many seminaries. While Wagner pays lip service to the idea that he is not promoting anti-intellectualism, it is hard to come to any other conclusion after reading his complaints about modern seminaries, in which he feels "skepticism is valued over belief.... Complexity is valued over simplicity (which is seen as 'naivete').... Committees are trusted over individuals (who are suspected of 'arrogance')" (Wagner, *Churchquake!* 233). For Wagner, the very skills that are at the foundation of the academic enterprise are a problem. It must be understood that even in evangelicalism, the extent to which Wagner wanted NAR seminaries to deviate from traditional accreditation schemas was incredible. At a time when many evangelical colleges and universities were aggressively and often successfully trying to enter the front ranks of academia, Wagner sought to drag NAR schools back to a degree of credulousness that far surpassed the ignorance shown at Dayton. Wagner's educational model combined a premodern understanding of science, the natural world, and academic research with a strangely sophisticated take on social science and the management of people groups. Wagner contended that for NAR churches, degrees should not "become prerequisites for ordination" (Wagner, *Churchquake!* 235). He suggested that in NAR seminaries historians were replaced by "visionaries," "theologians" with "entrepreneurs," "critics" with "cheerleaders," and "distinguished scholars" with "dynamic pastors" (235).

The role of the academic therefore changed in the process. Academics in NAR institutions were not interested primarily in a search for knowledge, as in most universities, but instead were individuals whose prime goal was explicitly to serve as movement "cheerleaders" and "hagiographers." As we have seen, the role of hagiographer is a common one among Charismatic academics. What makes Wagner's vision particularly reprehensible by evangelical standards is there is not even the pretense of the university being a place of learning. Even unaccredited fundamentalist institutions like Bob Jones University at least have respect for some areas of knowledge. Wagner, however, will have none of this. And this is reflected in the kind of curricular approach he supports. Wagner rejects telling the history of dogma, instead advising that people learn the history of revivals. He thinks epistemology is a waste of time and instead suggests schools teach "prophetic intercession." He is supportive of such classes as "Demonology Exposed," "Intercession for Revival" and "Communion with God" (Wagner, *Churchquake!* 237). The prime accountability for NAR academic organizations are not secular accrediting agencies—which often are the accrediting agencies for respectable evangelical colleges—but instead the local church or apostolic network, as well as today the Apostolic Council for Educational Accountability (ACEA), an organization that serves as a "functional substitute for traditional academic accreditation" for NAR institutions which feel that such accreditation is "a dead-end road and a hindrance to being all that God wants us to be" (Wagner, *Apostles Today* 96; Wagner, *Churchquake!* 237). Judgment of effectiveness for such organizations, in Wagner's eyes, should come through how well the graduates were doing with "the ministry to which they have been called, not by a manual of standards developed by an outside accrediting association" (Wagner, *Churchquake!* 236).

Thus when the WLI was formed it did not have academic requirements for entrance into the seminary. No college degree was necessary. Wagner rejected exams and grades, arguing that "I find it impractical to give exams or letter grades for the courses. The powerful impartation for ministry that the students receive validates the quality of their education, so exams and grades are not necessary" (Wagner, *Wrestling* 249). Wagner also did not require students to be residents, nor did the WLI have resident faculty. Different courses had different organizational formats, while curriculum was "tailor made to the needs of the students." What constituted the curriculum, however, were six core areas: "Apostolic Ministries, Prophetic Ministries, Intercession, Deliverance, Signs and Wonders and Spiritual Warfare" (251). These six subject areas can be translated in secular terms as: How to be an apostle, How to prophesy, how to pray, how to exorcise people, how to do miracles, and how to fight demons on a personal and geographical level.

According to Wagner, there were some organizational problems with WLI in the mid 2000s, and Wagner briefly considered phasing the program out. However, a new dean, Craig Davis, apparently was successful in reorganizing the institution. Soon there were regional WLIs across the country. Eventually there were 20 WLIS in the United States and 12 international WLI's (Wagner, *Wrestling* 251–252). Ché Ahn took over the chancellorship of WLI in 2010 ("About Ché Ahn"). Wagner's choice of Ahn had both personal and organizational motivations. Wagner was a long-time mentor of Ahn, and Wagner has said he is Ahn's "spiritual father." Both movement critics and supporters have traditionally admitted the closeness of the two men. From an organizational standpoint, Ahn represented an excellent choice to lead the WLI because he had been able to franchise the organization quite successfully. Ahn had established a WLI branch in Pasadena, as well as in Indonesia and Korea. The latter branch Wagner argued was the strongest branch of WLI in the world today, and the growing power of Korean Christianity globally—South Korean Charismatics are arguably the most globally influential group of Charismatics outside the West—doubtlessly gave added impetus to Wagner's choice of Ahn, whose Korean-American heritage and ability to network along multiracial lines has allowed him to create a number of WLI sites catering to the Korean-American community (see Wagner, *Wrestling* 284).

I have spent so much time detailing the ins and outs of WLI for two reasons. The first reason is self-explanatory: The WLI is a powerful institution within the NAR, and through its creation of numerous other sub-institutions, it is an increasingly influential one. Ignoring the power it has to influence future generations is something that both the left *and the right* ignore at their peril.

Secondly, in many ways the leadership model that WLI set up is the Achilles heel of the entire NAR. This is compounded by the fact, as Wagner relates, that the "Wagner Leadership Institute was only one of hundreds of new schools that had been springing up in recent years to equip the saints in the New Apostolic Reformation" (Wagner, *Wrestling* 252). Wagner is not exaggerating here. Practically all major apostolic networks eventually establish some sort of school or teaching organization. In the Revival Alliance, Global Awakening,

Iris Ministries, Ahn's Harvest Rock Church, and Bethel Church have all been involved in setting up some sort of "school of supernatural ministry," and as we have seen Georgian Banov would like to do the same thing. The Arnotts' Catch the Fire has also set up some unaccredited schools of ministry as well, although the online descriptions of them suggest they are more rigorous than other Revival Alliance institutions (see Bethel School of Supernatural Ministry; "Overview of GSSM"; Kantel 161–162; "Hrock SSM"; "Accreditation"; "Catch the Fire College").

The problem is Wagner's bias against theory has a real danger of leaving the second and third generation of NAR leaders intellectually and organizationally unable to run the movement as effectively as the first generation of movement leaders has done. Say what one wants about the beliefs of Otis Jr., Kraft, Wagner, or Silvoso, but these men were clearly brilliant at both marketing and branding the NAR as a powerful force in global Charismatic culture. Their generation of leaders had impressive organizational skills, often formidable education, and a high degree of creativity, especially when compared to modern movement leaders. There is a real danger for the NAR that the new movement leadership simply will not be able to mold the movement as skillfully as its originators intended. And the emerging generation of Charismatics looks even less likely to be able to do this effectively.

This may seem like good news to the movement's critics, since it would imply that the movement is likely to implode once the last of the first generation leaders pass on. However, there is a much more negative interpretation to give this development, which is that instead of the Charismatics within the NAR still having some control over their own movement, the movement's political agenda will instead be set by other political power players, particularly the Reformed movement. And this is something that Charismatics, non–Charismatic evangelicals, and the non-evangelical left, should seek to prevent. The theocratic bent of the Reconstructionist arm of Reformed Christianity obviously makes the movement unpalatable to progressives. And these same allegiances also mean the Reformed movement does not represent a politically effective base from which to launch an evangelical campaign for social transformation that will capture widespread support.

A second ministry under Wagner's leadership again shows the potential dangers of his lack of commitment to academic integrity: The International Society of Deliverance Ministers (ISDM). This is a "professional society" of Charismatic deliverance ministers/exorcists (Wagner, *Wrestling* 216). Originally the ISDM started as a "small roundtable" in 2000 and then expanded into a professional society in 2003. Doris Wagner, C. Peter Wagner's wife, was the original leader of the movement. This was not some honorary appointment

3. The Apostolic Networks

that she accepted however. Rather, Doris Wagner was at the forefront of some of the most radical and bizarre deliverance theology being promulgated. Wagner was the general editor of the deliverance anthology *How to Minister Freedom* (2005), which featured a virtual who's-who of prominent deliverance specialists and NAR supporters, including John Eckhardt, Frank Hammond, Cindy Jacobs, Charles Kraft, Ana Méndez Ferrell, Chuck Pierce, John L. Sandford, and the Wagner couple themselves (Doris Wagner, *How to Minister Freedom* 8–16).

Looking at the background of these individuals provide some context as to just how damaging the ISDM has the potential to be. Frank Hammond's book *Pigs in the Parlor* (1973), co-written with his wife Ida Mae Hammond, is a prime example of this. The book, one of the most popular exorcism manuals within evangelicalism, was one of the definitive manuals to come out of the seventies. *Pigs in the Parlor* is widely regarded as one of the most extreme deliverance manuals of the period. The manual warns that the seven "most common symptoms of indwelling demons" are "1. Emotional Problems ... 2. Mental Problems ... 3. Speech Problems ... 4. Sex Problems ... 5. Addictions ... 6. Physical Infirmities ... [and] 7. Religious error" (Hammond and Hammond 28). As Michael Cuneo, the foremost academic expert on exorcism, sarcastically noted after looking at this same list, "Is there anyone who wouldn't be a candidate for deliverance?" (Cuneo 108).

The Hammonds actively promoted prejudice against the mentally ill through their promulgation of the idea of a special demonic grouping for mental illness. Demon sub-groupings within this grouping included "insanity, madness, mania, retardation, senility, schizophrenia, paranoia, and hallucinations" (Hammond and Hammond 114). Homosexuality and lesbianism were also demonic sub-groupings as was masturbation, Mormonism, Unitarianism, Buddhism, Taoism, Hinduism, Islam, Shintoism, and Confucianism (Hammond and Hammond 115). And a special revelation given to Ida Mae Hammond seems especially suspect. This revelation held that schizophrenia actually was the result of split personalities. This was—and unfortunately still remains—a popular explanation for schizophrenia, one that lacks any medical credibility. The actual diagnosis that is associated with split personalities is dissociative identity disorder (DID), previously known as multiple personality disorder. Given that *Pigs in the Parlor*'s release date coincides with the release of *Sybil* (1973), the founding text of the DID craze, it is likely that a considerably non-theological influence affected the Hammond's demonology (see Hammond and Hammond 123–133).

Nor are the Hammonds the only, or even the most, controversial deliverance ministers to be anthologized in *How to Minister Freedom*. Peter Horrobin's

Ellel Ministry is also known for its bizarre beliefs. Ellel, which has long trained exorcists, includes in its training material, charts for tracing out one's family tree, in order "to locate possible demons that might have travelled down the generational line" (Howard 50). There is also a "special box to fill in one's marriage partner in case one has picked up any demon from him or her" (Howard 50). As British journalist Roland Howard points out, at Ellel: "alternative medicine, the New Age, traffic accidents, miscarriages, smoking, masturbation and just about any sexual position bar the missionary position can lead to demonization" (Howard 50). By the early 1990s Ellel was running courses "throughout the year at their seventy bed-centre near Lancaster, and it was becoming apparent that demand was outstripping supply" (Howard 92). Horrobin also taught that demons had entry points into the body, often through specific bodily orifices. One vicar Howard met told him that at an early Ellel course he "was told that sometimes it was necessary to pour Ribena (substitute communion wine) onto people's genitals to cleanse them of demons related to sexual sin which had entered there" (Howard 95).

Horrobin is also a prominent promoter of the idea of "soul ties" created through sexual abuse. According to Horrobin:

> whenever there has been sexual abuse, however light or heavy it may have been, there is a likelihood of demonization that will always seek to distort and damage godly relationships.... For example, a girl may have been sexually abused only once in early childhood. Traumatic though the event may have been at the time, it is likely to have been well buried among the other events of the past. However, the demon that came in through the incident has not forgotten so when the girl marries a Christian man, the demon ... will do all it can to interfere with their sexual relationship [Horrobin, *Healing Through Deliverance* 385].

It cannot be argued that Doris Wagner is somehow ignorant or in disagreement with Horrobin's views. Horrobin specifically states in Wagner's anthology that "when sexual relations have been forced upon a person in an abusive or rape situation, an ungodly soul tie is still established between the abuser or the rapist and the victim" (Horrobin, "Shedding Light on Soul Ties" 183). Wagner herself supports the soul tie idea: "I have prayer over a number of rape victims and let me assure you that a person who has been raped ... has indeed been seriously harmed both physically and emotionally.... The devil often uses such horrible experiences to open many doors to the demonic" (Doris Wagner, "Forgiving the Unforgivable" 92–93). It's clear therefore that Wagner was fully aware of the soul tie concept, and of the idea that it created demonic linkages between rape victims and demons—and often between rape victims and their attackers. Wagner also argues that forgiveness is necessary if the sex abuse victim is to receive healing. She argues, "When an injustice or serious sin has been committed, such as child sexual abuse, the child remembers the pain ... the trauma ... and visits that situation over and over again in his or her mind. Unforgiveness sets in and eventually invites a demon of unforgiveness to set up housekeeping in the soul of that person" (Doris Wagner, "Forgiving the Unforgivable" 99). Since Doris Wagner's statements are included in a manual that includes C. Peter Wagner himself, it can only be assumed that the NAR's founding father also believes that rape victims are demonically attached to their abusers.

The apostolic round table (i.e., its leadership) of Wagner's ISDM contained both a few of the more rational deliverance specialists, such as Charles Kraft along with the most extremist elements of the deliverance movement, such as Becca Greenwood. Foremost among these extremists however, is Chester and Betsy Kylstra. The use of the Kylstras' deliverance system is so outrageous that I will devote the next section just to describing it and its connection to ICA apostle Bill Hamon. However, the importance and influence of Hamon is so extensive within the NAR that I will have to return to him in Chapter 5, to fully flesh out his impact on the movement.

The Kylstras, Bill Hamon and Mercy Seriously Strained: The NAR's Excursion into Australia

At age 21, Naomi Johnson was working on a psychology degree at Edith Cowan University in Australia. Johnson was fairly independent despite struggling with an eating disorder, but could not afford specialty treatment for her anorexia, something she wanted to get under control. Because she did not have access to private health insurance, nor public funded service, she decided to go to Mercy Ministries. Nine months later, she left distraught, feeling little more than a child, and terrified to leave her bedroom because she was afraid of the "demons" that were causing her anorexia. A few months afterwards, Johnson entered a mainstream psychiatric unit (Pollard, "They Prayed to Cast").

Johnson eventually fought back against Mercy, who had labeled her struggles demonic (Weaver 86). Along with other survivors, Johnson went to the media. The three women's description of their time at Mercy Ministries was horrendous. They had been promised psychiatric treatment and clinical support, but instead were put in the care of Bible students, many under 30 and many with their own mental health issues. The counseling the program offered involved prayer readings, exorcism of clients, and tongues-speaking (Pollard, "They Prayed to Cast").

Australians were scandalized by the girls' stories. The controversy soon spread when the exorcism manual Mercy Ministries used were leaked to the media. And the exorcism manual was, of course, *Restoring the Foundations*. On November 26, 2008, Tim Brunero reported, "Handbooks allegedly used to perform exorcisms on sick girls at the controversial Mercy Ministries residences in Sydney and on the Sunshine coast have been leaked" (Brunero). The exorcism manual, according to Brunero, had sections like "'Identifying Additional Demons' ... Later, the book, *Restoring the Foundations*, published by an American Christian group, warns those exorcising demons to be firm. The 'ministers' commanding attitude [towards demons] resembles that of a person speaking to a little 'yappy dog'" (Brunero).

The controversy next made its way to the American Mercy homes. Mercy's founder Nancy Alcorn claimed that the Australian operation had been rogue, operating independent of American control.[5] A significant number of American graduates disagreed, as Caleb Hannan related in the October 2, 2008, issue of the *Nashville Scene*: "While the Australian press devoured the scandal's juiciest morsels—the money and the exorcisms—several former Nashville graduates were drawn to the familiar stories of neglect: the threats of expulsion, and the use of prayer as a substitute for psychiatric care" (Hannan, "Jesus RX"). Jodi Ferris, one of the older survivors and an important leader in raising awareness about Mercy's therapeutic methodology, related how Mercy had gradually acculturated women to the *Restoring the Foundations* therapeutic approach that was at the heart of the ministry, the last step of which is casting out demons, "a process that sometimes involved the bedrock of charismatic Pentecostalism: speaking in tongues" (Hannan, "Jesus RX"). Hannan's article also suggested that Nancy Alcorn might be gay, an explosive charge not only due to evangelicalism's anti-gay bias, but because Mercy Ministries promoted itself as a healing center for those "suffering" from homosexual attractions (see Hannan, "Jesus RX").

Though Mercy Ministries managed to preserve its reputation in the States, even with supporters claiming Mercy Australia had no relationship to Mercy America, its reputation was largely in tatters in Australia. Because of Mercy's poor Australian reputation, the homes in Australia eventually closed (Pollard, "Mercy Ministries Home to Close"). The American homes still remain open, as do Mercy "affiliates" in the UK, Canada and New Zealand (see "Locations"). Mercy Ministries now uses a curriculum called *Choices That Bring Change* ("FAQS Mercy"), which is apparently self-generated since unlike *Restoring the Foundations*, it is not readily available for sale in the United States.[6] Since the closing of the Australian homes, Mercy has aggressively tried to rebrand itself through several tactics, most notably promoting the now trendy evangelical cause of sex trafficking abolitionism (*Mercy Ministries* website; Sweatte). But for many of the ministries critics this is too little, too late.

Mercy has used or endorsed an eclectic mix of deliverance material over the years (see Alcorn, *Cut* 85, *Violated* 61, and *Starved* 81). The most troubling, however, is *Restoring the Foundations*. The Kylstras, for instance, promote a bizarre theory of demons' influence on the mind. The Kylstras believe that "some ... dear people have gone through life as analyzing machines. They analyze everything.... In addition a demon may be empowering the analytical thinking" (Kylstra and Kylstra 220). The Kylstras also promote the existence of "Skepticism demons" (227) and "mental-blocking demons" (307). For the Kylstras, the very existence of doubt is possible proof of possession. The more a client resists the RTF deliverance system, the more likely the RTF counselor/facilitator is to assume that the demonic, rather than the physical, is involved in the client's mental health problems (Weaver 98). The Kylstras' manual also promotes the existence of generational curses and the even more extreme concept of soul ties, in which a sexual abuse victim is often demonically linked to her abuser. As I have argued in *The Failure of Evangelical Mental Health Care*, Alcorn all but explicitly endorses the soul ties ideas in her theology (Weaver, *Failure* 99–100).

The RTF manual, which directly and intimately influenced Nancy Alcorn's own ministry, is unmistakably aligned with NAR theology. Bill Hamon wrote the introduction for *Restoring the Foundations* (Hamon, Foreword xiii). It's no surprise that he did, either, because the Kylstras freely admit that they were part of his apostolic network, Christian International:

> In 1993, they [Kylstras] were called by Dr. Bill Hamon to Christian International in Florida to minister to the CI leadership. This led to the first "Prophetic Counseling" conference in March of 1994, which included the launch of the "Christian International Proclaiming His Word Healing House." The relationship with CI and Dr. Hamon continues as Chester and Betsy are ordained by CI and serve on the CI Board of Governors [Kylstra and Kylstra 423].

The Kylstras established the Healing House Network in 2001 as a "covering membership organization" for RTF ministry teams. In NAR terms, this means that just as Bill Hamon apostolically covers the Kylstras, so too do the Kylstras cover those within the Network. In addition to being under Bill Hamon's leadership and serving on his board of governors, the Kylstras are also part of C. Peter Wagner's Apostolic Roundtable of Deliverance Ministries, and hold faculty positions at the CI [Christian International] School of Theology and Ministry Training College and Wagner Leadership Institute (Kylstra, *Biblical Healing and Deliverance* 277–278). They are thus involved in some of the more important ministries in the NAR today, with connections stretching up to chief NAR apostle C. Peter Wagner himself.

However, it is the Kylstras' close ties with Bill Hamon that are the most troubling. Hamon is one of the most fanatic apostles within the NAR and one of the most influential as well. As will be more extensively detailed in Chapter 5, Hamon promotes an unusually open version of "manifest sons" theology; in his particular formulation of that ideology, the church is equated with the "church race" (Hamon, *Prophetic Scriptures* 77) in a profoundly racialized discourse of church membership.

Hamon's gospel is profoundly restorationist, perhaps because of his extensive ties to the Latter Rain revival (see Hamon, *Prophetic Scriptures* 99–100; Hamon, *The Day of the Saints* 138–139). To realize the importance of Hamon's brand of restorationism, one must remember the concept of "spiritual fatherhip." The NAR's belief that the return of the apostolic office to the church has occurred is incredibly important to understanding this point. As Renee Holvast relates, the

> essential difference between the NAR and the traditional denominational churches concerned leadership and governance. The NAR was led not by a group but by an individual apostle. It was this divinely appointed apostle, as opposed to a board or a presbytery, a democratic vote or institution who was seen bearing responsibility for making decisions and guiding adherents [Holvast 158–159].

As we have seen, what has given the NAR its enormous organizational advantage over traditional mainstream churches has been its ability to mobilize people through transdenominational, translocal groups that focus on relational networks, rather than denominations, as their chief organizing component (Wagner, *Churchquake!* 126–127). However the effectiveness of the promotion of the NAR rested on the concept that the role of the apostle had been restored to the church due to the NAR (see Hamon, *Prophetic Scriptures* 128). The Latter Rain movement on which Hamon cut his teeth (see Hamon, *Prophetic Scriptures* 183 for his ties to Latter Rain preacher Reg Layzell), provided the prophetic fervor, ideology, and leadership skills to successfully pull off the promotion of this return to apostolic leadership, and Hamon, as one of the leading thinkers on restorationism within the NAR, was a crucial figure in this process.

It is important to note, therefore, that *Restoring the Foundations* deliberately and specifically invokes restorationism. According to the preface of the book:

> This restoration process [within RTF and the Charismatic movement at large], which is going on in each saint's life, also coincides with the restoration of the Church. It fits in with, and is a part of the restoration of the apostles and prophets. *Restoring the Foundations* ministry ... has been brought forth by God at this time to bring foundational healing and freedom to the Church.... Three levels of foundations are being restored today. The foundation of each saint, the foundation of the

local church, and the foundation of Christ's Church universal. As each individual saint is restored, all three of these foundations are being restored, healed, strengthened, enabled, and equipped [Kylstra and Kylstra xvii-xviii].

The Kylstras therefore see their ministry as a ground-level application of the wider church restorationist practices, such as SLSW, that are being practiced by the wider NAR. By helping individual saints, the Kylstras help restore the foundations upon which the Christian church was built, thus promoting a return to a more "authentic" form of Christianity based on a "primitivist" model (S.L. Ware 1019). Healing ministry paves the way for spiritual warfare on a grander scale. The Kylstras quote approvingly from SLSW experts such as George Otis, Jr. (Kylstra and Kylstra 147), and seem to be clearly aware of the "spiritual technologies" that characterize the NAR. *Restoring the Foundations* serves as a kind of "popular" NAR text that can reach audiences that might be turned off by Hamon's discussions of the "church race" or George Otis, Jr.'s digressions on spiritual mapping and thus sucks people into NAR ideas of spiritual warfare through the back door.

Not surprisingly, despite Mercy Ministries's claims to have forsaken the RTF model (Hannan, "Jesus RX"), Mercy still openly aligns itself with Christian International, despite that organization's historically close relationship with Chester and Betsy Kylstra. Christian International even calls Mercy, "our ministers," which denotes that Mercy Ministries is under Hamon's covering and answerable to him (Christian International Ministries, "Our Ministers: Mercy Ministries"). Apostle Jane Hamon has spoken at Mercy as well, along with her daughter Crystal (Christian International Ministries, "Suicide Bows Its Knee"). In fact, Alcorn received an award from Hamon's Christian International for being the "global impact ministry of the year" ("Mercy Ministries Surprised with Prestigious Award"). One must ask why Mercy maintains links to an organization so closely tied to the promotion of *Restoring the Foundations*, when *Restoring the Foundations* was the very treatment program that got Mercy Ministries in trouble in the first place.

Nor is this Alcorn's only link to NAR theology. Alcorn took a number of her residents to the Call, which she felt was "such a joy for our girls to be personally encouraged and ministered to by Lou Engle's wife, Therese, world-renown author and speaker Cindy Jacobs, and Lou's beautiful parents" (Alcorn, "Thousands Gathered to Pray"). Engle is closely linked to the extremist anti-gay legislation (including in some cases, the death penalty for homosexuals) in Uganda and has praised Ugandan leaders for promoting this legislation (Kron). Finally, according to Mercy, "Mercy Ministries has had the privilege of financially supporting Watoto ministries through the construction of two homes for orphans, but in July, we actually sent a team to do the work!"

("Unforgettable Message of Hope"). Watoto Ministries Marilyn Skinner has also spoken at Mercy ("Unforgettable Message of Hope"). Mercy advertises Gary Skinner's Watoto Ministries (also known as Watoto Church) as an organization devoted to ministering to AIDS victims, a claim that, while true, underlies a more sinister agenda ("Unforgettable Message of Hope"). According to the *Gay City News*, the Skinners' church is at the "forefront of the anti-gay movement in Uganda," a country that has narrowly avoided enacting the death penalty for homosexuals (Osborne, "A Ugandan Pastor with Global Reach"). Not surprisingly, Watoto has ties to Mercy's former close ally Hillsong, which donated over $700,000 dollars to the organization (Morris, "Focus on Justice"). Thus anti-gay efforts in Uganda, exorcisms in Australia, and the promotion of theocratic ideas at home are all tied into one tight bow, with uncounted numbers of potential victims.

Other ICA Networks, Institutions and Leaders

Beginning in 1999, Wagner started convening the Apostolic Council of Prophetic Elders (ACPE), a kind of fraternity of big-name apostles and prophets, who wanted to "build-relationships and establish mutual accountability" (Wagner, *Wrestling* 216; Holvast 160). The organization is fairly secretive, but a 2003 list of its very selective membership (it is invitation-only) reads like a who's who of NAR big-wigs, including (but hardly limited to) Mike Bickle, Paul Cain, Cindy Jacobs, Bill Hamon, Chuck Pierce, Dutch Sheets, and Doris and Peter Wagner (Shulltz). Like many large and powerful apostolic groupings, its main purpose is relational—ostensibly its aim is "to build relationships and establish mutual accountability" (Wagner, *Wrestling* 216). Wagner also markets the ACPE as a tool for integrating the apostolic and prophetic arms of the NAR, and given the prominence of early KCF leaders like Bickle and Cain in the 2003 membership list, that claim certainly is plausible, but it is also certainly not the only reason the ACPE is in existence (see Wagner, *Wrestling* 216).

Another crucial element of the ICA is the numerous prayer networks under its umbrella. Originally these prayer networks were known as spiritual warfare networks (SWN) (Holvast 106) and were part of the AD 2000 campaign. As we have seen previously, in 1997 Cindy Jacobs's U.S. branch was "reorganized under Jacobs' leadership into the United States Spiritual Warfare Prayer Network (USSPN)." This network would have 50 coordinators (one per state) and 14 "task forces" for ethnic and racial minorities (Holvast 106). In 2000, SWN officially changed its name to the Apostolic Strategic Prayer

Network (ASPN). As Holvast points out, this reflects the "new apostolic focus of the network" (Holvast 111). Also in 2000, Wagner was appointed "international apostle" over the Strategic Prayer Network (SPN). Wagner then delegated leadership of the USSPN to Cindy Jacobs and Chuck Pierce (Holvast 152). Later, Wagner changed the name of the movement to the Global Apostolic Prayer Network and put it under the leadership of Pierce, but by 2008, Wagner and Pierce, supposedly mutually, decided to step away from such an activist involvement in the "global prayer movement," and leadership passed to Cindy Jacobs who initiated the "Reformation Prayer Network" (known as the United States Prayer Reformation Network) (Wagner, *Wrestling* 281). However, as with all things NAR, there is a considerable degree of decentralization and relational networking within prayer networks. This has led to the formation of at least two other major prayer networks that have overlapping agendas with the RPN. The second major network was the aforementioned National Governmental Prayer Alliance. The NGPA, as previously mentioned, is explicitly nationalistic in overtones and served as a "clearing house" for intercessory information (prayer information) on the government of the United States (Holvast 121). Finally, in recent years, John Benefiel's Heartland Apostolic Prayer Network (HAPN) has become powerful as well, with branches in all 50 states (Rosenberg, "Rick Perry's Prayer-Rally Politics"). In practice, however, most state networks submit to multiple apostolic leaders, so that in reality each state has only one prayer network, in which the state leader is apostolically covered by all of the (current) major prayer network leaders.

Rachel Tabachnick, a PRA fellow, who along with Bruce Wilson is the leading American expert on the NAR, speculated to journalist Forrest Wilder that one of the major attractions of the apostolic movement to politicians is the movement's "valuable organizational structure and databases," a byproduct of the NAR's years of networking and spiritual mapping. Tabachnick says in reference to the 50-state prayer networks: "They've built such a tremendous communication network.... They found ways to work that didn't involve the institutional structures that many denominations have. They don't have big offices, headquarters. They work more like a political campaign" (Wilder). Today the NAR infrastructure includes prayer networks in all 50 states. Each state is under the authority of a statewide apostolic leader. Prayer warriors, according to a PRA report by Tabachnick, "regularly distribute guides in preparation for elections, 'educating' participants on political issues. They also sponsor training events and conferences and serve as a link between individuals and various NAR ministries" (Tabachnick, "Spiritual Warriors with an Antigay"). Tabachnick's point here bears emphasis. As both she and Rene Holvast make painfully evident, the supposedly apolitical Prayer Tracks and prayer networks of the '90s flowed rather smoothly into today's obviously political form of NAR networking. Spiritual mapping, though no longer necessarily the most important practice within the NAR, was the perfect tool for building these networks because the intelligence Wagner, Dawson, and in particular Otis Jr., advised people to get could so readily translate into more earthly forms of political mapping. That the left could not see this in the nineties; that indeed, the whole spiritual mapping movement largely flew under the radar of the national media, shows how critically progressives underestimated the Christian Right. Nor, arguably, was the left the only force that underestimated the NAR. Conservatives, particularly establishment conservatives, were caught offguard by the NAR's growth and organizational strength, and arguably the Christian Right itself has yet to harness the NAR's full potential.

The prayer movement also promotes prayer as a form of "intercessory activism." One can see this, for instance, with Mike Bickle's IHOP apostolic network, which uses "public displays of prayer and repentance" as one of the movement's "most vital organizing and energizing tool[s]" (Tabachnick, "Spiritual Warriors with an Antigay"). IHOP's apostolic network, which I will deal with in extensive detail shortly, organizes some 2,000 people to pray 24/7, literally every hour every day. This might seem like a noble effort to outsiders, which is exactly IHOP's intent, an intent it emphasizes, for instance, by promoting causes like sex trafficking abolitionism and local counseling services. However, these services are anything but benevolent when viewed through IHOP's particular cultural lens, a lens that decries social justice programs as being the spirit of the Antichrist, and decries Islam and Buddhism as "false religions birthed out of desire for social justice" (Greaves 45).

As for the leaders of the prayer networks, a mere sampling of their public comments convinces one that they are not the kind of people one would want in such influential positions. Dutch Sheets, for instance, argues that America is going to suffer punishment for the sins of "homosexuality, abortion and socialism" and the "toleration of immorality and perversion" (Tashman, "Newt Gingrich"). Sheets, in the same speech, also engages in typical Muslim-baiting (Tashman, "Newt Gingrich"). Yet Sheets was appointed to be the national co-chair of Newt Gingrich's Faith Leader's Coalition. Benefiel believes that the Statue of Liberty is a demonic idol (Tashman, "Jacobs, Benefiel"). He claims that homosexuality is an Illuminati conspiracy whose goal is to reduce the world's population to 500 million. Benefiel has asserted that homosexuality is a stronghold of the demonic figure Baal, a figure that he in other material has suggested geographical areas must divorce (Tashman, "Rick Perry Partner"; Mash). He also worked with the Call Detroit, which promoted the idea that demons should be cast out of mosques (Tashman, "The Call: Detroit"). Yet

Benefiel was an official endorser of Rick Perry, who certainly welcomed the support (Tashman, "Barton").

Cindy Jacobs is even more extreme than these leaders. She promotes the idea that Native Americans are afflicted by a "Leviathan spirit" that is responsible for the cultural trauma they currently suffer. In order to deal with this, they must repent for their ancestors' "sin of animism" or else the Leviathan spirit will be "very active in your bloodline" (Mantyla, "Jacobs: Those With"). Jacobs's husband has promoted the idea that the intercessory "prayer cover" that the various prayer movements have provided has thwarted numerous terrorist attacks (an idea that Cindy Jacobs appears to concur with) (Ariella). Cindy Jacobs herself has stated, "Time and time again we have sent our prayer network [to] a certain place and terrorists were exposed after that.... We have been able to avert a number of potential bombings" (Mantyla, "Jacobs: Our Prayers Stop"). Yet Jacobs is one of the most influential figures in the Christian Right today, and was a leading figure, by C. Peter Wagner's own admission, in the development of his own faith (Wagner, *Wrestling* 151–165).

Finally, brief mention should be made of the various Transformations networks. Transformationalism, as an idea, is discussed extensively in the next chapter. Basically, it is the most sophisticated form of dominionist branding for the NAR. Rachel Tabachnick positions the transformationalist movement as essentially hearkening back to George Otis's films *Transformations I* and *Transformations II* (Tabachnick, "Resource Directory"). As Tabachnick points out, there are various "brands" of transformationalism currently out there— networks promoted by George Otis, Jr., Ed Silvoso, Luis Bush, and others (Tabachnick, "Resource Directory"). Three things are important to understand about the transformationalist model. First, it is very sophisticated and can fool those on the left into thinking the economic model it offers is progressive. The reason transformationalism is able to do this is because of my second point— the leaders who market transformationalism are leaders traditionally associated with the NAR's intellectual arm—Silvoso and Otis Jr., specifically. Louis Bush's form of transformationalism can even market itself outside the movement entirely, given Bush's reputation as a more "traditional" evangelical (for Bush's theological positions as perceived by Wagner, see Wagner, *Wrestling* 170). Thirdly, despite the seeming liberalism of the transformationalist vision of the NAR, it is anything but that.

A brief glance at the various Transformations networks (courtesy of Rachel Tabachnick's scholarship), will highlight this point. In the early 1990s, Ed Silvoso began promulgating the Transformations philosophy in Argentina. Subsequently, he ended up founding the International Transformation Network (ITN), which he spread to Africa, Asia, and the Americas (Tabachnick, "The

Transformation Movement" 51). In the United States, the Transformations network is perhaps most famous for attempting to "plant" a candidate in the Republican run for governor in Hawaii. Duke Aiona lost the gubernatorial race following media coverage that highlighted Aiona's involvement in the Transformation campaign (Tabachnick, "The Transformation Movement" 52). Silvoso's Transformation network also helped Rick Perry kick off a day-long prayer event with NAR apostle Alice Patterson, a granddaughter of a KKK member who now promotes racial reconciliation while engaging in breathtaking historical revisionism that tries to make the left into the traditional opponent of egalitarian racial politics (Tabachnick, "The Transformation Movement" 52; Patterson passim).

According to Tabachnick, and in compliance with typical seven mountains ideology, specific assignments within transformation prayer networks include "selecting local leaders to head the effort of taking control over each of the seven mountains." Typically, this is done through assigning intercessors or prayer warriors to a local school or area. Leaders then "meet with local principals and administrators to set up church adoptions of schools. Transformation efforts are presented as charitable activities providing services to underfunded and struggling municipalities, often with inner city populations—which provides them access to public institutions necessary for establishing dominion" (Tabachnick 52). This ideology is then packaged and promoted through the *Transformations* films which send the same message and concentrate on what are seen as definitive examples of community change (Tabachnick 52). These films are long on anecdote and inevitably short on hard social science data that would justify their assertions. Yet these examples are prepackaged and sold as transformative "exemplars"—much like Heidi Baker is similarly sold on an individual level—in various NAR publications. It is difficult to quantify how many NAR books use the examples from the *Transformations* movies, but I would estimate that it is nearly half of them, mostly deriving from the first two *Transformations* movies. The example of miraculously giant vegetables originating from the transformations campaign in Almolonga, Guatemala is a particular favorite of the movement (*Transformations I*; Tabachnick, "Evangelicals Engaged"). As we will see, transformationalist ideology has too often had a devastating effect on the developing world, but what matters to NAR leaders is the mythos of social transformationalism. That mythos serves as the movement's self-justification, as its primary means of propaganda to social elites, and as a tool for communicating effectively with political and social elites. As Rene Holvast has pointed out, Silvoso's transformations network in particular focuses mainly on reaching those in power (Holvast 119). But while the powerful may be primarily concerned with economic and political influence, they also value political stability, and unless Silvoso, Otis Jr., and company are able to provide the promise of such stability, their movements will be left forlorn. Without the lie of successful social transformation, Silvoso would be unable to promote that myth.

Morningstar Network: The "Tea Party" Apostolics

Morningstar Network is a relatively powerful apostolic network that remains largely independent of the ICA or Revival Alliance. Its leader is Rick Joyner. Early media reports about Joyner indicate that he enjoyed a friendly relationship with Mike Bickle, arguably the most radical apostle in the movement at the time (Harmon, "God's Lightning Rod"). Joyner's ministry promoted mystical visions and like Bickle's strongly emphasized the prophetic, as compared to Wagner's more apostolic orientation (Harmon). Yet even *Charisma* magazine, whose coverage of the NAR is almost entirely favorable, admitted that some of Joyner's prophetic pronouncements had not come to fruition (Harmon).

The best way to view Joyner is to see him as the most explicitly Tea Party version of the NAR.[7] There is relatively little masking of NAR objectives within Joyner's writing or worldview. For instance, Joyner's solution for government reform in the wake of the 2007–2009 financial collapse was to push for financial deregulation and tort reform (Joyner, *I See a New America* loc 574, 1252, 1650–1695). As the Obama presidency "threatened" to enter a second term, Joyner's ministry became increasingly radicalized. Joyner warned Christians that Muslims were taking over the seven mountains of influence (Tashman, "Joyner: 'The Lord is Using Islam'"). According to a Right Wing Watch report, Joyner also feared that Obama was trying to merge Christianity with Islam (Tashman, "Joyner: Obama Helping to Merge"). Joyner, who is also involved in Transformations networking, was instrumental in the Call Detroit anti–Islamic campaign. This campaign was run by Transformations Michigan, the state affiliate of the Oak Initiative, an organization that is part of Joyner's apostolic network (Tashman, "'The Call Whines").

The Oak Initiative is the most disturbing of Joyner's many media and public outreach campaigns. It has ties with high ranking former military officials, most notably Lt. General William C. Boykin (USA) Ret., a board member ("Our Board Members"), who views the Obama administration as a Marxist insurgency and has stated, "Remember Hitler had the brown shirts and in the night of the long knives even Hitler got scared of the brown shirts and killed thousands of them. Well, so you say, are there any signs that that's actually happened? The truth is, yes. If you read the healthcare ... it's actually in the healthcare legislation" (Oak Initiative, "Marxism in America").[8] In other words, Joyner is helping promote "death panel"–type fanaticism on the part of his followers. The Oak Initiative also promulgates a variety of anti-Islamic material (see Joyner, "Volume 3, Number 2" where Joyner describes a sampling of such material) and has sponsored the article "Shariah: Threat to America," which "has been used by politicians as a legitimate source" (CAIR Michigan 3).

Among Joyner's extreme pronouncements was a call for a military coup in the United States ("Rick Joyner Praying"). Yet he is not some fringe participant in the NAR, whose ideas are unrepresentative of the movement. In fact, he was one of the chief apostles present at the commissioning ceremony of Todd Bentley ("Todd Bentley's Apostolic and Prophetic Commissioning 2/4"). Joyner has also shown an ability to cooperate quite effectively with members of other apostolic networks. The Call Detroit, for instance, represented a fusion of Lou Engle's and Joyner's organizational talents (Tashman, "Engle, Joyner Come Together"). One does have to ask why the movement continues to promote Joyner, whose ideology seems "hard right" even by NAR standards, instead of its more moderate elements. But in a larger sense, as one researcher has suggested to me, Joyner serves as a kind of testbed for promoting NAR doctrinal and policy innovations that may be too outside of the mainstream of the movement to be adopted immediately (Bruce Wilson, personal email, 21 Oct. 2013). If the innovations succeed, so much the better. If they do not, Joyner is powerful enough with his own constituency not to feel much blowback, and separate enough organizationally from the rest of the NAR for groups like the ICA and Revival Alliance to claim plausible deniability. In this maelstrom of political and religious radicalism, the future fate of millions of American Charismatics is tested, refined and sifted. Joyner's media presence makes that sifting possible and that is why despite his radicalism, it would be foolhardy to ignore him.

IHOP: Mike Bickle and the New Generation of Prayer Warriors

Mike Bickle's central involvement in the history of the NAR did not end with the Kansas City Prophets. In 1990, he helped found a leadership training program, Grace Training Center, at the same time his church had entered the Vineyard. By early 1991, attendance at KCF had reached some 7,000 people. By 1993, six additional churches had arisen as part of KCF's Kansas network (Riss, "Mike Bickle" 417). As we have seen, Bickle's Kansas City Prophets had a close connection to the Toronto Blessing (see Römer 26–27).

In fact, close does not begin to describe the relationship that developed between Bickle and the Toronto Blessing revivalists. According to Richard Riss, Bickle's church was a "prominent" player in the Toronto Blessing (Riss, "Mike Bickle" 417). Randy Clark, the leader of Global Awakening, was so impressed by a Mike Bickle sermon on Russia that he heard in 1990 that it served as a major motivational factor for his eventual ministry into that country (Bill Jackson 299–300).

This kind of mutual affinity and loyalty was shared by Mike Bickle, and played an important part in his decision to leave the Vineyard. In July of 1996, Bickle wrote the Executive Council of the Vineyard expressing his displeasure at the direction the AVC was heading. Bickle's concerns were numerous. He was bitter about the fact that the Vineyard was now downplaying its emphasis on the "prophetic and intercession," which had played such a key part of his own ministry, and of Wimber's early association with the Kansas City Prophets. Bickle also thought the movement was underplaying the importance of end-times evangelism, and was not sufficiently emphasizing the "fivefold ministry of Ephesians 4:11" (Jackson 337). Bickle believed this had led the AVC to rewrite the history of its relationship with Metro Vineyard (KCF's name under the Vineyard), especially in regards to the prophetic and intercessory elements of belief that the Vineyard had come to emphasize at the height of its alliance with KCF (Jackson 337). But central to Bickle's analysis of these spiritual failings on the part of the Vineyard was its treatment of the Arnotts, who he felt had received a "lack of honor" in their treatment from the Vineyard (Jackson 337). Bickle's willingness to go to bat for Revival Alliance members did not waver in the next two decades, as he closely aligned himself with HIM prophet Lou Engle and his Call Ministry (Eckholm).

In May 1999, Bickle founded the International House of Prayer (IHOP), based on a long-held desire to conduct 24/7 prayer sessions. IHOP members would call to God to help tornado victims or to help outlaw abortion (Eckholm). IHOP now regularly attracts tens of thousands of worshippers to its frequent revival meetings and hosts more than 1,000 staff members, which it labels missionaries, individuals who have left careers to live off donations as they spend "several hours a day in the prayer hall to revel in what they describe as direct communication with God." A Bible college nearby serves more than 1,000 IHOP students and functions as a powerful promulgation tool for IHOP ideology. Staff and students spend a minimum of 25 hours a week in the ministry's prayer room, frequently engaging in fasting as well, a major focus of IHOP ministry that it shares with Engle's the Call.[9] Bickle believes this focused worship affects "real-world events" by "weakening the demons and strengthening the angels that swirl among us" (Eckholm). Bickle's ministry also promotes the idea of what he calls forerunners, who he has cautioned the *New York Times* are not meant to be seen as a spiritual elite (Eckholm).

Yet, like so many of Bickle's assertions over the years, this claim is demonstrably false. In Bickle's book *Seven Commitments of a Forerunner* (2009), the elitist sentiments fly thick and heavy. According to Bickle, "Forerunners will imitate the lifestyle of John the Baptist and the New Testament apostles, who rejected the professional robes of religion for a lifestyle of radical obedience to Jesus and walking in the power of the Spirit. This will involve embracing a lifestyle that includes much prayer with fasting as they seek to go deep in the Word, while at the same time winning the lost, healing the sick, making disciples, church planting and operating in the power of the Spirit to meet the needs of people" (Bickle and Kim, *Seven Commitments of a Forerunner* 10). Besides the obvious allusions to spiritual elitism here—radicalness being a Charismatic buzzword for God's "elite" followers[10]—the specific elements of Christian practice that Bickle emphasizes are all important elements within first Latter Rain and later NAR systems for achieving spiritually transcendent states, namely church planting, discipleship, healing, and fasting. While Bickle's IHOP movement definitely emphasizes intercession—prayer—to a degree seldom seen in modern evangelicalism, this hardly defuses the charge of elitism, but only further grounds it within Bickle's theological system.

Indeed, it is clear that the Forerunner idea is little more than recycled Joel's Army rhetoric that Bickle himself promoted in the '80s. Though Bickle claims that he is not promoting spiritual elitism, and that the forerunner ministry is not reserved for the elite (Bickle and Kim, *Seven Commitments of a Forerunner* 11–12), out of the very opposite side of his mouth he emphasizes that the model for the forerunners are the apostles and John the Baptist, who are certainly spiritual elites to most Christians (Bickle and Kim, *Seven Commitments of a Forerunner* 10).

Bickle casts his Forerunner ministry in explicitly eschatological terms. According to Bickle, on May 7, 1997, the Holy Spirit in a "very powerful supernatural way" spoke to him and "said that He was going to raise up 10,000 Forerunners with the Spirit of John the Baptist and that He was inviting me to be a part of that with others in raising them up." These 10,000, therefore, are the spiritual cadre that God had promised Bickle as the prophetic voice for the future. To Bickle, these Forerunners are "central to our entire vision and all that's going to unfold in the years to come. They are the point of the arrow of all that God has promised us. Forerunners that would operate in the spirit of the friends of the Bridegroom [Jesus] that John the Baptist had" (Bickle, "The Coming Eschatological Revolution Part 1"). What concerns many critics of Bickle and IHOP is not so much the recycling of Joel's Army rhetoric, but the particular eschatology that the Forerunner idea is attached to. In traditional dispensationalism,[11] Christians are not encouraged to "date-set" the End Times. In other words, traditional dispensationalists are not encouraged to predict the specific date on which either the Tribulation or the Rapture comes. This has huge real world ramifications because it means in practice that many more traditional dispensationalists are not particularly concerned with hastening the approach of the End Times. Many believe that this is not only impossible, but also hubristic, in that one is seeking to change the will of God. Therefore traditional dispensationalism has had a strong tendency towards approaching politics and diplomacy apolitically, making dispensationalists relatively easy to politically neutralize vis-a-vis other prophetic schools of apocalypticism within evangelicalism.

Bickle comes from an entirely different vantage point, one he sums up with the slogan: "The Tribulation is not something that happens to us. The tribulation is something that happens through us" (Bickle, "Coming Eschatological Revolution Part 1"). This point about IHOP's eschatology, one that is shared by a growing number of NAR ministries that remain committed to the apostolic ideal, is crucial. In Bickle's system, Christians are not primarily victims of the End Times, but instead are perpetrators of End Times judgments on the Earth. The job of the End Times Christian is to serve as an intercessory prayer warrior, vying against the Devil for control of the Earth (Bickle, "Harlot Babylon"). In Bickle's eschatological system, the world will be divided between two houses of prayer, one led by Jesus (which will include both IHOP and many other End Times prayer ministries not affiliated with IHOP) and one run by Satan. These two houses of prayer will fight for control of the Earth in an eschatological worship war. Therefore, it is important to note that Bickle's promotion of 24/7 prayer is not a marketing trick, but is central to his whole theology. Similarly, IHOP's expansion into other areas of ministry and its relationship to those areas of ministry is almost always related to its eschatology.

Nowhere is this more clearly seen than in the area of social justice. Bickle teaches that the false worship movement that arises out of "Harlot Babylon"— the one world religion that will dominate the End Times—will be a "counterfeit justice movement" (Bickle, "Harlot Babylon"). Bickle warns his followers that just because "somebody says justice, somebody says feed the poor and somebody even says Jesus doesn't mean it's of the spirit of Jesus. The Devil's movement is going to feed the poor. You know why? It's good for business for the Devil to feed the poor.... He [the Devil] will raise the banner of justice for all the wrong reasons, in all the wrong spirit and that's what Revelation 17 reveals to us" (Bickle, "Harlot Babylon"). Stuart Greaves, IHOP's most prominent teacher on social justice issues, echoes Bickle, warning that "the present social justice movement is preparing the poor of the earth to receive the Antichrist" (Greaves 27). These teachings are in some ways not surprising. In many ways they reflect the biases of the evangelical movement as a whole. However, two things primarily distinguish IHOP's system from more traditional eschatologies on the issue of social justice. First, because IHOP is birthed out of a Charismatic theological system, there is a much greater emphasis on the demonic and signs and wonders. Issues of social justice within IHOP's eschatological system are filtered through these doctrinal lens. Secondly, the great emphasis that IHOP puts on intercession and prayer tend to mark the kind of activism the movement supports.

IHOP models what one could call "intercessory activism." According to Stuart Greaves, the primary strategy of Christ to "establish justice in the earth is by calling His people to a global 24/7 worship and prayer movement" (Greaves 84–85). IHOP therefore views social justice as coming about through prayer and worship. While the movement claims not to devalue social action, in reality the vast majority of the ministry's sermons and books speak more about the dangers of social action (vis-à-vis intercessory activism), which must be channeled through true justice movements if they are not to take on the characteristics of the false justice movement that motivate the forces of the Antichrist. Greaves also warns of the danger of emphasizing "social sin, at the expense of our personal sin, while failing to recognize that the fundamental cause of social sin is individual depravity" (Greaves 43). Thus, as is so common for the modern evangelical movement, IHOP views social justice issues in individual rather than structural terms (see Emerson and Smith 104 on this tendency of evangelicalism).

One particular IHOP ministry deserves special mention for the ambiguities of Christian social action it brings up: Exodus Cry. The Exodus Cry movement had its foundations in a 2007 intercessory event in which IHOP member Benjamin Nolot pushed for a "breakthrough" on the issue of human trafficking. Supposedly, this led to massive arrests worldwide thanks to Nolot and his fellow prayer warriors' intercession ("Exodus Cry: About"). Exodus Cry conceptualizes social activism as only being effective if it is tied to spiritual renewal. As David Sliker stated at the 2013 Exodus Cry Abolition Summit, "The measure to which you reform society is the measure to which you've been reformed by the gospel" (Sliker, Session 1). Therefore social reform without Christianity is ultimately futile; the corollary of this belief, which is implicit throughout a wide body of IHOP and Exodus Cry teachings, is that only Christians can meaningfully affect social change in the real world. When the "world"—secularists, non–Christians, or even liberal Christians—do this, they are actually merely making the world worse, by strengthening the false justice system and its messengers. Thus David Sliker warns people that if their "passion for people exceeds their passion for Jesus, you'll end up opposed to Him on the day of His glory" (Sliker, Session 1). Supporting social justice movements not linked explicitly to passion for Christ can therefore quite literally can put you in danger of hell-fire.

Exodus Cry argues that true freedom is impossible without a biblical message. Benjamin Nolot, the leader of Exodus Cry, warns Christians that they need to "draw a clear distinction between the humanism that is called activism and the righteous biblical, scriptural abolition movement…. We are either free in the righteousness that comes from God or we are enslaved in the unrighteousness that comes from our broken condition. But there is no such thing as freedom in unrighteousness" (Nolot, "Restoring the Ancient Path of Abolition"). Although the movement's commitment to ending slavery appears to be sincere, Exodus Cry largely sees physical freedom as being of secondary concern to spiritual freedom. One cannot truly be outside of bondage without the message of Christianity. Therefore, Nolot feels that when the movement makes "physical deliverance our primary objective, I believe we've already missed the point. What have we accomplished if we rescue people from hell on Earth, only to deliver them to hell under the earth" (Nolot, "Restoring the Ancient Path of Abolition"). A sense of keen eschatological futility is evident here. Exodus Cry counts its successes not so much in lives saved, as souls saved and/or transformed. Thus the primary goal of the movement is to help people spiritually first, and only secondarily to improve their social plight.

This may seem like a trivial point to many readers. Why complain about a movement that promotes ending sex trafficking just because its motivations differ from that of secular social justice ideologies? But the problem is that Exodus Cry's emphasis on spirituality at the expense of social justice deeply affects the movement's theological and counseling practice. Nolot, for instance, promotes deeply disturbing ideas about the spiritual consequences of undergoing sex trafficking. According to him, "The sad reality, as I look out, this is so tragic to me. That there's these people out there that have been quote rescued [from sex trafficking] but they're not free and the reality is many of them are nursing at the breast of demons." This is not some offhand reference either. Nolot also speaks approvingly of fellow Exodus Cry speaker Annie Lobert, who promotes the idea that women are frequently raped by demons (Nolot, "Restoring the Ancient Path of Abolition"). The latter belief has become increasingly prominent among Charismatics in recent years, leading to its promotion in no less an organ of Charismatic thought than *Charisma* magazine, the leading news source on spiritual issues for many Charismatics (Harmon, "Can You Be Raped by the Devil?"). Exodus Cry is not only apparently promoting a variant of "soul ties" theology but is literally preaching that doctrine to sex trafficking victims.

And in fact, it is clear from presentations by Kezia Hatfield, who runs Exodus Cry's Restoration program and does much of the program's counseling ("The Journey of Restoration" Track 6; Hatfield, Twitter Account), that this idea of "demonized" sex trafficking victims is present within their counseling material. Hatfield's presentations are all the more troubling in that she mixes clearly sincere compassion for her clients with what can only be considered an irresponsibility in treatment, commenting that

> there's such an importance for respecting their [victims'] choice, respecting their will, respecting all the things that have been taken from them ... so even in the things, especially related to like deliverance and different ways that we're you know praying through spiritual strongholds and other things, I have actually found.... I pray over the girls and ... lead them to the point that they want to be led and then actually the Lord has come and given them the language already [Hatfield, "Journey of Restoration"].

Thus Hatfield, according to her own testimony, promotes the deliverance—i.e., the exorcism—of sex trafficking victims (Hatfield, "Journey of Restoration"). Nor is this some off-hand reference to questionable counseling practices. Questionable counseling almost defines IHOP as a whole. Among the services it lists as available from the group are Sozo and Theophostic Prayer Ministry (TPM) ("Programs"). The problems with sozo have been delineated already. TPM, like sozo, relied extensively on recovered memory therapy (RMT)-like devices, which are now seen as suspect by many professional counselors. That IHOP is associated with such a ministry is not surprising, given the context of the Exodus Cry audio presentations. The 2013 Exodus Cry Abolition Summit included a presentation from Dan Allender (who also appears in the Exodus Cry documentary *Nefarious*. See Nefarious). Allender is well known for his support of recovered memory therapy (see Allender, *Wounded Heart* 144–145 on the startling amount of recovered memory cases he "treats"; see Priest and Cordill 392–395 on recovered memory therapy as Allender performs it) and his vast overestimation of the extent of child abuse in the modern world (Allender 25, Priest and Cordill 392).

Hatfield clearly herself promotes some of the more bizarre and socially damaging theories that came out of the recovered memory movement and the Satanic Panic it helped engender. According to Hatfield:

> When we look at the kinds of slavery and exploitation that is happening in the Earth right now, the depths and the depravity that it has manifested, as we have seen from

the beginning some of the most horrifying abuses but all done in a name of care and love.... We see things even in the area of ritual abuse and SRA [Satanic Ritual Abuse], these types of areas of exploitation, and abuses that really is in our opinion the very core, the very raw expression of trafficking. People are actually being sold to Satan and manipulated and controlled in ways that I won't go into right now [Hatfield, Track 5].

Hatfield therefore not only believes in deliverance and exorcism, but also in SRA and Satanic sex trafficking rings, both of whose existence has been repeatedly and thoroughly debunked since the early 1990s (see Nathan and Snedeker 245–246 on the end of the SRA controversy). Thus, there is the very real possibility that some of the abuse "uncovered" by Exodus Cry is not in fact abuse at all, which means the likelihood of Exodus Cry counselors making false allegations is fairly high; this is compounded by the fact that both TPM and Allender's therapeutic models are known among evangelical academics as models prone to encouraging false accusations, and these models have clearly influenced Exodus Cry. Sozo suffers from many of the conceptual flaws of Allender's model and TPM. What's ultimately most damning, however, for Hatfield's therapy, is that like almost all inner healing methodologies it promotes the idea of "presenting Jesus" in the memory. The idea behind presenting Jesus is basically to put Jesus within a memory and then to heal that memory by Jesus's presence within it (see Frecia Johnson 51–52, 64–65 for forms of inner healing practice similar to presenting Jesus; see McMichael and McMichael 44 and Reese 217 for the sozo version of it, which credits theophostic founder Ed Smith as an influence). While Hatfield's mention of Jesus within the memories is relatively brief—she states that love "was actually in the memory—Jesus—who was present—there is such a glorious shift where now we can remember love" (Hatfield, Track 5), her reference clearly places her in the inner healing camp of Christian practitioners. Given the track record of inner healing deliverance specialists, there is reason to doubt that sex trafficking victims who come to Exodus Cry are receiving proper therapeutic treatment. Thus even as Exodus Cry and IHOP promote themselves as intercessory activists, they needlessly retraumatize abuse victims by promoting clinically dubious and potentially damaging therapeutic models.

Brief mention should be made of one other aspect of IHOP: its force of economic theorists and business leaders. The prime ministry for this is the Joseph Company. The Joseph Company's philosophy is largely consistent with Seven Mountains doctrine—as is all of IHOP's ideology—and totally in sync with the marketplace ministry ideas of men like C. Peter Wagner and Ed Silvoso (Silvoso spoke at the 2004 Joseph Company summit. See Silvoso, "Redemption of the Marketplace"). There are one or two ideas that the Company emphasizes particularly though. Randy Sprague, one of its prominent leaders, speaks of a "Cyrus anointing" in which there will be a "Cyrus that's arising that's going to destroy Babylon.... We know that there are 2 Babylons. Here it comes. One is the city and one is the system and the new Cyruses, their calling is not to the city that no longer exists, but it is to the system that permeates our world. You live in Babylon. The money systems are Babylonian. The banking systems have their root in Babylon, and then into Western Europe" (Sprague, "The Cyrus Annointing Part 1"). Thus the Cyruses serve as roughly equivalent of the "new breed" in other marketplace ministries. Indeed, the terms are largely interchangeable. However, Sprague's reference is significant, in that the vision of Cyruses tearing down Babylon has an eschatological significance. Just as church forerunners tear down the harlot of the religious Babylon, so too do marketplace Cyruses tear down the harlot of the economic Babylon.

Bob Fraser, one of the early and most important leaders in Joseph Company ministry, who now runs Joseph International ("Meet the JI Team") has offered up the main book length study in IHOP economic philosophy. Most of it is identical to that found among other "marketplace ministry" leaders, such as Silvoso and Os Hillman. But Fraser is not unintelligent, merely deliberately derivative. One innovation that Fraser does introduce to his particular iteration of marketplace ideology is that he believes that there are "10 Kingdom Things Business Can Do" which "cannot be produced in ministries and ministry programs" (Fraser 19). Whereas Silvoso is more a strategic thinker and Hillman something of a propagandist, Fraser excels at the practical. Fraser promotes the idea that marketplace ministries can be a great place for learning "life skills" (19), which are not easily found outside of that arena. Fraser, after building up his list of arguments, skillfully suggests that businesses may provide ideal grounds for "mentoring and discipleship" (25). He believes, "As spiritual fathers and mothers, there are few joys greater than helping young people identify their heart desires, then helping them find their dream. This is one of the strengths of business, and it was one of my great joys as a CEO" (25). Fraser's use of the term discipleship may be innocent; he may be suggesting simply the kind of mentoring that goes on among typical non NAR-employers. But given the emphasis that the shepherding movement put on the same term, and the fact that it is frequently utilized by NAR apostles as theological code for embracing authoritarian language, there is reason to be concerned with the potential applications of discipleship within a business context. One should also wonder how much this model should be used in a pluralistic business setting. What is clear is that in Fraser's pragmatic writing, the NAR has found a skilled spokesman for their cause.

Conclusion

The NAR's apostolic networks represent an imposing, intimidating force of religious power. But to understand the movement's social significance, we must first trace out its economic philosophy. This philosophy is closely linked to the socioeconomic and political ideas of Christian dominionism. Shockingly, too, there are longstanding links between Charismatic and Pentecostal leaders, including those of the NAR, and the Reformed movement's Reconstructionist branch, long known for its explicitly theocratic overtones. The relationship between these movements, and the economic philosophies they spawned, represent some of the most dangerous threats to American democracy today.

4

NAR Economic Ideas

Marketplace Ministers, the Great Wealth Transfer and the Dangerous Economic Eccentricities of the Charismatic Right

In recent years, the NAR has begun to develop a coherent economic philosophy, one predicated on a variety of free market principles, some of which NAR leaders learned at the feet of early Reconstructionist leaders, particularly Gary North (for a particularly open manifestation of this link, see the references to North in Cindy Jacobs, *Reformation Manifesto* 173, 216). In and of itself, this should not be surprising. The shepherding magazine *New Wine* drew heavily on the writings of Rousas John Rushdoony, Gary North, and other members of the Calvinist right that were powerful in the seventies and eighties (Diamond, *Spiritual Warfare* 138, see also North, "An Economic Forecast for the Eighties" 9–13). It would have been surprising if the NAR had not inherited some of these ideas from its largely wholesale adoption of shepherding and Latter Rain ideas concerning fivefold ministry.

What makes the NAR's approach to economic and social justice issues so much more sophisticated than that practiced by either earlier forms of the Charismatic/Pentecostal movement or by the Calvinist Right was that the NAR managed to effectively cloak its extreme right wing economic philosophy in progressive-sounding rhetoric. Far more than George W. Bush's "compassionate conservatism," the NAR managed to sell itself as a new alternative to "failed" socialism and laissez faire capitalism. The fact that the NAR's economic message was often quite similar to the latter economic model has not gone unnoticed, but the rhetoric of positive social uplift espoused by the NAR struck a chord with an evangelical movement seeking to find a positive way of selling itself in a postmodern age.

Foundational Economic Assumptions of the NAR

Not surprisingly, C. Peter Wagner's writings provide both some of the foundations and also some of the clearest expositions of NAR ideas concerning economic issues. Wagner supports the idea of dominion theology (Wagner, *Dominion!* 59–63). In theological terms, the term dominionism usually posits the idea that God "is said to have given 'dominion' over the earth to humankind. The domionist interpretation formulated the idea that the world has to be subordinated to the rule of 'God's Word,' which is the Bible. The mandate is a privilege, but it is not only that. It is also an urgent responsibility. The de facto establishment of God's dominion was considered imperative" (Holvast 162).

Dominionism has been historically associated with conservative evangelical attempts to "change public life and to make society exclusively Christian" (see Holvast 162), though this association is not without controversy. Wagner's vision of dominionism is sometimes referred to as transformationalism or social transformationalism, though the term dominionism is also still used in reference to it (see Wagner, *Dominion!* 39–56). Wagner sees Christians as having an "assignment from God to take dominion and transform society" (Wagner, *Dominion!* 46). He refers to this as a "cultural mandate" (Wagner, *Dominion!* 46). It is notable also that Wagner explicitly invokes both John Calvin and famous Reformed Calvinist theologian and politician Abraham Kuyper as examples of the power of dominion theology. Kuyper, an enormous figure in Dutch Calvinism at the turn of the 20th century, would go on to influence such evangelical thinkers as C. Everett Koop, John Whitehead, Cal Thomas, James Dobson, and Ralph Reed (Detwiler 110, Wagner, *Dominion!* 46). Wagner's main problem with Kuyperian theology was not its theocratic bent, but the lack of attention it paid to Satan. As Wagner puts it, "For Kuyper, principalities and powers were sinful human social institutions rather than demonic beings per se. Because we are now correcting this, I strongly hope we will see the kinds of social changes that Kuyper brought sustained through succeeding generations" (Wagner, *Dominion!* 47). For Wagner, social and economic change could be affected far easier in the NAR than in Calvinist thought, because not being limited by Calvinist cessationist theology, it could directly confront the demonic forces that controlled oppressed or poverty-stricken economic systems.

Despite Wagner's attempts to quantify social transformationalism, in some ways his definition is quite vague. For Wagner, the term means that a city or nation state is "better off than it used to be" when socially transformed. The way to determine this is through sociologically verifying the transformation of a community. This can only happen if an "independent, outside, qualified observer using standard tools of social science or investigative reporting concludes that the social unit is now as different from what it used to be as a butterfly is from a caterpillar" (Wagner, *Dominion!* 55). The problem with this definition, is, of course, that the NAR's understanding of social science is radically different from traditional social science methodology, involving such factors as demons, spiritual mapping, and pseudo-scientific applications of concepts like animism (see Holvast 32, 305, on the problems with the term animism; see Holvast passim on demons and spiritual mapping). Therefore it is questionable to what degree the movement is willing to actually make its social or economic ideology subject to the scrutiny of the social science community.

A key component of the social transformationist/dominionist message, one that it shares with Reconstructionism, is the shift away from an individualist emphasis on salvation to a more communal-oriented idea of saving society. As Wagner puts it, "One thing that should help is for us to begin shifting our focus from redeeming individuals to redeeming society as our end goal" (Wagner, *Dominion!* 70). Lance Wallnau, in an introduction to Os Hillman's *Change Agent* (2011), similarly expresses concern with the individual-oriented nature of more "Salvationist" oriented churches, when he states, that

> while there is only one gospel, Os points out that the gospel we have primarily preached throughout the earth focuses on individual salvation. The gospel of salvation redeems souls but only indirectly redeems economic, educational, political or artistic institutions. The gospel of the kingdom, on the other hand, includes the gospel of salvation but encompasses the larger and more ambitious project of teaching to save nations, while preaching to save souls [Wallnau in Hillman, *Change Agent* xi].

The job of the church, in Wallnau's and Wagner's estimation, is cultural conquest. This does not necessarily mean direct theocracy; movement leaders have been careful to at least officially distance themselves from this idea (Wagner, *Dominion!* 15). What it does mean, however, is creating a society in which evangelical Christian values predominate, and where those values are used to directly influence the socioeconomic, media, and arts ideological state apparatuses (ISAs) that play such an important role in the maintenance of any contemporary Westernized society. Wallnau sees the salvationist gospel favored by more traditional evangelicals, particularly premillennial dispensationalists, as being a gospel of defeat, one that seeks only individual but not cultural transformation. As someone invested in the cultural triumphalism that the Christian Right has promoted since its heyday in the eighties and nineties, Wallnau is not simply satisfied with affecting culture at an individual level. Rather, he wishes to bring an entire societal shift to a different way of thinking.

Social transformationalism promotes itself as an essentially progressive ideological system, albeit one within the wider NAR framework. Perhaps the most influential advocate of transformationalism has been Argentine evangelist Ed Silvoso. Silvoso believes that there are five essential ideas that are paramount for "sustainable transformation":

> 1) The Great Commission is about discipling nations, not just people ... 2) The Marketplace (the heart of the nation) has already been redeemed by Jesus and now needs to be reclaimed by His followers ... 3) Labor is the premier expression of worship on Earth, and every believer is a minister ... 4) Our primary call is not to build the Church but to take the kingdom of God where the kingdom of darkness is still entrenched in order for Jesus to build His Church ... 5) The premier social indicator that transformation has taken place is the elimination of systemic poverty [Silvoso, *Transformation* 28–29].

Silvoso's agenda, therefore, like Wagner's and Wallnau's, focuses on national and corporate transformation, rather than individual transformation. Silvoso's message is essentially an optimistic-one, one tailor-made to appeal to poor audiences in the First and Third World who have already been bombarded with the even more optimistic ideology of the WOF "prosperity gospel" that has come to dominate much of the Charismatic world in recent decades. For Silvoso, not only can one's personal poverty or one's church poverty be transformed to riches; no, entire cultures can be economically redeemed through the power of the gospel. The crucial status of the marketplace in this ideological system cannot be overemphasized. In transformationalist NAR thinking (which is the currently dominant economic paradigm within the movement), the marketplace—a.k.a. the economy—is the area of society in which culture is redeemed. "Marketplace ministers"—both employers and employees, but mainly the former—are the individuals who are destined to bring about economic and cultural change. This change, according to Silvoso, ends up benefitting the poor, as well as the rich, through its elimination of "systemic poverty."

However, a close look at Silvoso's definition of transformationalism and systemic poverty leads the reader to doubt that Silvoso means the same thing by these concepts as would a progressive or a socialist. Silvoso significantly distinguishes between personal and systemic poverty. He defines systemic poverty as "the structure that perpetuates such deficiency [as lacking our daily bread]" (Silvoso, *Transformation* 117). While systemic poverty is not the fault of the individual, personal poverty is, as Silvoso claims that personal poverty is "usually self-inflicted" through such personality flaws as "laziness, addiction, or procrastination" (Silvoso 116). In addition, people are usually born into systemic poverty, unlike personal poverty (Silvoso 116). Yet Silvoso leaves unexamined what precise sociological criteria one is to use to delineate between the deserving and undeserving poor, those afflicted by systemic poverty and those merely suffering from personal moral failings. While it would be foolish not to admit that there have been abuses of social welfare systems, it would be even more foolish to see more than a small percentage of poverty as being caused by factors like laziness and procrastination. In addition, Silvoso does not acknowledge the possibility that such feelings of helplessness may result from growing up in economic systems that offer no chance for the poor to escape their fates.

Silvoso sees the poor as being potentially their own solution to poverty. This is because, according to Silvoso, "even though poverty is a problem, poor people are not, because according to the Bible, they constitute the greatest ... resource to *eliminate poverty*" (Silvoso 130). Silvoso's transformationalist ideology does have a kind of incipient class analysis, but one that differs radically from Marxist economic theory or liberation theology (the two prevailing economic theories it is clearly designed to compete with). Silvoso tends to downplay the need for or benefit of class conflict,[1] and prefers an economic model in which different social classes have different economic and social abilities. As Silvoso relates:

> Generally speaking, the poor score higher on the spiritual and relational dimensions, because faith in God is often the only source of hope available to survive the hopelessness that engulfs them.... On the other hand, people of wealth fare better on the material and motivational aspects. They have resources and the attitude and the know-how to leverage them so as not to approach the future with desperation, but they tend to score lower on relationships, and their faith in God is usually more "professional" than personal [Silvoso, *Transformation* 125].

What is notable about Silvoso's class analysis is how completely ahistorical it is. Whatever the faults of Marxist class analysis, it at least attempts to build a historical assessment of how modern class relations developed (the same could be said of some more sophisticated capitalist economic models as well). Silvoso, however, relies almost completely on class stereotypes in constructing his economic model of class relations. Whereas the poor have "soul," the rich have "intellect." Again, this is nothing new. What is amazing is that Silvoso and fellow NAR transformationalists attempt to build an entire economic ideology over so slim a justifying paradigm. Nowhere does Silvoso offer anything more than anecdotal evidence for the validity of this class analysis and what support he does offer mainly comes from the New Testament. This is quite problematic, since the Bible is a pre-capitalist text which it would be questionable to read as giving economic direction, even if one approaches Christian scripture from explicitly evangelical presuppositions.

Wagner's theory of poverty is even more extreme, and as his conceptualization of both poverty and the solution to poverty have become fairly central to understanding NAR economic ideas, it is important to examine Wagner's economic theology in detail. Wagner believes that there will eventually be a time when God releases wealth—that is, direct material wealth—to his Christian followers (Wagner, *Church in the Workplace* loc 574–576). At that point, Christians will "enter a time of abundance." However, not all Christians will receive this abundance. Some individuals, according to Wagner, will be left out, because they will be "bound by the spirit of poverty." This is not some metaphorical spirit. Wagner believes that those who do not gain wealth—in other words, the Christian poor of the future—will be literally demonized. Wagner states, "A poverty mind-set is not just a psychological problem. We are dealing with nothing less than a company of high-ranking demons assigned by the enemy to hinder the people of God from … taking their rightful dominion over God's creation" (Wagner, *Church in the Workplace* loc 576). For Wagner, demons are behind poverty (Wagner loc 583). Thus, transformationalist goals of societal reconstruction become even more essential, as apostles and prophets have to prove to their flocks that they can produce economic prosperity as proof of their flocks' Godly spirituality. But there is always a fallback position for the apostles and prophets, which is to claim that those who fail in this economic spiritual race were never sufficiently Christian to begin with. The system, in short, is self-perpetuating. Any failures in the system are simply attributed to individual believers, not the system as a whole, and thus the system has become immune to criticism from the inside.

Wagner and his allies in the NAR needed to make this idea of a golden era of wealth believable to their Christian constituency and therefore the movement came up with a concept variously known as the "wealth transfer" or the "great wealth transfer." For Wagner, there are two pillars for social transformation in society, "the church in the workplace" and "the Great Transfer of Wealth" (Wagner, *Dominion!* 18). These two elements of social transformation are connected by workplace apostles. It is the workplace apostles who "activate the … process" of transferring wealth from the workplace to the church (Wagner, *Dominion!* 19, 191–196, Wagner, *Church in the Workplace*, loc 656–692).

The need for, and consequent development of, workplace apostles has become an important development in the NAR in recent years. The term is pretty much what it sounds like. Workplace apostles are apostles who serve in occupations that would normally be considered secular, yet are considered to have apostolic authority over their followers. Wagner justifies this idea through a distinction between what he calls the "nuclear Church" and the "extended Church." The nuclear church consists of "the people of God, meeting in their congregation, whether in a church building or in a home" while the extended church would "be the people of God in the workplace, commonly called 'the

Church in the workplace'" (Wagner, *Dominion!* 141). The advantages of such a governmental system for the NAR are obvious. The concept of workplace apostles allows the movement to extend its apostolic powers beyond the four walls of a church and into parishioners' workplace environment. In addition, it gives the movement the capability to use the workplace as an evangelism platform for recruiting new members and affecting social change at an organizational and national level (Wagner, *Dominion!* 143–144). As Wagner points out, there are a number of ways of dividing the workplace. One method that has been advanced for a long time, mainly by Lance Wallnau, is the aforementioned "seven mountains" strategy. In the seven mountains vision, there are seven different "molders of culture," which include "religion, family, government, arts and entertainment, media, business, and education" (Wagner, *Dominion!* 144). What's crucial here is to understand that workplace apostles are seen as coequals with traditional nuclear-church apostles. Moreover, while it is theoretically possible for a workplace apostle not to be in a high position within his workplace, in practice such apostles almost always are. The material written by such apostles, such as Os Hillman's *Change Agent Engaging Your Passion to Be the One Who Makes the Difference* (2011), Ed Silvoso's *Transformation: Change the Marketplace and You Change the World* (2007) and *Anointed for Business* (2002), and C. Peter Wagner's *Church in the Workplace* (2006) all appear to be based on the assumption that the major people they are dialoguing with are businessmen and entrepreneurs.

But the real centerpiece of the economic ideology of the NAR, the idea that allows the movement to penetrate into working class environs, is the "great wealth transfer." Simply defined, the "great wealth transfer" is the idea of transferring "the control of wealth" from Satan and his minions to the "Kingdom of God" (Wagner, *Dominion!* 182). Wagner and his allies believe that the only way for societal transformation to happen and God's dominion mandate be achieved is via a transfer of wealth from the secular world to the Christian community (Wagner, *Dominion!* 182). Wagner sets up an elaborate system for this distribution of wealth composed of four core components: Providers, Managers, Distributors, and Field Marshals. The goal of this system is to get the economic wealth of the providers to the Field Marshals, who can "double or triple their successful efforts in extending the Kingdom of God if they had more money" (Wagner, *Dominion!* 192). Providers release this wealth to the field marshals (and the implication is, to the field marshal's apostolic followers) through two means. The first is through supernatural "transfers of wealth"; Wagner provides the example of the Israelites spoiling the Egyptians in the Old Testament as an example of this (Wagner, *Dominion!* 193). Secondly, and more crucially, the providers themselves will receive "extraordinary power to

4. NAR Economic Ideas 151

generate new wealth" (Wagner, *Dominon!* 193). While providers are not necessarily believers, this idea of supernaturally gifted wealth generators fits in well with emerging NAR beliefs about workplace apostles. Wagner has argued that workplace apostles will not simply be average everyday people, but will have the power to "perform signs and wonders" (Wagner, *Church in the Workplace* loc 339). Silvoso's language regarding these providers is even stronger and is reminiscent of the Kansas City Prophets, as he claims that the emerging marketplace "ministers" (a term often used interchangeably with marketplace apostles) will be a "new breed" (Silvoso, *Transformation* 147).

What is of concern in this extension of the apostle's rule into the marketplace is not so much church/state or church/employer conflict, though the problems these potential conflicts could cause are indeed considerable. Rather, the main problem stemming from the promotion of workplace apostles is the corresponding belief that workplace apostles, like "nuclear church" apostles, deserve unswerving obedience, obedience unregulated by church by-laws or denominational hierarchies. This leaves open the potential for workplace apostles to exercise versus unlimited control on employees, since they rule them not simply in the sacred sphere, but in the secular one as well. Indeed, the NAR in general does not recognize the sacred/secular distinction (see Wagner, *The Church in the Workplace* loc 148) at all. Wagner specifically argues that one of the powers of marketplace apostles is that they "exhibit authority" (loc 339). It would hardly take an overly paranoid individual to deduce that that authority will be partly used on behalf of the apostle in controlling his (or her) employees. What's more, Wagner argues that the authority of the apostles in both the nuclear church and the extended church (including the various workplace ministries) "comes from God" (Wagner, *Church in the Workplace* loc 1245). Thus, to oppose a workplace apostle is to oppose the will of God, which given the theology of the NAR, means that the laborer who protests against unfair treatment from his workplace apostle is likely to be seen as "demonized."

Yet the great wealth transfer obviously has real appeal to a large number of people, in part because it promises a supernatural solution to increasing economic distress. In addition, the pull-yourself-up-by-your-bootstraps idea that characterizes the wealth transfer idea is hardly foreign to Charismatic belief. The WOF movement has enjoyed wide acceptance among Charismatics for the same reason. Indeed, there are a number of similarities between the two ideas, including the fact that early forerunners of the prosperity gospel, such as E.W. Kenyon, promoted ideas that bore a striking similarity to the Latter Rain "manifest sons" doctrine (see, for instance, how Kenyon promoted the idea of spiritual supermen in Bowler loc 460). Indeed, Kate Bowler notes that the Latter Rain movement itself ended up deeply influencing much of the prosperity gospel that came in the wake of the Latter Rain revival (Bowler loc 954–974). Ideas of supernatural transfers of wealth, therefore, are hardly foreign to Charismatic circles. What Wagner's and the workplace apostles' vision of this idea makes plausible is the promotion of these ideas as a new form of social justice gospel that is more palatable to the American left than previous evolutions of the Christian right. The fact that this gospel actually in no ways promotes a social justice message has not stopped the NAR from injecting stealth candidates into the Democratic party under the banner of social justice (see Tabachnick, "Anti LGBTQ, Anti-Union"). As we have seen with IHOP's intercessory activism, the NAR uses its message of social justice to promote campaigns that produce exactly the opposite reaction from that which the left would believe these campaigns to be directed at.

Behind this social justice façade is a fairly thought out theory of both labor and economics that though sounding preposterous to many non–NAR readers, leaves the movement poised to exercise considerable socioeconomic influence. And like the praise-happy Charismatic movement that gives it birth, NAR economic ideas are influenced by what is to Charismatics the key element of their spiritual life: worship. It is to the idea of labor as worship that we now turn.

The NAR's Theory of Labor and Economics

Ed Silvoso's theory of labor as worship is one of the central theoretical insights of NAR economic theory. In a sense, this is not an ignoble goal; an increasing valuation of the value of all labor, which is what the NAR claims to predicate its philosophy on, could ultimately lead to a greater respect for the workforce. And indeed, Silvoso's idea of workplace worshipers sounds egalitarian. According to Silvoso, "labor is worship and every believer is a minister" (Silvoso, *Transformation* 97). However, much like the definition of apostleship favored by the NAR, this theory of worship is incredibly broad. According to Silvoso, this worship reflects not "simply the act of praising God in a church meeting…. Rather, it is to be an ongoing attitude and action of life—a *lifestyle*" (Silvoso, *Transformation* 101). Worship and work, for the NAR, are therefore identical. Thus, Silvoso promotes the amazing possibilities of a "college student serving a hamburger at McDonalds unto the glory of God. Visualize a maid cleaning rooms and making beds in a hotel unto the glory of God…. Or a captain of Wall Street submitting his portfolio to the Lord as the Lead Stockbroker" (Silvoso 101). Yet, as with Silvoso's theory of class relations, his theory of labor does not seem to distinguish between forms of labor that may be fundamentally exploitative (for instance, fast food work) and forms of labor that are not (working on Wall Street). Even if one accepts the capitalist presuppositions upon which NAR thinking is based, the movement's failure to come up with a theory of labor relations that does not invoke supernatural agency remains one of its biggest drawbacks to widespread acceptance.

Nevertheless the idea of work as worship is supported by other NAR apostles. For Os Hillman, for instance, workplace ministry involves serving others, and therefore represents an act of worship. Hillman wholeheartedly endorses the idea of work as worship (Hillman, *Change Agent* 34–35), seeing it as part of a wider vocational calling to use money to furtherance Christian ministry and transformation on earth (see Hillman, *Change Agent* 35–36). Societal transformation thus becomes a vocational attribute of the marketplace minister and therefore, whether the marketplace minister is acknowledged as an apostle or is one of the lowly sheep, he or she is in either case viewing the secular workplace as a battleground between Christian and secular, largely demonized forces.

Unfortunately, this is not merely hyperbole. Hillman literally believes that the American marketplace is controlled by demonic forces. In *Change Agent*, Hillman writes, "The spiritual stronghold that rules over the marketplace is mammon and pride. Mammon is actually a demonic principality. It motivates men and women in the marketplace to operate based on greed and pride. The economic crisis that began with the mortgage crisis in 2008 in America is clearly the work of these two spirits operating in men and women" (Hillman, *Change Agent* 168). The application of a theory of demonization to the marketplace makes it all too easy for the NAR to assign the blame for economic injustice on spiritual forces, rather than natural ones. Indeed, not only do NAR apostles frequently resort to such tactics, but they sometimes label left-wing economic dissident groups as demonized. For instance, Cindy Jacobs has warned that the Occupy movement is characterized by a "spirit of anarchy" which is fueled by a "principality, a power of darkness" (Mantyla, "OWS").

Even more extreme is Mike Bickle's IHOP movement; IHOP's leading economic thinker Stuart Greaves contends that "the present social justice movement is preparing the poor of the earth to receive the antichrist" (Greaves 67). Thus for Greaves, social justice is not simply demonic—it is a literal path to the Mark of the Beast and the apocalyptic conflict at the end of time. While other apocalyptic thinkers have occasionally associated social justice rhetoric with the Antichrist (notably in Tim Lahaye's *Left Behind* series), IHOP's emphasis on the power of "prophetic words" in the here and now, as well as its much more militant religious stance vis-à-vis fundamentalists like Lahaye, make the movement's militarism far more dangerous than that exhibited by traditional non–Pentecostal apocalyptic movements (Mantyla, "OWS").

The NAR has been consistently on message about the movement's relationship to capitalism, and their rhetoric is much more sophisticated than that promoted by the traditional Christian Right. The first element of their critique of capitalism is to admit that capitalism "in and of itself has no intrinsic social conscience" (Silvoso 135). Therefore, for the NAR, capitalism, without brakes, is essentially an amoral system. This represents a concession to left-wing critiques of evangelical economic theory, which have often pointed out the movement's failed attempts to reconcile capitalist ideology with what seems to be the largely anti-capitalist—or to be more historically correct, pre-capitalist—message advanced by New Testament writers. Silvoso thinks one of the core problems with traditional capitalism is that it does not prioritize ridding *"society of social evils by actively improving the lot of the disadvantaged through the intentional elimination of systemic evils"* (Silvoso 136, italics in original). Silvoso, however, concurs with evangelical economic guru and NAR-funder Ken Eldred, who argues that "like no other economic system in the history of mankind, capitalism is producing needed goods and services and improving the world's standard of living" (Eldred, *God Is at Work* 76; Silvoso 137; see *Uganda: An Unconventional War*, also covered in Chapter 6, for Eldred's funding of NAR initiatives). Thus, Silvoso feels that capitalism has to be attached to an ethic of social responsibility founded in Judeo-Christian culture (Silvoso 137); without such an ethic capitalism quickly degenerates into a system of greed and "amorality."

Eldred, an important influence on the NAR, argues that capitalism, unlike socialism, is founded on principles of "personal freedom and responsibility" (Eldred 76). But capitalism can evolve in any one of three directions: towards amorality, immorality or morality (Eldred 80). Immoral business practice, because it operates outside the legal bounds of a culture, ultimately provides no sustainable means for economic development (Eldred 80). The amoral model is what Eldred characterizes modern Western business practice as working under. This model is characterized, according to Eldred, by a concern for maximizing profits, and tends to obsess more over legality than morality (80). Eldred criticizes this amoral system for replacing morality with "the rule of law"; Eldred rather transparently suggests that this is responsible for the increasingly "complex legislation" that characterizes Washington regulations (80). He laments the fact that because amoral systems promote a lack of trust between employers, employees, and customers, there is a resulting "greater need for oversight, for legal checks and balances. This increases the transaction costs of doing business and puts the society at a distinct economic disadvantage. The number of laws being developed to regulate commerce in the United States is growing exponentially, all of which adds cost to the system and thereby reduces the economic value" (Eldred 81).

4. NAR Economic Ideas 155

Eldred is obviously arguing for economic deregulation. Nor would he be the only major NAR funder or participant to make this suggestion. Rick Joyner has made similar suggestions about the U.S. economic system, questioning the government's "micromanagement" of the economic system and supporting the economic ideas of stalwart libertarian thinkers like Ron Paul (Joyner, *I See a New America* loc 456,500). Joyner honestly thinks the United States can pump trillions of dollars into its economy simply by taking "the shackles of overregulation and unnecessary taxes" off the American economic system (Joyner, *I See a New America*, loc 1267). His ideas are self-serving, but the reason they work is because both NAR leadership and rank-in-file supporters have been trained to accept the idea that the economic system of the United States can survive if it adopts Eldred's third economic model: the moral model. In this model, businesses operate with moral standards and

> values such as service, integrity, and loyalty are observed not because they are mandated by the law (they are not) but because they are morally right.... This is an environment in which the human spirit thrives. Trust follows when other members of an economic system are known to operate under such a moral standard.... There is less need for costly security measures that guarantee performance. In a moral business environment, transactions are simplified and the cost of doing business decreases [Eldred 81].

What Eldred argues is that capitalism will work if we learn to be terribly decent to one another. He is smart enough to realize that this idea is not academically rigorous, so he adds an addendum to this argument, which insists that in order for this economic system to work effectively, it must be grounded in Judeo-Christian morality (Eldred 82), rather than self-interest,[2] or a universal secular morality.[3] The problem, of course, is that religion, just like secular ideological systems, has a poor track record of enforcing such utopian economic goals. Nor is it clear why Judeo-Christian economic theory is particularly slanted in this direction. Eldred's claim that there is biblical "support" for capitalism (Eldred, *God Is at Work* 76) is even more without foundation than the claims of Christian progressives that the Bible provides evidence for socialist values. In both cases, 21st century Western audiences are imposing their ideas about economics onto a first century text that not only is unconcerned about capitalism, but had no concept of what that term even meant. But leaving such "higher critical" concerns aside, it is questionable even from a biblically literalist position whether Eldred's argument has even marginal validity. The New Testament in particular, while having a few passages that could be slanted in favor of the rich, advocates an economic system that is totally incompatible with capitalism and only marginally more compatible with socialism. What NAR apostles fail to realize when reading the New Testament for economic wisdom is that in so far as the New Testament had an idea of economics, it was likely apocalyptic (on Christianity and apocalyptic thinking see Wells, *Cutting Jesus Down to Size* 280–295), a tradition hardly conducive to either dominionist or socialist views of economic relations.

Nevertheless, it is on this questionable hermeneutical basis the NAR founds its views of socialism. Even Silvoso, who superficially sounds more liberal than other NAR apostles, argues that "I am not advocating a socialistic approach that imposes a redistribution of wealth" (Silvoso, *Transformation* 119). Silvoso calls Communism an "evil and flawed system that pretended to have a social conscience" though he also faults capitalism for having only marginally better a conscience, one that "did not come naturally" to it (Silvoso, *Transformation* 136). Stuart Greaves similarly groups Marxism with other "false messengers" of justice, such as Islam and Buddhism (Greaves 45–48). For Greaves, the problem with such ideologies is that they start "with the plight of the poor, while ignoring Jesus' true agenda for the issue [of poverty], and they have ended up causing widespread confusion in the earth" (Greaves 44). Greaves suggests that in place of this more materialist oriented view of social class inequity, true social justice can be achieved via a "global 24/7 worship and prayer movement" inspired by Jesus (Greaves 84). Again, nowhere in this rhetoric is there any engagement with the actual beliefs of Marxists, socialists, or even simply nuanced pro-capitalist social justice advocates. Nor is there any attempt by Greaves or Silvoso to provide workable economic alternatives to social injustices. Instead both men expect their followers in the NAR to advance their economic prospects mainly through obedience to their apostles and faith. Since these concepts remain economically unverifiable, NAR leaders are left conveniently off the hook for any economic damage their beliefs might cause.

Eldred's criticisms of socialism are more rational, though these criticisms should ultimately be viewed skeptically. Eldred admits that in theory, the socialist idea of achieving economic equality is "laudable," but also ultimately unfeasible (see Eldred, *God Is at Work* Appendix B loc 5551–5609). Eldred argues that one of the main reasons for this unfeasibility is inherent within the socialist system itself, namely its tendency to focus on "wealth redistribution rather than on wealth creation." Because of these inherent flaws in socialism, Eldred argues that socialism ultimately does not provide either the "incentive to innovate nor the recognition that innovation advances every aspect of society" (Eldred, *God Is at Work* Appendix B loc 5606). Of course, to a certain extent, Eldred has a point, in so far as collectivist societies have been slow to accept economic innovation. What is problematic with Eldred's ideas is that he fails to acknowledge that socialism has never been truly tried out in a world free of capitalism. Because of this, socialist systems have always had to adopt a kind of hybrid functionality, never adopting socialism to the extent Marx envisioned. This may, in fact, be one of Marxism's flaws; but it also points to the inherently consumptive nature of capitalism, that simply devours any oppositional economic ideology and turns it into a mirror image of capitalism.

NAR visions of capitalism essentially suffer from some of the same flaws that characterize contemporary secular neo-liberal assumptions. The idea of self-correcting markets is, within the NAR, transformed into God-correcting markets, with the marketplace being conveniently controlled by a God-figure who is deus ex absentia and therefore as unappealable to as the International Monetary Fund or the Federal Reserve. God's followers are simply to assume that since He's all-powerful and all-benevolent, that all economic issues will work towards the glory of God. This is a very risky foundation on which to build an entire social movement; but given the perennial reemergence of restorationist thought within Pentecostal and Charismatic circles, it is understandable why the apostles think they can continue to milk these economic ideas for years to come, even as they risk ruining thousands of lives in the process. And unless secular culture becomes more aware of what is happening within the NAR that is all-too-likely to be the fate of the NAR's followers.

Who Watches the Apostles? Christian Reconstructionism, Fuller and Missional Policy Wonks and the Leadership of the Christian Right

Not surprisingly, considering how powerful the NAR is, it has established a number of links with other powerful Christian Right movements. The most important of these groups are Christian Reconstructionists and a set of church growth and missiologist specialists that come primarily out of Fuller seminary.

Many evangelicals would be surprised by the links between Christian Reconstructionists and the NAR. The movement, after all, was famed for its Van Tilian–based Calvinist presuppositionalism, an ideology not known for its great love of Charismatic theology. Exponents of the movement "propose to change the culture, then change the laws, and then—in the worst extreme versions—to expel, subdue, or perhaps even exterminate all those who do not share their vision" (Martin 353). The Reconstructionists believe their "mandate" is to "rebuild, or reconstruct, all of human society, beginning with the United States and moving outward" (Martin 353). In Reconstructionist ideology, the federal government would not regulate business, public education, or welfare and all its functions would be primarily contained in mail delivery and national defense, though local government would remain. However, in most instances, citizens, "would be answerable to church authorities on most matters subject to regulation." Only members of "biblically correct" churches would be able to vote. The most extreme idea proposed by Reconstructionist supporters is that homosexuality, adultery, blasphemy, and incorrigible disobedience by children would all be subject to the death penalty (Martin 353).

The fact is, however, that Reconstructionists had (and continue to have) fairly extensive ties with other Christian right leaders, including leaders who would later play a part in the NAR. This can be most carefully seen through a read-through of the crucial Coalition of Revival Manifesto, a founding document in the history of the Christian right. As Fritz Detwiler describes COR, it was seen by the Christian right as "an umbrella organization to unify and coordinate Christian right efforts in developing the theoretical models for transforming every sphere of American society" (Detwiler 136), featuring what could only be described as a "who's who of the Christian Right elite" (136). Prominent shepherding leaders Ern Baxter, Bob Mumford, and Charles Simpson all were signatories to the agreement (Grimstead, "A Manifesto" 13–16). This was hardly coincidental; even movement insider S. David Moore admits that the shepherding movement was making what he termed a "loose alliance" with the Christian Reconstructionist movement's intellectual founder R.J. Rushdoony (Moore 164). The numerous publications of *New Wine* that referenced both Reconstructionist and major Reformed Christian presuppositionalist leaders in the '70s and '80s suggest that this relationship is far closer than Moore would lead us to believe: Francis Schaeffer, Gary North, Edith Schaeffer, C. Everett Koop, and prominent Reformed anti-psychiatric advocate Jay Adams all appeared in *New Wine* over the course of the late 1970s and early 1980s (Diamond, *Spiritual Warfare* 138; North, "An Economic Forecast for the Eighties" 9–13; Schaeffer was excerpted in *New Wine*'s Feb. 1979 issue, "The Decline of Twentieth Century Man" 25–29; Edith Schaeffer was interviewed in the *New Wine* issue of May 1980, "Enduring as a Family" 3–6, 23–24; Jay Adams was interviewed in the *New Wine* issue of April 1982, 5–8. See Adams "Crowns Out of Crosses"; C. Everett Koop was interviewed in *New Wine* July/Aug. 1980, "The Domino Effect" 9–14; 16–17; see also Koop, "Memorandum from C. Everett Koop," which hints at close coordination between Koop and *New Wine* while Koop was in office). Moore also acknowledges that Bob Weiner, an ICA apostle (see the 2010 "International Coalition of Apostles Membership Directory," 15), and Larry Tomczak became allies with the movement. Tomczak's People of Destiny International, besides launching Ché

Ahn and Lou Engle to fame, would eventually morph into Sovereign Grace Ministries (SGM), a Calvinist organization that would combine the worst of Charismatic shepherding practice with extreme forms of Calvinist church discipline and social control (Charlton, "A Church Group, a Lawsuit"; Weaver 112, 154–158). Not coincidentally, both Tomczak and Weiner are signatories of the COR Manifesto (Grimstead, "A Manifesto" 16). Dennis Peacocke, another ICA apostle, was also a signatory (see 2010 "International Coalition of Apostles Membership Directory" 11; Grimstead, "A Manifesto" 13–16), as was Ralph Winter, whose work at Fuller in many ways drew on some of the same church growth ideas as Wagner. Biggest of all these connections was C. Peter Wagner himself, who also was a signing member (Grimstead, "A Manifesto" 16).

These links were not merely coincidental. Dennis Peacocke was one of Bob Mumford's top disciples (Diamond, *Spiritual Warfare* 127). Peacocke was leader of a group of churches in northern California, as well as in New York State, Mexico, Hawaii, and possibly other locations. Peacocke was also on the board of advisors for the Family Christian Broadcasting Network, at the time led by Ronald Haus, a former Assembly of God minister (Diamond 27–28). In 1987, Haus had the infamous anti-gay researcher Paul Cameron on his show; Cameron promoted the idea that gay people engaged in "worldwide sex tours" in which they "ingested the feces and urine of homosexuals on different continents." Diamond notes that Haus nodded his approval throughout Cameron's diatribe (Diamond 101–102). Yet, Peacocke thought nothing of allying with Haus. Indeed, apparently neither did the rest of the Christian right, since Haus was also a signatory to the COR Manifesto (Grimstead, "A Manifesto" 14). In 1984, Peacocke would conduct a seminar featuring the infamous Guatemalan dictator Efrain Ríos Montt as well as a host of intelligence operatives. Peacocke was a key Christian right player in efforts to destabilize Nicaragua, in compliance with the United States's foreign policy objectives in the 1980s (Diamond, *Spiritual Warfare* 128).

COR included a number of Peacocke's allies. Peacocke was the secretary of the organization. Ronn Haus was its treasurer, and political strategist Colonel Doner[4] was a Director (Diamond 128). Jay Grimstead, the leader of Coalition on Revival, took Dennis Peacocke as his personal pastor, according to Colonel Doner's own account (Doner loc 163). Doner himself admits to being Peacocke's disciple as well (Doner loc 1973). At a 1986 COR convention, Grimstead argued that one of the organization's goals was to facilitate a way of unifying politically active fundamentalists and Charismatics who shared wildly differing beliefs about the End Times. Grimstead spent years helping develop the Worldview documents that became the basis of COR (Diamond 128). Diamond found an unpublished draft of COR's Manifesto for the Christian Church that called specifically for "home cell groups" of no more than 12 members, in which individuals were accountable to each other—given the involvement of so many shepherding gurus in COR, Diamond draws the fairly obvious and correct conclusion that this was an implementation of shepherding on a more massive scale. The COR document also "recommends that sheep be required to sign a legal statement to the effect that he or she will not take legal action if the church staff administers 'discipline—including public excommunication—for behavior deemed unbiblical'" (Diamond 129).[5] This form of covenantal contractualism with one's church has been in recent years implemented to enormously abusive effects (see Weaver 154–157; Demar and Doner 13).

As Diamond points out, the relationship of the shepherds and the Reconstructionists were unusually close. R.J. Rushdoony had appeared on Peacocke's Bottom Line program and was also a contributing editor for the shepherding magazine *New Wine*. The November 1986 issue of *New Wine* featured a "postmillennialist manifesto" by Rushdoony (Diamond 138). Colonel Doner, a COR steering member,[6] argued that the Christian Right required a two-part solution to fix its structural problems. The first part was that the movement needed to be able to "command complete and total loyalty and selfless dedication and sacrifice to its objectives on the part of its supporters." Secondly, Doner argued that all Christians be "active." As Frederick Clarkson notes, Doner was advocating a form of Reconstructionism implemented through shepherding practice (Clarkson 101). In September 1987, COR chief Jay Grimstead would seek to experiment with this policy by organizing a meeting in Santa Clara in order to "set up a 'pastors committee' for long-range social and political takeover" (Clarkson 101–102). Grimstead therefore proposed an elaborate program of grounding pastors in "COR-approved theology and shepherding techniques over 18 months" (Clarkson 101–102). Part of this policy, which would later be adopted by the NAR (see Tabachnick, "The Transformation Movement" 51; Tabachnick, "Anti-LGBTQ, Anti-Union"), would be running stealth candidates for positions (Clarkson 101–102).

The end result of all this Reconstructionist and shepherding cross-fertilization is that the COR documents ending up serving as among the "most important forces for the theological transformation of the [evangelical] movement" (Detwiler 136). Detwiler, while cautioning that COR's influence waned after Grimstead more openly united himself with Rushdoony, points out that COR's greatest influence on the evangelical movement was the "unequivocal manner in which it expressed the dominion principle and applied it to seventeen spheres of society" (Detwiler 136). Even after Grimstead's involvement with Rushdoony, however, COR's influence did not disappear. James Dobson, for instance, began moving closer to Howard Phillips's United States Taxpayers

Party in the mid 1990s, and Phillips was an avowed Reconstructionist. As a result Dobson's own political language took on a distinct dominionist air. Detwiler contends, undoubtedly correctly, that COR's enduring legacy and main contemporary influence at the time of *Standing on the Premises of God's* publication (1999), was the influence it exerted on "the ideational dimension of the movement." According to Detwiler, "most of the contemporary leaders [of the Christian right] have been shaped by participation in COR or by the adoption of COR's main principles" (Detwiler 137).

It would therefore be incredibly naïve, considering the widespread involvement of shepherding leaders in both COR and the NAR, to believe that the NAR was not influenced by Reconstructionist thinking, even if we had not already previously seen that Lance Wallnau, Johnny Enlow, Cindy Jacobs and C. Peter Wagner, among many other NAR leaders, openly borrow Reconstructionist-style language and—in the case of Wagner and Jacobs— openly cite Reconstructionist leaders (Jacobs, *Reformation Manifesto* 173, 215– 216 and Wagner, *Dominion*, 59). This is not to say that the movement's lay members are necessarily on board with Reconstructionist ideology; they may not be, and in some cases may be horrified by the level of Reconstructionist influence over the Charismatic movement. The problem is that the NAR, like the shepherding movement, is a movement that by self-definition is not controlled or even much influenced by its laity. Since power is in the hands of the apostles, it is unlikely that the movement will steer itself away from these early influences in the near future.

But this does not mean that the way these influences will be marketed will not change. As Detwiler points out, the "dominion principle" is the key aspect of the COR documents (Detwiler 136–137); what form that principle takes is relatively unimportant for the Christian Right leadership. Kyle Mantyla, a People For the American Way researcher for Right Wing Watch, has pointed out a key organizational element of the Christian right, which is the movement's ability to back itself up with multiple redundant organizations (Mantyla, "The Religious Right's Organizing Philosophy; Mantyla, "Unity Through Redundancy"). Mantyla's point is a salient one, because this redundancy extends not just to movement followers but even to its orienting philosophies.

For the Christian right, a key organizational principle is the ability to "rebrand" previous political philosophies into more socially acceptable ideologies that still have essentially the same message. The public, more "respectable" form of Christian dominionism today is a loose alliance of Christian Right mission specialists and business thinkers, most of whom have some ties with Fuller Seminary. There are three sub-movements within this respectable branding of "mainstreamed" dominionism that are worthy of note, particularly since they greatly influence both the NAR and the Christian Right as a whole: a group of missions specialists that have borrowed Schafferian language for a kind of dominionist overseas missions (their prime advocate is Darrow Miller); the Business as Mission Movement (BAM), and the Insider Movement (IM, also referred to as IMP). Because these movements are influenced by some of the same ideology and thinking as the NAR, and have also in turn occasionally influenced NAR thinking themselves, I will describe both the BAM model and Miler here as a way of showing how concepts developed in the NAR have affected a wide swathe of evangelicals. Since the Insider movement has a wider applicability to the NAR as a whole, particularly its view of race, I will wait till Chapter 6 to describe it.[7]

Darrow Miller is a Christian missiologist and co-founder of Disciple Nations Alliance (DNA) along with Bob Moffitt and Scott Allen ("Leadership" Disciple Nations Alliance). Miller was a fellow at the evangelical retreat L'Abri, and was mentored by Francis Schaeffer. He also served as a director of Baptist Student Union before joining Food for the Hungry in 1981 (Mei 306). During his time with Food for the Hungry (FFH), Miller helped articulate the Christian Right's current strategy towards missions and overseas development, a strategy that remains in place to this day. In a 1988 position paper that Diamond obtained, Miller spelled out his development philosophy. Underdevelopment, for Miller, had its "root in the minds and hearts of individuals and in the moral and ethical ideals of cultures" (Miller, "The Development Ethic" 17 qtd. in Diamond 226). Miller explicitly rejected development approaches that stressed economic inequalities or that promoted the need for developing countries to gain access to advanced technologies. Instead, FFH argued that "poverty is rooted in individuals' belief systems and, by extension, in cultures supposedly conducive to underdevelopment and poverty" (Diamond 226).

Miller divided the world into two sorts of ethics, the development ethic and the poverty ethic. The development ethic saw the universe as God-created, with "unlimited resources and unlimited human potential to harness nature." Cultures of poverty, by contrast, promoted the ideas that humans were "basically good and that evil is rooted in social institutions" (Diamond 226). Miller's philosophy was cornucopian—it saw the universe as possessing unlimited natural resources, which if exploited properly could provide for everyone. He therefore explicitly rejected arguments grounded in materialist theories of development which argued that natural resources are finite; for Miller, theories that blamed problems "extrinsic to man" ultimately either fell into the "evolutionist" or the "revolutionist" trap. The former promoted Social Darwinism and eugenic policies, while the latter promoted revolution against imperialism (Miller, *Discipling Nations* loc 648–688). For Miller, poverty had little to do with structural or societal problems. Instead, the problem was people's worldviews.

Borrowing from his mentor Francis Schaeffer, whose "Christian worldview theory" was one of the organizing ideological paradigms of the religious right, Miller argued that worldviews were responsible for poverty. According to Miller, God "did not create poverty; man did. The problem is usually rooted in mindsets that retard and resist development, trapping people in destitution." But whereas Schaeffer would likely have had qualms about attaching a demonic explanation to poverty, Miller is happy to oblige, arguing that the poverty mindset and its values are "lies, and they ultimately come from the devil…. Aiding and abetting Satan in his deceptions are other malevolent spiritual beings, referred to in the Bible as principalities and powers" (Miller, *Discipling Nations* loc 760–765). Miller promotes the idea that Satan uses "spiritual principalities and powers," which he also refers to by the Greek word *stoicheion*, to "enslave whole cultures in webs of lies" which impact people not only morally or spiritually but at the "social, economic, and political" level (Miller loc 765–770). Thus, Miller, though allying with much more moderate evangelicals than those who make up the NAR, uses many of the same spiritual and political concepts that inform NAR thinking. Sara Diamond, more than two decades ago, pointed out scathingly that "Miller argues that the Africans are poor not because of concrete factors like faulty irrigation practices that make land barren, but rather because they have wrong thoughts" (Diamond, *Spiritual Warfare* 227). But the situation's actually worse—increasingly the poor are seen as not merely having bad thoughts, but demonized ones as well. Miller's worldview, as Diamond suggests, gives Christian right development agencies the impetus to think that they have the moral duty to "attack the belief systems of other societies" (Diamond 227).

One absolutely key part to understanding Miller's missions' agenda has been his promotion of holistic ministry (Miller, *Discipling the Nations* Foreword). Yujun Mei, one of the few academics who has studied Miller's ideas in any depth, tends to view this holistic ministry positively, not questioning FFH's Ted Yamamori's assertion that an earlier formulation of holistic ministry—symbiotic ministry—is simply a combination of Christian social action and evangelism (Mei 262). According to Yujun Mei, the concept of holistic ministry, was growing in Christian development circles during the late 1980s and early 1990s (Mei 304). As part of this growth, in the late 1980s, the Villars conference was held. *The Stewardship Journal* was also developed in order to promote an explicitly Christian view of relief and development. Holistic ministry emphasized that doing both physical and spiritual ministry were interlinked and important (304).

According to Yujun Mei the Samaritan strategy developed by Food for the Hungry "asserts that Christ's Great Commission in Matthew 28:18–20 is holistic. It is comprehensive and intended to impact all aspects of life and all levels of society as Jesus Christ is not just the King of future [sic]. He is the King now, and He is the Lord of heaven and earth: the Biblical Truth (the Biblical Worldview) can transform lives, cultures, and entire nations" (Mei 343). Such language is self-evidently dominionist, but replaces words like dominion, with transform. Holistic ministry thereby becomes a kind of internationalist dominionism, under the cloak of missiological theory.

The genius of the holistic model is that it promotes an idea that sounds like some self-help model of self-actualization, while actually promoting a rhetoric steeped in dominionist assumptions. Development, according to Yamamori, must be social, physical, and spiritual, and must also promote wisdom. However, according to Yamamori true cultural development requires "transformation"—a change of the individual's "heart." If such a change does not happen, countries will actually be more harmed than helped by development, even if it helps the "purses" of the people within these countries (Mei 340). Thus, for Yamamori, societies can only be transformed if individual hearts are transformed—thus neatly merging the rhetoric of American self-actualization with the Christian rhetoric of cultural dominion and manifest destiny.

Miller's book *Discipling the Nations* (2011), similarly, though not advocating violence as in the Reconstructionist model, openly uses dominionist language, referring to human beings as god's "vice-regents" on earth, whose responsibility is to spread "a gospel that includes but goes beyond evangelism and discipleship into nation building" (Miller loc 3412–3413). What Miller does is replace the Calvinist Kuyperian language of God's sovereignty, with the secular sounding euphemism of God's holistic ministry to the whole person, or the whole society. Kuyper advocated "the sovereignty of Christianity into all areas of public life" (Detwiler 106), just as Miller advocates the holistic ministry of God to every aspect of the person, community and nation (Miller loc 4352–4357). However, while Kuyper's approach was clearly not theocratic (Detwiler 106), its gradual adoption and modification by many members of the religious right, including Schaeffer and Rushdoony, often had such overtones. Given his mentoring by Schaeffer, who was somewhat, if not totally, enamored with Rushdoony (see Hankins 193–194; see also McVicar 308–309), it is doubtful that Miller means anything different by the term "holistic" than dominionism, though admittedly Miller may not want to see dominionism implemented to the degree promoted by Christian Reconstructionists.

Miller's form of transformationalism is important for a number of reasons.

First, it is seen as a perfectly valid and respectable ideology within evangelical circles, a safe transformationalism that lacks the kind of extremist pedigree that characterizes the NAR. Miller's book *Discipling the Nations* is recommended by two heavyweight evangelical leaders, Marvin Olasky, editor of the immensely influential *World Magazine* and the late Edith Schaeffer, whose reputation among evangelicals was scarcely less than that of Billy Graham at the time of her passing (Miller, *Discipling the Nations* Recommendations). Olasky and Schaeffer are Reformed royalty, which shows just how interconnected the evangelical movement now is, as Miller himself has also drawn himself into extensive links with the more Charismatically-aligned YWAM ministries.[8]

Secondly, Miller-style transformationalism helps soft-sell more hard-core NAR and Reconstructionist concepts under a safe, non-threatening umbrella. Those evangelicals or other conservative Christians who would be put off by the spiritual elitism and outward fanaticism of the NAR may find the faux social-justice rhetoric of Miller's holistic Samaritan strategy[9] to be a more appealing entry point into Christian right organizing than, say, Mike Bickle's IHOP ministry. In other words, just as there are different brands of apostolic networks for different individuals, there are also different branded economic ideologies that individuals within the Christian Right can today choose from, depending on their personality preference.

Finally, and most importantly, Miller's form of transformationalism represents the new direction of Christian right missions' strategy. Bruce Wilson, writing at the *Huffington Post*, has pointed out to me at least three major benefits of this kind of missions strategy for the Christian right. First, it furthers, U.S. foreign policy objectives. Secondly, it helps rebrand U.S., including U.S. missions, policy, from its formerly acknowledged status as a neocolonial ideology to a new form of "compassionate conservatism," in which local, small-scale economic development is emphasized, but where, as we have seen with Miller, there is still the idea that having a wrong culture/ideology/religion (as in Miller's or Reformed theology) or carrying generational curses (as with the NAR) is responsible for the victimization of colonized peoples. Thirdly, this policy is aimed at establishing "neoliberal privatization" through evangelical missions work (Bruce Wilson, personal email 12 Nov. 2013).

The Christian Right uses a number of ideological tools to accomplish these goals. One of the most formidable is the recent development of the Business as Missions movement (BAM). Charles Neal Johnson, one of the movement's major theorists and the author if its first comprehensive textbook, emphasizes the BAM movement's need to minister to each person "as a whole human being and by trying to address all of their pain." This can occur through "Jesus-centered prayer counseling and deep healing ministries" as well through the promotion of "international and economic development." Significantly, Johnson cites Charles Kraft and his own wife Frecia Johnson as important voices in the inner healing movement. Kraft, as we have seen, helped start the NAR; Frecia Johnson's doctoral work was considered important enough to warrant having Doris Wagner as an outside reader, and Frecia Johnson speaks of Kraft as a mentor (Frecia Johnson, title page vi; Charles Neal Johnson, "God's Mission to, Within, and Through the Marketplace" 103). Johnson also supports the use of spiritual warfare principles in business; given his wife's extensive writing on inner healing and her connections with high-placed NAR leaders, it would be foolish not to believe that her husband does not share a similar relationship to the NAR as well (see Charles Neal Johnson, *Business as Mission: A Comprehensive Guide* loc 1678–1680).

But what is the BAM model exactly? Charles Neal Johnson defines it as "a for-profit commercial business venture that is Christian led, intentionally devoted to being used as an instrument of God's mission ... to the world, and is operated in a crosscultural environment, either domestic or international" (Charles Neal Johnson, *Business as Mission: A Comprehensive Guide* loc 298–300). The important element here, from a theoretical standpoint, is that these are for-profit missions ventures. Such ventures are by no means totally unknown. Many evangelicals have for a long time supported what are called tentmaker ministries, where evangelical missionaries serve as professionals in other countries to gain evangelism opportunities. The difference between the BAM model and the tentmaker model is small, but crucial. Tentmakers are missionaries serving as business professionals; in the BAM model, one sees businessmen as missionaries. Thus capitalism becomes the means by which both the Good Book and the pocketbook are spread throughout the world. The idea in both models is for missions specialists to "serve" the community they are in, rather than be foreigners who serves no useful purpose to the community.[10]

Proponents of the BAM model (also known as the kingdom business model) argue that economic activity and missions activity should be integrated holistically. Business, they contend, is a divine calling, one that be honored. The BAM model creates overseas opportunities for spiritual (not to mention capital) advancement, because business owners are able to spread Christianity through their corporate endeavors, to people and to nations that might otherwise be unreachable (Wamutitu 164).

The BAM movement sees business as a means of developing networks of relationship that can play a vital importance in promoting Christian "witness and influence." These relational matrixes can involve shareholders, customers, suppliers and employees or can extend to other cultures and nations (Wamutitu 165).

Wamutitu argues that while a good concept, the BAM model is too westernized and has little help to offer churches in the developing world because of its over-reliance on "medium sized if not big business enterprises" (Wamutitu 168). Wamutitu also faults the BAM model for its cash-based assumptions, rooted in capitalistic mindsets. As he points out, many non-cash based societies do not have the capability of realizing the kind of profits envisioned by the BAM model (Wamutitu 169). Not surprisingly, he also sees the potential for imperialistic abuse in the BAM model:

> Finally business as mission, if not watched, can be a modern way of imperialism. Establishing large companies and running them in foreign countries can easily take advantage of the poor who may just provide labor with little pay and less decision making. Unless these businesses have a way of training and elevating local people to positions of leadership, and eventually make them partners in these companies, it will be another western expansion in foreign countries [Wamutitu 153].

The BAM model in many ways suffers from the same structural flaws that underlie the similar marketplace missions (MM) movement. In both the MM and BAM model, it is assumed that corporate leaders will look out for the good of their employees, apparently out of some sense of Christian *noblesse oblige*. Since in this Christian utopian relationship, there will no longer be as strained a relationship between employers and employees, increased workplace harmony will benefit both parties in the marketplace relationship. But this concept of economics is grounded in the assumption that employers and employees are driven by the same economic motives and are subject to the same economic laws. It totally ignores the vast power imbalances that exist between these groups of individuals.

There will, of course, always be ethical employers who are willing to sacrifice for the good of their employees. However, capitalism dictates they will be rare, because the nature of capitalism is predicated on enhancing profit and lowering production costs, both factors which lead to a need to periodically depreciate wages in order for businesses to maximize their profitability. Moreover, while there is absolutely no problem with being a Christian employer, the problems of employers proselytizing their workers are very much like those of superior officers doing the same with their military subordinates. Because of the gross power imbalances present, there is inherent potential for abuse that BAM supporters simply ignore.

The BAM model promotes a number of different development strategies, though ideologically many of these strategies have their foundational grounding in either Miller's "holistic" transformationalism or Silvoso's more popular NAR-inspired transformationalism.[11] Perhaps the one that has gained the most attention is microenterprise development, specifically Christian microenterprise development. MED is a developmental strategy that focuses on providing a wide range of financial services (savings, credit and insurance), as well as other business development services (business training, marketing assistance, etc.) in order to "help" entrepreneurs and the poor enhance their own productive abilities (Wamutitu 167). Christian microenterprise Development (CMED), borrowing from Miller and Yamomami, approaches development "holistically," with a strong emphasis on the role of the local church in poverty alleviation. This holistic understanding of poverty means that poverty is interpreted "not only from a socio-economic perspective but also from a spiritual perspective" (Wamutitu 168). The problem is that if we do live in a material universe, then such spiritual interpretations for economic inequity are absolutely useless to alleviating poverty; and even if we do not live in such a universe, the justifications for economic inequity used by both CMED-proponents and their ideological supporters among "holistic" transformationalists are little better than those advanced by neo-conservatives.

CMED organizations see themselves as missionaries to the "unbankable." Typically, CMED organizations aim themselves at the level just above the "poorest of the poor" (Eldred 184–186). Yet there are basic conflicts between the CMED model's missional goal and its simultaneous desire to be a profit-making enterprise. In CMED development (as in secular MED development), management ultimately "determines the extent to which such organizations succeed in reaching the entrepreneurial poor and also their sustainability over time" (Wamutitu 176). Wamutitu points out that a crucial byproduct of this model is that the success or failure of CMED's should be judged not solely by "effective loan repayment strategies but also their ability to reach the very poor." Therefore, CMEDs walk a tightrope between offering affordable services, "ministering" to the poor, and remaining "sustainable if not profitable" enterprises (Wamutitu 176).

Wamutitu illustrates this point by referencing the exorbitant interest rates NAR funder and business guru Ken Eldred advocates in CMED enterprises, which are often as high as 36 percent (Eldred 186, Wamutitu 176). Eldred realizes that such interest rates could be considered usury in the West (Eldred 186), but argues that "MED clients are all too happy to accept these lending conditions, and there is no shortage of potential borrowers" (Eldred, *God Is at Work*, 187). Of course, the fact that there is demand for such exploitative loans in the developing world is not a moral justification for charging such high rates. Wamutitu, himself a native of Kenya, clearly sees Eldred's justification as problematic, asking, "Are MEDs which are claiming to be serving the poor taking advantage of them given that the poor are vulnerable with limited choices and options? ... Since the poor often do not have access to normal banking services, their choices are limited. It is either they accept the high rates offered by the MEDS or be at the mercy of exorbitant money lenders" (Wamutitu 194). Wamutitu, not necessarily an opponent of either MEDs or the BAM model, nevertheless points out that he met a number of Nairobi pastors who lamented the high interest rates that MEDs were charging in Kenya. MEDs may therefore be popular among Kenya's poor, but mainly because, as Wamutitu points out, they are the "only option they [the poor] have" not because the poor are happy with them (Wamutitu 177–178).

The CMED model, as well the BAM movement, in a very tragic way, actually prove the wisdom of the salvific figure who inspired them. Jesus told us that the poor we would always have with us. The problem is that 2000 years of conservative Christian religion have taken that as a prophecy. But, if one takes Christ's words as wisdom from the heavens, there is another interpretation that could be suggested for them.

They could have been a warning.

Conclusion

As we have seen, the economic and social justice ideology of the NAR, not surprisingly, is largely in keeping with that of the wider religious right. While the NAR, and its allies among BAM and holistic missions' proponents can find endless ways of spinning dominionist language, the end result is still the same. Little of the NAR's economic philosophy conflicts with the aims of the Religious Right, though there is some reason to hope that corporate leaders may ultimately find its more bizarre manifestations—such as the "great wealth transfer"—antithetical to the furtherance of global business interests.

Perhaps more unusual than the NAR's view on economics, however, and certainly as dangerous globally, is the NAR's idiosyncratic view of race. We will see that NAR racial ideas distinguish the movement's beliefs from mainstream Americans like almost no other aspect of their beliefs. Yet this is not the typical racism associated with more fundamentalist aspects of the religious right, nor is the NAR the pluralistic paradise its proponents claim it to be. In reality it is both these things, a pluralistic racism or a racist pluralism if you will, and for the NAR the union of these two ideals is anything but impossible.

5

The NAR and Race
When Race Isn't Race (But Is)

The NAR's approach to race is both complicated and easily misunderstood. What is interesting about the NAR and its views of race is that in the NAR, race is no longer solely determined by the color of one's skin, apparent physical difference between ethnic groups, nor by traditional ethnological or anthropological concepts, but is instead dependent on one's allegiance to Christianity.[1] According to the NAR, if one is a true Christian one has the right kind of spiritual DNA. In NAR apostle Bill Hamon's words, one is a member of the "church race" (Hamon, *Prophetic Scriptures* 77). All those who do not subscribe to Christianity are members of an ultimately-to-be-defeated non-church race. Thus, racial conflict continues to be cast as a ruthless battle for power, even as the NAR positions itself as a post-racial group, with race not being defined by the color of one's skin, but the content of one's Christianity.

Generational Curses and Genetics

One figure absolutely crucial to understanding the rise of both the NAR and its view of race is William Branham. Branham's concept of "transgenerational demon possession," now typically known as "generational curses" (Collins 30) is foundational to NAR racial views. A fairly typical explanation of generational curses—here referred to as "Sins of the Fathers"—is given in Chester and Betsy Kylstra's *Restoring the Foundations*: "'Sins of the Fathers' represents the accumulation of all sins committed by our ancestors. It is the heart tendency (iniquity) that we inherit from our forefathers to rebel ... against God's laws and commandments. It is the propensity to sin, particularly in ways that represent perversion and twisted character. The accumulation continues until God's conditions

5. The NAR and Race

for repentance are met" (Kylstra and Klystra 104). For the Klystras, these sins of the father (or for other Pentecostals and Charismatics, simply generational curses) can be passed down through a number of means, including environment, genes, and through demonic inheritance (Kylstra and Kylstra 124–125).

What is crucial to understand here is that curses and demonic inheritance are often seen as mimicking or interacting with genetic and environmental factors as well. For instance, the Kylstras argue that sins of the father can alter genes themselves, causing changes to "the gene structure and order" (Kylstra and Klystra 124–125). Similarly, the Kylstras believe that "some demons apparently come down the family line. They often manifest soon after birth. We suspect that they are present even as the child is being formed" (Kylstra and Kylstra 279). Thus, for the Kylstras, demonic inheritance is seen as operating in a manner exactly analogous to that of genetics. Just as genetic factors like alcoholism, mental illness, and physical infirmities can be seen as being passed down the family line, so too can the demons who Pentecostals and Charismatics believe are responsible for these physical impairments.

Branham's concept of the serpent seed, though not explicitly adopted by most of those who subscribe to the ideology of the NAR, has in recent years also come to have an important influence on NAR views of race. As we have seen, this doctrine taught that Eve had sex with the serpent in garden, splitting the human race. The descendants of Cain were responsible for "the educational system ... and scientific development" and masqueraded today as "the educated and the scientists" (Weaver 113). By contrast, the "predestined believer" was heir to the "godly seed" (Weaver 123). As C. Douglas Weaver points out, Branham's theory of religious salvation was essentially genoist. Branham "was actually asserting that simple genetics determined one's eternal destiny" (Weaver 123). If one possessed the serpent's seed, one was destined to damnation, while the "heirs of Seth's seed [i.e., the godly seed] were bound for glory" (Weaver 123). Therefore, for Charismatics and Pentecostals who adopted elements of Branham's theology, particularly those NAR apostles closely associated with the Latter Rain revival, there was an implicitly racialized element of theology that came to characterize NAR theology, as it had the Latter Rain. This racial element however was not based on racial divisions defined by ethnic or color distinctions, but instead was based on divisions that arose between the saved and the damned. Crucially, there was often a note of genetic supremacism in these distinctions, as the "manifest sons" of God, or the "church-race," became the possessors of extraordinary powers unavailable to the racially "normal" (ordinary non–NAR Christians) or racial subnormals (the "damned").

Direct espousal of "Manifest Sons" and "church-race" theology is currently risky for NAR apostles, due to the attention the movement has recently received in secular quarters.[2] This has not stopped prominent supporters of the NAR from publicly aligning themselves with elements of "Manifest Sons" or "church race" theology, most notably those elements of the NAR most closely linked with the Kansas City prophets: leaders like Paul Cain, Bob Jones, and also major apostle Bill Hamon. However, one of the prime means of transmission of this ideology today is the seemingly innocuous description of "spiritual DNA" within Charismatic circles. This concept, goes by a variety of names—"apostolic DNA," "spiritual DNA," "Nazarite DNA," and so on—but the basic idea in all of these concepts is the same. While no one in the NAR has really provided a definitive explanation of this concept, probably the best description is provided by Ché Ahn, who writes that "I no longer merely confess that I am the righteousness of Christ. I realize that with His DNA in me through His blood, I could be nothing else. I realize the attributes of His DNA reside in me—whether dormant or active" (Ahn "Spiritual DNA"). For Ahn, therefore, there is a distinct genetic-like component to spirituality. Christ's DNA gives a Christian "supernatural DNA," but this DNA's power is predicated on one following the promptings of the Holy Spirit (Ahn, "Spiritual DNA").

Moreover, this spiritual DNA is subject to some of the same environmental influences that can in the popular imagination harm biological DNA as well. For instance, Ahn writes, "Just as there are anomalies and mutations in DNA that bring forth destruction and disease, we, too, must walk in the Spirit to maintain the purity of our distinct spiritual heritage" (Ahn, "Spiritual DNA"). For Ahn, there is a threat of spiritual devolution, of "church-racial" degeneration every bit as real to him as the threat of biological devolution envisioned in H.G. Wells's *The Time Machine* (1895). This devolution comes not from biological degeneracy, but from spiritual degeneracy that corrupts the spiritual genome of the Christian people. Though the church cannot ultimately and totally be corrupted in NAR thinking, spiritual devolution on an individual or corporate level slows the progression of the saints to their end times apotheosis.

Such DNA talk is common throughout NAR literature. For instance, C. Peter Wagner has frequently invoked the spiritual DNA concept. In *Apostles Today* (2006), Wagner uses the concept of spiritual DNA to explain the spiritual gift of evangelism, noting that "the gift of evangelist, therefore, becomes a personal attribute, a part of their [ministers'] *constitution*, their 'spiritual DNA'" (Wagner, *Apostles Today* 54). In *Churchquake!* (1999), one of the definitive NAR theoretical texts, Wagner quotes approvingly from Leo Lawson's description of Morning Star International, which Lawson says has "a spiritual DNA that is shared among those in our particular 'family' of churches.... The 'father' of the apostolic family ... is seen as imparting his spiritual DNA to those joined to him, and those joined to him see themselves as sharing both a common history as well as a common destiny" (Lawson 38 qtd. in Wagner, *Churchquake!* 119–120). Wagner also states that "there is great diversity among new apostolic churches. Each network has a distinctive DNA as a component of the whole Body of Christ" (Wagner, *Churchquake!* 63). To understand the importance of Wagner's support of the spiritual DNA concept one must first understand two things. First of all, one must realize the by now obvious influence Wagner has on the NAR. For Wagner to endorse the spiritual DNA idea means it has strong support from the apostles.

Secondly one must understand the concept of "spiritual fatherhood" which is becoming an increasingly important reason for the promotion of spiritual DNA and Latter Rain ideology within the NAR. The NAR's belief in the return of the apostolic office to the church is incredibly important. As René Holvast relates, the

> essential difference between the NAR and the traditional denominational churches concerned leadership and governance. The NAR was led not by a group but by an individual apostle. It was this divinely appointed apostle, as opposed to a board or a presbytery, a democratic vote or institution who was seen bearing responsibility for making decisions and guiding adherents [Holvast 158–159].

What has given the NAR its enormous organizational advantage over traditional mainstream churches has been its ability to mobilize people through transdenominational, translocal groups that focus on relational networks, rather than denominations, as their chief organizing component (Wagner, *Churchquake!* 126–127). As we have seen, because an apostle could act quickly, effectively, and (if necessary) outside denominational bounds, new apostolic churches proved to be highly adaptive in their responses to changing cultural situations.

The spiritual DNA concept helps further the idea of apostolic government because it promotes the idea that apostles are the spiritual "parents," often referred to (when male) as "spiritual daddies," of those under their leadership. Thus, those who possess the same spiritual DNA share a common familial and spiritual destiny, a spiritual manifest destiny, in which they will come into the spiritual inheritance of the Christian people. The concept of spiritual fatherhood thus allows the apostles of the NAR to position themselves as leaders of great, almost dictatorial, authority, whose commands are to be obeyed quickly and without question, since they contribute to the continued prosperity of one's spiritual *volk*.[3]

Simultaneously, the promotion of spiritual DNA concepts also helps further the agenda of those apostles who want to more aggressively market "Manifest Sons" ideology to a wider evangelical movement which is uncomfortable with Latter Rain theology, but is intrigued by pseudoscientific discussions of spiritual and supernatural DNA. Thus, it is not surprising that many apostles now employ discussions of spiritual DNA. Ed Silvoso, warns of the dangers of the "[spiritual] DNA first exhibited at Babel" (Silvoso 192). Dutch Sheets has stated that "we are descended from a king, Jesus, Creator and Lord over all, so it logically follows that deep in our DNA we have a desire and ability to rule" (Sheets 13). Dr. Francis Myles, another influential apostle, is one of the most explicit promoters of spiritual DNA concepts today. His book, *The Order of Melchizedek* (2010), is full of these references, and Myles is quite open in his linking of spiritual DNA to "Manifest Sons" theology:

> We have already established the fact that the New Creation is the spiritual identity of Kingdom citizens or what the Bible calls the manifest sons of God. The apostle Paul goes a step further in identifying or decoding the spiritual DNA of the new creation. Saint Paul calls this new nature the one new man and explains that God has abolished the cultural divisions of race, gender, and pedigree in the lives of those who are members of the new creation [Myles 286].

Myles's perception of NAR theology is particularly important to understanding why this theological system has been relatively successful at gaining non-white adherents. Myles is a black man from Zambia, while Silvoso is an Argentine (Sheets and Wagner are both white Americans). To those from outside the West, the gospel of "manifest sons" ideology sounds radically inclusive, destroying divisions of race, gender, class, and social distinction for the simple division between manifest sons, "normal" Christians, and the damned. For Myles what Manifest Sons theology promotes is nothing less than the kind of post-racial world envisioned by President Obama's more naive supporters. Thus, the promise of spiritual DNA is that it will unite the races together, grafting everyone "genetically" on to one racial branch in a way that more political visions of racial inclusiveness could not.

What is problematic is that while the NAR to a certain extent promotes itself as a racially inclusive ideological and organizational system, this is not always how the NAR operates in practice, nor how the ideology's long term cultural implications are likely to develop. Because NAR theology operates under a distinct vision of both race and demonic forces, it will ultimately be the confluence of these forces that proves to be the danger for all Americans, regardless of ethnic identity, who do not belong to the Christian *ethne* that is being promoted by the NAR.

Lou Engle's the Call: Nazirite DNA

Because of Lou Engle's prominence and relative openness about his allegiances to NAR ideology, his teachings are a good place to start in seeing how

DNA concepts are being employed within the NAR. Engle readily acknowledges the influence of Franklin Hall's *Atomic Power with God Through Prayer and Fasting* (1946), as well as the Latter Rain Revival that that work spawned, over his view of America (see Engle, *Digging the Wells* 5–6). That influence is easily seen, since Engle's book *Digging the Wells of Revival* (1999), a work explicitly about his NAR/Latter Rain derived view of fasting, has an entire chapter entitled "Atomic Power Through Prayer and Fasting" (see Engle, *Digging the Wells* 145–156).

Engle's view of race is embodied in his concept of "Nazirite DNA." Engle literally uses the term Nazirite DNA in an audiobook entitled "Nazirite DNA" (Engle, "Nazirite DNA"). Initially, the book does not seem to an outsider to have much to do with DNA, as DNA is not mentioned at all after the title. In reality, however, concepts of genetic salvation permeate the sermon. Engle states, "Whenever the Nation of Israel came under the Covenant of judgment of God, the divine prescription was to gather the consecrated ones to fast and pray in the day of trouble" (Engle, "Nazirite DNA"). Thus, the DNA of the Nazirite is consecrated spiritual DNA, the DNA of a spiritual elite willing to risk all for the Christian cause. Nazirite DNA is activated by extreme acts of fanaticism for the Christian religion. Crucial to affecting society for good or evil, is the way "entire generations risk everything to become the hinge of history" (Engle, "Nazirite DNA"). Though Engle promotes the viability of all age groups in Christian ministry, his particular form of activism centers on the young, and so he (like many participants in the NAR) promotes the idea that the forthcoming generations will be especially consecrated to God (hence his activism to the young in *Jesus Camp*).[4]

Engle, like NAR leaders in general, promotes the idea of a multiracial church united by theology, rather than divided into rival ethnic groups. Engle proclaims that

> in the Nazirite vow, God opened the door to anyone, male or female, from any tribe, who longed to be as radical in devotion and near to God as the priests were. The only qualification was to have a heart that intensely desired it. Nazirite consecration was not reserved for an elite club or a select few, but was an open invitation to anyone with a desperately hungry heart. No one was excluded or disqualified because of who they were [Engle, "Nazirite DNA"].

For Engle, therefore, being a Nazirite, possessing that DNA, is not explicitly about race. Entrance into the spiritual elite is not even about intelligence or social class, but is instead a process open to anyone of sufficient spiritual fanaticism. This is a conservative populist vision of Christian belief, one that fits well with America's Protestant tradition. It is therefore, fundamentally an *American vision* of spiritual unity, with the implicit racial assumptions of conservative American populists built into it. Foremost of these assumptions is that the ideal society is "color blind," a spiritual melting pot where everyone is judged by the same spiritual standard, regardless of culture, race, or social class. Only one judgment factor is relevant—one's commitment to Christ—and there are, as is typical in American racial politics, no excuses for those who fall short of the Judge's standards. For Engle, spiritual exclusiveness comes from cultural inclusiveness. Despite his claims, therefore the way of the Nazirite is quite clearly an elitist call, but the destiny of a Nazirite is determined not by his biological DNA—the Darwinian survival of the fittest model—but by the individual's spiritual DNA—the Christian survival of the fittest model.

Not only does Engle use biological and pseudo-racial terms in his description of Nazirite DNA, but his conceptualization of that idea takes on distinct elements of racial apocalyptic rhetoric. Engle, in his book *The Call Revolution* (co-written with Ché Ahn) (2001), writes:

> The Nazirites were not balanced. The extreme spiritual decline of the times called for an extreme reaction that was marked by holy violence.... A holy war has begun! Nazi or Nazirite? Satan is marching forward with a generation of skinheads, no hairs, willing to lay down their lives for the promotion of death and destruction. But God is summoning a counter youth culture—an extreme generation of longhairs who will sacrifice everything to promote love and life [Ahn and Engle, *The Call Revolution* 30].

Engle's pronouncements here are paradoxical in the extreme. Engle promotes the idea that his movement is fighting Nazi extremism through its own form of holy extremism. While Engle has been careful to note publicly that the term "spiritual violence" he does not mean "literal violence," there are very good reasons for seeing this claim as somewhat disingenuous (Engle, "A Global Prayer Movement"). As reporter Josh Kron of *The New York Times* notes, Engle backed the controversial death-to-gays bill in Uganda—coming out with a statement against the bill only to praise Ugandan pastors and politicians for their "courage" and "righteousness" in promoting the legislation (Kron). The casting of secular opponents of evangelicalism in Nazistic terms is also quite ironically a way of dehumanizing cultural opponents. To cast one's opponent as a Nazi, post–Holocaust, is to say that they are not worthy of being listened to or even respected, even if the oppositional ideology one dismisses is in fact in no ways similar to Nazism. Among the evils that Ahn and Engle condemn are abortion and homosexuality (Ahn and Engle 36–37, 41), even as they also condemn the sin of racism as well, in favor of "color blindness" (Ahn and Engle 45–46). Thus, the Nazis here are not Germans, and the Jews are not Jews. Instead, the oncoming apocalyptic race war is cast as a combat between militant skinheads, and the culture of abortion and homosexuality that promotes their ideology (here representatives of the old forms of racial identity) and the long-haired Nazirites, whose culture represents the new form of racial color-blind identity found in Christ.

Before moving on to Wendy Alec's *Chronicles of Brothers* series, one should note the oddly predestinarian elements of Engle's thought. By and large, the Charismatic and Pentecostal movements have rejected predestinarian thinking, though Pentecostal and Charismatic scholars have noted (correctly) that there was considerably more Calvinist influence on the movement than is commonly supposed. Reformed revivalism, particularly the influential though often maligned Keswick movement (which in its inception, at least was Reformed), played an important influence on early Pentecostal teaching (Allan Anderson 28–30). Though explicit endorsements of Calvinistic theology are still somewhat of a rarity in NAR circles, the NAR has inherited from both the Keswick movement and the often strangely Calvinistic thought of Branham (see Weaver 121–123 on Branham's view of Calvinism) its belief in "restorationism."

Anti–Quiverfull advocate Cynthia (Cindy) Kunsman has criticized elements of the Quiverfull movement for what she has termed "spiritual eugenics"—that is "those who view the Calvinistic concepts of grace and limited atonement as a means to justify cruel behavior toward those whom they esteem to be error, assuming that those persons are non-elect and therefore hated by God" (Kunsman). Essentially what Kunsman is pointing out—quite correctly—is how modern Calvinist theology and social Darwinist thinking resemble each other in their application of "tooth and claw" ideology to social, religious and economic models of cultural development. Because of the Latter Rain movement's similar application of Calvinistic ideas of spiritual determinism—here cast not in explicitly Calvinistic terms, but in the spiritual-racial ideology of Manifest Sons and "spiritual DNA"—it is appropriate to apply that term to the NAR as well. There is a danger in any spiritually eugenicist system—just as there is in racial eugenics—for the "elect" or "chosen" people to decide that ultimately their opponents are evolutionarily or spiritually unfit. Therefore, ironically, the supposed Nazistic elements Engle sees as implicit in secularism are themselves glaringly obvious in NAR thinking as a whole. And the very racial elitism that Engle so rightly condemns is actually merely translated into spiritual terms in his own belief system. The non–NAR observer should be pardoned if they do not see this as much of an improvement on traditional racialist ideology, because it is not.

Wendy Alec's Chronicles of Brothers: Revenge of the Serpent Seed Doctrine

Wendy Alec's *Chronicles of Brothers* series is an important text to understanding the NAR, despite its semi-self-published status.[5] Alec is the co-founder of God-TV, a 24-hour-a-day Christian network that has a potential audience of up to 200 million viewers in 212 nations ("Rory and Wendy Alec: God TV"). God TV is incorporated in the U.S. as a nonprofit group under the appellation Angel Christian Television Trust. One of its directors includes Francis Frangipane, a fairly prominent participant in the NAR, and the network has close ties with NAR leader Mike Bickle.[6] Alec, in other words, is no small player in evangelical power politics.

The concept of spiritual DNA in Alec's books takes on frightening aspects of racialist ideology in ways unseen in other NAR material. This is all the more telling because of Alec's relatively mainstream position within the contemporary Charismatic movement. Essentially, *The Chronicles of Brothers* tells the story of two sets of three brothers each. The first set is the angelic brothers, Michael, Gabriel, and Lucifer. The second set is the fictionally prominent 21st century de Vere brothers: Adrian de Vere, Nick de Vere, and Jason de Vere. Lucifer starts off the *Chronicles of Brothers* as a surprisingly sympathetic character, till his fear of humanity's usurpation of angelic prerogatives warps his mind and leads him to commit himself to a racial and spiritual conflict against humanity in which he attempts to corrupt the human genome; at each attempt, his brothers, with the blessing of Christos (Christ) and God, attempt to stop him. This conflict eventually culminates in the battle between Adrian de Vere (the anti–Christ) and his brothers during the End Times for control of the planet.

What is notable about this series of novels is the totally explicit racial manner in which the conflicts within them are framed. Lucifer's rebellion is motivated explicitly by his fear that "devastation" will fall upon the "angelic race" if God is allowed to continue creating human beings, as the "race of men" will "supplant our own" (Alec, *Fall of Lucifer*, 85). Lucifer is deeply jealous of humanity because they have been given "His [God's] genetic code" which God is "duplicating ... in matter" (Alec, *Fall of Lucifer* 83). For Lucifer, this is offensive both because angels do not have God's genetic code and because Lucifer sees the duplication of God's image in human beings as a challenge to the spiritual prerogatives of the angelic race. Lucifer warns his fellow angels of the coming racial apocalypse between humanity and the angelic hosts, stating, "Think of that very day and that very hour when this new race [humans] shall invade and occupy our own angelic sanctuary—and desecrate all that is pure and holy and sacred with their inferior creation" (Alec, *Fall of Lucifer* 95). Lucifer thus sees the conflict between angels and human beings as explicitly a racial one, one in which spiritual beings (the angelic) face off against human beings, who are a fusion of the spiritual and material. And the conflict, as in all racial apocalypses, is cast in terms of purity and holiness. The sacredness of the angelic "blood" is what is at stake.

Lucifer is of course the evil figure in the novel, yet his fears of racial supplanting also in some ways mirror that of colonized peoples throughout history. A critical reader can easily sympathize with Lucifer because clearly the goal of *The Chronicle of Brothers* is to promote the idea that Lucifer's "race" of beings— at least the demonic angels, anyway—actually are the human race's inferiors, thus supporting Alec's very real-world Christian genoism. Lucifer causes the Fall in order to corrupt the human genome and damn the human race, which to Alec is the worst possible action any being could commit (Alec, *Fall of Lucifer* 154), because it gives Lucifer the "title deed for Earth" while condemning humanity to God's wrath in heaven (Alec, *Fall of Lucifer* 155). Lucifer's demonic race then attempts to implant human beings with the demon seed. Part of this corruption of the human genome occurs through cultural influence. Lucifer plans to "introduce the race of men to evil. They shall sacrifice their sons and daughters to demons. Their lands shall be polluted.... Where there is vigor, we will ravage the bodies of the race of men with disease and every manner of malady" (Alec, *Fall of Lucifer*, 192). But Alec also plays into traditional evangelical ideas about the evilness of the biblical Nephilim, by arguing (in line with much of traditional evangelical theology) that the Nephilim were a byproduct of human-angelic mating. This produces a "demonized" genetic line that is apparently incapable of salvation, since God obliterates all the Nephilim with the Flood, at least in Alec's novels (Alec, *Fall of Lucifer* 195). Lucifer's goal with the Nephilim is to corrupt every human genetic line, to "demonize" the human seed with the demon seed, so that every human genetic line becomes demonized and thereby incapable of receiving salvation; were it not for Noah in the novel, Lucifer's plan would succeed (Alec 195, 201).

Christ's incarnation then becomes crucial to the plot, because undefiled blood—Godly DNA uncorrupted by the fall—is crucial if the damnation of the entire human race is to be avoided (Alec, *Fall of Lucifer* 236). Christos's "pure, undefiled DNA," his "unique seed" pays the legal penalty to Satan for humanity's transgressions (257). The idea here is that the purity of Christ's blood is transferred into Christians, thus giving Christians pure blood as well, rather than the demonized genetic lines of the Nephilim and those who choose to be damned rather than accept Christian belief. In a frighteningly open adoption of Branhamite theology, Alec even has Lucifer mimic serpent seed doctrine, by showcasing the damnation of the "crème de la crème of the Race of Men— the intellectuals.... Atheists, philosophers, agnostics—all rejecting the existence of a personal creator. Their god was their own minds and opinions. They scream the most volubly when they arrive in my domain and discover that I was real" (Alec, *The First Judgment* 346). For Alec, as for Branham, damnation of the intellectuals seems to be a given; they are the damned seed who Christians must defeat.

The third book in the series, *Son of Perdition* (2010), opens with the "Grande Druid council of Thirteen" composed of thirty-third-degree masons who are "the grand masters of the Illuminati," "the secret cabal that controlled the United States government" and the "elite who controlled the Federal Reserve, the Bank for International Settlements, the World Bank, the Council of Foreign relations, the Bilderberg Group, and the Club of Rome" conspiring to blow up the Twin Towers in order to bring about the rule of the Antichrist (Alec, *Son of Perdition* 17–18,19–24). Alec, despite being a prominent evangelical leader, here promotes outright 9/11 "Truther" rhetoric to a largely gullible audience. Furthermore, as Tabachnick points out, the novel's rhetoric of demonized bloodlines controlling humanity is a hallmark of anti–Semitic rhetoric about the Illuminati, the latter group playing a major role within Alec's series. This point is supported by Michael Barkun's research, a leading academic expert on right wing conspiracism, who has extensively linked anti–Illuminism to anti–Semitism (see Barkun, *A Culture of Conspiracy* loc 1144–1280; Tabachnick, "Part Two: The Prophecy/Conspiracy"). The idea of corrupted Illuminati bloodlines appears to have wide currency on the right, given the promotion of the idea among major conspiratorial theorists such as Alex Jones (see Springmeir, "Fritz Springmeier" in which Jones promotes 13 Bloodlines supporter Fritz Springmeier).

Although Alec's novel is not necessarily committed to anti–Semitism, the credence it gives to a number of conspiracy theory hobbyhorses (the Bilderberg Group, the Illuminati, Trutherism) that have become a playground for anti–Semites, is reason enough to have serious qualms about Alec's fiction. But here these ideas take on the spiritualized form of racial politics that characterizes NAR thinking. For instance, Satan's genetic scientists, the Twins,[7] conduct a deliberate eugenics and bioengineering program in the series in order to battle God and prepare for the last days. The Twins are supposedly genetic "purists," yet what they create is described by Alec as racial monstrosities that she clearly abhors: "They spawned an army of misshapen inbreds. Millions of depraved new species—grotesque, deformed monsters" (Alec, *Son of Perdition* 112). For Alec, the racialized demonic Other bears resemblance to the characterization of Jews and blacks promoted by Neo-Nazi and Neo-Confederate authors. Physical monstrosity is in Alec's text, as in all racist literature, equated with moral monstrosity.

By the fourth novel of The *Chronicles of Brothers*, *A Pale Horse*, Alec's conspiratorial threads take on bizarre proportions. Lucifer, in order to obliterate Christ's work within the human genome, launches two plans. The first is the use of demons as poseurs for extraterrestrial beings (literally aliens), as a means of fooling the human race into worshiping demons instead of God, thus

5. The NAR and Race

re-demonizing the human race (and presumably their genome as well). Lucifer believes that

> the revelation of an ancient civilization will prove that intelligent life other than man exists in the universe. Proof of artificially built structures on the moon and Cydonia, Mars,[8] will eventually lead the Race of Men to the conclusion that the entities responsible designed and guided them throughout history—that our presence on Mars and in UFOS confirms that we are their gods. Then we shall wreak our final revenge. We shall instruct them that the Nazarene was one of our own. No more, no less. We shall persuade them that we are the gods they seek. They will worship us.... The truth of the Nazarene ... will be obliterated [Alec, *A Pale Horse* 64].

Alec here plays upon a number of classic conspiratorial fears, particularly that of alien abduction. Alec's explanation of alien abduction is roughly consistent with that of mainstream evangelicalism, which historically (among noncessationists) has seen alien abduction encounters as being the result of demonic influence over human beings. But more importantly, Alec also plays to alien abduction conspiracy theories themselves, theories which like Alec's own novels, are often profoundly racialized (see Matthews 11, 17), expressing white fears of racial others (such as the "Greys"), while supporting the existence of alien racial elites, such as the Nordics, or Space Brothers, whose name and appearance explicitly invoke racial elitist ideology. These theories currently are trending upwards in the conspiracy theory marketplace, particularly due to influential conspiracist David Icke, who believes in the existence of reptilian beings who are dominating the human species.[9] Alec's fiction therefore fits easily into an already racialized discourse of abduction and alien encounter.

However, Alec uses one final, unique twist to distinguish her vision of race and racial politics from that of other NAR supporters, though it is one that would doubtlessly meet with many of these supporters approval: an idiosyncratic view of the Mark of the Beast. Using a combination of a false-flag program and a thinly veiled version of "FEMA death camps" (which literally appear to have been built during the Obama administration, if one follows Alec's timeline), the one world government institutes a genetic rewiring of the human race under the cover of a vaccination program. Anyone who is vaccinated in this program takes on the Mark of the Beast, that mark being a literal rewriting of their DNA into the creation of a demonic race of human beings. As Lawrence (an angel posing as a human being) tells a stunned group of human dissidents: "Every human being who receives the vaccine will have their human genomic source code mutated forever, altered by the insertion of DNA belonging to the fallen angelic host.... I'm talking billions of demonized human beings" (Alec, *Pale Horse* 267). Alec thus uses the threat of pandemic (another popular theme of conspiracy theorists, most notably the anti-vaccination movement) as the means by which humanity's, and in particular Christians', racial enemies attempt to corrupt the genetic stock of "pure" Christians. Those who succumb to the mark take on not simply the spiritual degeneracy found in traditional narratives of the End Times but unmistakable elements of racial degeneracy as well. Those human beings who do not accept Christ, for Alec represent a real threat to Christians, because as long as they resist God, there is the chance that Satan may demonize their "spiritual DNA."[10] The idea of someone being vaccinated into genetic inferiority has powerful racist and anti–Semitic resonances. As Peter Cohen's award winning documentary *Architecture of Doom* points out, the Nazi party frequently invoked the threat of the "racial bacillus" as a means of promoting fear of Jews and other minorities (see *Architecture of Doom* on how the Nazis conceptualized Judaism in viral terms). Such propaganda plays into long-standing white fears of biological contamination that have in recent years been transmuted into currently more socially acceptable—though increasingly marginal—fears of contamination by homosexuals. What Alec's novels do is open up the door for future NAR theorists to promote a new form of socially acceptable genoism—this time directed against the widely hated figure of the secularist—through which the NAR can continue to promote the demonization of Othered peoples under the guise of a supposedly color-blind ideology.

Bill Hamon: The Emerging Church-Race

Bill Hamon is one of the foremost apostles within the NAR, with only a handful of apostles having remotely near his influence. His books have been personally endorsed by C. Peter Wagner (Endorsements, *Day of the Saints*). Wagner wrote the forewords for several of Hamon's books, including *Prophetic Scriptures Yet to Be Fulfilled* (Wagner in Hamon, *Prophetic* 17–19) and *Apostles, Prophets, and the Coming Moves of God* (Wagner in Hamon, *Apostles* xxi-xxiii). In addition, Hamon's work is endorsed by numerous other important NAR figures, such as James Goll, Chuck Pierce, Ed Silvoso, and Cindy Jacobs; Hamon's work has also been endorsed by more mainstream Charismatic figures such as Oral Roberts, showing the wide sway NAR theology has come to hold over mainstream Pentecostal and Charismatic churches (see Commendations in *Apostles* xv-xix; Hamon, Endorsements, *Prophetic Scriptures*). Therefore, Hamon represents a mainstream figure in the NAR. Hamon's value to the NAR, besides his promotion of Latter Rain theology, is as an apostolic strategist. As with C. Peter Wagner and George Otis, Jr., the non–Charismatic observer should not be deceived by the apparently bizarre beliefs of Hamon. Hamon is, short of Wagner, Kraft, Silvoso and Otis Jr., one of the leading intellectual lights of the movement, his apparent anti-intellectualism non-withstanding.

To understand Hamon's application of NAR racial theories, one must understand two important parts of Hamon's theology. First is Hamon's conceptualization of race itself. For Hamon, "the church is now God's holy nation and chosen generation" (Hamon, *Prophetic* 33). Thus, the church is a nationality, and equivalent with a nation state. But the church is also a race, the "church race." Hamon contends, "Just as Jesus was God's perfect man, so the Church is to become Christ's perfected human race. The perfected Church-race of humanity will fully satisfy the original desire and plan that God had in his heart when he created the human race…. Those born of the Second-Adam – Jesus Christ receive His DNA nature, but they must grow and mature into Christ's likeness and image of character and maturity" (Hamon, *Prophetic* 76–77). Hamon's idea of race, therefore is contingent on the church race achieving a kind of theosis in which the race becomes literally God-like as it takes on elements of Christ's "DNA nature." Theosis has always been an implicit element of Manifest Sons theology, particularly during the Latter Rain revival. What Hamon does is codify that theosis concept into explicitly racial terms. But again, the church race is not to be defined in terms of traditional racial distinctions. Indeed, "all race distinctions are dissolved when people become members of the body of Christ. They become citizens of a new race, the church race. In the Church people are no longer black or white, Asian or European, male or female…. They are neither superior nor inferior to one another, but fellow citizens of the Church-nation" (Hamon, *Eternal Church* loc 2965–2967). Therefore, the church-nation dissolves all other groupings. There is only one nation, and in that nation there can only be one race. That race is a super-race and that nation is a super-nation, a church "superpower," with both the race and the nation aiming for spiritual transcendence through the theosis to be achieved by the Manifest Sons of God.

Hamon, in fact, explicitly promotes a form of spiritual racism, claiming, "The Church is the highest realm, the most privileged people, and the greatest race of beings in God's eternal universe" (Hamon, *Prophetic Scriptures* 97). For Hamon, the church-race is the Aryan people of Christianity, the "new breed" and it should therefore see itself as racially superior to those who are not of the church-race. But this form of racial superiority is not open simply to Caucasians, but to anyone who wishes to take on the mantle of the "church race." Thus spiritual racism allows everyone who wants to, to enjoy the benefits of racial elitism, regardless of their individual ethnic identification or apparent physical difference from other human beings. Institutional spiritual racism is encouraged in this movement, but is directed not against ethnic others, but religious others. Within the church-race, the solidarity of the church *ethne* is maintained through identification with the spirituo-organic body of the church race.

The *völkisch*-like element of identification of the church body with the spiritual race is by no means unintentional. Indeed, it is the second key element of Hamon's vision of NAR-derived race theory. For Hamon, the idea of race is not synonymous with people, but with a person. As Hamon describes, it "God never did create a being called 'people.' He created a person, one man. The Church is viewed as 'one man,' for the Church is destined to be a 'perfect Man' ... The Church is one Body made up of individual members" (Hamon, *Eternal Church* loc 244–245). Hamon's theory of the Church therefore sees it not simply as one nation, or even one body, but fundamentally as one person with individual members making up the body. Of course, the metaphor of the church as a body is a longstanding one in Christianity, deriving directly from the biblical text itself.[11] What is unique and troubling in Hamon's application of that theory is his over-emphasis on the degree of theosis possible for human beings,[12] as well as the equation of a single body with a single race. Given the NAR's similar preference for individual over democratic (corporate) leadership, one sees here the three elements—one race, one body, one leader—that were implicit in Nazi and other biologically-derived racialist ideologies. While it is doubtful that Hamon or any other NAR leader could ever get the entire NAR to accept an identification of the church as coequal with God, this application of the idea of theosis to the idea of race is dangerous. It is no coincidence, for instance, that the idea of theosis found such willing followers in the initially heavily racialized theology of the Mormons (see Ostling and Ostling 310–314 on Mormonism and theosis). Hamon, operating in a post–Holocaust context, should have known better than mix the idea of race and theosis so casually. But for Hamon, like many leaders of the NAR, what ultimately matters is the continued prosperity of the church race and its precious "spiritual DNA." Any threat to that race, or that purity, is a threat to the church as a whole and leaves the NAR free to do whatever it needs to defeat that spiritual opponent.

Conclusion

Strangely enough, despite the NAR's claim to color-blindness, one of its most important practices, which was central to the "spiritual mapping" movement, is that of identificational repentance, a practice with profoundly racial implications. As we have seen, in this practice, a spiritual intercessor, standing

5. The NAR and Race 185

in "as a substitute, [asks] for forgiveness for a geographical area or people. The practitioner [identifies] with the area and its sin, and then asked God for forgiveness. A process of social, political and economic progress ('healing') was expected to result" (Holvast 100). According to the theory of identificational repentance, an affinity group (some family, clan or nation to which a trip is organized) is purported to "be guilty of some form of 'corporate sin.' The practitioner [of identificational repentance] prays that God will use his personal prayer to forgive the sins of the past, such as for the Crusades, wars, or ancient slavery. The practitioner identifies with people groups or territories and repents on their behalf" (Holvast 201). The reason for this, according to John Dawson, one of the leading theorists of identificational repentance within the NAR, is that "unless somebody identifies themselves with corporate entities, such as the nation of our citizenship, or the subculture of our ancestors, the act of honest confession will never take place" (Dawson 30).

What Holvast leaves unclear, but which is explicit if one reads practically any NAR work on identificational repentance, is that this practice is intrinsically tied to Pentecostal demonology. For instance, the Kylstras contend that "applying this principle [of identificational repentance] to an organization or a geographical area—a church or business, or a city or region—can yield great results in clearing out demonic principalities and paving the way for awakening and spiritual revival" (Kylstra and Kylstra, *Restoring the Foundations* 144). Even more explicit in making these links to demonology are George Otis, Jr.'s *Transformations* documentaries. These documentaries promote the idea that various communities, usually racially othered and living in the developing world (Columbia, Uganda, Guatemala, and Fiji feature prominently in various *Transformations* videos), are demonized. For instance, Cali, Colombia is afflicted with troubling drug problems caused by the drug lords' consultations with the occult (*Transformations* DVD). Similarly, a purported witch in these videos, who is being condemned by the NAR leader in them, Thomas Muthee,[13] presumably for practicing native Kenyan religious practices, is vilified in the first *Transformations* film for her use of "targeted witchcraft" against Muthee. In reality, this "witch," Jane W. Njenga, was no witch at all, but "a pastor with the African Mission of Holy Ghost Church" (Alsop). What is tragic is not this purported witch's fate—to this day she remains unharmed by the efforts of Muthee—but the fact that in 2008, eleven "elderly Kenyans, mostly women, were burned to death ... after locals accused them of being witches" (Alsop). While Muthee may not be directly responsible for these burnings, his own witch-hunt for Mama Jane certainly added considerable fuel to the smoldering fires of NAR revivalism within Kenya (see also Ongere). Thus, the concept of identificational repentance, when attached to the idea of demonized human beings or people groups, can literally be used as a justification for murder, both on a small scale and potentially on a much more massive and problematic scale as well. Therefore, the continued promotion of "spiritual DNA" rhetoric, right alongside the idea of identificational repentance (seen explicitly in the very opening of the first *Transformations* video. See *Transformations I* DVD) leaves open the possibility that the NAR will in the future label specific people groups as inherently and irredeemably demonized. At that point, the whole distinction between spiritual racism and racism based on apparent physical difference will cease to matter, because in either case the targeted group will be equally dead.

What are we to make of the wider cultural significance of NAR theories of race? Nell Irvin Painter, in *The History of White People* (2010), points out that whiteness studies holds "white race, ordinarily invisible in the black/white dichotomy, up to the light. In them it appears as social, not biological, a powerful social construct letting whites think of themselves first and foremost as individuals. Although white people may exempt themselves from race, white privilege comes into view as a crucial facet of white race identity" (Painter 388). Like most research today, this book supports a social constructionist view of race, while acknowledging that race has a powerful real-world influence on how human beings interact culturally. What, NAR concepts of race tell us, however is the power of the narrative of race to survive the death of the concept of biological race.

As Painter points out, race, though an idea deeply embedded in contemporary culture, is not a stable construct. In antiquity, people did not think of themselves as "white" nor did they relate their moral or intellectual character to their color, because "neither the idea of race nor the idea of 'white' people had been invented, and people's skin color did not carry useful meaning" (Painter 1). What mattered to the people of antiquity was "where they lived" (Painter 1). Painter's view of the relatively recent origins of the concept of race seems to represent an emerging, though not uncontested, consensus in academia, especially among anthropologists ("American Anthropological Association Statement"). However, because race is not a stable social construct, the interpretation of it as being linked to biology or ethnicity or even geographical location is not necessarily a permanent one. What NAR theology tragically shows is that the concept of race can survive its own demise. Because racial taxonomies have proven infinitely adaptive over time, despite their lack of scientific validity, such taxonomies can be translated into future ideological systems, like NAR racial theology, that are willing to reject biological racism or racism based on apparent physical difference, for new forms of racism predicated on spiritual or ideological difference. New racial elites can be built, elites that cross the traditional lines of race, but create new races born not of ethnicity but ideological commonalities.

NAR theology serves as a death knell to the white fantasy of a post-racial society. Whether or not racism based on apparent physical difference or color of skin survives, race as a concept seems doomed to survive the death of its previous pseudoscientific taxonomical classifications (e.g. color, ethnic group, etc.), so long as the new spiritual and/or ideological racists of the future can construct new theories of racial supremacism that appeal to members of many different traditionally-defined ethnic groups or races. Racism, in short, will survive by becoming sincerely multicultural and multiracial. The potential of such racism to affect the world at a global level cannot be underestimated.

6

From the Others of the Americas to the Others Overseas

The NAR's Global Campaign for Reconciliation and Identificational Repentance

In this concluding chapter, I examine the NAR's policy towards racial and religious others, as well as its activities in various countries throughout the world. This is not an attempt to unite disparate "p.c." themes (namely race relations, religious pluralism and concerns over globalization). Rather, the NAR's concepts of racial and religious others are intrinsically related and help inform how the movement conducts itself overseas. The NAR's stretch is now global. This chapter can do no more than hint at that power, and I caution the reader that what I relate here barely scratches at the surface of the NAR's reach. In the first section of the chapter, I discuss the NAR's views on racial reconciliation. In the second section, I explore the so-called Insider Movement (IM), another Fuller Seminary offshoot, which though not always aligned with the NAR, has borrowed much of the NAR's missional ideology and drinks at the same ideological springs as the NAR—namely the anthropological and social theories of Charles Kraft and Donald McGavran respectively (see Holvast 17, 28–34; Coleman 2, 4). This movement seeks to convert members of non-evangelical, including non–Christian, religious traditions to evangelical ideology by advocating the idea that one can believe in Christ while still calling oneself a Muslim, a Jew, a Hindu, etc. While the Messianic movement is the most well-known of these efforts, and the one most openly aligned with the NAR, the Insider movement model is now applied to virtually every religious tradition imaginable. In the final and longest section of the chapter I explore the activities of the NAR in various countries. Like René Holvast's approach towards spiritual mapping, my approach to NAR activities overseas will be descriptive and suggestive. It is impossible to comprehensively outline the apostles' international reach; the movement is too large and diffuse to do that. But the evidence I provide here should point to real concerns about the apostles' growing power.

The NAR's View of Racial Reconciliation

Crucial to understanding the NAR's view of racial reconciliation—and to a lesser extent, the insider movement's view of religious relationships—are two concepts: identificational repentance and contextualization. As the reader will recall, identificational repentance is a "two stage intercessory action" in which individuals first acknowledge the sin of their "affinity group (clan, city, nation or organization)" and then pray to God that He will use their repudiation of that sin as a "redemptive beachhead from which to move into the larger community" (Otis Jr., *Informed Intercession* 251). The NAR's view of race and nationality is grounded in the belief that both individuals and *even geographic territories* can be spiritually traumatized via demonic oppression, possession, or demonization (see Petrie 30 on territorial demonization; see Otis Jr., *Twilight Labyrinth* 136 on collective trauma). Otis Jr. communicates this idea by making an analogy between sexual abuse and idolatry, writing that "whereas individuals, particularly abused children, tend to cope with their pain through sexual promiscuity or multiple personality disorder, communities are more inclined to some form of idolatry. In both cases the rule is the same: The more traumatic the circumstance, the greater the number of 'saviors' solicited" (Otis Jr., *Twilight Labyrinth* 141). Thus communities are judged primarily in terms of how demonically afflicted they are perceived to be. While some NAR leaders have attempted to be pluralistic in their demonic taxonomies, assigning demonic proclivities to a wide number of civilizations, including Western ones, it must be acknowledged that the primary anti-demonization campaigns are directed at the developing world. The 10/40 Praying Through the Window campaign, for instance, which provided the impetus for much of the spiritual mapping movement and later NAR organizing, centered almost exclusively on Asian and African countries with small or non-existent Caucasian populations.

Yet the NAR has had a massive appeal both among non-whites overseas and at home. As Tabachnick notes, "Pentecostalism has a history of racial diversity and women ministers, and [the] NAR itself has broad appeal in terms of gender, race, and ethnicity, for example ... women and minorities are prominent in its leadership" (Tabachnick, "Spiritual Warriors"). How does one explain this appeal? A large part of it, of course, comes from the element of multicultural racism that characterizes the NAR's peculiar version of identity politics. Since race is conceptualized in large part through the lens of the church family (particularly for Bill Hamon, but even somewhat for other apostles), racial difference among both blacks and whites is sublimated for the wider identity of the church *ethne*. In this model of racial politics, NAR churches become the proverbial racial melting pots, but also provide a degree of racial and cultural unity that might not otherwise be possible.

There are also more pragmatic reasons that minority and developing world communities often ally with the apostles, which point to the continuing power imbalances between whites and non-whites even at this late historical date. To illustrate this point, it is fruitful to look at the experience of Native American/First Nations people with the NAR.[1] Andrea Smith has noted in an interview with Richard Twiss and Randy Woodley (both Native evangelicals involved in the Native American Contextualization movement described below)[2] that both men in part saw their Native evangelical writings which critiqued syncretism (seen by many evangelicals, including the NAR, as the blasphemous, sometimes even demonic, blending of two religious traditions) as "strategic." As Smith relates, these texts were written "to be persuasive specifically to evangelicals who might reject the inclusion of all Native cultural practices within Christianity" (Smith 84). For Twiss and his allies, therefore, a significant part of the reason for partially assimilating the NAR's ideology is so that the Native American community can still retain a part of its cultural identity as distinct from this assimilating tendency. In other words, partial assimilation is seen as a better alternative than total assimilation or total annihilation, both prospects which are real threats for indigenous communities throughout the Americas today.

The problem is that this situation sets up a lose-lose situation for the Native American community, in which proponents of a Christianized Native identity and a more traditional Native religious identity are strategically divided, thus diffusing the possibility of a unified cultural resistance against white imperialism that is focused on achieving real social justice for Native communities. The primary means by which such cultural division is achieved is via a process called contextualization (see Twiss, "Native-Led Contextualization" 30). While Twiss's work references more than one model of contextualization, his references to Kraft's particular version of that are frequent within his dissertation, and since it is Kraft's model that is in almost all cases being used by the NAR, I deal primarily with the Kraftian model below.

Twiss saw the contextualization model as addressing "the challenge of communicating the gospel message in ways and terms that unbelievers understand. Its challenge is avoiding the foreignness of a gospel dressed in Western clothes that characterized the era of noncontextualization. It seeks to overcome the ethnocentrism of a monocultural approach by taking cultural differences seriously and by affirming the good in all cultures" (Twiss, "Native Led Contextualization" 30). In the Native context, therefore, contextualization serves in part to further missionary efforts towards Native peoples (see Smith 85 for a somewhat different formulation of the same point). The incorporation of Native cultural practices is seen as essential in contextualization efforts, since the incorporation of these practices into Christian missions increases the likelihood of Natives adopting Christian beliefs (see Andrea Smith 85 on this as well). Smith points out that this creates the situation of Native peoples being used: "to missionize other indigenous peoples" (Smith 85); indeed the NAR sees Native Americans as ideal missionaries precisely because of this point.

Contextualization however, is used in a far broader sense by the Christian Right as a whole and may in fact be one of its crucial organizational insights over the last forty years. Roughly speaking, contextualization is the same idea as "transculturation." According to Twiss, "contextualization addresses the challenge of communicating the gospel message in ways and terms that unbelievers understand" (Twiss, "Native-Led Contextualization" 30). Contextualization advocates claim to find good in all cultures and thus reject a monocultural approach to Christian missiology (Wolfe 19).

Kraft's translational model of dynamic equivalence is unarguably the most popular contextualization model in the evangelical movement. As we have seen, Holvast credits Kraft's anthropological insights, of which dynamic equivalence was the most important, with being crucial to the spread of spiritual mapping and thus the birth of the NAR (Holvast 28–34, but especially 31). Similarly, academic J. Henry Wolfe credits Kraft's model as being the "most influential force behind Insider methodology" (Wolfe 190).

Kraft's anthropology starts with a number of assumptions, not all of which were outlined in Chapter 1. One of the most crucial of these insights is a concept Kraft borrowed from Paul Hiebert (who took the idea from mathematics): the distinction between bounded sets and fuzzy sets. Traditionally, Christianity has used a bounded set model to determine who is a member of a faith community. In other words, membership in a faith community is established through determinate, explicit acceptance of certain cultural and ideological ideas of a religious community, and also the rejection of other ideas (Wolfe 195–196). In a fuzzy set, on the other hand, what matters is the "direction and orientation of movement." Fuzzy sets are "drawn, not by proximity to the ideal, but by direction toward it" (Wolfe 196–197). Therefore, God will be all right with sub-optimal behavior, so long as someone is "traveling in the right allegiance direction" (Wolfe 197). Therefore, while Kraft believed that one must start with a faith in Christ, he sees this as the only necessary entry point for Christian belief (Wolfe 197). Thus for Kraft, and even more for the Insider Movement that borrowed his ideas, salvation no longer is defined in event-based terms, but in process-based terms. This allows groups like the NAR and the Insider Movement to comfortably interact, and even join, other cultures that are seen as being spiritually sub-optimal, though ultimately for the goal of raising these cultures up to the evangelical understanding of Christianity. This idea in both movements is commonly coupled with McGavran's homogenous unit principle insight, whose paraphrase by C. Peter Wagner is particularly relevant to understanding the NAR and Insider movements' approach to missions: "People like to become Christians without crossing, racial, linguistic or class barriers" (Wagner, *Wrestling* 109). Because of this, both the Insider movement and the NAR typically like to use pre-existing members of "people movements" or religions—that is, insiders—as the first wave of conversion, seeing such individuals as ultimately more likely to be effective in missions' efforts.

Contextualization, as envisioned by Kraft, allows evangelical ideology to be incredibly chameleon-like in its application, fitting itself to any cultural system, while seeking at the same time to subvert that system from within. Each of the movements that has thrived on contextualization tends to specialize in a specific area of contextualization. What the NAR specializes in doing is creating dynamically equivalent translations of evangelical ideology that fit comfortably into a wide range of worship styles, ethnic groups, and racial groups. The Insider movement applies the dynamic equivalence model at the level of religion (Wolfe 190).

This brings us back to Twiss and Native contextualization. Native religion represents an interesting challenge for incorporation within the Insider Movement and the NAR, challenges largely the byproduct of these movements' own internal prejudices. This is because both of these movements, like the larger evangelical movement in general, tend to distinguish between "high" and "low" religions. High religions are concerned with "cosmic questions" about life, have written texts, are institutionalized, and provide ethical guidelines for life and conduct. Low religions, by contrast, primarily focus on "health, fertility, wealth, and power" in this unabashedly Western reading of religious development. Such systems are seen as frequently involving an "intermediate realm of spirit intercessors" (Wolfe 24). The concept of power encounter developed by Alan Tippett and also utilized by John Wimber in a somewhat different context is also important here. Tippett believed that when people served gods "invested with spiritual power (from Satan), it was crucial for them in considering Christianity to discover which god had the greatest power" (Kraft, *Anthropology of Christian Witness* 452). Ultimately, the NAR only sees Christianity and Judaism as high religious movements; Islam, though technically a high religious movement, is seen as needing to be confronted with "power encounters" because of the amount of folk elements that the movement has incorporated into itself. In Kraft's model, this kind of syncretism opens believers up to the occult (Wolfe 24–25, 221). When the NAR and the spiritual mapping movement bought into this paradigm they began to explicitly associate "low religion" practices from around the world with occultic and demonic powers.

Since NAR supporters believed (and continue to believe) that there could be demonically inhabited people, geographical locations, customs, and even objects—the movement had two immediate and rather obvious problems. First, not every culture in the world makes the Western distinction between sacred and secular. Native evangelicals, for instance, in some cases "do not separate Native spirituality and Native culture" and therefore "do not see the practice of traditional Native spirituality as a contradiction to Christianity" (Smith 84–85). Therefore, for cultures that see all life and all culture as spiritual, what the NAR asked for was not merely a forsaking of religious identity, but also cultural identity. More importantly for NAR leaders (as well as for the leaders of the Insider Movement), was the concern that in seeking to create "Muslims for Jesus" or "Natives for Jesus" one might inadvertently create the opposite effect: Allah for Christians, for instance, or a Native American equivalent thereof. It is perhaps one of the greatest ironies of the NAR that despite its obsession with avoiding syncretism, no religious movement in the U.S. is more profoundly syncretic. Because the movement's foundational assumptions have always been fundamentally pragmatic, its leadership has ultimately placed results above doctrinal orthodoxy, thus creating a tension in religious praxis that seems unlikely to be solved in the near future.

In the Native American community, this is played out to tragic effect. Leaders like Twiss and Randy Woodley end up supporting contextualization efforts that ultimately are aimed at colonizing the very communities that these men have dedicated themselves to protecting. Woodley, for instance, "goes so far as to say that missions to Native peoples should adopt the 'Muslims for Jesus' and 'Jews for Jesus' approach to mission work" (Smith 86). Woodley therefore argues that Christians should encourage Natives to "follow Jesus" rather than embrace Christianity (Smith 86). As Smith points out, some of these appeals to mission work may be seen as strategic on the part of these leaders, necessary compromises in the face of grotesque power imbalances between Native peoples and whites (Smith 86). While Smith's contention is undoubtedly true, she underestimates the effectiveness of current Charismatic missions' strategy towards Native Americans (including that of the NAR).[3]

NAR Native apostle James Chosa, for instance (2010 "International Coalition of Apostles Membership Directory" 4), is a graphic reminder of the effectiveness of NAR rhetoric. Chosa attempts to render NAR rhetoric as inherently indigenous. For Chosa, "true identity rightfully connects us in the love of God to our indigenous spot in the earth" (Chosa and Chosa xiv). Chosa reinterprets the term indigenous as applying "to all equally since the problem of disconnection and identity knows no racial or national boundary." Christians have both an "indigenous heavenly and earthly identity in Christ Jesus." Chosa therefore sees the application of the term indigenous solely to Native Americans, as limiting Christians, particularly Western Christians, access to their "identity and dominion destiny," which for him involves "territorial deliverance and transformation" (Chosa and Chosa xiv).

Chosa (and his wife, who is the co-writer of *Thy Kingdom Come They Will Be Done in Earth*) thus sees not just the NAR, but the whole message of dominionism and SLSW as profoundly liberating for the Native community. He sees the project of the NAR as an indigenizing of whites, rather than a Westernizing of Natives, and thus embraces the dominion mandate of territorial deliverance and transformation that is virtually textbook NAR rhetoric. A selling point offered up by many of the newer generation of Charismatics[4] is exactly their emphasis on "spirit and spiritual warfare," which as Smith indicates at least acknowledges "the power of Native spiritual traditions" (Smith 84). The result of these beliefs, however, is that the New Charismatics Smith discusses in *Native Americans and the Christian Right* (2008), who are definitely no more fanatic than the NAR,[5] encourage Natives to burn Native "paraphernalia" and reject even traditional Native healing practices as "demonic or idolatrous" (Smith 84).

Indeed, the NAR's subversion of Native populations throughout the Americas is easily traceable. Current NAR apostles were subverting indigenous peoples even before the spiritual mapping movement took off. Perhaps the most graphic, and certainly the most well documented example of this occurred in Guatemala. Initially this activism centered around the Guatemalan dictator General Efrain Ríos Montt, who ruled Guatemala from 1982 to 1983 (see Diamond, *Spiritual Warfare* 164–168 on Montt). Evangelicals began taking an especial interest in Guatemala in 1976, when a group of missionaries called "Gospel Outreach" arrived in Guatemala in order to do relief work after a major earthquake (Diamond, *Spiritual Warfare* 164). Having earlier networked through a 1962 massive evangelical crusade launched by the Latin American Mission (LAM), evangelicals living in 1970s Guatemala adopted much of the outlook of North American evangelicalism. Missionaries espoused an apolitical position since Social gospel outreach was seen as potentially offensive to Guatemalan authorities (Brouwer, Gifford and Rose 54). Along with the foreign aid that came in after the 1976 earthquake, Guatemala also received an infusion of "disaster evangelism." Missions strategist Jim Montgomery described the earthquake as "another upheaval the Holy Spirit used to awaken Guatemalans to their spiritual needs" (Montgomery 3–4 qtd. in Diamond, *Spiritual Warfare* 215).

By the early 1980s, many Catholics, concerned with the increasing authoritarian nature of the Guatemalan government, were "actively political at the grass-roots level, on a continuum ranging from mild reformism to explicit liberation theology" (Brouwer, Gifford and Rose 55). Evangelicals, on the other hand, still held an apolitical worldview but clearly benefitted from the efforts of right-wing elements in Guatemala, which included "members of the landed elite, the military, and upper-class business and professional groups united to oppose the advance of Mayans, small-scale ladino farmers, and all sectors of private and public wage earners" (Brouwer, Gifford and Rose 55). This apolitical orientation abruptly ended with the coming to power of Efrain Ríos Montt in 1982. Montt a neo-Pentecostal, openly espoused evangelicalism (Brouwer, Gifford and Rose 55). Montt quickly became the shining star of the Christian Right, particularly its Charismatic wing. Pat Robertson flew to Guatemala a bare five days after Montt seized control of the country, and penned the introduction to Montt's biography (Brouwer, Gifford and Rose 56). Robertson was so enamored of Montt that he told the *New York Times* he hoped to send the country over a billion dollars in aid through his Christian Broadcasting Network (CBN). While this act of aid never came to fruition, it did allow Montt to reassure the U.S. Congress that he would not have to rely on American foreign aid, but could instead count on private donations from U.S. evangelicals (Diamond, *Spiritual Warfare* 164–165).

In June 1982, Montt's aide and Gospel Outreach elder (Montt was a leader in Gospel Outreach's Guatemalan Verbo Church) arrived in the United States for a meeting with a number of high ranking U.S. officials and Christian Right activists, including presidential counselor Edwin Meese, Interior Secretary James Watt, and evangelical leaders Pat Robertson, Jerry Falwell, and Loren Cunningham (leader of Youth with a Mission). Cunningham, besides leading the increasingly NAR–influenced YWAM movement, also was one of the influences on the seven mountains idea now so heavily promulgated by the NAR (Cunningham, "Transcript of Interview"). Almost simultaneously, the State Department conducted a special briefing for Christian right leaders, in which they emphasized "the need for private support for the Ríos Montt regime" (Diamond 165). Gospel Outreach, with the heaving backing of Pat Robertson and his 700 Club, raised millions for a "humanitarian aid" project euphemistically labeled Operation Lovelift. On the same day that President Regan lifted a ban on U.S. military aid to Guatemala (January 8, 1983), 350 evangelicals set out for Guatemala with a boat that held more than one million dollars' worth of food, clothing, medical supplies, and housing materials destined for refugee camps in Guatemala's Ixil triangle (Diamond 165).

The money raised in operation Lovelift helped support Montt's pacification plan, which forced the relocation of Indians to the highlands, for the explicit goal of wiping out the communist menace. Montt's regime killed thousands and forced millions of Indians to flee their homes. This campaign, dubbed "guns and beans" (*fusiles y frijoles*) eventually led to displaced Indians being placed in "resettlement villages" where Natives were "provided food, shelter and work in a tightly controlled, highly monitored environment" (Brouwer, Gifford and Rose 56).

Montt's genocidal campaign was helped by Israeli advisors, who helped him construct "Plan Victoria 82," characterized by Victoria Sanford, Assistant Professor of Anthropology at Lehman College, City University of New York, as "the most closely coordinated, intensive massacre campaign in Guatemalan history" (Victoria Sanford). The Israelis, who had been long time allies of the Guatemalans, helped the Guatemalans formulate Plan Victoria's scorched earth policy; the army's implementation of this policy involved, among other things, using "Israeli and American planes to bomb, strafe, and burn hundreds of villages and drive those who survived into the model villages administered by so many good [evangelical] Christians" (Weissman; Rubenberg). Of course the evangelical movement did not want any bad PR for their genocidal campaign against the indigenous peoples of Guatemala, so *Christianity Today* claimed that Montt had been "undeservedly libeled in the press" (Diamond, *Spiritual Warfare* 166).

In the Ixil Triangle, Gospel Outreach, the Wycliffe Bible Translators/Summer Institute of Linguistics and the Berhost Foundation, sought to coordinate with the government through the creation of the Foundation for Aid to the Indian People (FUNDAPI). Through that organization, Berhost was responsible for all medical care, while Wycliffe controlled education for Indian children up to the third grade (Diamond 166–167). After Montt left the presidency in 1983, a report on Montt's reign published by the Chile-based Instituto Lationoamericano de Estudios Trasnacionales contended that Gospel Outreach's Verbo Church took "jobs in espionage and torture and accompanied Israeli and Argentinean experts during interrogation sessions." At least one of the reports of evangelical torturers came from an evangelical pastor (Diamond 167).

Montt left office in 1983 after being ousted from the presidency. He then went back to his role as a church elder. In 1984, the National Religious Broadcasters invited Mott to attend their 1985 convention, and its executive director helped him lead a speaking tour in the U.S., sponsored by evangelical heavyweights Jimmy Swaggart and Pat Robertson. Crucially, Montt was also the keynote speaker at a conference entitled "Marxism on the Doorstep: Conflict to the South," which was sponsored by leading shepherding advocate and future ICA apostle Dennis Peacocke and, as mentioned previously, featured speeches from various intelligence operatives (Diamond 128, 167).

After helping to oppress Guatemala's Native population, one might have hope that evangelicalism would develop a sense of caution in Central America. But instead, Guatemala became one of the centers of spiritual mapping ideology. Holvast argues spiritual mapping in Guatemala was characterized by three aspects. The first was an obsession with the city of Almolonga, which was thought to be demonically gripped by the deity Maximon (Holvast 129–130). As Holvast points out, Almolonga provided the spiritual mapping movement with some of the same self-justifications for its existence as the efforts attributed to Resistencia in Argentina, albeit on a lower scale. Once the territorial demons were successfully confronted in Almolonga, prosperity supposedly resulted (Holvast 129–130). Both C. Peter Wagner and George Otis, Jr., expressed concerns about the demonization of Almolonga (Holvast 129–130) and Otis Jr. narrated and produced *Transformations I*, which had an extensive section documenting the alleged miracles in Almolonga, including abnormally large vegetables that spontaneously started growing there (*Transformations I*).

The second major factor in spiritual mapping in Guatemala was the role Harold Caballeros played in the movement. Caballeros was founder and pastor of El Shaddai church in Guatemala City, which was a focal point of spiritual mapping in Guatemala. Wagner saw Caballeros as being on the "cutting edge" of global Christianity and claimed Caballeros had discovered spiritual mapping on his own (Holvast 130). Caballeros's archaeological research in to the spiritual mapping process led him to deduce that a Mayan spirit named Quetzacoatl was responsible for controlling a "spiritual stronghold" in his area. Caballeros then marketed his own derivation of the spiritual mapping model, which focused on historical, physical, and spiritual factors (Holvast 130).

The anti–Native rhetoric in Caballeros's *Victorious Warfare: Discovering Your Rightful Place in God's Kingdom* (2001) is disturbing. Not only is Mayan culture seen as demonized in the book, but Caballeros also promotes the idea that "principalities and powers" (i.e., evil spirits/demons) were responsible for "the cult of the feathered serpent" that he sees as a major facet of Aztec and Inca culture as well (Caballeros 15). This serpent spirit "inspired all art in the Mayan, Aztec, Toltec, and Inca cultures" (Caballeros 17). Caballeros promotes the idea that this worship of the flying serpent had effectively handed over Meso-America to this spirit and was responsible for the suffering in Guatemala. The Mayans therefore went through a spiritually "degenerative process" that was provoked by their "idolatry" (Caballeros 20). As much as a half or more of Guatemala's population is Mayan (Holvast 131), which obviously makes Ladino (mixed Hispanic-Mayan) Guatemalans enormously nervous ("Guatemala" [Brittanica]; "Guatemala" [CIA World Factbook]). Even more disturbing for Guatemala's Native population, Caballeros eventually achieved the rank of foreign minister of Guatemala, a rank he held as of 2012 (Clinton). This is significant because Caballeros eventually became an NAR apostle, and is identified as such in René Holvast's careful study of the spiritual mapping movement (Holvast 130–131).

Obviously Caballeros's rhetoric is advantageous to European-descended Guatemalans. But it is also significant for the neo-colonialist agenda of both the American government and the evangelical movement. The incredible achievements of Mesoamerican culture have always put the lie to ethnocentric Western valuations of Amerindian peoples as being primitive or barbaric, and thus have served as a powerful rebuke to the civilizing missions of the Americas' various would-be colonizers. Denying the strength and moral dignity of these cultures is an important part of delegitimizing Amerindian peoples' rights to their own lands in the minds of both European and Native descended peoples in the Americas.

Added fuel for the spiritual mapping movement in Guatemala was the election of President Jorge Serrano Elías in 1990. Serrano was an active member of Caballeros's El Shaddai Church. Elías's election was preceded by an extensive spiritual mapping campaign in Guatemala against three human beings who the movement identified, according to Wagner, with "the spiritual forces of darkness as strongmen," two of whom happened to be running against—and leading—Elías in the polls. After these extensive bouts of warfare prayer, the two candidates dropped out, which Wagner attributes to the spiritual mapping efforts made in Guatemala (Wagner, *Churches that Pray* 209; Holvast 131). Wagner used this incident to promote the effectiveness of spiritual mapping in cultural transformation (see Holvast 131).

As Holvast points out, Liliana R. Goldin and Walter E. Little's research indicates that the prosperity of Almolonga had more to do with a longstanding tradition of the city being industrious and prosperous, combined with the city's "keen marketing, specialization in cash crop production and the timely adoption of new agricultural technology." The two researchers make clear that Almolonga's prosperity predates the spiritual mapping movement (Holvast 132). Thus, as in the case of Resistencia, the supposed model of success for cultural transformation is an illusory one.

In addition, much of the power of spiritual mapping and later on the NAR could be explained by Guatemala's "relative proximity to the US" (see Holvast 132). Despite Wagner's claims for Caballeros's independent development of spiritual mapping, Guatemalan spiritual mapping practices were clearly influenced by the U.S. Guatemalan evangelicals and neo-Pentecostals joined U.S. spiritual mapping networks, hosted the 1998 SWN conference, and entertained important NAR leaders, including C. Peter Wagner and George Otis, Jr. (Holvast 132–133). At El Shaddai's 2006 World Congress, the story of Almolonga and "the promise of Guatemala's church growth" were the highlight of an international conference that attracted such NAR notables as James Goll, Cindy Jacobs, and Bill Hamon (O'Neill loc 4111, 4133). Holvast contends that the continued relevance of spiritual mapping in Guatemala can in large part be explained by its "public adoption by Caballeros," one of the evangelical movement's most influential leaders in the area and an important figure in Guatemala. In addition, Guatemalan spiritual mapping was given a sense of urgency by the "revitalization" of Mayan culture—that is, Amerindian culture—within Guatemala, which was viewed with great alarm not only by Caballeros, but also by Otis and Wagner as well (Holvast 132–133).

Spiritual mapping in Guatemala continued into the 2000s and became an important political tool for El Shaddai. In 2006, as the 2007 Guatemalan national elections approached, El Shaddai proclaimed the foundation of a new political party, VIVA Guatemala (O'Neill loc 2555). As a result, El Shaddai began what ethnologist Kevin O'Neill described as a "covert spiritual warfare campaign" to clean up Guatemala in preparation for Dr. Caballeros's run for president. O'Neill specifically notes that spiritual mapping was used during this campaign (O'Neill loc 2567).

Unfortunately, Guatemala is not the only nation in the Americas where the NAR is promoting anti–Amerindian rhetoric. Gideon Chung Keun Chiu's dissertation "A Strategy for Effective Evangelism in Vancouver" details with spiritual relish the literal demonization of Native cultures in Vancouver, and Western Canada generally. According to Chiu, Vancouver is influenced by many different spirits. Swedish spiritual mapping activist, Kjell Sjöberg of Sweden, contended that Vancouver was filled with more New Age activities than any place in the world. Rick Joyner saw one of Vancouver's main "strongholds" as the city's seeking after pleasure. Bob Birch, a major player in NAR politics in Canada, identified: "the spirit behind the gays as one of the strongholds" and issued a warning against "submitting to the spirit of Jezebel and worldliness" (Chiu 68). Vancouver, therefore was seen by the spiritual mapping movement and by important NAR apostles as a thoroughly demonized city, no doubt in part to its reputation for cultural pluralism.

Chiu pinpointed a crucial problem for spiritual mappers in Vancouver: the Thunderbird spirit, which he characterized as one of the "original strongmen of the Native Indian Religion" (Chiu 69). This spirit, together with other Native spirits, formed "the original stronghold which is considered as one of the most powerful satanic strongholds in the world, with its headquarters in Victoria, B.C" (Chiu 68). Chiu asserts that an "obvious fact" about the Native Indians of Canada was that they were "at the bottom of the economic and social scale" (Chiu 75). Rather than blame this problem, however, on social inequities and colonialism—which are the fairly obvious causal factors for most indigenous suffering in Canada—Chiu notes that the Natives "are in bondage to spirits both through deception and by intent" (Chiu 75). Chiu blames the Natives' plight on the shedding of innocent blood—not by Europeans, but by Natives against Natives (Chiu 75–80). Chiu advocated that "representatives of the forefathers [of those who committed bloodshed] need to acknowledge the sins and confess on their behalf. They need to repent, forgive and bless each other, and bless the land" (Chiu 81). This latter point of blessing the land is extremely important, because in much of NAR rhetoric involving indigenous peoples—one sees this particularly in Chosa, but its present in other apostles' writings, including those by Caucasian writers—only the host people of a country can ultimately bless all its inhabitants and help cleanse the land of territorial spirits (Chosa 98–106,110; see Dawson, *Healing America's Wounds* 25–27, 30 for a rough model of this process applied in a Maori context). Thus any crimes committed by indigenous peoples are taken especially seriously, ironically because it is these people who are seen as being most able to bless the land.

But what was truly bizarre about Chiu's demonization of Native cultures was the promotion of totem poles as a demonic communication system. According to Chiu, who based his findings on the spiritual mapping research of Darryl Jones, totem poles were strategically erected at key points in Vancouver, particularly the "city gateways and high places" (Chiu 85). Kjell Sjöberg, with the blessing of NAR leader Bob Birch, came to Vancouver to attend a prophetic prayer conference. At this conference, Sjöberg revealed that the Vancouver totem poles were "directly connected with those in Japan" and served as demonic "communication links across the globe" (Chiu 90). This belief was taken literally by spiritual mapping advocates in Vancouver. Chiu contended that in a "similar manner as the telephone poles and satellite links linking the nations together in communication, the totem poles have linked strongholds into a network that has held the nations in bondage" (Chiu 97). Quite literally, the spiritual mapping movement in Vancouver, led by Canada's foremost NAR apostle (see McDonald 131–135), believed that numerous nations were demonized by a demonic telecommunications system constructed out of totem poles.

Chiu does not note the horrible racism implicit in characterizing indigenous religious practices in this manner, and increasingly, neither did Canada's Native population, as a number of First Nations people in the Canadian arctic participated in *Transformations II*, another one of George Otis's documentaries that furthered the very policy of cultural annihilation these First Nations people saw Otis's organization as protecting them from (see *Transformations II*).

So thoroughly and tragically had the NAR hoodwinked Native Christian leadership that James Chosa and his wife spend an extensive amount of time in their *Thy Kingdom Come Thy Will Be Done on Earth* (2004) attacking the contextualizing of the Gospel in native communities, arguing that the Native community does not need "religious forms, regalia, special songs, instruments or any material thing to worship God" (Chosa and Chosa 143–145) indicating the Chosas' alignment with the hardline elements of Native Charismatic belief that rejected attempts at syncretism. Yet Chosa and his wife appear oblivious to the fact that the ideology of contextualization is grounded in the same Kraftian assumptions that fuel the NAR, of which he is an apostle (see Wolfe 58 on Kraft's ideas of contextualization; see Kraft, *Christianity in Culture* 295–296, for his most explicit discussions on contextualization, though contextualization is in many ways the subject of that entire book), and that there is in fact significant overlap in these movements' leadership. John Dawson, for instance, who practically invented spiritual mapping, wrote the foreword to Richard Twiss's *One Church, Many Tribes* (2000); Twiss also received an endorsement from C. Peter Wagner, who argues that the book is an "excellent orientation to the Native American worldview, written in terms the rest of us can understand and appreciate. God is using Richard Twiss in a remarkable way as a leader who is hearing what the Spirit is saying to the churches" (Twiss Endorsements *One Church, Many Tribes*).

Thus, Chosa, an NAR apostle under Wagner's discipleship (2010 "International Coalition of Apostles Membership Directory") and therefore presumably approved of by Wagner, ends up doing battle with Twiss, whose ideology is simultaneously also approved of by Wagner, even though the two men's approach to Native/evangelical relations are both mutually irreconcilable and totally antithetical to each other. It takes skill to play two opponents off each other; but it takes a man of Wagner's political genius to make two allies sincerely think they are pursuing opposing ideological aims when in fact they are fighting for the same thing: the annihilation of their own culture. Perhaps Chosa and Twiss were willing participants in Wagner's Machiavellianism, but I think Smith's cautions about Native evangelicals limited options in choosing allies are valuable here (Andrea Smith 84). Leaders like Chosa and Twiss had to choose between the devils that they knew—the spiritual mapping movement and its eventual NAR descendants—and those that they did not. But in the process of dealing with these earthly devils, Chosa and Twiss were transmuted—and in Chosa's case transmuted himself—into the very demonic figures the NAR invoked in its perpetual, and to this day, still ongoing, campaign against Native peoples.

The Insider Movement (IM) and the NAR: Beating up Other Religions with the Good Cop/Bad Cop Strategy

In this section, I briefly discuss the Insider movement strategy developed by evangelical missiologists as a means for converting populations previously seen as evangelism-adverse. While the Insider Movement is not necessarily or even primarily aligned with the NAR, its foundational assumptions for converting non-evangelicals overlap significantly with the NAR. As mentioned previously, the Insider Movement takes the idea of dynamic equivalence developed by Kraft and takes them beyond their NAR context. The NAR saw dynamic equivalence as a way of adapting the "gospel" to different racial and cultural groups that might otherwise be resistant to the spread of the evangelical message. The IM merely expanded this idea to the religious context, allowing individuals to stay within their particular religious contexts while accepting Christ as their "personal Savior."

The reason I cover the IM here is twofold. First, the IM can be productively viewed as the Good Cop strategy that Christian Right missions' theorists use to convert members of non-evangelical religions, while the NAR's typically more aggressive form of evangelism can be seen as a more strident, bad cop approach. The second reason for covering the IM is its closer parallels with the "Messianic Jewish" movement (which is itself largely the prototype for the Insider movement). At this current juncture, the Messianic movement is thoroughly embedded in the NAR. Because of the enormous political and religious problems this poses for Israeli, Palestinian, and U.S. policy makers, it is imperative to note these movements' similarities.

The IM, as Doug Coleman points out, was not an overnight phenomenon. IM supporter Kevin Higgins, arguably the most influential advocate of this particular mission paradigm, noted the influence of Donald McGavran and Alan Tippett on the movement, whose ideas about the homogenous unit principle and the need for Christian people movements were reinterpreted to add non– Christian religions as possible places in which to form new people movements

(Coleman 2). The influence of McGavran especially is crucial, and not simply because of the influence he had on Kraft and Wagner. The IM, like the NAR, assumes that it needs to build up critical bases of support in non–Christian or insufficiently evangelized communities before those communities will be sufficiently enamored of the Christian message to convert to Christianity. In order to facilitate this process it is important to minimize potential conflicts between people within these emerging people movements and their surrounding culture, which may be hostile to the evangelical message or even Christianity in general. McGavran makes this point explicitly in *Understanding Church Growth* (1970) (McGavran 335–337). He argued that Christian individuals within people movements should make a joint decision to enter into a Christian lifestyle without "social dislocation" allowing them to remain in "full contact with their non-Christian relatives, thus enabling other groups of that people, across the years, after suitable instruction, to come to similar decisions and form Christian churches made up exclusively of members of that people" (McGavran 335). McGavran's genius insight was to realize that evangelistic efforts might be more successful if these efforts were reinterpreted more at the level of the group than at the level of the individual. While obviously rejecting the idea of communal salvation, McGavran realized that evangelical missions' efforts overseas worked best when they involved a gradual building up of a faith community through its methodical assimilation of surrounding cultures. Thus, for McGavran, as for the IM, while conversion was an individual decision, it was a decision best made within the context of community, the broader the communal base the better.

McGavran believed that one of the major problems of colonial evangelism had been that it had been extractionist, forcing the individual to choose between his faith and his community. McGavran believed that such extractionist practices "failed to understand the sociological nature of decision-making within a society" (Wolfe 32). The advantage of using people movements was that they were grounded in minimizing the social differences between the converted individual and his community; ideally, this would serve as a "light" by which the converted individual would be able to shine the Christian message to his unredeemed neighbors (see Wolfe 32).

The IM differed from people movements by the fact that it encouraged "family and community groups" that came to believe in Christ to "remain inside their socio-religious communities, retaining the entirety of their former religious identity" (Wolfe 40). Thus for the IM it was not at all contradictory to say that one believed in Jesus Christ as one's personal savior while at the same time also claiming a dual identity as a Muslim follower of Jesus. It must be understood that this is not a form of pseudo-universalism. Rather it is an attempt to Christianize other religious systems to the point that those systems ideologically collapse from within or at least surrender large numbers of their own members to Christianity via gradual attrition. It is, in other words, an explicitly colonialist religious practice, but one that uses more subversive tactics than the more open and confrontational methods of evangelism favored by traditional evangelical missionaries.

A seminal essay by Charles Kraft in 1974 made the startling suggestion that missionaries "bend every effort toward stimulating a faith renewal movement within Islam." Kraft suggested that the missiological establishment should "encourage some Christians to become Christian Muslims in order to win Muslims to Muslim Christianity" (Kraft, "Psychological Stress Factors" 143–144; Wolfe 58–59). As Kraft's ideas on contextualization were gradually refined over the next two decades, more and more elaborate and sophisticated theories of cross-religious evangelism were developed. The formation of the Insider methodology itself can be in great part attributed to the development of the C1–C6 Scale pioneered by John Travis. Travis's C1–C6 Scale, better known as the C scale, was designed "to assist church planters and Muslim background believers to ascertain which type of Christ-centered communities may draw the most people from the target group to Christ and best fit in a given context" (Travis 407; Coleman 4.). Travis emphasized that conversion of Muslims would require a wide variety of missionary approaches, thus cautioning against a too ready preference for any one model.

Each form of outreach reflected a different form of approaching Islam. The C1 church included traditional Orthodox, Catholic or Protestant churches, some of which might predate Islam in selected geographic territories. Most reflected a Western worldview, which often created a chasm between the church and the surrounding community. "Muslim background believers" could be found in C1 churches in some cases. C1 believers unambiguously called themselves Christians. C2 was essentially the same as C1 except for language. These churches might use insider language, but their religious vocabulary was probably non–Islamic and also "distinctively 'Christian.'" The use of insider language, however, meant that these churches might contain somewhat more Muslim members than C1 churches. The C3 model focused not on churches but on "contextualized Christ-centered Communities." These communities would use Insider language and what was interpreted as "religiously neutral Insider Cultural Forms." These forms might be folk music, ethnic dress, artwork, etc. In the C3 model Islamic elements, when present are "filtered out." The goal of the model is to make Christianity seem less foreign by using contextualization to minimize cultural difference. C3 communities may still meet in churches, but may also meet in more neutral areas. C3 believers, however still do call themselves Christians. C4 Communities are similar to C3, but also allow "biblically permissible Islamic forms," such as avoiding pork and alcohol or praying with raised hands. In C4 communities meetings are not held in church buildings and the meetings are composed almost exclusively of Christians from Muslim backgrounds ("Muslim Background Believers"). Although this is a highly contextualized version of Christianity, C4 believers are seldom seen as Muslim by the Muslim community. C4 believers also begin incorporating more fuzzy language in their relationships with Muslims, for instance using terms like "followers of Isa the Messiah." C5 is the most controversial of these "Christ-centered communities" and the real center of controversy. The C5 community are Messianic Muslims who live within "the community of Islam." Those parts of Islam which are incompatible with evangelical interpretations of the Bible are rejected, while other parts are reinterpreted when possible. Messianic Muslims may participate in corporate acts of Islamic worship, but often subtly reinterpret the meaning of that worship. C5 may sometimes lead to the formation of Messianic mosques, though this idea seems to have been somewhat downplayed by certain Insider advocates in favor of converting Muslims by subtler means. What is crucial about C5 identity is that these Messianic Muslims are meant to be seen as Muslim by the Islamic community (Travis 407; Coleman 4–6). C6 believers are largely synonymous with the idea of a secret church where people remain totally silent about their religious belief. They also are seen as Muslims and may identify themselves as Muslim (Coleman 5–6).

IM advocates interpret the Pauline epistles as providing a justification for staying within a religious community whose beliefs Christians have largely rejected. They contend that so-called "unbiblical" aspects of Islam must be rejected, but contend that such rejection can be undertaken without completely renouncing Islam as a whole (Coleman 11). What is important to understand is that many IM supporters perceive Islam more as a sociological descriptor than a religious one, identifying Islam as more a cultural than a religious identity. Similarly, their own religious identity is in some ways seen in these terms. Thus, what is important for the IM movement, is that Muslims are converted to Christ, not to Christianity. IM thereby replaces an institutional definition of religion, with a relational one. This move is crucial for two reasons. First, it allows the movement the ideological "wiggle-room" to claim what seems to be mutually exclusive institutional identities. But secondly this move gives the IM a real advantage in missions, because a relational definition of religion is inherently beneficial to religious movements that are incarnational in character. Since Christianity emphasizes an incarnational relationship between Christ and humanity, it is ideally poised to benefit from such an arrangement. Simply put, when religion is viewed not institutionally, but relationally, the deck is already stacked in favor of Christianity, because of its greater tendency to anthropomorphize its deity figure.

The NAR, like the IM, is a flexible theological movement. While I did not find any evidence of NAR incorporation of IM rhetoric in reference to Islam, such rhetoric is clearly seen in the NAR's approach to so-called "low religious traditions" like Native American belief systems. It is also evident in the movement's approach to Judaism. Given, however, the almost identical ideological wellsprings from which the IM and NAR draw, it would be extremely unlikely if there is not much more interconnections between these movements than this work documents, especially considering that many IM proponents move in the same Fuller Seminary circles that gave birth to Kraft, Wagner, and Wimber. Given the NAR's highly pragmatic nature and the apostles' ability to quickly adapt to changing strategic situations, it is also likely that IM methodologies will be adopted in the future by some NAR supporters. What might prevent a fullscale adoption of IM ideology is not the unwillingness of the NAR's leadership but the fact that in the United States the NAR has had to take a hard ideological line to keep the faithful energized, which means, among other things, demonizing Islam to the extent that IM strategies are too likely to be seen as syncretism by many of the leaders of the NAR. In addition, some of the more hardline apostles, particularly Rick Joyner, are deeply embedded with the American far right and are unlikely to support any form of religious proselytization that takes the kind of nuanced approach to conversion favored by IM proponents.

The defining NAR text on Islam is *The Last of the Giants: Lifting the Veil on Islam and the End Times* (1991). *The Last of the Giants* was one of Otis's most early texts on spiritual mapping and helped pioneer the field. Written in the wake of the first Iraq war, Otis Jr.'s text comes heavily recommended, including endorsements from C. Peter Wagner and Darrow Miller ally Ted Yamamori (who wrote the preface for the book) (Otis Jr., *Last of the Giants* 19–20). For Otis Jr., the fall of Soviet Marxism left a spiritual void in the world. Three forces were contending to fill that void—Islam, Hinduism and materialism. Of the three, Otis Jr. labeled Islam as the largest threat (Otis Jr. 52–58; Kidd 128). Otis suggested that Muhammad's revelations were demonically inspired. He also warned that evil spirits within geographical areas rarely have their original "invitation" to inhabit those areas revoked. Therefore, when Muslims exchanged "their pre–Islamic heathen rituals for the Hajj" they were merely "repackaging ancient rites of spirit welcome and appeasement as popular, and seemingly more benign, festivals and pilgrimages," thus reaffirming demonic control over these areas. Because many Muslim cultures had obviously engaged

6. From the Others of the Americas to the Others Overseas 207

in rituals like the Hajj, as well as erected "sacred sites" which were dwelling places for what Otis called "unclean spirits," large parts of the Islamic world were conceptualized as "captive strongholds" for Islam, that is "areas where human partnerships with evil spirits have resulted in dense demonic populations and the domination of surrounding societies." A widely disproportionate number of locations deemed as captive strongholds by Otis were located in areas populated primarily by Muslims, including Mecca and Medina themselves (as well as Tehran and "Babylon") (Otis 94–95). Otis openly supports the idea that the reemergence of "the demonic prince of Persia" was responsible for the Iranian revolution (Otis 121). He blamed the brutality of Saddam Hussein on Satan and the demonic as well, as he writes: "Those who believe that traditional weapons of warfare will put an end to the brutality that is Iraq are sadly mistaken.... Like a spiritual hydra, so long as the demonic principalities at the root of the land flourish, the spirit of Saddam and his vision of Babylon will live on" (Otis Jr. 117). Thus, even in its embryonic state, the NAR conceptualized of Islam largely in supernatural terms, seeing it as a demonic religious system that needed to be dismantled in order for evangelism to be truly effective.

However, despite the notes of warning in Otis's work, evangelical global missions in the 1990s was obsessed with Islam, in large part due to the idea of the 10/40 window popularized by Louis Bush and his AD 2000 campaign. Since the majority of the unreached people groups within the 10/40 window were Muslim, the NAR saw Muslims as a prime target for conversion. 10/40 brochures promoted the idea that such conversions would require "overcoming Satanic strongholds." Despite Otis's forebodings about the Middle East, as the new millennium approached, evangelical leaders began calling for prayer in the major cities of the 10/40 window (Kidd 128–129). As Thomas Kidd points out, the events of 9/11 helped push the evangelical movement in an increasingly apocalyptic direction when it came to Islam, a direction in any case it had always had a propensity to head, given evangelicalism's longstanding apocalyptic outlook (Kidd 151, 155–160).

But the specific rhetoric of SLSW and spiritual mapping that Otis Jr. added to the NAR's understanding of Islamic-Christian relations immensely amped up the potential tension points between the two religions. Secular critics, while having reason for concern about traditional dispensationalist rhetoric, have overrated its potential influence over Middle Eastern affairs. While evangelicals have remained constantly energized about "defending Israel," the key point to understand about traditional dispensationalism is that most dispensationalists do not want to hasten the day of Christ's return.

The new form of Charismatic apocalypticism is not necessarily dispensationalist in character, though it is often premillennialist in outlook. The important part in understanding current Charismatic eschatological beliefs and their potentially world-ending significance is to realize two things. First of all, the exact eschatological scenario among individual NAR leaders is not so much the issue, though secular critics would be remiss in not tracing such differences. The second point is even more crucial: For most NAR believers who do hold to some sort of apocalyptic End Times scenario, the End Times is something to be looked forward to, not feared. Traditional dispensationalist eschatology is defeatist; NAR eschatology is triumphalist. They could not be further apart. What this means in real world terms is that the NAR views opposing religious ideologies through an apocalyptic prism that is prone not to political apathy (as with traditional dispensationalism), but total political fanaticism against opposing worldviews. Since opponents are seen as not simply serving corrupt or evil religions, but literally demonic ones, practically any tactic is deemed acceptable to convert them.

The NAR's actions in Turkey and Iraq provide particular evidence of this point. C. Peter Wagner's *Confronting the Queen of Heaven* (1998) is a particularly notorious example of Islamophobia, which Wagner somehow manages to promulgate as NAR religious pluralism. During the late 1990s, the city of Ephesus in Turkey became an important target for Wagner's Spiritual Warfare Network (Wagner, *Confronting the Queen* 9). Wagner came to believe that the chief territorial spirit over Ephesus was Diana of the Ephesians, who the movement equated with the Queen of Heaven (and with the worship of the Virgin Mary) (Wagner, *Confronting the Queen* 12, 31–32). The only way the movement saw of defeating such a demonic force was through SLSW combat against the Queen of Heaven (Wagner, *Confronting the Queen* 12). Part of this involved the aforementioned Operation Ice Castle (Wagner, *Confronting the Queen* 12, 36–37). But the NAR also "puffed" its actions in Turkey as proof of the ongoing outpouring of the Holy Spirit in the 10/40 window. One effort was the euphemistically entitled Reconciliation Walk, which Wagner dubbed the "most massive prayer expedition of the decade." Its goal was to "mobilize Christian intercessors to walk every known route of the First Crusade with only one agenda item: repenting (or apologizing) to Muslims and Jews for the sins which our Christian ancestors committed against them in the First Crusade 900 years ago, and in the subsequent crusades" (28). These reconciliation efforts bore enormous fruits with the Native American community, even as the NAR effectively labeled them as a demonized people; thus it is not surprising that the NAR applied the same model in Turkey.

Wagner claimed to have shown Cindy Jacobs a map of where the Garden of Eden might have been located, as well as Mount Ararat, after which he showed her pictures of Diana and an "idol of Mary," as well as "other things related to the Queen of Heaven" (39). Jacobs then proclaimed it was time to stop skirmishing with the Queen of Heaven and confront her in her own palace. What this entailed, according to Wagner, was a massive spiritual mapping effort by George Otis to find fifty sites in Turkey to send prayer journey teams to as part of a spiritual mapping effort. Wagner then used the Turkey effort as a spur to conduct spiritual warfare in other countries, especially those that were sending out prayer warriors to Turkey. Thus even as Wagner was claiming to promote peace between Muslims and Christians, he was promoting the idea that the Turks were being demonized by the Queen of Heaven (Wagner 39–40).

Meanwhile at Fuller Seminary, research was undertaken into the exact nature of Turkey's demonic strongholds. Won Ho Kim's 1999 Masters thesis "A Strategy for Spiritual Warfare in Istanbul, Turkey," directed by Charles Kraft, was the first of two Fuller-derived works to discuss the problem of demonized Turks. Kim makes clear that he felt global mission would not be completed until the church had ascertained "the strongholds in those areas where Satanic powers are prevalent." These areas included Turkey, since Kim relates that he sees spiritual mapping as a "useful instrument for understanding these powers of darkness," a tool that has developed into an "effective strategy for reaching Turkey" (15).

Kim recommends using a form of contextualization (given his advisor, probably but not certainly Kraftian) in reaching Muslims (120), not unlike the strategy adopted by the IM, but with the proviso that this strategy needs to be molded through a spiritual mapping paradigm. According to Kim, in order "to engage in effective spiritual warfare in Turkey, missionaries must break down the connections between evil spirits and cultural forms and people. In addition, Christian workers must use the cultural forms in accordance with local custom in order to have a positive effect and break the stronghold of evil" (12). Such forms of contextualization were critical, because Kim believed that "demonic strongholds that hinder people from coming to the Lord are deeply entrenched in Turkish society" (62). Remember, all of this was written under the tutelage of the anthropological founder of NAR ideology and clearly reflected the then dominant view of Turkish society being promoted by Wagner and his allies. Deriving his model of Satanic strongholds from Cindy Jacobs, Kim lists nine potential types of satanic strongholds in Turkey, the most offensive of which his assertion that a satanic seat of power was located in Turkey, because the city of Pergamos was located there (Kim 66).[6]

Kim also quotes an email he received from C. Peter Wagner himself which is something of a bombshell. Wagner told Kim that the spiritual roots of Islam is the territorial spirit "Artemis." Wagner claims that Muslim leaders would not allow archaeological excavations in Mecca because "the connection between the moon goddess and Islam would then be highlighted scientifically, while Islam desires to maintain its public image of monotheism." Wagner makes explicit that the reason the NAR was praying for Turkey had little or nothing to do with reconciliation, but instead was rooted in the movement's attempt to cleanse Turkey of demons, as he notes that "we knew that the power of the Queen of Heaven had to be broken in order for the gospel to spread in Turkey" (68). Wagner also again connects Islam with supposed Mariolatry, pointing out that Mary worship increased in Ephesus after the ecumenical council of 431 that was held in that city. Having been thoroughly hoodwinked by Wagner by this point, Kim concludes that "after 8 years in Turkey, I came to the conclusion that the obstacles to evangelizing the nation lie in the satanic power in Islam" (Kim 122). Despite the unclear justifications Kim offers for seeing more than one billion of the world's human beings as being demonized, he never wavers in his belief that spiritual mapping and other SLSW practices are the best tactics for evangelism in Turkey.

Kim followed this Masters' thesis up with a doctoral dissertation on Turkey that he completed in 2006, again under the directorship of Kraft. In a post 9/11 atmosphere in which it should have been obvious to any dissertation director that greater sensitivity was needed in approaching Islam, Kraft nevertheless signed off on a work that was every bit as inflammatory as Kim's Master's thesis. According to Kim, "Turkey is very resistant to the gospel. Satan holds the nation under a veil of spiritual deception by using a false religion to generate bondage. Satan maintains his strength and control among people in Turkey through Islamic ritual practices, through fundamental Muslims who commit themselves to Islam, and through more than sixty thousand mosques and political leaders" (Kim, "Spiritual Dynamics" 2). Kim's targets had not changed, they had just grown in number. With 60,000 mosques and political leaders as potential enemies for evangelicals in Turkey, Kim leaves evangelicals with plenty of enemies to choose from in that nation. Worse, Kim promotes the idea that conversion of Muslim family units is difficult because Turkish families have "been demonized through soul ties that are transferred through generations." He therefore advises Christian workers that if they "do not destroy demonically empowered bondage ... evangelism in Turkey will be ineffective" (87–88). Thus soul ties theology, a core element of some of the most repugnant aspects of NAR ideology, is used to demonize families for their religious beliefs.

However, the most dangerous and potentially worrisome actions the NAR has undertaken in the Islamic world are not in Turkey, but in Kurdistan—that is, northern Iraq. When the U.S. occupation started there, American evangelicals began establishing schools, printing presses, radio stations, bookstores, medical and dental clinics, and churches in northern Iraq. These efforts were assisted by the Kurdistan government, and some of these efforts were partially funded by U.S. taxpayer dollars that were channeled to these evangelicals through State Department grants and construction contracts authorized by the Defense Department (Reynolds, "American Evangelicals in Kurdistan").

These efforts had important antecedents. In 1988 Saddam Hussein launched an assault on the Kurds, which included a chemical weapons attack that slaughtered thousands. Some 14,000 refugees from Kurdistan ended up coming to Nashville, Tennessee, now the largest Kurdish population center in the country. Four years later, a group of Nashville evangelicals (who investigative reporter Mike Reynolds explicitly labels "dominionists"), called Servant Group International left Nashville's Belmont Church for the mountainous terrain of Northern Iraq, where they soon entrenched themselves (Berkowitz, "What in the Name of?").

Northern Iraq was prime 10/40 real estate and also held much prophetic significance because of its proximity to "Babylon," which some evangelicals believe will be the seat of the One World government during the end times. Servant Group International was specifically campaigning with the 10/40 idea in mind. Evangelicals settled in Kurdistan with the blessing of the Nechirvan Barzani-led Kurdistan Regional Government (KRG) and the Bush administration, even though policy experts thought that the expansion of such an aggressive form of evangelism into Kurdistan was "like striking matches in a room full of gasoline" (Berkowitz, "What in the Name of?").

At a September 2003 gathering of evangelical leaders in Kirkuk, George Grant, a leader of Servant Group International, declared that "Jesus Christ is Lord over all things; He is Lord over every Mullah, every Ayatollah, every Imam, and every Mahdi pretender; He is Lord over the whole of the earth, even Iraq!" Needless to say, such statements can do little to improve U.S./Islamic relations. Documents that reporter Michael Reynolds obtained showed that between 2005 and 2007, the United States Department of Defense paid the Kurdish company Daban Group a minimum of $465,639 to construct Grant's School of the Medes. Two years earlier, the State Department-funded program Healthcare Partnerships in Northern Iraq funneled tens of thousands of dollars into various Servant Group evangelizing and humanitarian endeavors (Reynolds).

Servant Group was notable for a number of distinct points, among them that it used a military model of evangelism—what they self-labeled spiritual warfare; that it incorporated tent making and Kingdom Business into its overseas missions; that it used spiritual mapping; and finally that it adhered to a "Kingdom Now" worldview with distinct ties to the NAR (Reynolds). The group also made shrewd ties with the Bush administration, particularly through

Belmont Church's former pastor Stephen Mansfield who wrote the bestselling *The Faith of George W. Bush* (2003), which was required reading for evangelicals in the mid-2000s (Reynolds). Mansfield was also responsible for producing a hagiographic biography of shepherding leader Derek Prince, *Derek Prince: A Biography* (2005) (Mansfield passim). Prior to taking Belmont's pulpit in 1997, Mansfield worked in northern Iraq with Servant Group, bringing bibles and the famous *Jesus* film to the Kurds (Reynolds).

Douglas Layton was the founder of Servant Group International and drew praises from Christian Reconstructionist leaders for his efforts in Iraq; this is not perhaps surprising considers his relationship with Grant, who had published books for the Reconstructionist Dominion Press and co-wrote *Rebuilding the Walls* with Christian Reconstructionist Peter Waldron (Berkowitz). In 2005, Layton helped produce a promotional campaign called Kurdistan: The Other Iraq, which "featured smiling Kurds waving American flags and thanking the United States for its invasion of Iraq" (Reynolds). Layton also helped tout the rich opportunities awaiting corporate multinationals in northern Iraq (Reynolds).

As disturbing as all this is, the open involvement of Grant in such an evangelism effort is what is most cause for concern. Grant has been a Christian Reconstructionist for decades and runs the Classical Schools that SGI has set up in Iraq from more than half a world away. Grant's 2001 book *The Blood of the Moon* argues for conquering the Islamic world by military might to bring about Muslim conversion. Mark Potok of the Southern Poverty Law Center argues that Grant's schools are "deeply influenced by white supremacist ideas," pointing to Grant's association with the notorious Douglas Wilson, a fellow Reconstructionist whose *Southern Slavery: As It Was* (1996) tries to justify Southern slavery as a wonderful cultural system that promoted racial harmony and provided great health care for slaves (Hayes and Saul; Wilkins and Wilson 11; Reynolds). The combination of NAR and Reconstructionist forces in the same country is not a good sign. Each alone can do damage, but the combined theocratic aggression that heralds those efforts in which they are successfully able to put aside their theological differences beggars description. When one adds to this point the fact that both Grant and George Otis, Jr. (who has connections with Layton) (Reynolds, "How American Christian Right"), also seem to have connections with more mainstream evangelical leaders like Darrow Miller and his fellow holistic transformationalists, there is real cause for concern that dominionist doctrine is becoming systematically mainstreamed within at least the Christian missions world, to possibly devastating effect. What the final result of that mainstreaming will be, no one can tell.

As of 2009, Reynolds described the SGI as having virtually the "run of the country" in Kurdistan, where the Kurdistan Regional Government (KRG) often backs "their ministries and schools with grants of land, buildings, and other favors" (Berkowitz). Between the subversion from within through the IM, and the subversion from without through the NAR and its allies, the missiological establishment within evangelicalism has done nothing less than declare full scale war against Islam. But in doing so, the evangelical movement has politicized itself to an unprecedented degree, gutting evangelical doctrine out in favor of a politicized religion that is willing to either kill or flatter in order to achieve its aim of eradicating Islam. The question is, what kind of Christianity would that leave the world in its wake? Such acts of theistic conquest against other faith traditions have very real consequences, not just to those being converted, but to surrounding societies and nation states that are left dangerously unbalanced in the wake of these efforts.

Israel: NAR Insiderism at Its Most Dangerous

As we have seen, the NAR's potential outward adoption of IM methodology has been made problematic by the fact that while the movement has little problem in using insider methods with "low religious" traditions—what the movement often condescendingly calls animist traditions—the NAR is much less comfortable applying Insider methodology to large religious traditions such as Islam, Hinduism, and Buddhism. This likely arises out of fears on the part of the NAR leadership that they will be charged with religious syncretism. While the NAR can assimilate some Native American or African religious traditions under its banner without receiving too much criticism from fellow evangelicals, the same could be not said if the NAR attempted to merge larger religious traditions into its thought system.

The one exception to this, however, is Judaism. Indeed, the NAR promotes syncretic fusions of Judaism and Christianity to an amazing degree. The main way the NAR has attempted to infiltrate Judaism is through the so-called Messianic movement. This attempt at religious subversion, as well as the NAR's increasingly radical eschatological beliefs, represent the *single most dangerous aspect* of the movement as a whole, whose potential effect on Middle Eastern politics cannot be overstated.

The NAR, like evangelicalism in general, has always claimed to be acting from a philosemitic standpoint, as if philosemitism were somehow the opposite of anti–Semitism. Yet philosemitism has hardly always served that purpose. Early Anglo-Israelism attacked anti–Semitism, yet used the idea of racial chosenness that its genealogical-centric beliefs promoted to attack groups that were then not allied with whatever group was then on the "in" with the Anglo-Israelites. It was not uncommon to see such philosemities attacking anti–Semitism. But as we have seen, Anglo-Israelism proved all too capable of evolving into anti–Semitism when it suited those in power. *The Dearborn Independent*, a notorious anti–Semitic newspaper had a British Israelite for an editor and the movement ended up creating perhaps the most reprehensible theological system in modern Christianity: The Christian Identity movement (Tabachnick, "The New Christian Zionism").

As Tabachnick points out, Christian Zionist media is actually a major promoter of anti–Semitic and anti–Jewish media. This can be seen in well-known works like the non–NAR inspired *Left Behind* series, whose anti–Semitism is obvious (see Mleynek passim), but also in more subtle ways, such as evangelical jeremiads against esteemed Jewish religious figures like Hillel. In particular, anti-pharisaical rhetoric has become incredibly popular among Charismatics and Pentecostals in recent years. The Pharisees are often equated with a literal demon, with this Pharisaical demon supposedly being responsible for "legalism and division in the church." Such beliefs are promoted even by more scholarly NAR leaders like Wagner, despite the fact that even a cursory knowledge of New Testament criticism would acquaint Wagner with the fact that Christ himself was philosophically closer in many ways to the Pharisees than many other of Jewish groups operating in the New Testament Palestine (Tabachnick, "The New Christian Zionism"; MacCullough 72).

Tabachnick explicitly identifies the NAR as a major force behind the Messianic movement and the case she makes for this point is compelling. One-time CUFI director Stephen Strang is a prominent NAR Apostle, and his magazine *Charisma* has been little more than a mouthpiece for the NAR for more than a decade. Another CUFI director, Robert Stearns, edits the "popular Apostolic and Prophetic magazine," and co-founded the Day of Prayer for the Peace of Jerusalem (DPPJ). According to Tabachnick, the DPPJ is "the largest single Christian Zionist event with advertised participation of 200,000 churches in 175 nations"; shockingly the event also has gained the endorsement of the Knesset's Christian Allies Caucus (Tabachnick, "The New Christian Zionism").

Tabachnick is even more alarmed by a 2005 CBN interview, in which Stearns told that Christian network that all participating churches in the DPPJ would receive the book *Your People Shall Be My People* (2001) by Don Finto as their prime entryway into "Messianic ministries." Tabachnick's concerns here are not difficult to fathom. Finto's book is published by Regal, a Charismatic publisher with a long history of supporting NAR authors. The book's blurbs also signify its alignment with the movement. Prominent Apostles Francis

Frangipane, Jim Goll, and Cindy Jacobs all give Finto's book glowing reviews, as does NAR ally Jack Hayford (Finto, blurbs). Finto is a member of Stephen Mansfield's Belmont church, which as we have seen had ties to politically explosive Christian missionary efforts in Kurdistan, efforts that have been tied to the NAR by respected journalists (Reynolds "How American Christians"; Finto 15).[7] Finto's book is also heavily promoted by and in turn heavily promotes the work of John Dawson and his International Reconciliation Council. Dawson was one of the earliest promoters of identificational repentance (see *Healing America's Wounds*, for example), and if identificational repentance towards Jews resembles the practice as used towards Native Americans and other socially marginalized groups, then there is no way for the NAR to deny that the current Messianic movement's agenda is anything other than explicitly evangelistic.

Finto seeks to make the relationship between NAR theology and the state of Israel clear by noting the simultaneous occurrence of the Latter Rain Revival and the creation of the state of Israel in 1948. Finto calls the Latter Rain Revival a "great healing ministry," yet totally neglects to inform his readers, many of whom might be otherwise uninformed, about the many negative critiques of Latter Rain theology. Finto also uses the book to promote the AD 2000 movement as another major force in world Christianity, which has been "accompanied by the greatest prayer effort ever launched in history" (Finto 45).

Sarah Posner has noted that the existence of two houses of prayer in Israel modeled after Mike Bickle's ministry, which historically has had an extreme emphasis on End Times theology (see Posner, "Kosher Jesus"). Posner also notes that Asher Intrater, another NAR aligned Messianic believer promotes the idea that the Jews will undergo a second Holocaust during the End Times (Posner, "Kosher Jesus"). Again, Intrater's NAR alignment is fairly easy to decipher, based partly on the fact that Intrater has frequently collaborated with Daniel C. Juster, president of Tikkun International, who is an ICA apostle and whose Tikkun International is one of many ministries under the ICA's wider banner. Also, Intrater was on Tikkun International's board as of the mid–2000s (see Tabachnick, "God's Plan for Israel" 31; See 2010 "International Coalition of Apostles Membership Directory"; see also "Tikkun International Board"). As Posner points out, for the Messianic movement—and again this is a clear sign of its takeover by the NAR, as their eschatologies are exactly alike—the Rapture really is not typically the big issue. Instead, Messianics believe, like many in the NAR—particularly IHOP—that they are preparing the way for a "purified church" (Posner, "Kosher Jesus").

Dan Juster's Tikkun International, though by no means the only Messianic group out there, is one of the more prominent, and Juster is seen by the Messianic movement as its major theologian. As of the mid 2000s, Juster provided "oversight to 15 congregations in the USA" which given his position in the ICA assuredly means that he's providing apostolic covering for those congregations (Tabachnick, "God's Plan for Israel" 31).[8] Finto was also on Tikkun International's Board, as was Asher Intrater and his wife ("TIkkun International Board"). Juster is the vice-chairman of the Messianic Jewish Bible Institute (MJBI) ("Board of Directors") and was one of its co-founders (Yanover). That organization, in addition to being the premier educational site for Messianic Jews, has garnered considerable criticism for its promotion of proselytization and its political dalliances with figures like Glen Beck and former president George W. Bush (Yanover). Considering the fact that Juster is indisputably the most prominent theologian in the Messianic community, and that Intrater and Finto are widely seen as influential voices in that community as well, it is impossible to reject Tabachnick's conclusion that the Messianic community has become thoroughly saturated with NAR philosophy. And in spite of Posner's mild skepticism on the NAR (see Butler), her own research damningly indicts such skepticism, as almost all the groups and individuals she names in her expose are either led by NAR apostles (IHOP), members of apostolic networks (Intrater), or allies (John Hagee).

Israel has been the site of major events by other NAR leaders as well. Lou Engle held a major Call event, Call Jerusalem, in Israel during 2008 ("CWN, 2008 Global Day of Prayer"; Tabachnick, "God's Plan for Israel" 18).[9] Coverage of the Call was broadcast on God TV, whose alignment with the NAR and questionable racialized theology have already been outlined in Chapters 5. The Call Jerusalem 2008 meeting was also attended by Mike Bickle (Tabachnick, "God's Plan for Israel" 18) and received CBN coverage ("CWN, 2008 Global Day of Prayer"; Hart, "Global Day of Prayer Unites Millions").

Much of the rhetoric surrounding Judaism coming out of the NAR, as well as the messianic movement itself, is concerning because of its references to special Jewish spiritual DNA. While the movement claims not to view such DNA in terms of racial biology, the equation of Jewish DNA, with a "unique ability" for "success and survival," as seen in books like Perry Stone's *Breaking the Jewish Code* (2009), is a strikingly irresponsible use of biological metaphors as applied to spirituality (Stone 1–4). Stone's claim that the kohen members of the Levite tribe carry a special god gene is equally troubling (Stone 11). While there is always a fair amount of metaphor mixed with NAR descriptions of genetics, the fact is that many contemporary Charismatics and Pentecostals take such metaphors literally.

There are far too many Messianic organizations and leaders with NAR affiliations to cover in one chapter, but brief mention should be made of one other figure that represents perhaps the most formidable force in NAR–aligned

Messianic activism in Israel. That is Calev Myers. Myers is the director of an influential organization called the Jerusalem Institute for Justice and a self-described Messianic Jew. Myers has made a reputation off of defending supposedly persecuted Messianic Jews in Israel who are suffering "discrimination" at the hands of the Orthodox establishment. Myers allegiance to the Messianic movement, despite some prevarications on his part, is rather transparent. Most notably, he appeared in the 2011 IHOP documentary, *Nefarious*, as an expert on sex trafficking (Ain; Nolot, *Nefarious*). Myers has pushed for citizenship for messianic missionaries (Kravitz; Roach), which in turn has led to controversial modifications in Israel's Law of Return, modifications that would entitle Messianic Jews to citizenship if their father is Jewish (Izenberg). Obviously such changes are highly controversial to the Orthodox and ultra-Orthodox communities in Israel and with good reason, as Myers seems to be bending at least the religious definition of Jewish identity to its breaking point. Yet Myers continues to be a sought-after figure in the Charismatic community because of both the success he has had at marketing Messianic beliefs in Israel and the sophistication with which he has undertaken that marketing.

Nowhere in the world is NAR theology singularly more dangerous than in Israel. Already populated by more "traditional" forms of Christianity, as well as Judaism and Islam, Israel has always been a powder keg waiting to go off. The deliberate and systematic targeting of Jews for conversion by the Messianic movement is a continuation of Christianity's 2000 year campaign of theocide against Judaism. Millions of people have paid with their lives for this campaign, yet it shows no sign of ending. Israel, however, is hardly the only country to be touched by the NAR over the last several decades. The movement has its claws in seemingly every country in the world. We have already seen its effect on Turkey, Guatemala, Argentina, and the United States. Below I provide a sampling of the NAR's influence overseas, an influence that will continue to shape the world for many years to come.

Canada: From the Latter Rain to Todd Bentley, the Surprising Story of Canadian Charismatic Fanaticism

As the United States' nearest neighbor and one of its closest allies, it is not surprising to find that NAR activity has featured prominently in Canada compared to most Western countries. Indeed, arguably the NAR could not have been created without Canadian Charismatics. As we have seen, the 1948

Latter Rain Revival originated at the Sharon Orphanage and Schools in North Battleford, Saskatchewan, Canada, on February 12 and 13, 1948 (Riss 13). That revival was greatly influenced by William Branham's Vancouver B.C. campaign in the fall of 1947 (Riss 12), which testifies to the surprising power of the most extreme forms of Charismatic belief in Canada. And we have also seen that Canada was the springboard for the Toronto Blessing, the most important modern "renewal" movement within the Charismatic movement, and a revival directly responsible for the creation of the Revival Alliance, one of the two most powerful apostolic networks within the NAR. This section, while not rehashing the events of these two renewal movements, seeks to examine some of the NAR's more recent activities in Canada.

Outside of the Latter Rain revival and the Toronto Blessing, one of the most obvious NAR outreaches in Canada is the Watchmen for the Nations. Watchmen for the Nations was founded by Bob Birch, who in the late 1960s turned his Vancouver church into a center of the Jesus movement in Western Canada. Although Birch was not an immediately identifiable figurehead for the Jesus movement—he was something of a dour figure and was not a fan of the sexual revolution—his church quickly gained popularity for its welcoming in of flower children and other youth living on the margins of Canadian society. Birch soon won international acclaim and proved more than willing to put it to political use. He tried to stop nude sunbathing at Vancouver's Wreck Beach and played a large role in an effort to stop a Rolling Stones concert. By 1990, in his eighties, Birch tried to stop Vancouver from hosting the international Gay Games. Birch took out full-page ads in Vancouver newspapers warning of Armageddon and demanding that the games be banned "in the name and authority of Jesus Christ" (McDonald 127–133). As a result, Watchmen for the Nations was founded in the early 1990s (McDonald 133–134).

For a while, the group's main focus was its monthly spiritual warfare events, which drew as many as two thousand Charismatics to each event. However, as Marci McDonald points out in her expose of rightwing Canadian Christianity, *The Armageddon Factor: The Rise of Christian Nationalism in Canada*, from the beginning Birch's organization was not an ordinary one. Birch soon became focused upon invitation-only weekends in which assembled Pentecostal leaders sought spiritual guidance from God as to where to next take their movement. According to McDonald, they eventually came to the conclusion that Canada "must atone for its transgressions against its First Nations" (McDonald 134). McDonald correctly points out that this was in line with the wider policy agenda of the NAR, particularly the ceremony of identificational repentance (McDonald 134). What McDonald did not know, but what we have already seen, is that the NAR's efforts towards First Nations people were even less conciliatory than McDonald suspects.

Indeed, the campaign against Native culture and totems in Vancouver was just one small part of an extremely aggressive campaign of early activity in the area by NAR activists. Besides Kjell Sjöberg's visit to Vancouver in February 1991 (Chiu 91), a number of other prominent NAR leaders visited Canada in the early 1990s, including Francis Frangipane, Rick Joyner, and Cindy Jacobs (Chiu 149–150). In January 1991, the leaders of Watchmen for the Nations were invited by the N.W. Prayer Gathering Network meeting. This network was led by Jim Watt, the only surviving elder of the 1948 Latter Rain movement in North Battleford. Chiu indicates that Watt's network was the American equivalent of Watchmen for the Nations, thus linking the Canadian group to some of the most hardcore Charismatics south of the border (Chiu 150). In September of 1992, a "Warfare Prayer" conference was held in Vancouver that introduced Ed Silvoso to the local community. The conference had connections with Cindy Jacobs' Generals of Intercession organization as well. Silvoso urged members of the Vancouver Charismatic community to "focus on city-wide inter-denominational efforts to preach the gospel" (Chiu 150–151). In other words, Silvoso was urging for SLSW on a city-wide scale in Vancouver. Silvoso urged Vancouver Charismatics to visit Argentina as well, thus allowing for the forming of some of the international relationships that were so essential to the NAR's eventual global spread (Chiu 151). Such a concentrated effort by the eventual leaders of the NAR highlights the importance of Canada to the NAR, and testifies to the national impact of Charismatic teachings in Canada, which goes far beyond simply the Toronto Blessing or John Arnott's Catch the Fire ministries.

The repentance ceremonies towards Natives ended up provoking a rash of Pentecostal missionary efforts to Native communities in Canada (McDonald 134). Some of these efforts would later be featured in *Transformations II* (2001), which stops just short of claiming that Native culture is demonized; the implication is obvious for those familiar with other movies in the *Transformations* series, but may not be clear to someone who watches the treatment of First Nations people in the video independent of other *Transformations* material (*Transformations II*). Like other *Transformations* efforts, the missions work done among First Nations people in Canada was used by Otis Jr., and his allies as proof of the effectiveness of NAR ideology in transforming other cultures.

In 1998 Birch, then in his nineties, passed leadership of Watchmen for the Nations to David Mohsen Demian, an Egyptian surgeon who Birch saw as his "spiritual son." Demian took Watchmen for the Nations in a more political, but also more low-key, direction. Demian conducted a campaign called La

Danse for reconciliation between the French and English populations of Canada, which according to McDonald, "acted out a mock courtship and wedding between the two founding nations, complete with an exchange of vows presided over by televangelist David Mainse, one of Watchmen's most high-profile members" (McDonald 134–135). Demian would credit these efforts with helping to vanquish the threat of Quebecois separatism (McDonald 134–135). McDonald's description of these efforts sounds virtually identical to the racial reconciliation and identificational repentance strategies of the NAR, making it likely that these efforts were interpreted as such by NAR-leaning Charismatics within Canada.

Demian also urged Canadian reconciliation with Israel. For Demian, the chief obstacle to Christian revival in Canada was the "stain of anti–Semitism," which he traced to a 1939 decision by Frederick Charles Blair to turn away a German ship filled with Jewish refugees, most of whom ended up perishing in Europe (McDonald 134–135). In 2000, Demian led a reconciliation ceremony with Jewish leaders, but this was part of a much bigger long term objective. In 2001, Demian led 500 hundred other conservative Christians on a trip to Israel where he stopped at Yad Vashem and pled for forgiveness from the country's chief rabbi on behalf of Canada. Following this event, Watchmen for the Nations became one of Canada's leading Christian Zionist organizations. Demian twice hosted the Knesset Christian Allies Caucas in its visits to Canada, an organization of Israeli parliamentarians whose chief objective is fostering links with governmental counterparts in other countries; Demian also vigorously supported Stephen Harper's pro–Israel policy in the Middle East (McDonald 135–136). Yet given the NAR's eschatological leanings it is extremely doubtful that Demian's primary concern is for Israel; rather it is that Canada be on the right side of history when the eschatological end comes (a point that McDonald also makes explicit. See McDonald 136–137). Such eschatological concerns are evident in Demian's prophetic pronouncements, particularly following the 2008 economic crisis, after which Demian pushed for greater governmental authority on the part of Christians involved in politics (McDonald 137).

Watchmen for the Nations has a number of political and religious ties throughout Canada. One of the foremost of these ties is to the Canadian National House of Prayer. Since taking over a former Ottawa convent in 2005, the Canadian National House of Prayer has marketed itself as a prayer mission to the members of Parliament, whose goal is "to bring a positive presence by a caring church to our nation's government." The organization is led by Rob and Fran Parker. The Parkers' organization has been given almost unprecedented access to the Canadian halls of power. The Parkers contend that their mission is non-partisan, but as McDonald points out, the National House of Prayer has a marked tendency to support Harper and his agenda; Harper in return, is not shy to show his gratitude, especially when it leads to good photo-op opportunities (McDonald 123). The Parkers helped organize The Cry, a Canadian version of the Call. The Parkers do not mention their link to Lou Engle and his allies south of the border, but in 1999, the same year IHOP was founded in Kansas City, Rob Parker conducted a "spiritual pilgrimage from Calgary to Ottawa, where the Canadian version was born," after a prayer walk he attended along with the B.C.-based Watchmen for the Nations (McDonald 127–131). Shortly after 9/11, with the memories of terrorist attacks fresh in their mind, the Parkers attended a Watchmen conference at a Kelowona B.C. Bible college. At the meeting, the group decided to found a National House of Prayer, which would eventually come to fruition in the Parkers' ministry (McDonald 137–138). Prominent Canadian politician Stockwell Day has also been closely linked to the New Apostolic Reformation, including receiving a confidential prophecy from Cindy Jacobs (McDonald 138–139).

Meanwhile, the Cry organization also retains an active presence in Canada as the youth arm of the NAR there (McDonald 13). In fact, on the Call's website, the Cry's leader Faytene Kryskow is mentioned as the "chief Canadian" at an event sponsored by Engle (McDonald 15–16). Yet despite Kryskow's links to Engle and other extremist elements within the NAR, she "seldom fails to snag a guest appearance from one of the evangelicals in [Steven] Harper's caucus" (McDonald 16). Indeed, despite Stephen Harper's well known aversion to being seen as too directly affiliated with the more extreme wings of the Christian Right, Harper has lauded Kryskow's organization for its "thoughtful, faith-filled citizens," as well as its political activism (McDonald 16). Yet, as McDonald points out, Kryskow was linked to a network of radical Pentecostals which included NAR heavyweights Stacey and Wes Campbell. The Campbells were tied to John Arnott's Toronto Airport Christian Fellowship (formerly TAVF), and were involved in the infamous commissioning ceremony of Todd Bentley, which involved virtually every NAR figure imaginable (McDonald 157–160).

This brings us to our last Canadian link to the NAR, Todd Bentley. Bentley is a Canadian evangelist who was for a brief time the brightest emerging star in the NAR. Bentley's 2008 Lakeland, Florida, revival was one of the most talked about religious revivals in recent memory, and much like the Toronto Blessing, ended up dividing the Charismatic movement. Bentley promoted the idea that through God he could cure cancer, heal the deaf, and even raise the dead. This belief was shared by hundreds of thousands people who visited his Lakeland revival meeting (Reed). Bentley's revival was streamed via Internet and live broadcasts on the satellite channel God TV. According to God TV, its viewership more than doubled once Bentley began being televised. At the height of the revival, Bentley's web page was getting more than eight million hits a month, showing how incredibly popular Bentley had become (Reed).

As Travis Reed reported, however, this "ease of Internet communication cuts both ways for Bentley." Bentley's critics circulated a Youtube video of him kneeing a purported terminal stomach cancer patient in the stomach, after God purportedly advised him to do so. Another clip showed Bentley explaining how he "kicked an elderly lady in the face, choked a man, banged a crippled woman's legs on a platform, 'leg-dropped' a pastor and hit a man so hard it dislodged a tooth" (Reed). Bentley's ministry expected criticism of its miracle cures, so it distributed a list of fifteen people it claimed to have been cured, all but three of whose stories were supposedly medically verified and vetted. Reed and his fellow members of the Associated Press, however, made extensive efforts to contact these individuals. As Reed relates, "two phone numbers given out by the ministry were wrong, six people did not return telephone messages and only two of the remainder, when reached by the Associated Press, said they had medical records as proof of their miracle cure. However, one woman would not make her physician available to confirm the findings, and the other's doctor did not return calls despite the patient's authorization" (Reed). Bentley also claimed to have seen King David personally and to have met the Apostle Paul in heaven, who, according to Bentley, "was looking very Jewish" (Sanchez). Bentley also had tattooed across his sternum military dog tags, embellished with the phrase "Joel's Army" (Sanchez).

On June 22, C. Peter Wagner and his wife Doris attended the Lakeland Revival. According to Wagner:

> As we observed and participated in the meeting in the tent, we became very nostalgic about Wimber and Argentina, even noting some physical resemblance between Todd and Wimber. His accuracy in words of knowledge reminded us of both John Wimber in the past and Robert Henderson in the present.... We saw or felt nothing that would cross the lines we have previously experienced in high-profile revival. We have learned that God-driven revival is often messy, tending to pull some out of their religious comfort zones, but at the same time opening gates for new seasons of the movement of God [Pierce and C. Peter Wagner].

The fact that Bentley was promoting the whole Joel's Army ideology (with its explicit links to Latter Rain thinking), that he promoted physical violence in the pursuit of healing and that his healings could not be attested to, did not faze Wagner. For Wagner, Bentley represented a force that needed to be controlled and harnessed, both to prevent further damage from his revival, but also to utilize the fanaticism of Bentley's followers. Instead, Wagner brought up a host of apostles to commission Bentley's ministry, including Rick Joyner,

Doris Wagner, Wesley Campbell, and a number of other prominent NAR leaders. Ché Ahn, Bill Johnson, and John Arnott laid hands on Bentley and anointed him with a "special new 'Be Revived'" oil that Chuck Pierce had sent them for the ceremony (Pierce and C. Peter Wagner).

Indeed, Wagner saw the commissioning ceremony as an important event in the NAR's growth and development, writing:

> We are now in a place in what I see as the Second Apostolic Age that apostles can agree publicly to bring alignment. The seventeen apostles involved in this event represented three distinct apostolic streams: ICA (10 were ICA members), Revival Alliance, and Morningstar. Even though we are not networked formally, we believe in and support each other and we stand together when a crisis such as this one comes along [Pierce and C. Peter Wagner].

For Wagner, Lakeland was an important display of unity between the various apostolic "streams." It showed that different apostolic networks could coordinate effectively even in regards to extremely contentious events like the Lakeland Revival. Wagner's comments about informal links were, of course, deliberately deceptive: The whole point of the NAR is relational networking built on authoritarian figures with Charismatic personality. It therefore would be extremely unlikely that Wagner would admit to any formal relationship between Revival Alliance, Morningstar and the ICA, even though those links, as we have seen, are plentifully evident.

Bentley's ministry eventually imploded once it was revealed he was having an affair with a staffer (Charisma, "Todd Bentley Enters"). The fact that Bentley had committed sexual assault while a teenager—a fact that had been well known since at least 2002—apparently did not faze the NAR leadership, but adultery did (Billy Bruce). However, since Bentley's name was now tied to a vast swathe of the NAR leadership in the States, as well as several leaders in Canada, the movement decided to try to rehabilitate him, and after a three-year restoration process, Rick Joyner tentatively brought Bentley back as a revivalist (Joyner, "Rory and Wendy Alec Interview"). The movement had not really had a choice. With a leader as tied to them all as Bentley, forgiveness was the better part of valor.

Canada is an odd story. Three of the five most important Charismatic revivals of the last sixty years—the Latter Rain revival, Toronto, and the Lakeland outpouring—either started in Canada or were directly birthed by Canadian evangelists. This may seem implausible to American audiences; indeed its implausibility played a part in the hostile reception accorded McDonald's excellent study of NAR activities in Canada (see McDonald loc 5560–5654). Canadians do not want to believe that they have a religious right; nor do secular Americans, who see Canada as a bastion of tolerance. Unfortunately, wishing things away does not make them not so. And the religious right in Canada is all too real a phenomena, one that may be with us for many years to come.

Uganda: The NAR and Killing in the Name of Christ

The history of NAR activism in Uganda is tragic and is tied to more longstanding Christian Right activism in that country. When it comes to Uganda, one does not ask what Christian Right movements are involved in the country, but which ones are not. Below, I outline the post-colonial history of Uganda, before moving on to discuss the NAR's involvement in that country.

The various people groups that make up present-day Uganda were composed of a variety of different "political units." Some of these were governed by strong centralized monarchies, the largest of which was the kingdom of Buganda. The other polities were smaller and somewhat more egalitarian. By the mid–1800s, Muslim traders and slavers had reached Buganda, allowing Islam to take root by the early 1860s. Henry Morton Stanley opened the country for Christianity in the mid 1870s. Anglican missionaries arrived in 1877, followed two years later by the Catholics (Gifford, *African Christianity* 112).

For a long time eastern Africa proved relatively impenetrable for Western interference. Germany's interest in East Africa, however, prompted Britain to obtain control of the area, a process that started in the 1890s and culminated with the effective total control of modern Uganda by 1919. However, this process was only achieved with difficulty and with the help of the Baganda, the natives of Buganda. The Baganda, by collaborating with the British in the conquest of what is now modern Uganda, obtained an elite position within the British protectorate, as well as gaining much new territory. However, they also gained a great deal of enmity from other Ugandan ethnic groups, an enmity which continues to this day. According to Paul Gifford it is this ethnic division, that after religious division, remains "the second enduring tension in Ugandan politics" (Gifford 113).

Regional allegiances and division prevented for some time the formation of any nationwide nationalist movement in Uganda. The first nationalist party, the Uganda National Congress, was finally founded in 1952, but was soon divided by factionalism. In 1954, the Democratic Party (DP) was founded, but again its aims were somewhat factional as well, as its primary goal was to protect Catholics against Anglican ascendance. A third party, the Uganda People's Congress (UPC), was founded in 1959, merging with a part of the older UNC. This party was led by Milton Obote, the first Prime Minister of Uganda. In the era leading up to independence, proper nationalist sentiment never really had a chance, as it was hindered by the Bagandas' attempts to form a separate state. In 1963, one year after independence, Uganda established itself as a republic with Kabaka Mutesa II as its federal President. However, the country suffered from continued division, leading to a February 1966 coup by Obote against Mutesa. Obote banned opposition parties in 1969 only to be overthrown himself by Idi Amin in January 1971. Amin's famously brutal regime directed much of its violence against the Acholi and Lango peoples. Intellectuals were slaughtered and the Ugandan infrastructure crumbled into dust. After a failed invasion of the Tanzania's Kagera salient, Uganda was invaded by the Tanzanian army in cooperation with the exile army known as the Uganda National Liberation Army (UNLA). This led to the formation of another provisional government, led again by Obote. However the elections that brought Obote into power were largely seen as being rigged and a number of opposition groups went into the Ugandan bush to resist Obote's regime. Of these groups, the most important was Yoweri Museveni's National Resistance Army (NRA). Obote's government, in turn, tortured and killed thousands of civilians. The army overthrew the Obote government in 1985 and established a Military Council. In 1986, however, the NRA took over Kampala and dissolved the Military Council. Museveni established a cabinet and gained control of the country. He encouraged guerrilla forces to join the NRA, and overall was fairly successful in this effort, but there still remained some dissident forces, the most notable of which was the Lord's Resistance Army, formed out of the remains of Alice Lakwena's Holy Spirit Movement, a dissident movement which was crushed by government troops as it advanced on the capital. The famous Joseph Kony, the subject of the controversial Kony 2012 media campaign, ended up taking over the resistance movement (Gifford 113–115; Craine).

In 1989, Museveni held local elections and began the process of establishing a new Constitution. He also extended the government's term of office for another five years, while reestablishing the ban on party political activity, which Museveni felt was the cause of the divisions which had wrecked Uganda. The Constitution was reestablished in October 1995 and in May 1996 Museveni won a presidential election that was seen to be, by African standards, relatively free and fair (Gifford 113–115). Museveni remains in power to this day.

According to Gifford, writing in the late 1990s, it was the rise of Pentecostalism in Uganda that gave Christianity its high profile there at that time (which has only increased exponentially since Gifford wrote *African Christianity: Its Public Role* [1998]). Much of the expansion of Christianity in Uganda was also tied to development work. Christian groups were not permitted in

Uganda just to evangelize; there was an expectation that there would be a return in development and aid in exchange for allowing missionaries in. Thus, much "Christian development work is not the result of any theology but simply needed to enable Christian groups to enter the country" (Gifford 154). Much of this development work was fueled by groups like Disciple Nations Alliance (DNA) and clearly had at a political agenda. DNA networked in Africa with Gary Skinner's Kampala Pentecostal Church. In 2000, members of KPC attended a DNA Vision Conference at which Miller's model of holistic ministry and biblical worldview were taught (Miller and Allen et al. 49). Miller's vision of Africa *explicitly blamed* Africans for their poverty, stating, "The root of the problem [in Africa] is not material, nor is it primarily located outside the continent. The root of the problem is inside the minds of the people of the continent" (Miller and Allen et al. 37). Much of this supposed mental evil was rooted in African "animist" beliefs (Miller and Allen et al. 39). For Africa, to be redeemed, therefore, its "traditional belief systems ... must be replaced with an equally comprehensive biblical worldview" (Miller and Allen et al. 43).

Miller's worldview-oriented critique of African culture fit in well with prevailing NAR transformationalist ideas in Africa. As Kapya Kaoma's PRA report "Colonizing African Values: How the U.S. Christian Right is Transforming Sexual Politics in Africa" indicates, the transformationalist movement, rather than "address the root causes of poverty in most African countries ... blames poverty on evil powers and demons." Ugandan government and business leaders are taught by these transformationalist experts that they "have no control over challenging poverty except by developing their spiritual fitness like anybody else" (Kaoma 4). Ed Silvoso contends that in Uganda, "church leaders have joined hands with those involved in business, recognizing that they have a key role to play in the transformation of the nation. Together they are working to see God establish His Kingdom in the area of business, education and government" ("Transforming in Uganda" qtd. Kaoma 4). Silvoso is hardly exaggerating here. President Museveni and his devout born-again wife Janet Museveni held an official state dinner for representatives of the ITN Network in March of 2007. The NAR organization College of Prayer, headquartered in Atlanta, Georgia, is used to promote NAR ideology in the Ugandan parliament. According to ITN's Africa Representative Werner Swart (today the leader of Harvest Evangelism Africa. See "Werner Swart"), ITN saw in Africa a potential for the union of marketplace and religious leaders in Uganda, stating that: "We realized that the marketplace and the pulpit in Uganda needed to be united. And so they formed in Uganda what is now known as the Transformation Network Uganda ... which is basically an ITN chapter" (Bruce Wilson, *Transforming*

Uganda). The scale of this effort in Uganda was massive, with the ITN itself admitting to having 80 districts in Uganda each with its own mini-ITN chapter (Bruce Wilson *Transforming Uganda*).

As, Kaoma and his fellow writers from PRA point out, much of the strength of SLSW, Transformations, and other NAR teachings in Africa derive from "widespread belief in demons, ancestral curses, and witchcraft" on the continent. In addition, the strong element of self-actualization present within the Pentecostal tradition, particularly in its more WOF-oriented elements, may appeal to many Africans. As Kaoma points out, "It is natural to want to move from poverty to economic prosperity; here [in Transformation teachings] is a spiritual path to reach that goal. Don't blame the corrupt and broken government system for your poverty, says the Transformation movement. Blame the demons and evil powers around you—blame LGBT people, blame abortion" (Kaoma 4). Thus, the Transformation movement's ideological beliefs allow Africans to externally scapegoat minority and or vulnerable populations in their countries as being the true cause of national decline, even as Africans themselves, as we have seen, are often scapegoated by the very people—the NAR in general and the transformationalist movement specifically—who are behind the promotion of the scapegoating of LGBT people in Africa. Yet while the focus on demonology may play on indigenous traditions, the literal demonization of African LGBT people as evil is not in keeping with African tradition (Kaoma 5). Jeffrey Siker, writing in *Homosexuality and Religion: An Encyclopedia* (2007), notes that "significant fluidity is often found in gender identity within African traditional religion" and that individuals with such fluid identities are often honored in these traditional belief systems (Siker, "African Traditional Religion" 52). Thus the repeated demonization of LGBT people, which is currently at the forefront of the controversy about NAR actions in Uganda, has little root in traditional African culture.

Silvoso's ITN has gained influence in Uganda by placing its African operations under the control of Ugandan President Yoweri Museveni's nephew Joseph Okia. At the 2008 Transformations conference, Okia stated that "Uganda is critical and important for world conquest." Janet Museveni, the first lady, has also attended ITN conferences as well (Kaoma 5). Yet, Silvoso's influence represents merely a tiny part of NAR and transformationalist influence in Uganda. Further evidence of this influence can be deduced by looking at George Otis Jr.'s *Transformations* video series.

Otis's *Transformations* series, starting in 1999 (Holvast 91) has produced a number of films to showcase the *Transformations* ideology, some of which have been previously highlighted in this text. But Uganda plays a very special role in the *Transformations* films, much like Resistencia did for the spiritual mapping movement. Jeff Sharlet, in his expose of the Christian right power-brokering organization known as the Family, has noted that for evangelical Americans, "Christian Africa has been appropriated for a story with which American fundamentalists argue for domestic policy, a parable detached from American realities, preached for the benefit of Americans" (Sharlet, *The Family* 328). Sharlet has Uganda specifically in mind with this critique (328) and it's hardly difficult to see why. Indeed, Otis Jr.'s *Transformations II* provides support for Sharlet's thesis about Christian right activity in Uganda, when the narrator states, "Having observed God's willingness to transform discrete territories and cultures, only one question remains: Can this happen at a national level? Is there any evidence of God at work in a modern state, a sovereign nation?" (*Transformations II*). The documentary then proceeds to highlight why Uganda is becoming the model for the new transformational state worldwide. Like many videos in the *Transformations* series, *Transformations II*, simultaneously promotes its indigenous subjects as both gifted and potentially demonized. The narrator explains that "this one time pearl of Africa has spent decades in a deep spiritual crisis, its very name has become synonymous with death.... Uganda's history, like that of many African nations, is filled with magic practices and secret rituals. Fetishes ... were everywhere and kings even to the days of Idi Amin are known to have offered human sacrifices." The video ends in hagiographic fashion as President Musevini and his wife covenant the next thousand years of Africa's history to Christ (*Transformations II*).

Even more inexcusable than *Transformations II* was another video in the Sentinel Group's *Transformations* series, *Uganda: An Unconventional War* (2006). Engaging in classic slacktivism, the documentary told the story of the Acholi people in Uganda, paying particular attention to the atrocities committed by Joseph Kony's LRA. The LRA, as we have seen, was a resistance movement/militia that roamed northern Uganda and its neighbors through much of the late 20th and early 21st centuries, terrorizing local inhabitants. After the quashing of Alice Lakwena's Holy Spirit movement, Kony joined another Ugandan faction and in 1987 declared himself a prophet for the Acholi people group, taking effective charge of what would eventually become the LRA. Significantly not documented in *Uganda: An Unconventional War* was the fact that the LRA in its early years enjoyed a decent amount of support in northern Uganda (Craine). This comes as no surprise to anyone who has studied even cursorily Ugandan history, since Museveni himself promoted highly discriminatory views of northern Ugandans, equating them with "biological substances to be destroyed" (Ochala-Lukwiya 52). Museveni has been frequently accused of using derogatory language against the northern people of Uganda (51). Also missing from *Uganda: An Unconventional War* is any shading of Museveni's character. Because of Museveni's close alliances with the Christian right, his efforts in northern Uganda are cast in the best possible light, while the Acholi people are literally portrayed as demonized (*Uganda: An Unconventional War*).

This is not to say that Kony is any saint. After the LRA's initial years of limited popularity, the militia began to plunder local populations as its supply of resources dwindled. The movement was reinvigorated in 1994 with the support of the government of Sudan, angry at the Kampalan government for its support of Sudanese rebels. Kony ordered the LRA to attack villages, "murdering, raping and mutilating in a campaign of intimidation that displaced some two million people. Children were abducted and brainwashed into becoming soldiers and slaves." Resisters were beaten to death. In 2005, the International Criminal Court (ICC) issued a warrant for Kony's arrest, bringing him under international scrutiny and cutting off much of his support. Kony made peace offers, but the ICC's warrant also complicated matters by making it harder for Kony to come out of hiding. By the end of 2006, Kony and the LRA had left Uganda and based themselves in the Democratic Republic of the Congo and Sudan. In November 2008 Uganda's neighbors, now the targets of LRA violence despite its quickly lessening numbers, told Kony that a failure to sign the ICC peace agreement would lead to a military conflict. However, the proposed conflict failed to dislodge Kony (Craine).

What made *Uganda: An Unconventional War* reprehensible was that it blamed the Acholi people for the very attacks they suffered under Kony's Lord's Resistance Army (LRA). This of course played into the anti-northern narrative of the Museveni government and also ignored the fact that Museveni and the National Resistance Movement (NRM) that now leads Uganda had a marked tendency to favor one ethnic group over another, making Acholi fears of Museveni's regime hardly unreasonable. *Uganda: An Unconventional War* also shockingly fails to document the fact that Museveni's own NRA movement was responsible for atrocities itself, in its bid for power in the early 1980s (Ochala-Lukwiya 31–33, 103), which again casts doubts on the anti-northern and anti–Acholi narrative of both Museveni and Otis's documentary itself.

Even more reprehensible is the information *Uganda: An Unconventional War* leaves out about the camps in which the Acholi are forced to live in by the Ugandan Army. According to the narrative of the film, while everyone agrees that the camps "cannot and should not last forever, some believers see a redemptive purpose in whatever days … may be remaining" (*Transformations II*). The need for this redemptive interpretation is made graphically clear by the documentarians, as the dread threat of Islam is brought up as the main reason why the camps are needed to convert the Acholi people (*Transformations II*). Appallingly lacking in this narrative is any understanding of what the Acholi people suffer daily in these camps. The official line about the camps, which is countenanced by Western powers like the United Kingdom and the United States, is that the camps were formed voluntarily in order to provide protection to the Acholi from the LRA. Conveniently left out of this story is the fact that the Ugandan army has established a free-fire zone outside the camps. People caught outside a camp after sunset are seen as rebels. When Burundi tried a similar tactic against its rebels, international protest quickly moved to quash it, but Uganda, as a Western success story, got away with it. Meanwhile more than a 1,000 Acholi died in the camps each week, as of 2006. Forty-one percent of the dead were children under five (Dowden).

What makes the documentary even more farcical is that it promotes the idea that it was spiritual warfare undertaken by Ugandan evangelicals, particularly by NAR apostle Julius Oyet, which helped to defeat the LRA forces (Kaoma 6). Oyet is a close ally of Os Hillman, the prominent marketplace ministry leader and a major player in NAR politics (Bruce Wilson, "Everything You Need to Know"; Hillman, "Marketplace Meditations"). *Uganda: An Unconventional War* strongly implies that the government campaign against the LRA would have been impossible without Oyet's help, since Kony himself was demonically possessed and had supernatural powers because of it (Kaoma 6).

In short, *Uganda: An Unconventional War* played an equivalent, though earlier role, for evangelical youth, as did *Kony 2012* (2012) for both evangelical and secular young people.[10] It was a cheap means of inducing evangelical activism in Africa, activism that rather than helping the Ugandan people, is being directly funneled into a number of right wing causes, the most notable of which is the suppression of LGBT people in Uganda. Meanwhile, the video promulgates the transformationalist message of empowerment of the poor, all the while receiving major funding from the NAR funder and honorary workplace apostle Ken Eldred's Living Stones Foundation, one of the chief architects of the BAM model and hardly a friend of the poor (*Kony: An Unconventional War*).

On October 14, 2009, Ugandan parliamentarian David Bahati introduced a piece of legislation called the Anti-Homosexuality Bill. Its provisions included a three-year prison sentence for failing to report a homosexual within 24 hours; seven years of imprisonment for the "promotion" of homosexuality; life imprisonment for one homosexual act; and the death penalty for "aggravated homosexuality" (this included "sex while HIV-positive, sex with a disabled person, or simply sex, more than once, marking the criminal as a 'serial offender')" (Sharlet, *C Street* 130). Many credit the visit of an obscure evangelical hatemonger, Scott Lively, with fomenting the hatred in Uganda. Lively was the author of the infamous Holocaust revisionist text *The Pink Swastika* (1995), which argued that Nazism was rooted in homosexuality and warned of the "homo-fascist" menace now threatening the United States (Sharlet, *C Street*, 145; David Smith). Despite the historical unreliability of that claim, it did not stop Lively from being well-received in Uganda, where he outlined the different type of gay men, which ranged from 'monster' to 'super-macho' to 'butcher.' According to Lively, the last mentioned group of gay men was composed of the kind of people "it takes to run a gas chamber" (Sharlet, *C Street* 145). This conference was held at Kampala Pentecostal Church (Watoto), Gary Skinner's church, which as we have seen, is aligned with Hillsong in Australia, an NAR-affiliated Australian megachurch that itself had close ties with American NAR deliverance ministry Mercy Ministries (Lively, "Report from Uganda"). Human rights activists "saw the [death-to-gays] bill as the direct result of a March 2009 conference in Kamapla featuring Lively and American ex-gay activists" (Sharlet, *C Street* 146–147). Sharlet sees the conference more as a catalyst than a cause, pointing out how homosexuality in Uganda was increasingly characterized as a form of neo-colonialism on the part of the West (Sharlet 146–147). In either case, what is clear is that an NAR-aligned church played a key part in promoting the bill.

Stephen Langa, an elder at Kampala Pentecostal Church/Watoto Church, organized the infamous conference (Burroway, "Lively Responds; Burroway "American Evangelical Connections"; Burroway, "Religious Groups"). Langa was a member of Darrow Miller's DNA and ran its Uganda affiliate called Transformation Nations Alliance (Burroway, "Religious Groups"). After Langa started receiving negative attention from secular commentators, Miller tried to distance himself from his association with Langa. But as Michelle Goldberg notes, this distancing effort was at best lukewarm (Goldberg; Allen, Miller and Moffitt). While Miller and his allies claimed that they did not support the criminalization of homosexuality (Allen, Miller, and Moffitt), a simple search of Miller's *Darrow Miller and Friends* website absolutely contradicted this assertion. Miller's site promotes an essay by Langa decrying Western sexual colonialism and criticizing the West for its own negative critique of the anti-gay bill (Miller, "Sexual Colonialism"; Langa). Miller decries LGBT sexual activity as "Sexual Colonialism: The New Legacy of Western elitism" (Miller, "Sexual Colonialism"). It therefore is extremely unlikely that Miller disapproved of Langa's plans for Uganda's LGBT population.

Miller, of course, was close friends with Ted Yamamori. Yamamori's connection to Uganda is extensive. Yamamori helped pen the preface to George Otis, Jr.'s *The Last of the Giants* (Yamamori 19–20 in Otis Jr.); Otis Jr., as we have seen, is extensively involved in crafting the NAR's Ugandan agenda, through his promotion of the *Transformations* movies. This is not some casual link either; Yamamori played an important role in helping refine Ken Eldred's (the funder of *Uganda: An Unconventional War*) *God Is at Work* (2009), which in turn served as one of the prime foundational texts for the Business as Missions movement (BAM) and which also has had some influence on the Marketplace ministries movement as well (Eldred, *God Is at Work* 15). Langa was listed by FFH (of which Yamamori was president until 2001) as an honorary advisor. Langa's Family Life Network and Samaritan Strategy Africa are listed as partners by FFH (Osborne, "US Right Wing Charities"). This is hardly surprising, since Samaritan Strategy Africa's goal is to spread "DNA training across the continent of Africa," according to a DNA report that gay news website *Box Turtle Bulletin* obtained (Burroway, "American Evangelical Connections"; also see Darrow Miller and Friends, "Restoring the Breach," which lists Samaritan Strategy Africa as a DNA affiliate). In 2008, FFH gave just under $340,000 to Watoto Church (formerly Kampala Pentecostal Church) (Osborne, "US Right Wing").

Of course, where Miller, Yamamori, and the NAR are, Reconstructionists would be also. Reconstructionist Peter Waldron, a Michelle Bachmann campaign staffer, was allegedly involved in an effort to capture Joseph Kony and claim the $1.7 million bounty on his head. The *Kampala Monitor* reported that Waldron was "suspected of links to a group [the] neighboring Democratic Republic of Congo (DRC) and 'planned to set up a political party here based on Christian [Uganda] principles'" (Franke-Ruta). Waldron was on the steering committee of the Coalition on Revival ("National COR Steering Committee"; Franke-Ruta) and co-wrote the book *Rebuilding the Walls: A Biblical Strategy for Restoring America's Greatness* (1987) with Reconstructionist George Grant. Not surprisingly, Grant has fairly well documented ties with both Yamamori and Miller. All three men were co-signers of The Villars Statement (Olasky and Co. 147–148), a foundational document in Miller's holistic transformationalist approach to international development.

Other evangelical leaders—surprisingly "mainstream" in the movement—have also supported the increasing oppression of LGBT people in Uganda. Foremost of these is Rick Warren, who played a major part in dividing African Anglicans on the issue of homosexuality (Kaoma, "Globalizing the Culture Wars" 16). Warren supported radical Charismatic leader Martin Ssempa in Uganda. Ssempa was known for such stunts as "burning condoms in the name of Jesus and arranging the publication of names of homosexuals in cooperative local newspapers while lobbying for criminal penalties to imprison them" (Blumenthal). According to Max Blumenthal, writing for the Daily Beast, "When Warren unveiled his global AIDS initiative at a 2005 conference at his Saddleback Church, he cast Ssempa as his indispensable sidekick, assigning him to lead a breakout session on abstinence-only education as well as a seminar on AIDS prevention" (Blumenthal). As a result of anti-condom and pro–"abstinence only" efforts in Uganda, largely fueled by Warren, Ssempa and other Christian right activists, Uganda's success in combatting AIDS in the 1990s (when President Museveni backed safe sex) is largely unraveling (Blumenthal).

Sssempa pushed for harsh regulations on gays in Uganda, leading to two of Museveni's top officials demanding the arrest of gay activists who Ssempa had named. Warren claimed that he did not harbor anti-gay sentiments, but he was crucial in legitimizing Ugandan Anglican bishops attempts to leave the Church of England and traveled to Kampala specifically to give their efforts legitimacy (Blumenthal). And not surprisingly, given Rick Warren's church growth background, his dissertation mentor was C. Peter Wagner himself (Rick Warren dissertation abstract).

As we have seen, Lou Engle's the Call has been able to rally massive support in Uganda for the anti-gay legislation (Kron). The recent documentary *God Loves Uganda* (2013) has also traced the relationship between Mike Bickle's IHOP ministry and Uganda (*God Loves Uganda*), including the pouring of millions of dollars into its Ugandan missions, "much of it filtered into local churches and missions with explicitly anti-gay agendas" (Lybarger). Lou Engle's former roommate, Senator Sam Brownback, appears in *Uganda: An Unconventional War*, promoting the transformationalist message about the Acholi in Uganda, so the NAR has obviously been able to link with U.S. governmental powerbrokers as well (*Uganda: An Unconventional War*; see also Lybarger for *God Love Uganda*'s director Roger Ross Williams' take on this situation). Many African pastors, including Ssempa and NAR Apostle Joseph Mulinde (who has given sermons at IHOP presided over by Mike Bickle himself. See "John Mulinde"), have promoted "transformation teachings on LGBT people as cursing their nations." Both Apostles Oyet and Joseph Mulinde were at the forefront of those pastors claiming credit for the "Anti-Homosexuality Bill"; both men also spoke alongside Engle at the aforementioned Kampala rally he held in support of the bill (Kaoma, "Colonizing Africa's Values" 5).

But perhaps no greater evidence of the sheer scope of NAR influence in Uganda can be offered than the testimony of Museveni's nephew Joseph Okia, who admitted outright to PRA that: "Definitely there is a link between conservative Christians in American and conservative Christian leaders in Uganda. And a lot of strategic geopolitical thinking that is pioneered by people like Ed Silvoso and Peter Wagner. [They have] had a profound impact on the thinking of leading Christians in Uganda…. For sure, there has been a close intellectual and mentoring relationship between people like Ed Silvoso and myself, and different Christian leaders in Uganda" (Kaoma, "Colonizing Africa's

Values" 6). That the nephew of Uganda's president, the head of ITN's East African wing, would so openly admit his country's alliance with the NAR speaks volumes about how thoroughly the Christian Right has now penetrated Uganda, and indeed much of Africa.

Why has the Christian Right been so successful in Africa? Jeff Sharlet argues that much of this success is due to the fact that the secretive Christian Right organization, the Family, helped recruit Museveni into its environs (Sharlet, *The Family* 53–54). There is undoubtedly some truth to Sharlet's accusation. The point to be made here, as Kyle Mantlya has contended, is that the religious's rights efforts have built-in redundancy. These efforts cannot fail if undertaken with effective enough support from their wider evangelical faith-based constituency and U.S. policy makers. Since both of these groups seldom perceive the Religious Right as acting against evangelical or American policy interests, the Religious Right is allowed the opportunity not simply to operate on a community-level overseas, but to treat foreign countries like Uganda, as *Huffington Post* contributor and documentarian Bruce Wilson put it, as "prototypes" for national and international evangelical objectives. In short Uganda has proven to be an evangelical test tube of sorts, one that a wide variety of groups—not just DNA, not just the Family, not just Reconstructionists, and not even just the NAR—have utilized effectively. But the combination of so many theistic chemical recipes may prove disastrous for the Ugandan people, if the country cannot figure out a way of more democratically and pluralistically relating to the issue of church-state relations. If this does not happen, Uganda could very well turn into a 21st century Charismatic version of Calvin's Geneva. And despite Reconstructionistism's claims to the contrary, that's a place absolutely no one would want to live.

The United Kingdom: Apostolic Networks, the Subversion of Anglicanism, and the Story of the NAR in the U.K.

As with Canadian Pentecostalism, British Pentecostalism dates far back in history. As Allan Anderson correctly points out, the road for Pentecostalism in Britain was paved long before the Pentecostal movement was even founded, mainly through the Keswick Conventions of the 1870s, which "taught a distinct baptism in the Spirit as 'enduement with power'" and the famous 1904–1905 Welsh Revival which gained Christianity a 100,000 people in Wales, if reports are to be believed (Allan Anderson 91). Obviously the entire history of British

Pentecostalism is beyond the scope of this book, but it is important to understand at least somewhat how Charismatic belief developed in Britain between the 1970s and today, to fully understand the appeal of the NAR in certain British churches.

The Charismatic Renewal's initial strands can be traced in Britain as far back as the 1950s, through, for instance, the ministry of Arthur Wallis, who would play an important role in the British Restorationist or house church movement (Hocken 489; Kay 10–13). In the mid–1960s, the growth of the Charismatic Renewal was "slow but steady" within the United Kingdom (Hocken 490). The initial major impetus for the movement came out of the ministry of Michael Harper at Fountain Trust (Hocken 490). The conferences held by Fountain Trust attracted well known British promulgators of Charismatic Renewal as Arthur Wallis and Campbell McAlpine (Hocken 490). Initially, the Charismatic Renewal's strongest impact was felt among evangelical Anglicans (Hocken 490). Besides Michael Harper, perhaps the most important early supporter of the Renewal in Anglican circles was David Watson. However the Renewal also provoked opposition among other evangelical leaders, notably the well-respected John Stott (see Hocken 490).

Among those affected by the Charismatic Renewal, a restorationist wing soon developed, which is usually initially distinguished from the Renewal itself in much of the literature (this distinction gradually disappeared over the course of the '70s until the Charismatic Renewal and Restorationist wings of Charismatic thought were virtually identical. See Walker 34) (Hocken 490). Restorationists resembled renewalists in that they were middle class and emphasized the experiential. However, like classic Pentecostals, they emphasized evangelism considerably more than renewalists and grouped themselves "into enclaves that were sociologically sectarian in character" (Walker 32). Although never directly stated in the secondary literature, it does seem that British Restorationism's sectarianism was greater than parallel theological developments in America, such as the shepherding movement, and thus in some ways perhaps more resembled the earlier Latter Rain movement in this particular characteristic than the more ideologically flexible American shepherding contingent

British sociologist Andrew Walker drew a basic distinction between two blocks of the Restorationist movement, which he labeled R1 and R2. According to William Kay's account of these distinctions (which like most Pentecostal historiography is hagiographic), "R1 was the more exclusive, organized, authoritarian and radical of the two groups and R2, centered largely in London, was more flexible, more expressive and more willing to work in conjunction with other Christian groups and agencies" (Kay 20). Nigel Wright, while clearly respecting Walker's pioneering research into the Restorationist movement, argues that the ideological diversity in the movement is now so great that it is best to see each Restorationist network as a "distinct entity with a particular ethos" (Wright 66).

British Restorationism was devoted to an apostolic system of leadership, one that included prophetic leadership and sometimes shepherding practice as well (Hunt, *A History*, 355). According to William Kay, there were some fairly extensive links between the Fort Lauderdale Five and the early apostolic networks in Britain which emerged in the 1970s and 1980s (see Kay 20), links that Kay characterizes as "direct and personal" (Kay 197). Ern Baxter preached to congregations within the British apostolic networks and British apostolic figures traveled to America to meet with leaders of the shepherding movement (Kay 197). Kay argues that "no formal links were established" between the British networks and the United States and given the number of conflicting egos involved, this is quite possible (Kay 197). In any case, as Kay admits, shepherding concepts and practices did influence Britain, thanks to the influence of publications like *New Wine* (Kay 197). Nigel Scotland also notes the rabid popularity with which shepherding doctrine was sometimes greeted in Restorationist circles (Scotland 109–110). Hunt indicates that shepherding practice was implemented quite widely throughout British Restorationism, but proved too controversial for the movement to ultimately permanently sanction (Hunt 366–367). In any case, the adoption of shepherding provided the grounds for a number of the major shepherding leaders to influence Britain (Hunt 365).

Hunt argues that one of the attractions of Restorationism to British Christians might have been the postmillennial flavor that characterized it (Hunt 355). As we have seen previously, the Pentecostal and Charismatic movements have always been ambivalent about the hopeless eschatology offered up by traditional dispensationalists; Restorationism in Britain helped to mitigate the hopelessness of traditional dispensationalist eschatologies, which had never had much luck in Britain. Simply put, the postmillennialist vision could be more easily accommodated into a British evangelicalism that was keenly concerned with respectability; the rapture-ready eschatology of premillennial dispensationalists did not allow for the interpretively flexible scriptural hermeneutics that were needed for the Charismatic gospel to take root in the United Kingdom.

Between 1972 and 1974, a distinct leadership structure was developed by the Restorationist movement, which complemented what the movement saw as the "'horizontal' relationship with God through his Apostles, Prophets and Elders" (Hunt, *A History* 361). The most significant southern leader would be John Noble and in the north Bryn Jones would be the most influential. The core leadership of the movement, which would eventually encompass the leaders of more than 12 important British apostolic networks, felt that they were in a "covenant relationship with a vision for a worldwide Church founded on a model divinely revealed during their discussions together" (Hunt 361, Kay 19). However, as Hunt points out, the British apostolic networks of the seventies and eighties, much like the shepherding movement, did not really develop a "uniform structure" (Hunt 361). Nevertheless, the Restorationist movement developed a number of important central tenets that seemed to unify the movement. For the purpose of linking British Restorationism to the NAR, the most important of these beliefs were a belief in a "world-wide End Times revival"; the return of apostolic and prophetic gifts and ministries; the "establishment of apostolic teams to supplement and complement the work of godly leaders of local churches"; and a commitment to the idea that denominations were not part of God's plan for humanity or the church (Hunt 362). As in America, apostleship was related to the return of fivefold ministry and was also related to the special anointing of individuals (Hunt 364), suggesting that British Restorationism was more than a little influenced by the 1948 Latter Rain Revival.

Originally, the British restorationist movement was led by a group of seven apostolic leaders: Arthur Wallis, Bryn Jones, Peter Lyne, David Mansell, Graham Perrins, John Noble, and Hugh Thompson (Kay 24–25, Hocken, "House Church Movement" 773).[11] The movement shortly thereafter admitted in seven other major leaders: George Tarleton, Gerald Coates, Barney Coombs, Maurice Smith, Ian McCullogh, John MacLaughlin and Campbell McAlpine (Kay 24; Hocken, "House Church Movement" 773). In 1980, Terry Virgo, with the blessing of Jones, developed an apostolic team called New Frontiers which was established in the south of England. Along with the development of another (more ill-fated) apostolic team called Cornerstone (under the leadership of Tony Morton), the development of Virgo's network led to the distinction of R1 and R2 eventually becoming less relevant. By the 1980s, some Restorationist leaders, particularly Noble, were seeking to build bridges to the rest of the Charismatic movement while rejecting the ardent anti-denominationalism that so characterizes British Restorationism. Other leaders adopted a more intermediate position, characterized by "fewer links to denominational charismatic renewal than Noble but, unlike Jones, taking an active part in the Evangelical Alliance [arguably the most important evangelical organization in Britain] and the British Charismatic Leaders Conference" (Hocken, "House Church Movement" 774).

By the early 1980s every faction of Charismatics in Britain was ready for a change, be it Charismatic Renewal or Restorationist, Anglican or non–Anglican, denominational Pentecostal or not (Hunt, *A History* 416–417). The figure that was seen as emblematic of the Pentecostal "New Way" was John Wimber. The path for Wimber's phenomenal impact on Britain was paved in part by the influence of Donald McGavran and his church growth ideology on significant elements of the British evangelical movement, but Wimber's charisma and appeal to the British Charismatic public cannot be overestimated. Hunt suggests that what Wimber offered British Charismatics was a reinvigoration of the Renewal movement that lacked the "rigid structure and dogma of Restorationism" (Hunt 417). Meanwhile, for Restorationists, Wimber's teachings were seen as potential stimuli to the long-awaited revival that their particular rendering of postmillennialist enthusiasm sought (Hunt 417).

Wimber was invited to Britain in 1981 by Anglican evangelical David Watson and by the Baptists in 1982 (Hunt 418–419). A six day Third Wave conference held in October of 1984 allowed the British public their first large scale opportunity to interact with Wimber's teachings. The meeting was characterized by a number of characteristic phenomena of Wimber's particular style of ministry—visions, prophecy, etc.—which caught the attention of British evangelicals even more than Wimber's effective church growth strategies (Hunt 419–420). Wimber's ministry was particularly attractive to Anglican Charismatics (Hunt 421). Hunt offers a number of reasons why this might have been the case, the most likely of which is the attractiveness of healing ministry to Anglicans. Healing ministry—including faith healing and deliverance—had played an important part in the early success of the Charismatic Renewal within the Church of England. As Hunt points out, there was a "latent demand within a number of Anglican congregations for healing," but this demand was partially hampered because many Anglicans did not want to be associated with the kind of brash forms of healing revivalism that characterized the more colorful healing evangelists in the American tradition, such as Benny Hinn. Wimber's style of deliverance, as Hunt notes, must have seemed remarkably restrained compared to the kind of deliverance practice undertaken by men like Hinn (Hunt 421). Indeed, Wimber's influence on healing ministries in Britain was hardly limited to the Anglican church; Hunt credits Wimber with partly influencing Peter Horrobin's founding of Ellel Ministries (Hunt 421–422), an organization with extensive NAR links.

Wimber was so influential on British Anglicanism that he practically founded a form of Third-Wave Anglicanism. By the early 1990s, 1200 Anglican clerics had joined the Vineyard's regular mailing list. The Vineyard's own organization in Britain was even led by a former Anglican cleric, John Mumford (Hunt 422). Among Restorationists, Wimber offered a plausible escape-hatch to get the movement out of its self-imposed trap of shepherding practice, which had alienated British and American Charismatics alike (Hunt 423).

Wimber's efforts in Britain were not without controversy, particularly after some of the prophecies made during the "Kansas City Prophet era" of Wimber's ministry proved to be inaccurate (Hunt 428–429). British Charismatics proved less willing than their American counterparts to accept the lackadaisical approach to prophetic accuracy utilized by the Kansas City Prophets and their associates. Yet even here there must be some major qualifications, for major British evangelical and Charismatic leaders played an important role in facilitating the success of the Kansas City Prophets ministry. David Pytches, for instance, a former Anglican bishop of Chile, Bolivia, and Peru, penned *Some Said It Thundered: A Personal Encounter with the Kansas City Prophets* (1991), an influential book on the Prophets penned during the height of their popularity (Hocken, "David Pytches" 1013; Pytches passim). Pytches also gives what can only be called selective testimony in his characterization of the Ernie Gruen controversy, leaving out any significant information about the exact accusations Gruen made against Bickle and his allies, which were explosive (see Pytches 146–148).

Which Anglican and Restorationist Charismatics were, or are, involved with the NAR then? This is a somewhat difficult question to answer. Given Pytches's willingness to write a book supporting Bickle, one of the most radical supporters of the NAR, Pytches's sympathy for the movement can be assumed. Among Restorationist leaders, the situation is rather interesting. Hunt believes that in Europe, Charismatics who might be associated with the term "New Apostolic" or postdenominational are "in the region of 36 percent of the total." In England, he argues this would "undoubtedly include the so-called 'New Churches' that have come to rival mainstream Charismatic Renewal" (Hunt 12). Thus for Hunt, the Restorationist movement clearly represents a form of new apostolic ministry. Kay's book on *Apostolic Networks in Britain* (2007) concurs in that assessment, showing how intimately linked apostolic networks there were with the development of Restorationism. The question then, is not whether British apostolic networks are not New Apostolic—they clearly are—but the degree to which they align with major U.S. apostolic networks, such as the ICA and Revival Alliance.

Indeed, several of the major networks seem to have fairly definite links with American-style New Apostolic thinking. Barney Coombs's "Salt and Light" group almost definitely has such links, given Coombs fascination with R.J. Rushdoony in the late 1980s and early 1990s (Wright 68). Coombs's group was deeply involved in shepherding and given the shepherds links to both Wagner and Rushdoony it would be highly unlikely that Coombs was not at least sympathetic with the America right's agenda (including now the NAR), particularly at the height of his involvement with Reconstructionist thinking (68).

Indeed, Kay seems to indicate that Coombs may have influenced in a Reconstructionist direction by the Fort Lauderdale Five, particularly Bob Mumford, though Coombs claims to have avoided the worst parts of the shepherding controversy (Kay 89). Since Kay apparently did not bother to research this claim, there is no way of knowing how serious Coombs was in his retraction of these beliefs; given the shepherds' record in that regard, an authentic change of heart seems unlikely.

One group that was almost certainly deeply imbedded with U.S. apostolic networks within the NAR and sympathetic to their most radical ideals was a group of British Charismatic leaders who signed a statement defending the Kansas City Prophets, even after the revelations made by Ernie Gruen were publicized. This group of leaders included Gerald Coates, Roger Forster, Sandy Millar, Pytches, and Terry Virgo of New Frontiers (Hillborn, "A Chronicle" 141–142).

This is a rather formidable list. As we have seen Pytches had considerable power in the Anglican church. Terry Virgo leads what is today considered one of the most successful Restorationist groups in Britain (see Hunt 374–375). According to Kay, Virgo was not sympathetic with the doctrine of territorial spirits as promoted by Wagner (Kay 78); even if this contention is true, its ultimate merit is questionable. Wagner and Wimber definitely did have differing views on territorial spirits, as Wagner himself acknowledged; however, it cannot be denied that Wimber's own view of spiritual warfare powerfully influenced Wagner's and vice versa (Wagner, *Wrestling* 189–190). Nor can it be denied that many of the explicitly NAR aligned ministries that have arisen in the last 20 years either were aligned with the Vineyard (for instance, Mike Bickle's KCF church) or grew out of the Vineyard-inspired Toronto Blessing, which amounted to the same thing (practically the entire Revival Alliance is proof of that). Virgo also endorsed Todd Bentley's ministry (as did Gerald Coates), despite Bentley's aforementioned alignment with Joel's Army ideology (Hunt, *A History* 600).

According to Hunt, teachings on spiritual warfare were particularly attractive to the Icthus Fellowship and Pioneers streams of Restorationism, with Roger Forster, the leader of Icthus, playing a major role in the spread of spiritual warfare doctrine in Britain (Hunt 492–493). The Pioneers, led by Gerald Coates, meanwhile served as a speaking platform for "prayer warriors" such as Cindy Jacobs (Hunt 493). However, perhaps the most visible example of British Restorationism's adoption of American style spiritual warfare is the so-called March for Jesus organization. This idea was formulated by Roger Forster in the mid–1980s. Potentially following the lead of Carlos Annacondia of Argentina, Forster and his congregation would "prayer-walk" before trying to establish new congregations or church plants in any specific geographical area. In 1986, for instance, Icthus went toe to toe with Soho, the center of the sex industry in London. In 1987, Forster got together with 3 other evangelical leaders who shared his view of spiritual warfare, including Gerald Coates and Lynn Green (who was a director in YWAM). The first March of Jesus was conducted "against the influence of greed and corruption in the banking and financial institutions." When there was a global monetary panic, March for Jesus saw this as "God acting in response to their vanquishing of the demonic forces in the City" (Howard, *Charismania* 33–34).

Subsequent marches made equally questionable claims for the effectiveness of spiritual warfare. Coates argued that a 1988 hurricane and Margaret Thatcher's dismissal from political office were "human fallout from the spiritual battles affected during the marches" (Howard, *Charismania* 35).[12] March for Jesus soon spread—to Europe, then to the States, and by 1994 it had gone global. The 1994 march was particularly significant because the march's supporters predicted that a march would occur in every capital city of every country. Howard clearly indicates that the March for Jesus was part of the broader objectives of the AD2000 Campaign of which Wagner played such a large part (Howard 36).[13] Linking Forster even further with the development of the NAR is the organization Challenge 2000, which was led by his son. Challenge 2000 was a UK attempt to use "demographic computer-based technology in spiritual warfare," modeled on the spiritual mapping practice of American organizations like AD 2000 and the Sentinel Group. The goal of the project was to "produce a database which holds marketing profiles of geographical areas as well as spiritual mapping charts" (Howard 36). Howard notes that the Challenge 2000 database deliberately recorded demographic information (based on the government census) and then used this information precisely as a marketing agency would, "to locate what type of people live in particular environments and what their needs and aspirations are. This information is fed through to churches in particular areas to see how they can best serve their constituency and what methods of evangelism seem most appropriate" (Howard 36–37). Similarly, churches could feed this information back to Challenge 2000, giving the organization a potential data gold mine (Howard 36–37).

However, the most intriguing links to the NAR in the United Kingdom come not from Restorationism but from Anglicanism and its relationship to the Toronto Blessing. As Roland Howard indicates, "the main route for the blessing into the UK was through the leaders of Holy Trinity Brompton and Bishop David Pytches, then priest of St. Andrews Chroleywood and a number of 'New Church' leaders" (Howard 111). Holy Trinity Brompton (HTB) became a major pilgrimage site in Britain for those seeking the Toronto Blessing (ed. Hillborn, "Toronto in Perspective" 136). While much of the initial activism on behalf of Vineyard-style spirituality took place under the auspices of Sandy Millar, it is now Nicky Gumbel who is most associated with the church. That HTB was closely involved in the Blessing is not disputed. Indeed, David Hillborn sees Nicky Gumbel's interaction with Eleanor Mumford at a meeting of church leaders, in which Mumford pronounced the wonders of the Blessing, as the crucial event in the spread of the Blessing in Britain. Gumbel was already by this point the well-known coordinator of the immensely popular Alpha Course—a course meant to introduce people to Christianity within a 13 week period (Hillborn, "A Chronicle" 160). It is also clear that HTB maintained Sandy Millar's support for the Kansas City Prophets for an unusually long period of time, well after the Gruen controversy had worked its way through most of the evangelical world. In an article written before the TAV-AVC breach, but clearly after the start of the Blessing (since it references Randy Clark, who became prominent only after the Toronto Blessing began in 1994), Millar praised the Kansas City Prophets, stating that "we watched them at close quarters when they were here and saw them demonstrating a degree of prophetic anointing that in my view we have yet to see in this country, even—or should I say especially?—among some who might criticize them" (Millar qtd in. Hillborn 278).

To understand why these links are so important one must understand the influence HTB's Alpha Course has had. As of November 2001, Alpha's flagship press organ, *Alpha News*, reported that 7,300 Alpha courses were running in the United Kingdom. At its height in the U.K. there were as many as 10,500 such courses being run (Hunt, *The Alpha Enterprise* 11). Alpha's reach internationally was equally impressive. Even before the launch of its 1998 massive national marketing campaign, Alpha had spread internationally to 75 countries. By mid–1999, Alpha had claimed to have established 11,430 courses internationally. By 2003, the number of Alpha graduates had reached nearly 4 million (Hunt 13). In recent years, Alpha's main growth market has been America, largely with the cooperation of the AVC. By the end of 2003, Alpha was claiming that it was running in 5,000 U.S. churches and in 2001 some 40 Alpha conferences took place in America alone. Alpha meanwhile received endorsements from such evangelical leaders as Bill Hybels (a megachurch pastor), Luis Palau, and Jack Hayford (an ally of C. Peter Wagner) (Hunt, *Alpha Enterprise* 14). Gumbel's *Questions of Life* (1993), his first book, had sold more than 500,000 copies by the time Hunt's *Alpha Enterprise* (2004) was published in 2004 (14).

Alpha is meant to be a safe, non-confrontational way of bringing non–Christians into the evangelical faith (Ronson). While, this work does not subscribe to the "cultic" analysis of Alpha that is popular in some circles, it cannot be denied that Alpha does borrow a few of the methods popularized by such groups. For instance, the famous cult tactic of "love bombing" people with initial affection is undoubtedly a partial motivator for the Alpha Supper which traditionally is served at the beginning or end of each course (see Hunt, *Alpha Enterprise* 58–59 on the Alpha Supper. Ronson's "Revelations: How to Find God" documentary also provides some interesting footage of an Alpha Supper). What is even more apparent is that there is a certain amount of bait-and-hook to the Alpha Course, with the program's most controversial and Charismatic element, the Holy Spirit Weekend, not being implemented until one third or halfway through the course (see Hunt, *Alpha Enterprise* 69).

Hunt, who has no delusions about the Alpha Course's essentially Charismatic nature, argues: "The Holy Spirit weekend is in many respects the centerpiece of the Alpha Programme. It has two principal functions: firstly, to bring a greater integration to the Alpha group ... secondly, to provide a series of teachings on the Holy Spirit which emphasize the charismatic core of the Alpha course" (Hunt 233). The Holy Spirit Weekend offers up a "Ministry time" that focuses on healing, particularly emotional healing, and now forms the centerpiece of the ministry, even as Alpha tends to minimize its connection to Wimber's power-evangelism (the more outwardly "spiritual warfare" component of Wimber's ministry). Thus the focus in the Holy Spirit Weekend is heavily on healing, particularly of emotional pain (241–242).

While Hunt admits the possibility of cult-like influence through the Alpha Course, he ultimately argues that this probably overstates the case against the course (Hunt, *Alpha Enterprise* 244–246). This work agrees with Hunt's assessment. Certainly the Alpha meetings I myself attended in my youth were about as non-threatening as could be. But then, I was never confronted with a room full of tongue-speaking Anglicans, and I also came from an evangelical background where such tongue-speaking would have been less threatening than to more vulnerable people than me. And to be fair, if Alpha is like every other evangelistic enterprise, it is precisely vulnerable people it will target, not out of cruelty but because Alpha Course promoters sincerely believe it is such people that the ministry can most readily help. Combine these facts with Alpha's emphasis on healing, particularly *emotional healing*, and one has a potential for disaster. As I have noted in my book *The Failure of Evangelical Mental Health Care*, the use of deliverance/inner healing practices in evangelical circles has led to notorious abuses of clients; there is little likelihood that Alpha would be different in this regard (Weaver 27–105 passim).

However, a more immediate problem with Alpha is perceptively noted by Hunt. This is its application of church growth ideology. Specifically, Alpha plays out the "homogenous unit principle," particularly its notion of "like attracts like." Alpha implements such strategies not simply by its ministries to youth and students, but through other ministries aimed at distinct social groups such as young mothers, the unemployed, the elderly, etc. (Hunt, *Alpha Enterprise* 37).

Alpha supporters may claim that it does not deliberately support the NAR. While such a claim is dubious, given Alpha's close relationship to the Toronto Blessing, the reality is that whether or not Alpha feels it belongs to the NAR, many apostolic networks clearly feel that Alpha belongs to them. In a revealing passage in Kay's *Apostolic Networks in Britain*, Kay highlights why apostolic networks are attracted to Alpha:

> So far as apostolic networks were concerned, Alpha was an ideal complement to their own discipleship or church planting programs. Alpha could be used with small or large groups, in the settings of a private home or a rented hall, and the discussion generated by the presentational materials could be owned and customized by course leaders. The Holy Spirit weekend of ministry within the course ideally suited the experiential dimension of apostolic networks while the meal together easily fitted in with their existing church style.... Alpha led the way in late 20th century and early 21st century evangelism and apostolic networks found its presumptions and methods entirely to their liking [Kay 236].

Kay is likely here referring only to British apostolic networks, but as we have seen many of those networks have connections with American apostolic networks, and most of the others likely have sympathies with American NAR ideology. Moreover, considering its widespread influence on the Vineyard and its wide usage in America, it is impossible to believe that Alpha is not being similarly implemented by U.S. apostolic networks. Alpha offers such apostolic networks a number of advantages, not least of which is organizational flexibility. Alpha's Amway-like approach to recruiting also allows for a re-introduction of a gentler, modern form of discipleship practice to be re-introduced into churches which might be normally gun-shy of anything that smacks of shepherding. But perhaps Alpha's most important feature for NAR supporters is that it puts a middle class, largely respectable face on some of the more extreme doctrines of the modern Charismatic movement, including the NAR. Gumbel is far too slick to be caught by even the most aggressive interviewers. Compared even to Wagner or Silvoso, he has been able to mainstream extreme NAR-derived beliefs into the center of evangelicalism. Further, by providing a kind of "spiritual warfare-lite," an urbane model of Charismatic Renewal, Gumbel's ministry provides a convenient entry point into the NAR for any mainline Protestant who might otherwise be put off by some of the more extreme claims made by more fanatical NAR supporters. In short, in the Alpha Course, the NAR has its perfect recruiting tool, one that it can use with impunity even as it denies its connection to Gumbel and vice-versa.

Before closing this section, brief mention should be made of Peter Horrobin and his Ellel Ministries. Horrobin has been included in the Wagners' major anthology *How to Minister Freedom* and the Wagners have also endorsed Horrobin's *Healing Through Deliverance: The Foundation and Practice of Deliverance Ministry* (2008), which is similarly endorsed by NAR stalwart Alistair Petrie (Wagner, *Healing Through Deliverance* Endorsements). He is definitely therefore a major influence in NAR circles. Ellel Ministries was founded in 1986; by 1991 it was running courses throughout the year, at its spacious seventy-bed location near Lancaster. It soon expanded into Eastern Europe as well. Ellel is notable because Howard argues that at the time of *Charismania's* publication (1997) it was the U.K.'s—and possibly the world's—biggest exorcism ministry. While the Wagners ISDM may now surpass Ellel in influence there can be little doubt that Horrobin's theories on deliverance have been enormously influential. His *Healing Through Deliverance* seeks to carry on the legacy of Derek Prince and other of the more erudite old-school deliverance supporters; Horrobin's work is frequently mentioned in other deliverance material.[14] Horrobin claimed not to have encountered any psychiatric condition that did not involve demons and in a seminar stated, "I haven't yet ministered to anyone who was seriously sexually abused who did not also need deliverance" (Horrobin 96–97). As I have pointed out, whether or not Horrobin invented the whole soul ties concept is unclear; what is clear is that he has been one of its most effective proponents. That the Wagners would support such an extremist so openly does not speak well for the future of the American Charismatic Church; and that Horrobin proved so phenomenally successful in the U.K. speaks to the continuing danger New Apostolic beliefs play, even in the relatively secular nations of Europe.

Australia: The Controversy That Is Hillsong

I will only deal briefly with Australia, as much of the influence of the NAR in Australia has been documented in both Chapter 3 and in my book *The Failure of Evangelical Mental Health Care*, which explored the NAR's disastrous counseling misadventures in Australia, courtesy of Mercy Ministries and Bill Hamon's apostolic network.

The most important thing to understand about the Australian experience of the NAR is that the NAR's success in Australia was achieved mainly through the institutional denominational structure in Australia, namely the Assemblies of God. Wagner argues that after battles over leadership and the "routinization" of Charismatic experiences in the Assemblies of God, apostolic ministries became popular in the Assemblies of God in Australia. Notably, he points to Brian Houston (the founder of Hillsong Church) and his father Frank Houston, as examples of this growing trend. As a result, the Australian AOG developed its own apostolic networks, which could choose to affiliate or not affiliate with the Australian AOG if they so chose (Wagner, *Chuchquake!* 150–152).

As much as Australians might hope that this is ridiculous hyperbole on Wagner's part, there is some solid evidence to back it up. Shane Clifton's article "The Apostolic Revolution and the Ecclesiology of the AoGA" has noted the influence of this new apostolic paradigm on Australian churches. According to Clifton, Australian Pentecostal David Cartledge (a crucial figure in Australian Christian in general) credited the apostolic "revolution" with helping the church fight against centralized bureaucracies. Cartledge, and those who followed in his wake, preferred theocratic church government structures which he felt maximized the amount of power available to "God-appointed" apostolic leaders. Cartledge, like Wagner, credited the apostolic revolution in the decades following the AGA's (Australian Assembly of God) 1977 Biennial Conference as being responsible for the huge amount of growth the movement has subsequently achieved (Clifton no pagination).[15] Clifton points out that part of the problem with establishing the truth of Cartledge's contention is that he applies the term apostle somewhat retroactively, in much the same way Wagner did with the NAR. But whereas Wagner was likely correct in saying that something like the NAR had had previous manifestations in the evangelical church, Cartledge's use of the term apostle was more problematic, as Australian pastors had seldom if ever used this terminology about themselves prior to Cartledge's adaptation of the new apostolic narrative in the 1990s (Clifton no pagination). In any case, while Clifton is not always entirely unsympathetic to NAR ecclesiological concerns, he admits that the new apostolic revolution did lead to increasing centralization of power in the hands of pastors, particularly in megachurches (Clifton no pagination).

Today, undoubtedly the biggest player in Australian NAR power politics is Hillsong Church, and its influence is quite considerable. Hillsong's history goes back more than 30 years. In February 1978, Brian and Bobbie Houston emigrated from New Zealand to Australia and became part of the "ministry team" of Sydney Christian Life Centre. In August 1983, they founded Hills Christian Life Centre, what would become Hillsong ("About Hillsong"). Hillsong is now said to be Australia's largest church (Maddox 223). It is hard to underestimate the influence of Hillsong worldwide. Celebrities like Justin Bieber have been mentored by Hillsong leaders (Bailey; Menzie, "Justin Bieber Breaks Down"; Menzie, "Justin Bieber Tried"). Even more influential than Hillsong's influence on musical celebrities is its own highly touted worship music, which according to Hillsong is sung by more than 45 million people each week in the United States alone, leaving the church with extremely lucrative licensing fees (Bailey).

While it is difficult to explain how much Hillsong is loved by the evangelical community, it is perhaps even more difficult to communicate how loathed the church is by the Australian public. Much of this loathing, of course, is a direct response to the Mercy Ministries controversy, which outraged many Australians. Indeed, so hated has Hillsong become in Australia, that *The Chaser's War on Everything*, a popular comedy show in Australia during the mid 2000s, did a scathing parody send-up of Hillsong's musical style that expressed considerable ire at Hillsong's prosperity-gospel infused message (see Chaser's War).

In large part, the negative view of Hillsong within the Australian media and public is a direct result of the ministry's repeated inability to interact honestly with the Australian public. Particularly concerning to many Australians was Hillsong's friendships with important Australian political figures. Australian Prime Minister John Howard praised Hillsong in 2002 at the opening of its $25 million complex, for its growth from 45 members to 14,000, saying, "I've got to tell you that I don't think there's any side of Australian politics that could do a branch stack as good as that" (Maddox 224–225). This statement, even Howard's appearance at the event, was made all the more remarkable by the fact that it occurred right after the 2002 Bali bombing, which killed almost 100 Australians ("Bali Death Toll Set"), an event that for Australians was equivalent to the distress felt by Americans after 9/11 and which should have been occupying all Howard's time at that point. Howard and his ministers, over the course of his third term, increasingly aligned themselves with Pentecostal and non-denominational evangelical churches that would have been previously seen by Australia's Liberal Party as fringe elements. Besides Howard opening Sydney's Hillsong, Australian Federal Treasurer Peter Costello would sing paeans to the Ten Commandments as the salutation for Australia's problems at a Hillsong conference (Maddox 164). Meanwhile, Howard also conducted a cloak-and-dagger "subterranean assault" on Australia's new religious other—Islam—which partly relied on appealing to a return to Australian "traditional values," as well as the support of private Christian education, as a weapon in the Australian culture war against the Muslim "Hun," both programs of thought that worked in hand in hand with the Australian Religious Right's political goals (Maddox 182–192). Marion Maddox also has expressed concern with the almost total control of the Australian Family First Party by the Australian Assemblies of God (which is itself largely New Apostolic in orientation) (225), as well as with the involvement of Hillsong member Alan Cadman in the Lyons

Forum, a kind of Australian right wing think-tank out of which Cadman advocated for the kind of "'faith-based' welfare programs'" that were implemented in the U.S. during the Bush administration (Maddox 38–39).

Australians were also considerably put out by the financing of Hillsong. Hillsong is not required to publicly disclose its finances in Australia, and this lack of disclosure, as well as calls for megachurches and other Christian organizations of Hillsong's size to be taxed, have been a matter of considerable controversy in Australia (Bailey). Hillsong's Sydney location alone (it has several locations worldwide) claimed to have had $64 million in revenue in 2010, but this statistic significantly omitted worldwide music sales, which are a huge profit source for Hillsong. Hillsong is a leading player in Charismatic missions in Africa, and disturbingly, given current Charismatic theology concerning sexual abuse, is at the forefront of anti-sex trafficking efforts as well (Bailey). All of this has led to a great deal of criticism in Australia, including an entire expose of Hillsong on the Australian news show *The Current Affair* ("Hillsong Money Machine"). For Americans, the idea of taxing a church might seem counterproductive, violating longstanding American conceptions of "separation" of church and state. However, the questions the Australian secular public is asking about ministries like Hillsong are far from lacking in merit. There seems to be little practical reason for granting churches tax exempt status, even in the United States. Indeed, getting rid of the tax-exempt status of churches might arguably be a boon to both leftwing and rightwing churches alike, as they would finally be able to espouse political views directly, so long as they paid the IRS or its overseas equivalents. What the Australian public is asking, essentially, is just that Pentecostal churches—including those in the NAR—be regulated like any other charity. Whether such regulations will move beyond the shores of Australia remains an open question.

South Korea: Prayer, Power Evangelism and Cell Churches, Korean Style

And finally, we come to South Korea, where the NAR has developed extensively but largely undocumentably. That the NAR has a large presence in South Korea is likely indisputable for a number of reasons. First, according to the International Dictionary of Pentecostal and Charismatic Movements, neocharismatics account for 42 percent of South Korea's Pentecostal/Charismatic population, a plurality of that population (Pentecostal Encyclopedia 239 "South Korea"). While the Encyclopedia does not define Neocharismatics as being analogous to the NAR, the term does include the NAR within its environs, as well as the house church movement and the prophetic African Independent Churches (AICs), both of which occasionally (in the case of house churches, considerably) cross over into the NAR. Therefore, it is highly likely that a large percentage of South Korean Charismatics align themselves with the NAR. What is even more indisputable is that regardless of the South Korean church's alignment with the NAR's leadership structure, it is *intensely on board* with the NAR's vision of demonology. This point has been well documented in the secondary literature. For instance, Brouwer, Gifford and Rose's study found that of the largest Presbyterian, Methodist, Holiness, Baptist megachurches they found in South Korea, all of them except the Presbyterian church were Pentecostal in theology and promoted exorcism as a major practice. Furthermore "power evangelism," the major tool of John Wimber and, in distilled form, of the NAR as well, is not just practiced by David Yonggi Cho, but even by pastors like Ki Dong Kim of the Sung Rak Baptist Church, who promoted power evangelism techniques that seemed indistinguishable from those of more traditional Pentecostal denominations like the Assembly of God (see Brouwer, Gifford and Rose 119). According to Ig-Jin Kim, a scholar not unsympathetic to the Korean Charismatic movement, power evangelization is "in general" accepted by Korean Pentecostals and even evangelicals (Ig Jin Kim 281–282). Kim directly invokes Wagner and makes clear that Korean Pentecostals and Charismatics, as is common within the NAR and the Third Wave in general, preach about territorial spirits (Kim 281–282).

Before turning to Paul Yonggi Cho, who though not operating within an NAR apostolic network, has done more than any South Korean Pentecostal to advance the cause of the NAR, I should briefly point out two important NAR ministries with connections in Korea. The first is the Korean branch of the Messianic Jewish Bible Institute (see "Korea"). The school operates a school of messianic theology in South Korea ("Korea"). Dan Juster, arguably the most well-known Messianic Jew in the world and a major supporter of NAR theology, is on the organization's board of directors ("Board of Directors"). As we have seen in the section on Israel, Juster is also definitely aligned with the NAR, as is the Messianic movement in general. For outsiders, the collaboration between Messianics and Korean Pentecostals is bizarre, but it is actually relatively easy to document. Indeed, perhaps the most bizarre and in many ways sinister part of this alliance is the documentary *Restoration* (2010), produced by South Korean producer Joan Lee (Bradley Kim). While the film tells the story of a real life attack on a Messianic Jew in Israel that harmed a young teenager, the filmmakers seem oblivious to the fact that the way they portray the incident turns what essentially was a fairly isolated incident into an eerie invocation of the blood libel (Kim; "Justice for Ami Ortiz"; Israel Today Staff).

The second NAR group that seems to have a particular interest in Korea is Mike Bickle's IHOP movement, which has an extensive collection of translated material for Koreans available on its website. The affinity IHOP apparently feels for Korean Pentecostalism may be attributed in large part to the very similar philosophies of prayer that govern IHOP and much of Korean Pentecostalism. Korean Pentecostal emphasis on prayer has a long history, going back to the prayer mountain movement, which emphasized fasting and prayer (Eim, "South Korea" 240), and the strong emphasis on prayer continues to this day. Prayer plays an important role, for instance in Cho's classical Pentecostal adaptation of power evangelism, which as in the NAR variant thereof, sees prayer as an effective tool of spiritual warfare against the Devil and territorial spirits (Ig-Jin Kim 281–282).

However, it is Paul Yonggi Cho's theology that has most profoundly interacted with the NAR. Cho's relationship with the NAR is in many ways similar to that of Silvoso. Unlike some NAR adherents in the developing world, who are promoted as leaders when they are really followers, Cho, like Silvoso, has had a genuinely profound effect on the development of the NAR, even though his status within the movement would best be described as an allied co-belligerent. The most obvious area of Cho's influence, of course is the cell church movement. Cho proved remarkably successful at adapting the homogenous unit principle of Donald McGavran to the South Korean religious context. Cho, significantly, however, did not use the homogenous principle for the entire church, just for the cell system itself. He therefore was able to sell his congregation, Yoido Full Gospel Church, as a church that genuinely did not differentiate between rich and poor, well-educated and uneducated, etc. Homogenous cells were thereby combined into more heterogeneous elements in the church polity at large (Brouwer, Gifford and Rose 118). Through Cho's organization Church Growth International, he managed to brand his form of church growth policy throughout much of the world (Brouwer, Gifford and Rose 45). Cho's ministry, as well as other Korean Charismatics, have also increasingly interacted with power evangelism supporters through the Fuller School of World Mission, where many Korean students study.[16] Yoido has also aggressively put itself at the forefront of world missions with as many as 500 missionaries already sent from the church as of 1992 to the United States alone (Brouwer, Gifford and Rose 120).

Cho also played some role in the success of the spiritual mapping movement, though less in its development. A 1987 visit he made to Argentina led to a fair amount of media hype (much of it possibly self-generated) (see Holvast 56–57). The First International SWN meeting was held in South Korea, thanks to Wagner's UPT and SWN (Holvast 101–102). Wagner considered himself an admirer of Cho's church growth tactics and was a member of the board of Church Growth International for many years (Wagner, *Wrestling* 142–143). In 1995, AD 2000 organized the Global Consultation on World Evangelization II, also held in Seoul (Holvast 104) and it is clear from much of both the spiritual mapping and evolving NAR discourse in this period that Korea was seen as the next new thing in evangelical circles, the place to be.

However, as Holvast points out, though Pentecostalism was enormously successful in Korea, and though spiritual mapping was not unknown in Korea, there was a sense in which the latter was virtually absent. Koreans, were of course, active in the AD 2000 network, as seen from the conferences they hosted, and they staged a number of "impressive prayer marches, on account of which hundreds of thousands and even millions were reported to participate" (Holvast 139). Cho joined the SWN network and several other Korean leaders played a notable role in spiritual mapping, notably Pastor Kim of the Kwang Lim Methodist Church and Pastor Hwan of the Myong-Song Presbyterian church (Holvast 139).

However, Korean Pentecostals and evangelicals conceptualized spiritual mapping much differently than Westerners, much of their conceptualization involving Cho's concept of the "fourth dimension." This was the belief that "there are powers in another dimension." These powers were not just available to Christians, but could be used by anyone. However, Christians had the ability to use these powers more effectively than others, and such techniques were used to help one progress in one's faith. Cho therefore heavily emphasized prayer in this particular worldview, combined with visualization techniques, which Holvast sees as standing in hand-in-hand with the general WOF aspect of Cho's teachings. Therefore, even though Korean Pentecostalism shared with U.S. Pentecostalism a belief in power evangelism, the Korean model of spiritual warfare was based on Korea's own idiosyncratic take on territorial spirits, one not necessarily shared by the West (or vice versa). In addition, the huge amount of church growth in Korean Christianity, according to Holvast, meant that many Americans who went to Korea at the height of the spiritual mapping movement were more interested in learning and adapting Korean evangelistic strategies than they were in exporting their own to Korea (as happened in the case of Argentina, for instance) (Holvast 140–141).

Wagner came to believe that the major benefit South Korean Christianity provided to the world was not its practice of spiritual warfare—which for Wagner, in any case, would not have proved easily exportable—but its fervent and easily culturally transmissible theology of prayer (Holvast 141). Typically for Wagner, he was prescient in this prediction. As we have seen, movements like IHOP are seeking to both export themselves to Korea and to implement styles of worship that are quite similar to the fervent prayer style embraced by many Koreans, such as all-night prayer (which was practiced in Korea long before IHOP adopted this prayer method) (see Ig-Jin Kim 110 on the all-night prayer tradition in Korea). IHOP, for instance, has recently opened a whole school dedicated just to Korean-language and Korean ministry ("Forerunner School of Ministry"). Given the continued power evangelism and Pentecostalism have in South Korea, and the fervency of many Korean believers' beliefs, it is likely that South Korean forms of New Apostolic thought will continue to play a large part in the development of the movement for years to come.

Conclusion

Of all the countries mentioned here, Australia in many ways represents perhaps the most hopeful outcome to the problem the NAR presents to the West and the developing world. Although the NAR has had success in Australia, as well as in neighboring countries like Fiji and New Zealand, it has also met in Australia considerably more skepticism and organized opposition than anywhere else in the Western world, including other secular cultures like the United Kingdom. Part of this is likely due to higher educational standards in Australia, as well as potential concerns by left-wing Australians that greater influence by the NAR and its allies may lead to delays in social progress on issues like Aboriginal rights or better social welfare provisions. Because of the NAR's considerable overlap with the prosperity gospel of the WOF movement, it is usually not seen as conducive to progressive politics by serious observers of the Charismatic movement.

Whether the success that Australians have had at limiting the political effectiveness of the NAR can be duplicated in other countries, particularly in the developing world, is open to question. Part of the problem that scholars and progressive activists face and will continue to face in dealing with the expansion of Third Wave Pentecostalism and the NAR into the developing world is that NAR political and socioeconomic theories can often seem superficially benign. However, if one looks deep enough into the documentation on the movement, as well as the political views of many people participating in the NAR, this progressive framing of the NAR simply cannot be sustained.

This, however, has not prevented some scholars—mainly those aligned with the Templeton funded Flame of Love Project—from attempting such a framing. For instance, Matthew Lee, Margaret Poloma, and Stephen Post, in *The Heart of Religion: Spiritual Empowerment, Benevolence and the Experience of God's Love* (2013), write in glowing terms of how "instead of a few Pentecostal

6. From the Others of the Americas to the Others Overseas   253

leaders working to change communities through their benevolent organizations, Steve Witt, Bill Johnson, and others in the NAR challenge all Christians to dream big and work with God to change the world" (Lee, Poloma, and Post, *The Heart of Religion*, 177). Such scholarly naiveté—which is characteristic of Poloma's entire scholarly oeuvre—highlights the continued need for progressive scholars to challenge the NAR's self-narrative of a benign movement intent only on bringing the gospel to the suffering and hope to the needy. This means that scholars will have to both challenge the NAR's narrative, but also sympathize with the many sincere and well-meaning people in the NAR who cannot understand how potentially destructive the policies they advocate are to the populations they serve. The failure to communicate this need for dialogue would be nothing less than catastrophic. As evangelical Protestantism seeks to find itself at the beginning of the 21st century, no question about its global implications is more pressing than what is to be done about the NAR. And no question may have worse repercussions, both for those within the NAR and those outside it, if society fails to understand the theology and politics of this new shift in global Christianity.

Conclusion
Where Does the NAR Go from Here?

In the final analysis, what are we to make of the NAR? Will it continue to be an influential force in the future or will the apostolic paradigm play itself out? My fear about premature predictions of the NAR's demise are similar to my concerns about predictions concerning the collapse of the Christian Right. The latter group has been declared dead repeatedly, only to engage in a karmic rebirth in which it recycles the same ideologies that it produced in previous generations. The NAR's development is strikingly similar to that of the wider Christian Right. Indeed, the NAR is but the latest form of an apostolic revolution that can arguably be traced at the very least as far back as the Latter Rain Revival, and certainly to the shepherding movement. Yet lay Charismatics and Pentecostals are continually willing to buy into the NAR as a new manifestation of God's spirit. I have witnessed this at NAR services that could have come straight out of the shepherding movement or even the Latter Rain Revival. Doctrinally, little has actually changed; but the branding has become infinitely more sophisticated.

The threat NAR theology poses is not simply local but global. The exporting of Charismatic ideology, particularly its NAR variation, to the developing world, has had devastating effects on a number of countries, particularly Guatemala and Uganda. In the process American prejudices about issues like homosexuality, racial relations, non–Christian religions, and capitalist economics are transposed onto developing world cultures in a fundamentally imperialistic and exploitative manner. While Uganda's "death-to-gays" bill or Harold Cabelleros's discriminatory campaigns against Mayan culture in Guatemala may benefit NAR apostles, as well as the social elites who run these countries, it is difficult to see how such campaigns help further the interest of impoverished, often war-torn communities.

A quarter century ago, Sara Diamond's *Spiritual Warfare: The Politics of the Christian Right* (1989) pointed out the relationship then emerging between Religious Right activism overseas and right wing American foreign policy objectives. The Religious Right was then in the vanguard of supporting the Nicaraguan contras. Christian Right groups were supportive of numerous counter-revolutionary pastors in Nicaragua who were oppositionally united against progressive Central American Christianity (as exemplified by liberation theology). The Christian Right devoted a good deal of money to backing up the South African apartheid government and used much of its missionary relief and development work in the developing world in a manner that led, according to Diamond, to "disastrous implications" (Diamond vi). The NAR represents the latest iteration of this union between Christian right activism and the kind of Reaganite military-industrial capitalism that has characterized the American right for at least the last thirty years.

What is perhaps most disturbing about the NAR is how naked its union with governmental foreign policy and economic objectives truly is. The advantage for businesses in having employees who believe their employer is their apostle is obvious. Similarly, the Great Wealth Transfer idea is an ingenious way of diverting working class people, particularly in the developing world, from more pragmatic, and for Western governments, *more inconvenient*, ways of redressing economic imbalance. And the increasing sophistication of the transformationalist model of evangelical economic development, which may eventually cause another "paradigm shift" for the NAR, is evident by even a casual reading of transformationalist material. Similarly, NAR theology helps to keep developing world countries destabilized, promoting the kind of "low intensity conflict" in these areas that is at the heart of U.S. foreign policy in the developing world. Sara Diamond pointed out in the 1980s that in the developing world, "Christian Right 'humanitarian' suppliers and promoters of anti-communist ideology use religion to mask the aggressive, cynical nature of 'humanitarian' projects" (Diamond, *Spiritual Warfare* 162). Currently, this cynicism is seen most markedly in the NAR's "aid" to Uganda, but transformationalist ideology as a whole is widely popular in Africa and has the potential to destabilize large swathes of the continent if left unchecked, allowing the United States to continue exploiting that continent, as well as Latin America, as it has done for more than half a century.

There are real reasons to be concerned with the NAR's ever-increasing expansion. Perhaps nowhere is this more evident than in Israel. Mike Bickle's IHOP has maintained close ties with messianic Jews in Israel and is clearly trying to establish a major presence there (see Posner, "Kosher Jesus"). Yet the ever-present apocalyptic nature of Bickle's theology makes him potentially a very dangerous ally for Israel. The almost complete subversion of Messianic Judaism by the NAR threatens to transform a Middle Eastern situation that was already a powder-keg into an ideological time bomb just waiting to go off. Are these the allies best suited for maintaining a rational foreign policy? Can productive trade relations, exploitative or not, be maintained when such unpredictable allies form a crucial part of contemporary right wing political—and increasingly economic—organizing? I would hope that this book has convinced the reader that such alliances are ultimately not productive in the long term.

One could hope that the increasingly middle class character of American Charismatic faith might eventually dim the apostolic movement's attraction in evangelical communities, but so far that has not happened. Indeed, in many ways the NAR's adoption of pragmatism and a "me-centered" theology plays into the largely bourgeois sensibilities of America's suburban jet-setters, where church and mall are synonymous theological terms. While these sensibilities may not be in keeping with academia, or the fashionably counter-cultural groups of evangelical cultural elites, they certainly play well with the economic elites of the evangelical movement, who if Ken Eldred and company are any indication, see Pentecostal and Charismatic Christianity as limitless picking grounds for ruthless exploitation of working class evangelicals. Sean McCloud has called for the reapplication of class analysis to religious studies and in reference to the NAR that sentiment is a badly needed one ("Divine Hierarchies"). Such scholarship is not simply needed from a methodological perspective, but is ethically imperative if we are to understand the modern Charismatic movement.

The reason such class-based analysis is so desperately needed is because too much scholarship in Pentecostal studies falls into either reprehensible caricatures of Charismatic culture, or alternately, as in the scholarship of Candy Gunther Brown, equally ridiculous pictures of valorized utopian Charismatic communities whose beliefs are to be interpreted as uniformly benign. Neither of these pictures gives us an accurate analysis of how the NAR will develop in the future.

Such an analysis is needed. There are real questions to be asked about how permanently such a top-down system of dictatorial authority can be maintained. If the apostolic networks do collapse, what will take their place (if anything)? How will the most modern forms of the NAR, such as transformationalism, adapt to the changing religious climate we find ourselves in? What will Wagner's followers do if they realize that the Great Wealth Transfer is little more than an elaborate pyramid scheme? There are a limitless number of such questions that the NAR's development invokes, questions in desperate need of answer (Tabachnick, "Large RW Christian Group").

Where Does the NAR Go from Here?

In dealing with any potentially extremist movement, academia should play a critical public role of critique and analysis. It is perhaps the lack of this role in relationship to the NAR that has been the most disheartening aspect of the movement's continuous triumph in the American political and religious scene. It is not just that academia failed to note the rise of the new politics of spiritual warfare. This was bad enough, but understandable given the context of the mid 1990s, when few non-evangelical scholars even understood the difference between Pentecostalism and fundamentalism, let alone knew how to theorize those differences. Academia has not just given the NAR a free pass, it has in many ways given the NAR the keys to the Ivory Tower. One can see this through Harvey Cox's close association with the Flame of Love Project, as well as the continuing countenancing of suspect Pentecostal scholarship via the gargantuan grants the Templeton Foundation has advanced to Pentecostal scholars in recent years.

But at a more fundamental level, academia did not simply countenance the NAR; *it caused it*. Without the application of McGavran's homogenous unit principle, without Kraft's brilliant misapplications of anthropological theory, without the misuse of Hiebert's concept of the Excluded Middle, and most of all without Wagner's and Wimber's ability to fuse these ideas into cohesive, easily digestible ideological packages, the NAR would have never been born.

The NAR's rootedness in the admittedly sometimes twisted anthropological and sociological theory of the Christian right should give academics pause. The NAR is hardly the first academic ideology to morph into a political philosophy, though it is arguably the first sophisticated mass application of social sciences theory to the political agenda of the Christian Right. With the academy's ever increasing ability to quantify and describe human behavior in ever-more concrete terms, there is presented the very real possibility that slightly "pseudo-scientificized" versions of mainstream science will be used as means of social control by right wing religious groups. It is all too likely that the NAR, like other evangelical movements based on questionable pseudo-scientific assumptions—the biblical counseling movement, reparative therapy, etc.—will utilize these same assumptions to reinforce existing church power structures, particularly the authoritarian forms of church discipline that, for differing reasons, are becoming prevalent in both NAR and New Calvinist circles.

So perhaps the story of the NAR is not solely a story about Charismatics, or a story about oppressed peoples and questionable politics. Perhaps the NAR's story is a story about knowledge itself, and the pursuit of it. If the history of the NAR teaches us anything, it is of the danger of approaching scholarship solely from a pragmatic standpoint, one unconcerned with the effect the research academics, social scientists, economists, and public policy thinkers engage in has on the theological 99 percent who are not part of the NAR leadership. Time and time again throughout this book, we saw scholars and pseudo-scholars create new scholastic fields and spiritualized sciences that combined subtly thought out political plans with pseudoscientific principles. The result was the evolution of a theological movement that was paradoxically at once both modern and pre-modern. But whether both feet will come forward in the new century, or take two steps back, only time will tell. And the cost for taking those steps may be incalculably more than we bargained for.

List of Abbreviations

BAM Business as Missions
CHCP Christian Healing Certification Program
CMED Christian Microenterprise Development
COR Coalition on Revival
DNA Disciple Nations Alliance
FFH Food for the Hungry
FGBMFI Full Gospel Business Men's Fellowship International
HIM Harvest International Ministry
HTB Holy Trinity Brompton
ICA International Coalition of Apostoles (now known as ICAL, the International Coalition of Apostolic Leaders)
IHOP International House of Prayer
IM Insider Movement
IRUL Institute for Research on Unlimited Love
ISDM The International Society of Deliverance Ministers
ITN International Transformation Network
KCF Kansas City Fellowship
LGBT Lesbian, Gay, Bisexual, Transgender
LRA Lord's Resistance Army
MED Microenterprise Development
MM Marketplace Missions
NAR New Apostolic Reformation
NRA National Resistance Army
PDI People of Destiny International
PIH Partners in Harvest
PIP Proximal Intercessory Prayer
PRA Political Research Associates
RTF Restoring the Foundations
SGM Sovereign Grace Ministries
SLSW Strategic Level Spiritual Warfare

List of Abbreviations

SRA Satanic Ritual Abuse
TACF Toronto Airport Christian Fellowship
TPM Theophostic Prayer Ministry
WLI Wagner Leadership Institute
WOF Word of Faith

Glossary

Alpha course—A phenomenally successful evangelistic course that originated at Holy Trinity Brompton (HTB). The course was largely shaped by HTB's current leader Nicky Gumbel (Hocken, "Alpha Course" 312; Pentecostal Encyclopedia). Although mainly a recruitment tool, the course's Charismatic ties are extensive and have deep roots in New Apostolic teachings. For these roots, see Chapter 6. As New Apostolic efforts go, the Alpha Course has been unusually successful at mainstreaming itself in evangelical and even mainline Protestant circles.

Apostle—The head of an apostolic network. Typically, the NAR dates the recovery of the apostolic role to the 1990s and early 2000s, though historically this is a dubious contention, as several successive movements have adopted variants of the apostolic idea, some of them dating as far back as the 1940s.

Apostolic networks—A group of churches and Christian believers who are under the "covering" of an apostle. Apostolic networks, as Holvast points out, differ from traditional denominational churches mainly in how they conceptualize "leadership and governance." Apostolic networks are typically not led by a group but by "an individual apostle." It is this "divinely appointed apostle, as opposed to a board or presbytery, a democratic vote or institution" who is seen as being responsible for making decisions for the movement and directing its adherents (Holvast 158–159). This work, while not supportive of the idea of apostolic networks, argues that organizationally apostolic networks have a number of advantages over traditional denominational structures that has led to the adoption of this organizational model by the NAR.

Business as Missions movement (BAM)—Charles Neal Johnson defines BAM ventures as "a for-profit commercial business venture that is Christian led, intentionally devoted to being used as an instrument of God's mission ... to the world, and is operated in a crosscultural environment, either domestic or international" (*Business as Mission: A Comprehensive Guide* loc 298–300). The important element here, from a theoretical standpoint, is that these are for-profit missions' ventures. Unlike traditional tentmaker ministries, which emphasize the role of missionaries as business professionals, BAM emphasizes the role of business professionals as missionaries.

Charismatic Renewal movement—The Charismatic Renewal was a major revival movement which incorporated many traditional Pentecostal practices that occurred outside the established Pentecostal denominations, beginning in the 1960s. It was characterized by a pragmatic ability to unite across disparate denominational and ideological groups within Christianity at large (including mainline Protestantism and even Catholicism), and had a strong missionary focus (Holvast 35, see also Synan 177–231).

Charismatics—In typical evangelical parlance, Charismatics are usually seen as Pentecostals-lite, that is, the less radical element of the wider Charismatic/Pentecostal movement. In reality, however, if one is defining Charismatics by the more technical sense of those who indulged in the Charismatic Renewal, the exact opposite impression emerges. In general, Charismatic is used in the popular sense of the term (or alternately to refer to the entire Charismatic/Pentecostal movement), since it's so ubiquitous, but readers should remember that denominational Pentecostalism is in many ways less radical than its Charismatic descendants. Regardless if one is talking about the Charismatic movement, Charismatic Renewal, or Pentecostalism, all three groups are characterized by a strong belief in the gifts of the spirit, such as speaking in tongues, prophecy, the casting out of demons, etc.

Church Growth movement—The church growth movement was a movement pioneered by evangelical thinker Donald McGavran, which sought to maximize the growth of evangelical churches. McGavran concluded that the key to doing this was by mobilizing large "people movements" by which people made collective decisions to commit their community to Christianity (Holvast 17, 18). Equally important to McGavran was the homogenous unit principle, which the NAR would come to understand as the ability for non–Christians to convert without having to cross "racial, linguistic or class barriers" (Wagner, *Wrestling* 109). As Holvast points out, the church growth movement would lay the foundation for spiritual mapping (see Holvast 17–18). Two of its leading proponents, Charles Kraft and C. Peter Wagner, would play a foundational role in helping create the NAR. The church growth movement's emphasis on pragmatism (see Holvast 28) meant that the movement was willing to experiment with a number of ecclesiological, worship, and liturgical innovations, so long as these innovations did not interfere with the essential political conservatism of the movement's leaders.

Deliverance—Casting out (or alternately casting away) of evil spirits (Collins 4). Cuneo specifically refers to deliverance as a "form of exorcism" (Cuneo 42). Collins tends to emphasize deliverance's differences from exorcism slightly more than Cuneo (Collins 4), but even he admits the terms are closely linked (4). It is crucial to understand that in most, though not all Protestant deliverance practice, the sufferer is demonically oppressed or "demonized," rather than possessed (4). Most deliverance practitioners in evangelicalism today are Charismatic, or sometimes neo-evangelical.

Demonization—"To be oppressed, influenced or, even, controlled by demons in some way" (Collins 4). Significantly, Charismatics typically argue that Christians can be demonically oppressed, but not possessed.

Dominionism—"In its broadest sense, dominionism is the theocratic idea that regardless of theological view or eschatological timetable Christians are called by God to exercise dominion over society by taking control of political and cultural institutions. The term is sometimes used interchangeably with Christian Reconstructionism and its offshoots.

Glossary

Reconstructionism was crucial to the spread of Dominionism among Neocharismatics and subsidiary movements within Pentecostalism. But the Latter Rain movement of Pentecostalism is also a root of contemporary Dominionism. The fusion of these roots has found its most recent expression as the 'Seven Mountains Mandate'" (Rachel Tabachnick and Fred Clarkson, Personal communication).[1]

Fort Lauderdale Five (FLF)—The five main leaders of the shepherding movement: Don Basham, Ern Baxter, Bob Mumford, Derek Prince, and Charles Simpson. On the uses and misuses of this term, see Moore 33–42.

Fundamentalism—Fundamentalism was a conservative Protestant movement that, during its period of national prominence during the 1920s, opposed theological modernism and evolutionary theory (Marsden 3–4). Detwiler lists "insistence on the Virgin Birth, the miracles of the Bible, the bodily resurrection of Jesus, and the power of Jesus' sacrificial death to remove the stain of sin from us," along with personal conversion, as the main markers of fundamentalism (Detwiler 151). Fundamentalists are chiefly distinguishable today by their wholehearted support for biblical inerrancy (in the original texts), creationism, and traditional as opposed to higher critical hermeneutical strategies.

Generational curses—A common term in current Charismatic parlance, in which demons are seen as being inherited from ancestors. In Cuneo's work it is variously referred to as "intergenerational evil" or "congenital demonism" (see Cuneo 149). The concept is the same.

Great Wealth Transfer—Simply defined, this is the idea of transferring "the control of wealth" from Satan and his minions to the "Kingdom of God" (Wagner, *Dominion!* 182). The Great Wealth Transfer is utilized by the NAR to appeal to working class and disadvantaged audiences who are moved by its promise of a bright economic future.

Ground-level deliverance/spiritual warfare—Delivering individual human beings and/or animals of their demons (see Holvast 189 on ground-level demons); Otis Jr. refers to it as "ministry activity that is associated with individual bondage and/or demonization" (Otis Jr., *Informed Intercession* 253). This form of spiritual warfare is opposed to occult level deliverance/spiritual warfare and deliverance from "principalities and powers," (pretty much synonymous with strategic level spiritual warfare), the highest form of deliverance, which typically involves "intercessory confrontations with demonic power concentrated over given cities, cultures, and peoples" (Otis Jr. 257).

Identificational repentance—According to NAR movement theorist George Otis, Jr., identificational repentance is a "two stage intercessory action that involves: an acknowledgment that one's affinity group (clan, city, nation or organization) has been guilty of specific corporate sin before God and man, and 2) a prayerful petition that God will use personal repudiation of this sin as a redemptive beachhead from which to move into the larger community" (Otis Jr., *Informed Intercession* 251). In actual practice, the NAR's belief in identificational repentance tends to promote the idea that a variety of populations, particularly in the Third World, are "demonized."

Intercessor/intercession—An intercessor is someone who prays. Intercession is the act of praying, usually on behalf of something. This work occasionally uses this term, rather than praying, as the connotation in Charismatic culture is slightly different than the standard term prayer, which is seen as less radical. The term intercession is frequently invoked by Charismatics when praying on behalf of a nation or a people group.

Kansas City Prophets—"The Kansas City prophets are a group of individuals that includes Mike Bickle, Paul Cain, John Paul Jackson, and others associated with the Kansas City Fellowship" (Gohr 816–817). The Kansas City Prophets were a major influence on the development of the NAR, through Mike Bickle's and Paul Cain's influence on John Wimber. Kansas City Fellowship (KCF) eventually birthed the IHOP movement, which is one of the most important apostolic networks currently operating, and a major power player within the NAR.

Lakeland Revival—A 2008 revival that occurred under the leadership of Canadian evangelist Todd Bentley. While it attracted many followers, Bentley for many Charismatics and non-Charismatics alike has come to represent what is wrong with the Charismatic movement as a whole. Bentley's NAR connections are extensive and are documented at several points throughout this book.

Latter Rain movement—"A Pentecostal movement of the mid 20th century that, along with the parallel healing movement of that era, became an important component of the post-WWII evangelical awakening" (Riss, "Latter Rain Movement" 830). William Branham and Franklin Hall (see chapter 1; also Riss, "Latter Rain Movement" 830) were important influences on the movement, which explicitly promoted Manifest Sons theology (Riss, *Latter Rain* 95–97). Latter Rain teaching was immensely influential on the NAR (see Holvast 164).

Mainline Protestantism—Here used to refer to the major liberal denominations, such as the Congregationalists, Episcopalians, Lutherans, etc. The NAR has made surprising inroads into the mainline churches at times.

Manifest Sons of God—"A belief in a new kind of Christian elite who wield special spiritual power in order to subdue the earth and who will actually conquer the earth in the end times" (Holvast 164). Manifest Sons theology was an important influence on both the 1948 Latter Rain Revival and the NAR.

Neo-evangelical—The term is used here approximately as the term born-again evangelical is deployed Fritz Detwiler's *Standing on the Premises of God*: Neo-evangelicals would be characterized by a "conversion experience" similar to other evangelicals, but would not (necessarily) have the hard line position on inerrancy and creationism that fundamentalists would have, nor the emphasis on spiritual gifts that is a part of Charismatic and sometimes Holiness practice (Detwiler 153). The term is a nebulous one in many ways, and the rule of thumb that an evangelical "was [once defined as] anyone who identified with Billy Graham" (Marsden 234) still holds some validity even today.

New Apostolic Reformation (NAR)—The New Apostolic Reformation is a movement of evangelicals, primarily from the Charismatic tradition, who sought to restore the role of the apostles to contemporary church life. In practice, what this means is a different vision of church ecclesiology, focusing on relational networks over close denominational affiliations and controlled through the natural charisma and authority invested in the apostle (for the relational aspect, see Holvast 159). Holvast relates that in the NAR, one is not "led by a group but by an individual apostle. It was this divinely appointed apostle, as opposed to a board or presbytery, a democratic vote or institution who was seen bearing responsibility for making decisions and guiding adherents" (Holvast 159). The NAR's leadership structure allows it to quickly react to changes in contemporary Christian culture; the movement is further aided by its rather pragmatic approach to church growth, an approach inherited by NAR leader C. Peter Wagner from his mentor Donald McGavran.

Occult-level spiritual warfare—According to major NAR theorist and policy wonk George Otis, Jr., occult level spiritual warfare refers to "intercessory confrontations with demonic forces operating through Satanism, witchcraft, shamanism, esoteric philosophies ... and any number of similar occult vehicles" (Otis Jr. 253). Occult-level deliverance has generally been less studied by scholars than SLSW or ground level deliverance, but for the NAR it is quite important. Often occult level spiritual warfare involves the burning of "pagan" artifacts. This can refer variously to the relics of Eastern cultures, Satanic or Wiccan paraphernalia, or indigenous artifacts.

Pentecostalism—A major subset of modern Christianity characterized by a strong belief in the gifts of the spirit, such as speaking in tongues, prophecy, the casting out of demons, etc. Pentecostalism can most productively be contrasted with Charismatic belief by pointing out Pentecostalism's stronger allegiances to traditional denominational structures, something that's becoming less and less a characteristic of Charismatic practice. Charismatic practice and ecclesiology also tends to be more ecumenical than traditional Pentecostalism, so long as the groups the Charismatic church allies with reflect conservative moral values.

Postmillennialism—The idea that "the prophecies in the book of Revelation concerning the defeat of the anti–Christ ... were being fulfilled in the present era, and were clearing the way for a golden age.... Christ would return after this millennial age (hence 'postmillennialism') and would bring history to an end.... Postmillennialists typically were optimistic about the spiritual progress of the culture" (Marsden 49). Postmillennialists tend to be more optimistic about social change than premillennialists and therefore are more willing to alter society to bring about positive social change.

Prayerwalking (also sometimes phrased as prayer walking)—According to NAR theorist George Otis, Jr., prayerwalking is "the practice of on-site, street level intercession. Prayers offered by participants are in response to immediate observations and researched targets" (Otis Jr. 254). Prayer walking played an important part in promoting spiritual mapping. The practice is still fairly widespread and has occasionally been documented by secular sources, such as in the extras section of the *Jesus Camp* DVD (*Jesus Camp*).

Premillennialism—Premillennialists "believe in Jesus Christ's bodily return before His Thousand-year earthly reign" (Boyer 2). Please note that not all premillennialists are dispensational premillennialists. Dispensational premillennialists believe that the history of the world is divided into a number of divinely-decreed historical eras (dispensations), and that we are currently in the Church Age, stuck between one crucial event—the Crucifixion—and another, the Rapture (where Christians will be taken bodily up in the air to be with God). The Rapture will be followed by the Tribulation, a seven-year period of great suffering. This will give way to the Battle of Armageddon, where Jesus and his saints will return to earth and defeat the Antichrist. Following this is the Millennium, in which Christ reigns a thousand years. A brief final revolt will then be conducted by Satan, the dead will be resurrected, and history's final event, the Last Judgment, will occur (Boyer 88). Please note however, that this is merely the most popular narrative of the "End Times." "Post-Trib" premillennial dispensationalists believe that the Rapture will occur only after the Tribulation, even for Christians. "Mid-Tribbers" believe the Rapture will occur halfway through the Tribulation.

Prophet—Within the Charismatic movement, a prophet is typically seen as someone providing prescient guidance on how to direct the future of the church. The office of apostle is typically seen by NAR supporters as being returned to the church in the 1980s. Depending on who one talks to, the return of this role is credited to the Kansas City Prophets or more commonly the ministry of John Wimber. It should be understood that the role of prophet and apostle have a large overlap, and some apostles have claimed both mantles. If a prophet does not claim the role of apostle, his typical role in the movement is providing support for the authority of the various apostles. It should also be noted that the accuracy of prophetic ability is frequently interpreted differently by NAR supporters than other evangelicals. NAR supporters typically do not demand 100 percent accuracy on behalf of the prophets, and indeed do not see that as necessarily being part of the prophetic mandate as laid down by the Christian scriptures. This differs the movement sharply from mainstream evangelicals, who believe that for a prophet to be a prophet, no prophecy can be inaccurate.

Prosperity Gospel—"Name It and Claim It" or "Health and Wealth" gospel. The prosperity gospel emphasizes the power of a motivated spiritual life to gain the adherent wealth and influence. Often this is done through donating to the ministry which promotes the prosperity gospel, leading to the charge that prosperity ministries exploit their members.

Reconstructionism—"Broadly speaking, Reconstructionists believe that Christians have a mandate to rebuild, or reconstruct, all of human society, beginning with the United States and moving outward. They contend that the Bible, particularly Mosaic Law, offers the perfect blueprint for the shape a reconstructed world would take" (Martin 353). Reconstructionism is most well-known for its infamous desire to make homosexuality, adultery, blasphemy, and repeated disobedience on the part of children punishable by death (Martin 353). Reconstructionists have frequently allied themselves with both the shepherding movement and the NAR.

Reformed Christianity—This tradition "draws its defining characteristics from the theological teachings of John Calvin" (Detwiler 154). It is noted mostly among other evangelicals (to a certain extent, too simplistically) for its emphasis on God's power to predestine individual salvation. Reformed Christianity, though the smallest part of the "Christian Right" (Detwiler 154), is also the most theologically influential on the movement as a whole (Detwiler 154). This work follows Detwiler in arguing that Reformed Christianity has disproportionate influence to its relative size.

Restorationism—A set of ideas prevalent within all of Protestantism, but particularly among Charismatics and Pentecostals, that something went dreadfully wrong with the early church, but that the church has been successively reviving itself since the Reformation to a better and better form of Christianity in preparation for Christ's return (Ware 1019). Restorationist thought within the NAR, even more than in most Charismatic movements, is distinguished by an intense hopefulness about the future, which distinguishes it from the pessimistic viewpoint of premillennial dispensationalists

Seeker-Sensitive Church—Evangelical Churches devoted to gaining new followers and maintaining current membership. There is no set denominational affiliation for such churches, though many do seem to straddle a middle ground between neo-evangelicalism and a "charismatic-lite" gospel. Seeker sensitive churches are often associated with the church growth movement and sometimes with the prosperity gospel. In recent years some of these churches have become more hardline due to Charismatic, particularly NAR, influence.

Serpent seed doctrine—In the context of the Latter Rain movement, the idea that Eve had "sexual intercourse with the serpent in the Garden of Eden." The result of this sinful breeding practice was the division of the world between the descendants of Cain (the intellectuals and their allies, the serpent seed) and the godly seed carried through the bloodline of Abel. Branham taught a quite literal form of Christian genoism, where salvation was dependent upon one's bloodline (Douglas Weaver 123–125).

Seven Mountains campaign—A campaign, also variously referred to as the 7-M Mandate or the Seven Gates philosophy. The Seven Mountains campaign was an attempt to utilize the language of dominionism in the furtherance of the NAR's larger goal of sociopolitical and economic transformation. The two primary articulators of the idea were Lance Wallnau and Johnny Enlow. Based on a message from God that was supposedly imparted to both Loren Cunningham and Bill Bright, the seven mountains campaign held that there were "seven molders of culture or seven world kingdoms and he who could take those kingdoms could take the harvest of nations" (Bruce Wilson, "Lance Wallnau Explains"). According to Wallnau, the seven mountains are religion, education, government, family, media, art, and business. The Seven Mountains campaign has been very successful, but widespread concern about its dominionist nature makes it likely that other brands of transformationalism will replace the seven mountains campaign in the future, in order for the movement to avoid getting negative exposure form the Seven Mountains movement.

Shepherding movement—The shepherding movement, sometimes called the discipleship movement, put a particular emphasis on "accountability and submission to church leaders." Churches were centralized under a "pyramid-like authority structure," with progressively higher levels of shepherds, submitting to progressively even higher levels of leadership above them. There were widespread complaints of abuse and cultic manipulation against the shepherding movement, which continue to this day. Shepherding played an important part in the acceptance of deliverance ministries in the States. Two of its major leaders were also major leaders within the deliverance "movement" as well, namely Derek Prince and Don Basham (Balmer 523–524). Shepherding practice was an important influence on the NAR.

Spiritual mapping—A movement, primarily among evangelicals and "neo-Pentecostals," "that specialized in the use of religious techniques to wage a territorial spiritual war against unseen non-human beings" (Holvast 1). Spiritual mapping was a popular practice of strategic level spiritual warfare (SLSW) in the 1990s, and it's partly due to its influence that the NAR is so powerful today.

Spiritual warfare—"The concept of a dualistic war between good and evil" (Holvast 6). Arguably, some doctrine of spiritual warfare has always been present in the Christian church. However, Charismatics emphasize the idea to extents unheard of since at least the Dark Ages.

Strategic-level spiritual warfare (SLSW)—SLSW practices aim to "effect power encounters" that will essentially disempower territorial demonic spirits which hold possession over certain "social groups or geographical locations with which they are identified" (Collins 103). SLSW has been frequently been used by the NAR, particularly at the height of the spiritual mapping craze.

Third-Wave Pentecostalism—A term generally used to refer to evangelicals who "recognize the role of the Holy Spirit in divine healing, receiving prophecies, even casting out demons." Unlike traditional Pentecostals, however, they believe that believers "are baptized in the Holy Spirit at the moment of conversion," thus bypassing some of the more, to mainstream evangelicals, alienating elements of denominational Pentecostalism (Balmer 576). Contrary to Balmer and mainstream historians of the Charismatic movement, this work does not see denominational Pentecostalism as suffering from "schismatic tendencies" (576); quite to the contrary, this work asserts that it is precisely some of the Third Wave's later incarnations, particularly the NAR, which are most responsible for the currently huge problem of factionalism within denominational Pentecostal churches.

Transformationalism—Transformationalism is the newest and most ideologically sophisticated form of NAR economic philosophy. While essentially agreeing with capitalist economic models, transformationalism concedes to left wing economic critics that capitalism itself has no underlying moral conscience (Silvoso, *Transformation* 135). Transformationalists therefore contend that the way to transform society economically is by applying a moral model of economic theory to economic interchange, one based on Judeo-Christian principles (Eldred 81–82). In principle, transformationalism is as rabidly capitalistic as other NAR economic models, but does a much better job at masking this. Note that there are also non–NAR forms of transformationalism, which present there ideas in even "smoother" forms.

Word of Faith (WOF) movement—A movement that "believes that the power of Christ is not limited to eternal life. Instead—God intends for all faithful believers to live healthy and wealthy lives in this world" (Souders 28). The WOF movement is basically akin to the prosperity gospel, or the gospel of health-and-wealth (Souders 28). There is oftentimes significant overlap between WOF teachings and NAR leaders, both of whom predicate their message on Charismatic presuppositions about the physical and spiritual world.

Chapter Notes

Preface

1. Rachel Tabachnick's Talk to Action link provides video of Ammerman speaking, which is why I use it.

Introduction

1. Not to be confused with the actual denomination called the New Apostolic Church. For information on the New Apostolic church, whose roots lay in the teachings of Edward Irving, see Dorries 928–930.

Chapter 1

1. Although not a scholar in any sense, Bill Randles's *Weighed and Found Wanting* (1995) provides an interesting look at how spiritual elitism has warped modern Pentecostalism, from a Charismatic critic of the contemporary Restorationist movement. My thinking on this elitism concept has been influenced both by Randles and by my interactions with secular researchers, such as Rachel Tabachnick.

2. Presumably he was referring to Indians as a whole here, though I cannot be certain.

3. See shepherding magazine *New Wine* "Contributing Editors: October 1969," 3. Boze was still a contributing editor as of at least January 1971, so the link was a long-lasting one. See *New Wine* "Contributing Editors: January 1971," 3.

4. It is significant, and all too typical, that Moore's account of the scandal at HSTM is almost entirely derived from the testimony of the founding four teachers of the shepherding movement: Don Basham, Derek Prince, Bob Mumford, and Charles Simpson. The possibility that the shepherds might have ulterior motives for presenting evidence in a light conducive to their advantage seems not to occur to Moore here. This tendency characterizes much of Moore's *The Shepherding Movement* (2003), which is massively over-reliant on the major shepherds' recounting of the shepherding movement. Moore's inability to deal with the criticisms leveled at shepherding practice, even though they were vociferous during this period (even appearing in secular sources) remains a major flaw of his work.

5. On the deep influence that the Latter Rain, particularly Reg Layzell, had on Hamon, see Hamon, *Day of the Saints* 138–139. According to Wagner's own account, Hamon was the one who suggested Wagner take on the role of apostle. See Wagner, *Wrestling* 209–210.

6. Hollenweger cautions, however, that there were not nearly as many healings attested to as most people thought. See D.J. Wilson 440.

7. An idea which has a long and notorious reputation, including within the "White Power" Christian Identity movement.

8. See also Branham "Leadership" available at this Branhamite website link: http://Churchages.Com/En/Sermon/Branham/65-1207-Leadership, which supports Weaver's quotation and appears to be from the same sermon.

9. See in *New Wine*, the October 1975 issue, "God's Order for Husbands" by Christenson 25–30, and the September 1975 issue "Pray for the Lordship of Christ," 13–17.

10. For the effects of the Lakeland revival on the NAR, see Chapter 6.

11. McGavran's status as an evangelical is

somewhat contestable, with Holvast's naming of him as a neo-evangelical, a generous appellation of that term, though ultimately a correct one. See Holvast 18.

12. At least in Wagner's rendering, which does have scholarly support. See, for instance, Cook 66–67.

13. Note that this account is also given by Bickle's critic Albert Dager, with almost identical terminology. See Dager 127.

14. Significantly, in Bill Jackson's *Quest for the Radical Middle*, point 4 is left out. See page 194. Jackson does talk about these 4 points on the next page, but attributes the extra point not to the unknown prophet, but Bob Jones, a now very well-known figure in the prophetic movement.

15. See Dagar 146 as well. I have listened and transcribed the original audio, but have deferred to Dagar's transcription of it here because I believe his transcription was more accurate than mine.

16. It has been clearly identified as aligned with the NAR in secular news media. See Tietz. This is an important point to note, as it is sometimes claimed by Bickle's supporters that his ministry is not aligned with the NAR.

17. Later the Toronto Airport Christian Fellowship (TACF).

18. The ICA is now known as the International Council of Apostolic Leaders. I have utilized its original acronym throughout this text, since the ICAL appellation is recent.

Chapter 2

1. I would note that the Argentinan evangelical community is certainly capable of exercising independence when it needs to; indeed, it is partly because of that ability to exercise independence that there are very conflicting narratives about the nature of the late 1980s Argentine revival.

2. Annacondia himself does not claim to have practiced spiritual mapping. This is Wagner's interpretation of Annacondia's ministry. See Holvast 62.

3. See Holvast 88 on Murphy's promotion of spiritual mapping.

4. For information on this burning, see Bruce Wilson's "Burning Buddhas, Books, and Art" on the progressive site, Talk to Action.

5. A notable difference between Arnold and other deliverance proponents is his rejection of SRA and MPD, which shows his intellectual superiority to credulous deliverance promoters who support these diagnosis. See Collins 104–105.

6. It should be noted that Dawson was a New Zealander in origin, not American. Dawson back cover.

Chapter 3

1. This will be described in greater detail later in this chapter.

2. See for instance, Johnson, "Creating a Supernatural Mindset" on the "Supernatural Mindset" which the wealth mindset seems to be based See also Johnson, *When Heaven Invades Earth* 32.

3. Because all of these organizations were under Wagner's apostleship, they effectively were part of his apostolic network in principle, though not in name. Wagner himself is careful to note that these organizations are separate from the ICA, but as they are under his authority, there was a good deal of apostolic overlap while he controlled them all, some which of remains even now.

4. The WLI is now under the leadership of Ché Ahn who is a member of Revival Alliance. As of April 2010, it was also part of the ICA as well. See the 2010 "International Coalition of Apostles Membership Directory," 2.

5. Hannen's article "Jesus RX" also is clearly very skeptical about Alcorn's claims that Australia represented a rogue organization.

6. Mercy Survivors has, however, recently obtained a copy which they believe to be genuine. See Mercy Survivors, "Mercy Ministries Counseling Manual Exposed." The Survivors Network believes the changes in the manual to be largely superficial (as do I) and spin control, but it's hard to prove that without more extensive leaks from within the organization.

7. I wish to thank researcher Bruce Wilson for helping me decipher just what purpose Joyner serves in the NAR.

8. I have included a reference to Tabachnick's transcript of Boykin's words in the Works Cited in case the online YouTube video is deleted. See Tabachnick, "Transcript."

9. These practices almost assuredly in the case of IHOP and definitely in the case of the Call, hearken back to the teachings of Franklin Hall. See Engle, *Digging at the Wells* 5, for Hall's specific influence, which is in any ways obvious throughout all of Chapter 11 of that book, whose chapter title is "Atomic Power Through Prayer and Fasting."

10. For examples of the use of "Radical" in the same sense, I would direct the reader to the Charismatic-friendly ministry Teen Mania. See "Inspire the Fire in Your Teen." See also Orme, published in *Relevant Magazine*, a leading Charismatic journal founded by Cameron Strang.

11. Bickle claims to be a premillennialist, but distances himself from historical dispensationalism. His own version of premillennialist thinking sounds much like traditional evangelical End Times Theology, but with an emphasis on a "Supernaturally"-powered End Times church. This whole theology is mediated from Bickle's post-tribulation outlook, which holds that the Church won't be raptured until after the Tribulation (as seen previously) (Bickle, "Historical Premillennialism" 3, 12, passim).

Chapter 4

1. See for instance, Silvoso, *Transformation* 119–120, where he deemphasizes the need for the rich redistributing their wealth.

2. This can lead to situational ethics, when economic crises provide incentive to dishonest companies like Enron. See Eldred 82.

3. A type of morality it would be impossible to get everyone to agree on, and which for Eldred, leaves humanity with no higher value to drive this "Universal Ethic." See Eldred 82.

4. Note that Colonel Doner's first name is literally Colonel. This is not a military rank.

5. I was also able to find what appears to be that same document.

6. Doner now has a rather complicated relationship with his history as a Christian right activist. See Doner 19–25, though note that some of the people who helped supposedly lead him out of the Christian right are actually deeply part of it.

7. I wish to especially thank Bruce Wilson for input on this section without which it would have been impossible to trace these movements.

8. YWAM has published many of Miller's books. See YWAM Publishing "Darrow Miller." Note that Cunningham has endorsed even relatively extreme NAR leaders like Mike Bickle. See "Endorsements." Cunningham also spoke at the 2009 Onething conference (an annual event of IHOP) according to an IHOP Facebook advertisement. See "Loren Cunningham Is Speaking."

9. See Darrow Miller, "Discipling Nations" 4352–4362, on his version of the Samaritan Strategy; see also Mei 318–319; See Lienisch, *Redeeming America: Piety and Politics in the New Christian Right* 126–127, on Colonel Doner's similar concept.

10. My thanks to Joseph Warui Wamutitu's remarkably objective dissertation "Economic Empowerment for Missions: Empowering the Church in Kenya for Holistic and Crosscultural Ministry," 154, for raising this last point in my mind, if only indirectly.

11. Neal Johnson seems to be in the latter camp; Ken Eldred straddles both, though he's given a good deal of support to the NAR and is considered a workplace apostle by the movement. See Wagner, *On Earth as It Is in Heaven* loc 2046.

Chapter 5

1. I have carefully used the term "apparent physical difference" in this chapter at several points to distinguish traditional forms of racial politics, including racism based on such differences, which have for the last several hundred years been based primarily on faulty biological and aesthetic standards of racial difference, from the kind of racial politics and racism on which NAR theology is predicated, which as we will see has important differences from traditional racial classifications.

2. See, for instance, Sanchez. There are two main reasons why supporting Manifest Sons theology remains dangerous for apostolic leaders. First of all, Manifest Sons theology, even in its earliest incarnations, was so nakedly dominionist that it is all too likely to gain notice among those outside the NAR (especially other evangelicals) if it is too openly adopted. Secondly, the obvious racialist elements of "Church Race" theology, if too openly advocated, interfere with Charismatic efforts at racial reconciliation. For more on these efforts, see Chapter 6.

3. I use the term *Volk* cautiously, but deliberately. Though the NAR movement is not automatically or even predominantly racist in the traditional sense of that term, there are undercurrents of *Völkisch*-type ideology within NAR thought that would intrigue any student of German history.

4. It should be noted that this is not necessarily the kind of millennial expectation promoted by premillennial dispensationalists, as there are a wide variety of viewpoints concerning millennialism within the NAR.

5. It's actually unclear whether this book is self-published or not, but it appears to be published by a publisher, Warboys Publishing,

that from what I can tell is a vanity publisher. In any case, the books seem to be fairly popular if the number of amazon reviews is any indication. They were sufficiently influential to be found in my secular research university's book store at one point.

6. Note that Bickle still clearly supports the NAR, despite his denials. See Tietz.

7. An almost certain reference to Mengele.

8. Demons live in outer space in this series.

9. See Lewis and Kahn, 46, on Icke's popularity, which has only increased since the publication of their article in 2005.

10. In these novels, the term DNA is being used quite unmistakably literally.

11. See for instance, Ephesians 4:13, on which Hamon bases this theology.

12. Which would be considered scandalous by the Eastern Orthodox church, the chief modern proponent of the idea of theosis.

13. Muthee famously prayed over Sarah Palin, while she was at a Pentecostal church in Wasilla, Alaska, to be protected from witchcraft. See "Palin Pastor Prayed for Witchcraft Protection."

Chapter 6

1. I use the Native American community specifically here, because it's actually relatively hard to find NAR material on racial reconciliation written by African Americans, Asian Americans or Hispanics, though material referencing other issues is produced relatively frequently by all three communities, especially African American apostles. Most material on racial reconciliation between whites and non-whites, outside of the Native American context, is usually written by whites.

2. See "Eagle's Wings Ministry: People" on Woodley and Twiss "Native-Led Contextualization" Abstract. Note that Richard Twiss is now deceased.

3. This is no small compliment to the NAR, since Smith is an astute observer of evangelicalism.

4. Smith uses the term "New Charismatic Traditions" which seems to be roughly equivalent with how I describe Third Wave Pentecostalism.

5. Indeed, since Smith was apparently unaware of the NAR at the time of Native Americans and the Christian Right, there is a high likelihood that many of these New Charismatics may have been members of the NAR, or at least followed their teachings.

6. I am not sure that Kim is spelling this city's name correctly here, but I've seen several variant spellings in Christian and non–Christian material alike.

7. Note that all references to Reynolds' work are for "American Evangelicals in Kurdistan," unless otherwise noted.

8. Note that this is grabbed from a screen shot, not Tabachnick's writing, so there can be no doubting its authenticity.

9. Note that Hart, a pro-evangelical source, confirms a Call event was held here at the time. Also note that Jewish Israel, which provides the video of the Call, is a somewhat biased website. The video provided was clearly, however, undoctored. In any case Tabachnick's academically reliable account confirms this chain of events.

10. See Bruce Wilson's extensive documenting of Kony 2012's links to the evangelical movement in his special report for the LGBT activist site Truth Wins Out. Bruce Wilson, "Special Report": also Wilson "Kony 2012 Effort a Ministry."

11. All references to Hocken are to his article on the Charismatic movement unless otherwise noted.

12. Coates is also linked to the NAR through John Arnott's Partners in Harvest, of which he was listed as a member of its Advisory Council as of 2001. The council also included Ché Ahn as well. See Römer 225.

13. See also Hunt, *A History* 494, who points out Wagner's favorable view of the March for Jesus.

14. See for instance, McMichael and McMichael, 8, for its use in the sozo movement.

15. Note that the version of Clifton's article I was able to obtain had no pagination. I understand that the Australian version may have such pagination.

16. See Brouwer, Gifford and Rose, 120, on this score, though this fact is in any ways obvious from a perusal of recent dissertations from Fuller which have a large number of Korean and Korean diaspora writers producing Fuller's ever-expanding amount of theoretical material.

Glossary

1. The reader should note that this is a working definition provided to me courtesy of Frederick Clarkson and Rachel Tabachnick. It will likely be further refined over the upcoming months.

Works Cited

"About Bethel Sozo: Autism." *Bethel Sozo*. N.D. Web. 3 May 2013. http://bethelsozo.com/about#/4.

"About Ché Ahn." *Wagner Leadership Institute*. N.D. Web. 6 May 2013. http://wagnerleadership.com/Che.htm.

"About Exodus Cry." Exodus Cry. N.D. Web. 12 Nov 2013. http://exoduscry.com/about/.

"About Hillsong." *Hillsong*. 2009. Web. 8 Mar 2014. http://web.archive.org/web/20090406021415/http://myhillsong.com/more-hillsong.

"About ICAL." *International Coalition of Apostolic Leaders*. N.D. 8 Aug 2014 http://www.coalitionofapostles.com/about-ical/.

"About the Institute." *Institute for Research on Unlimited Love*. N.D. Web. 6 May 2013. http://www.unlimitedloveinstitute.org/aboutus/index.html.

"About Us: Global Awakening History." *Global Awakening*. 2013. Web. 8 Mar 2014. http://globalawakening.com/home/about-global-awakening/history-of-global-awakening.

"Abridged List of Deliverables for the Flame of Love Project." *Flame of Love Project*. 15 June 2011. Print (Web link taken down).

"Accreditation." *Catch the Fire*. 2011. Web. 18 Aug 2014. http://catchthefire.com/college/accreditation-programs.

Adams, Jay. "Crowns Out of Crosses: An Interview with Jay Adams." Interview. *New Wine Magazine* 14.4 (April 1982): 4–8. Web. 8 Mar 2014. http://www.csmpublishing.org/res_newWine.php.

"Advisory Board." *Flame of Love Project*. N.D. Web. 2 May 2013. http://www3.uakron.edu/sociology/flameweb/board.html.

Ahn, Ché. *Into the Fire: How You Can Enter Renewal and Catch God's Holy Fire*. Ventura, CA: Renew, 1998.

Ahn, Ché. "Spiritual DNA." *Ministry Today*. N.D. Web. 8 Aug 2013. http://ministrytodaymag.com/index.php/first-priority/15390-spiritual-dna.

Ahn, Ché. *When Heaven Comes Down: Experiencing God's Glory in Your Life*. Grand Rapids: Chosen, 2009.

Ahn, Ché, and Lou Engle. *The Call Revolution*. Colorado Springs: Wagner Publications, 2001.

Ain, Stewart. "Jewish-Evangelical Alliance Fraying as UN Session Opens: Jewish Groups Balk at Joining Anti–Durban III Rally Featuring Reputed Messianic Jew, Even as Israeli Pols Support It." *The Jewish Week*. 13 Sep 2011. Web. 8 Mar 2014. http://www.thejewishweek.com/news/international/jewish_evangelical_alliance_fraying_un_session_opens.

Alcorn, Nancy. "Beauty Is in the Eye of the Beholder." nancyalcorn.com. 6 Feb 2009. Web. 8 Aug 2013. http://www.nancyalcorn.com/2009/02/beauty-is-in-eye-of-beholder.html.

Alcorn, Nancy. *Cut: Mercy for Self-Harm*. Enumclaw, Washington: WinePress Publishing, 2007.

Works Cited

Alcorn, Nancy. "Don't Wait for Tomorrow." nancyalcorn.com. 23 Feb 2009. Web. 9 Aug 2013. http://www.nancyalcorn.com/2009/02/dont-wait-for-tomorrow.html.
Alcorn, Nancy. *Echoes of Mercy*. 1st Edition. Nashville: Mercy Ministries of America, 1992.
Alcorn, Nancy. *Echoes of Mercy*. Revised Edition. No location listed: Mercy Ministries, 2008.
Alcorn, Nancy. *Keys to Walking and Living in Freedom*. 4 CD set. Disk two. Sermon Mercy Ministries. Nashville, Tennessee. N.D.
Alcorn, Nancy. *Mission of Mercy: Allowing God to Use YOU to Make a Difference in Others*. Charisma House, [2013]. Kindle Edition.
Alcorn, Nancy. "Nancy Alcorn Sets the Record Straight: An Open Letter from Nancy Alcorn, Founder and President of Mercy Ministries." nancyalcorn.com. 25 Feb 2009. Web. 8 Aug 2013. http://www.nancyalcorn.com/2009/02/nancy-alcorn-sets-record-straight.html.
Alcorn, Nancy. "On the Road Again." nancyalcorn.com. 13 Apr 2009. Web. 25 Aug 2013. http://www.nancyalcorn.com/2009/04/on-road-again.html.
Alcorn, Nancy. *Starved*. Enumclaw, Washington: Winepress Publishing, 2007.
Alcorn, Nancy. "Thousands Gathered to Pray for Our Nation—Update from the Call." nancyalcorn.com. 8 Sep 2010. Web. 8 Aug 2013. http://www.nancyalcorn.com/2010/09/thousands-gathered-to-pray-for-our.html.
Alcorn, Nancy. *Trapped: Mercy for Addictions*. Enumclaw, Washington: WinePress Publishing, 2008.
Alcorn, Nancy. *Violated: Mercy for Sexual Abuse*. Enumclaw, Washington: WinePress Publishing, 2008.
Alec, Wendy. *The Fall of Lucifer*. London: Warboys Publishing, 2005.
Alec, Wendy. *The First Judgment*. London: Warboys Publishing, 2007.
Alec, Wendy. *A Pale Horse*. Dublin: Warboys Publishing, 2012.
Alec, Wendy. *Son of Perdition*. London: Warboys Publishing, 2010.
Allen, Scott, Darrow Miller, and Bob Moffitt. "Thoughts on the Uganda Anti-Homosexuality Bill, 2009." *Darrow Miller and Friends*. 16 Dec 2009. Web. 8 Mar 2014. http://darrowmillerandfriends.com/2009/12/16/thoughts-on-the-uganda-anti-homosexuality-bill-2009/.
Allender, Dan B. *The Wounded Heart*. Colarado Springs: Navpress, 1990.
Alsop, Zoe. "Kenyan Who Blessed Palin Chases Witches at Home." *We News*. 12 Oct 2008. Web. 18 Aug 2013. http://womensenews.org/story/campaign-trail/081012/kenyan-who-blessed-palin-chases-witches-at-home#.Uhj2jNhLi3E.
"American Anthropological Association Statement on 'Race.'" *American Anthropological Association*. 17 May 1998. Web. 19 Aug 2013. http://www.aaanet.org/stmts/racepp.htm.
Anderson, Allan. *An Introduction to Pentecostalism*. Cambridge: Cambridge University Press, 2004.
Anderson, Neil. *The Bondage Breaker*. Eugene: Harvest House, 2000.
"Area Five: Evolutionary Perspectives on Other Regard." *Institute for Research on Unlimited Love*. N.D. Web. 2 May 2013. http://www.unlimitedloveinstitute.org/news/pdf/Area_Five.PDF#page=1&zoom=auto,0,33.
Ariella. "Jacobs Claims to Have Thwarted Numerous Terrorist Attacks." *Right Wing Watch*. 9 Nov 2012. Web. 8 Mar 2014. http://www.rightwingwatch.org/content/jacobs-claims-have-thwarted-numerous-terrorist-attacks.
"The Azusa Street Revival and Its Legacy." *USCC College*. Spirit in the World: The Dynamics of Pentecostal Growth and Experience Conference. 6 Oct 2006. Web. 8 Sep 2014. https://www.youtube.com/watch?v=xVIOjrwlj0c.
Bailey, Sarah Pulliam. "Australia's Hillsong Church Exports Its Influence Through Praise and Preaching." *Religion News Service*. 4 Nov 2013. Web. 8 Mar 2014. http://www.religionnews.com/2013/11/04/australias-hillsong-church-exports-influence-praise-preaching/.
Bains, Sunny. "Questioning the Integrity of the John Templeton Foundation." *Evolutionary Psychology* 9, no. 1 (2011): 92–115.

Works Cited

Baker, H.A. *Visions Beyond the Veil*. Minneapolis: Ostherhus Publishing House, N.D.
"Bali Death Toll Set at 202." *BBC News*. 19 Feb 2003. Web. 8 Mar 2004. http://news.bbc.co.uk/2/hi/asia-pacific/2778923.stm.
Balmer, Randy. *Encyclopedia of Evangelicalism*. Louisville: Westminster John Knox Press, 2002.
Barlow, David H., and V. Mark Durand. *Abnormal Psychology: An Integrative Approach*. 2nd Edition. Pacific Grove, CA: Brooks/Cole Publishing Company, 1999.
Barkun, Michael. *A Culture of Conspiracy: Apocalyptic Visions in Contemporary America*. 2nd Edition. Berkley: University of California Press, 2013. Kindle Edition.
Barkun, Michael. *Religion and the Racist Right: The Origins of the Christian Identity Movement*. Chapel Hill: University of North Carolina Press, 1994.
Barnhart, Melissa. "John MacArthur Responds to Critics Who Believe His Strange Fire Conference Is Divisive, Unloving." *Christian Post*. 20 Oct 2013. Web. 8 Mar 2014. http://www.christianpost.com/news/john-macarthur-responds-to-critics-who-believe-his-strange-fire-conference-is-divisive-unloving-107051/.
Barrs, Jeremiah. "Shepherding Movement." *New Dictionary of Theology*. Ed. Sinclair B Ferguson, David F. Wright, J.I. Packer. Downers Grove, IL: Intervarsity, 1988. 369.
Bebbington, D.W. *Evangelicalism in Modern Britain: A History from the 1730's to the 1980's*. London: Unwin Hyman, 1989.
Bellant, Russ. "Sarah Palin and the New Apostolic Reformation." *The Free Press*. 28 Oct 2008. Web. 13 Aug 2013. http://www.freepress.org/departments/display/19/2008/3255.
Berkowitz, Bill. "Heads Up: Prayer Warriors and Sarah Palin Are Organizing Spiritual Warfare to Take Over America." *Alternet*. 28 Feb 2010. Web. 8 Mar 2014. http://www.alternet.org/story/145796/heads_up%3A_prayer_warriors_and_sarah_palin_are_organizing_spiritual_warfare_to_take_over_america.
Berkowitz, Bill. "What in the Names of the Crusades Are Tennessee Evangelicals Doing in Kurdish Iraq?" *Religion Dispatches*. 20 Feb 2009. Web. 8 Aug 2014. http://www.religiondispatches.org/archive/politics/1134/.
Besen, Wayne. "Kim Daniels Scandal Grows as Bizarre and Bigoted Views." *Truth Wins Out*. 22 Apr 2011. Web. 8 Mar 2014. https://www.youtube.com/watch?v=RIf1FxHgk_k.
Bethel School of Supernatural Ministry. *The Bethel School of Supernatural Ministry*. 2014. Web. 8 Mar 2014. http://bssm.net/.
Beverly, James A. *Holy Laughter and the Toronto Blessing*. Grand Rapids: Zondervan, 1995.
Bickle, Mike. "The Coming Eschatological Revolution: Part 1." Sermon. Video. Onething Conference 2008. Private Collection.
Bickle, Mike. "Harlot Babylon: A Coming One World Religion." Sermon. Video. Onething Conference 2008. Private Collection.
Bickle, Mike. "Historic Premillennialism and the Victorious Church." Joseph Company Conference. Transcript. 4 June 2011. Web. 8 Aug 2014. http://www.mikebickle.org.edgesuite.net/MikeBickleVOD/2011/20110604-T-Historic_Premillennialism_and%20the%20Victorious%20Church.pdf.
Bicke, Mike, and Bob Jones. "Visions and Revelations: Mike Bickle with Bob Jones, 1988." 1988. http://archive.org/details/VisionsAndRevelations-MikeBickleWithBobJones1988.
Bickle, Mike, and Brian Kim. *Seven Commitments of a Forerunner*. Kansas City: Forerunner Publishing, 2009.
"Biochemistry." *Encyclopaedia Britannica. Encyclopaedia Britannica Online Academic Edition*. Encyclopaedia Britannica Inc., 2013. Web. 31 Aug 2013. http://www.britannica.com/EBchecked/topic/65785/biochemistry.
"Biology, Philosophy of." *Encyclopaedia Britannica. Encyclopaedia Britannica Online Academic Edition*. Encyclopaedia Britannica Inc., 2013. Web. 5 May 2013.
Blumenthal, Max. "Rick Warren's Africa Problem." *The Daily Beast*. 7 Jan 2009. Web. 8 Mar 2014. http://www.thedailybeast.com/articles/2009/01/07/the-truth-about-rick-warren-in-africa.html.

Works Cited

"Board of Advisors: David Sloan Wilson." *John Templeton Foundation*. http://www.templeton.org/who-we-are/our-team/board-of-advisors/david-sloan-wilson.

"Board of Directors." *Messianic Jewish Bible Institute*. 2014. Web. 8 Mar 2014. http://mjbi.org/board_of_directors.php.

Bowler, Kate. *Blessed: A History of the American Prosperity Gospel*. New York: Oxford University Press, 2013. Kindle Edition.

Boyer, Paul. *When Time Shall Be No More: Prophecy Belief in Modern American Culture*. Cambridge: Harvard University Press, 1992.

Branham, William. "Leadership." TSW 7:7. n.d. (Note: This appears to be a sermon quoted on this pro–Branham website: http://churchages.com/en/sermon/branham/65-1207-leadership. If the citation information on that site is true, Branham gave the sermon on 7 Dec 1965 at Covina Bowl in California. I have used the citation information as provided by Weaver for this citation, but they appear to be identical sermons.)

Branham, William. "Spoken Word Is the Original Seed #2." Jeffersonville, Indiana. 18 Mar 1962. Weblink to sermon audio available at: http://www.messagehub.info/en/read.do?ref_num=62-0318A.

Brin, David. "J.R.R. Tolkien– Enemy of Progress." Salon.com. 17 Dec 2002. 31 Aug 2008. dir.salon.com/story/ent/featyre/2002/12/17/tolkien_brin/print.html.

Brouwer, Steve, Paul Gifford, and Susan Rose. *Exporting the American Gospel: Global Christian Fundamentalism*. New York: Routledge, 1996.

Brown, Candy Gunther. "Global Awakenings: Divine Healing Networks and Global Community in North America, Brazil, Mozambique, and Beyond." In *Global Pentecostal and Charismatic Healing*, ed. Candy Gunther Brown. Oxford: Oxford University Press, 2011. 351–369.

Brown, Candy Gunther, ed. *Global Pentecostal and Charismatic Healing*. Oxford: Oxford University Press, 2011.

Brown, Candy Gunther. "Introduction: Pentecostalism and the Globalization of Illness and Healing." In *Global Pentecostal and Charismatic Healing*, ed. Candy Gunther Brown. Oxford: Oxford University Press, 2011. 3–26.

Brown, Candy Gunther. *Testing Prayer*. Cambridge: Harvard University Press, 2012.

Brown, Candy Gunther, PhD; Stephen C. Mory, MD; Rebecca Williams, MB BChir, DTM&H; and Michael J. McClymond, PhD. "Study of the Therapeutic Effects of Proximal Intercessory Prayer (STEPP) on Auditory and Visual Impairments in Rural Mozambique." *Southern Medical Journal* 103.9 (September 2010): 864–869.

Brown, Malcolm. "Dingo Baby Ruling Ends 32 Years of Torment for Lindy Chamberlain." *The Guardian*. 12 June 2012. Web. 8 Mar 2014. http://www.theguardian.com/world/2012/jun/12/dingo-baby-azaria-lindy-chamberlain.

Bruce, Billy. "Healing Evangelist Todd Bentley Reveals Facts About Past Assault." *Charisma*. 31 Dec 2002. Web. 8 Aug 2014. http://www.charismamag.com/site-archives/154-peopleevents/people-and-events/814-healing-evangelist-todd-bentley-reveals-facts-about-past-assault-.

Brunero, Tim. "Mercy Ministries Exorcism Books Leaked." *Live News*, Australia. 26 Nov 2008. Web. 6 May 2013. Accessed through http://www.rickross.com/reference/hillsong/hillsong41.html.

Burkhalter, William Nolan. "A Comparative Analysis of the Missiologies of Roland Allen and Donald Anderson Mcgavran." Diss. Southern Baptist Theological Seminary, 1984. Print.

Burroway, Jim. "American Evangelical Connections: The Disciple Nations Alliance and Uganda's 'Kill Gays Bill.'" *Box Turtle Bulletin*. 14 Dec 2009. Web. 8 Mar 2014. http://www.boxturtlebulletin.com/tag/stephen-langa.

Burroway, Jim. "Lively Responds to Lawsuit." *Box Turtle Bulletin*. 15 Mar 2012. Web. 8 Mar 2014. http://www.boxturtlebulletin.com/tag/stephen-langa.

Burroway, Jim. "Religious Groups Push for Uganda's Anti-Gay Bill Revival." *Box Turtle Bulletin*. 6 Sep 2011. Web. 8 Mar 2014. http://www.boxturtlebulletin.com/tag/stephen-langa.

Butler, Anthea. "Beyond Alarmism and Denial in the Dominionism Debate." Interview by Sarah Posner. *Religion Dispatches*. 29 Aug 2011. Web. 8 Mar 2014. http://www.religiondispatches.org/archive/atheologies/5026/beyond_alarmism_and_denial_in_the_dominionism_debate/.

"C. Peter Wagner: Japan Is Cursed Because the Emperor Had Sex with a Demon." *Righwingwatch.Org*. N.D. Web. 6 May 2013. http://www.youtube.com/watch?v=3yIgZPTqUIc.

Caballeros, Harold. "Pentecostalism's Role in Guatemala's Social Transformation." *USCC College*. Spirit in the World: The Dynamics of Pentecostal Growth and Experience Conference. 6 Oct 2006. Web. 13 Sep 2014. https://www.youtube.com/watch?v=1wsJjR6QrWQ.

Caballeros, Harold. *Victorious Warfare: Discovering Your Rightful Place in God's Kingdom*. Nashville: Thomas Nelson, 2001.

Cain, Paul. "Joel's Army." Teachings of: Paul Cain. Research Library: Discernment Ministries, Inc. N.D. Track 9 (but the sermon clearly came out before the Ernie Gruen document, as he references it. See Gruen 123).

CAIR Michigan. "Islamophobia in Michigan: The Oak Iniative." *CAIR Michigan*. 2013. Web. 8 Aug 2014. http://vc-cairmi.s3.amazonaws.com/files/2013-06-06-16/theoakinitiative.pdf.

"Cal Pierce, Director." *Healing Room Ministries*. N.D. Web. 8 Mar 2014. https://healingrooms.com/index.php?page_id=421.

Capone, Alesha. "Borders Passes the Hat for Anti-Gay, Pro-Life Charity." crikey.com. 14 Nov 2007. Web. 8 Aug 2013. http://www.crikey.com.au/2007/11/14/borders-passes-the-hat-for-anti-gay-pro-life-charity/.

Caron, Christina. "Large Group Denouncing Islam Mobilizes in Detroit." *ABC News*. 11 Nov 2011. Web. 8 Aug 2014. http://abcnews.go.com/US/large-group-denouncing-islam-mobilizes-detroit/story?id=14933906.

Casciotta, C.J. "The Movement Behind Jesus Culture." *Relevant Magazine*. 2 Mar 2011. Web. 8 Mar 2014. http://www.relevantmagazine.com/god/worship/features/24868-the-movement-behind-jesus-culture.

"Catch the Fire College." *Catch the Fire*. 2011. Web. 19 Aug 2014. http://catchthefire.com/College.

Charisma. "Todd Bentley Enters Restoration Process." *Charisma*. 30 Nov 2008. Web. 8 Aug 2014. http://www.charismamag.com/site-archives/218-peopleevents/news/2719-todd-bentley-enters-restoration-process.

Charlton, T.F. "A Church Group, a Lawsuit, and a Culture of Abuse." *Religion Dispatches*. 5 Mar 2013. Web. 8 Mar 2014. http://www.religiondispatches.org/archive/atheologies/6788/a_church_group_a_lawsuit_and_a_culture_of_abuse/.

Charlton, T.F. "Evangelical Church Accused of Ignoring Sexual Abuse, 'Pedophile Ring.'" Salon.com. 12 Mar 2013. Web. 25 Apr 2013. http://www.salon.com/2013/03/12/evangelical_church_accused_of_ignoring_sexual_abuse_pedophilia_ring_partner/.

Charlton, T.F. "Sovereign Grace Sexual Abuse Lawsuit Just Got More Complicated." *Salon*. 13 June 2013. Web. 8 Mar 2014. http://www.religiondispatches.org/dispatches/guest_bloggers/7138/sovereign_grace_sexual_abuse_lawsuit_just_got_more_complicated/.

Chaser's War on Everything. "Hillsong Church Parody—Praise the Lord Song." 27 May 2006. Web. 8 Mar 2014. https://www.youtube.com/watch?v=xEAWPcbTw8k.

"Ché and Sue Ahn." *Flame of Love Project*. N.D. Web. 6 May 2013. http://www3.uakron.edu/sociology/flameweb/research/ahn.html.

Chiu, Gideon Chung Kuen. "A Strategy for Effective Evangelism in Vancouver." Diss. Fuller Theological Seminary, 1997. Print.

Chosa, Jim, and Faith Chosa. *Thy Kingdom Come Thy Will Be Done in Earth: A First Nation Perspective on Strategic Keys for Territorial Deliverance and Transformation*. Billings: Day Chief Ministries, 2004.

Christenson, Larry. "God's Order for Husbands." *New Wine Magazine* 7.9 (October 1975). Web. 8 May 2014. 25–30. http://www.csmpublishing.org/res_newWine.php.

Christenson, Larry. "Pray for the Lordship of Christ." *New Wine Magazine* 7.8 (September 1975). Web. 8 Mar 2014. 13–17. http://www.csmpublishing.org/res_newWine.php.

Christian Healing Certification Program. "Deliverance Ministry 2 Course Syllabus." *Christian Healing Certification Program.* 9 Oct 2013. Web. 8 Mar 2014. Currently available at: http://www.healingcertification.com/academics/deliverance#3-level-2.

Christian Healing Certification Program. "Deliverance Ministry 3 Course Syllabus." *Christian Healing Certification Program.* N.D. Web. 8 Mar 2014. Currently available at: http://www.healingcertification.com/academics/deliverance#4-level-3.

Christian Healing Certification Program. "Deliverance Ministry 4 Course Syllabus." *Christian Healing Certification Program.* 9 Oct 2013. Web. 8 Mar 2014. Currently available at: http://www.healingcertification.com/academics/deliverance#5-level-4.

Christian Healing Certification Program. "Inner Healing and Soul Care Course 1 Syllabus." *Christian Healing Certification Program.* 9 Oct 2013. Web. 8 Mar 2014. Currently available at: http://www.healingcertification.com/academics/inner-healing#2-level-1.

Christian International Ministries. "Our Ministers: Mercy Ministries." *Christian International Ministries.* 2011. Web. 18 Aug 2013. http://www.christianinternational.org/index.php?option=com_content&view=article&id=1069:mercy-ministries530&catid=3:our-ministers.

Christian International Ministries. "Suicide Bows Its Knee! Apostle Jane Hamon at Mercy Ministries, February 2011." *Christian International Ministries.* 2011. Web. 25 Aug 2013. https://www.christianinternational.com/index.php?option=com_content&view=article&id=470%3Asuicide-bows-its-knee-apostle-jane-hamon-mercy-ministries-february-2011&catid=26%3Amarketplace.

Clark, Randy. *Global Awakening Ministry Team Training Manual.* Mechanicsburg, PA: Global Awakening, 2009.

Clark, Randy. "A Study of the Effects of Christian Prayer on Pain or Mobility Restrictions from Surgeries Involving Implanted Materials." Diss. United Theological Seminary, 2013. Print.

Clarkson, Frederick. *Eternal Hostility: The Struggle Between Theocracy and Democracy.* Monroe, ME: Common Courage Press, 1997.

Clarkson, Frederick, and Rachel Tabachnick. Personal Communication. 19 August 2015.

Clifton, Shane. "Pragmatic Ecclesiology: The Apostolic Revolution and the Ecclesiology of the Assemblies of God in Australia." *Australasian Pentecostal Studies* 9 (2005/6):23–47.

Clinton, Hillary Rodham. "Western Hemisphere: Remarks with Guatemalan Foreign Minister Harold Caballeros." Einnews.com. 21 Feb 2012. Web. 8 Aug 2013. http://world.einnews.com/pr_news/81957221/western-hemisphere-remarks-with-guatemalan-foreign-minister-harold-caballeros.

Coleman, Doug. "A Theological Analysis of the Insider Movement Paradigm from Four Perspectives: Theology of Religions, Revelation, Soteriology and Ecclesiology." Diss. Southeastern Baptist Theological Seminary, 2011. Print.

Collins, James M. *Exorcism and Deliverance Ministry in the Twentieth Century: An Analysis of the Practice and Theology of Exorcism in Modern Western Christianity.* Eugene: Wipf and Stock 2009.

Cook, David Lowell. "The Americanization of the Church Growth Movement." Diss. Auburn University, 1998. Print.

Cox, Harvey. Foreword. *Global Pentecostal and Charismatic Healing.* Ed. Candy Gunther Brown. Oxford: Oxford University Press, 2011. xvii-xxi.

Coyne, Jerry. "Can Darwinism Improve Binghamton?" *New York Times.* 9 Sep 2011. Web. 6 May 2013. http://www.nytimes.com/2011/09/11/books/review/the-neighborhood-project-by-david-sloan-wilson-book-review.html?pagewanted=all&_r=0.

Works Cited

Craine, Anthony G. "Joseph Kony." *Encyclopaedia Britannica. Encyclopaedia Britannica Online Academic Edition*. Encyclopaedia Britannica Inc., 2013. Web. 3 Dec. 2013. http://www.britannica.com/EBchecked/topic/1017670/Joseph-Kony.

"CRCC: Future 50." *Center for Religion and Civic Culture*. 2014. Web. 19 Sep 2014. http://crcc.usc.edu/initiatives/future50/.

"CRCC Newsletter." 1, no. 13. (Fall 2006). Web. 8 Aug 2014. http://crcc.usc.edu/docs/CRCCNewsletter_Fall06.pdf.

Cuneo, Michael W. *American Exorcism: Expelling Demons in the Land of Plenty*. New York: Doubleday, 2001.

Cunningham, Loren. "Transcript of Interview of Loren Cunningham on Original 7 Mountains Vision." Interview by Os Hillman and Kelle Hughes. 19 Nov 2007. Web. 8 Mar 2014. http://www.7culturalmountains.org/apps/articles/Default.asp?columnid=4347&articleid=40087.

"CWN, 2008 Global Day of Prayer in Celebration in Jerusalem." *Jewish Israel*. Video. 9 Oct 2009. Web. 8 Nov 2013. http://jewishisrael.ning.com/video/cwn-2008-global-day-of-prayer.

Dager, Albert James. *Vengeance Is Ours: The Church in Dominion*. Redmond, WA: Sword Publishers, 1990.

Daily Mail Reporter. "'It Could Come Back to Haunt Him': Rick Perry's Alleged Ties to 'Demon Seeing' and KKK-Linked Religious Leader Could Derail Campaign." *Daily Mail*. 30 Sep 2011. Web. 8 Mar 2014. http://www.dailymail.co.uk/news/article-2043435/Rick-Perrys-alleged-ties-demon-seeing-KKK-linked-religious-leader-derail-campaign.html.

Daniels, Kimberly. "Why Celebrating Halloween Is Dangerous." *Charisma*. 30 Oct 2013. Web. 18 Mar 2014. http://www.charismamag.com/spirit/spiritual-warfare/7134-why-celebrating-halloween-is-dangerous.

Darrand, Tom Craig, and Anson Shupe. *Metaphors of Social Control in a Pentecostal Sect*. New York: Edwin Mellen, 1983.

Darrow Miller and Friends. "Restoring the Breach: A Conversation Between Practitioners in Africa." *Darrow Miller and Friends*. 5 Dec 2011.Web. 8 Mar 2014. http://darrowmillerandfriends.com/2011/12/05/restoring-the-breach-a-conversation-between-practitioners-in-africa/.

Dawkins, Richard. *The God Delusion*. Boston: Houghton Mifflin, 2006.

Dawson, John. *Healing America's Wounds*. Ventura, CA: Regal Books, 1994.

Dedmon, Theresa. *Born to Create: Stepping into Your Supernatural Destiny*. Shippensburg, PA: Destiny Image, 2012.

Demar, Gary, and Colonel Doner. "The Christian Worldview of Government." Ed. Jay Grimstead. *Christian Worldview Documents*. Coalition on Revival. Murphys, CA: Coalition on Revival, 1989. http://www.reformation.net/COR_Docs/Christian_Worldview_Government.pdf.

De Silva, Dawna, and Teresa Liebscher. "Sozo: Advanced, Healed, Delivered." Session 8 ("Shabar Wrap Up"). N.D. Mp3.

De Silva, Dawna, and Teresa Liebscher. "Sozo: Advanced, Healed, Delivered." Session 9 ("Sozo Q + A"). N.D. Mp3.

De Silva, Dawna, and Teresa Liebscher. *Sozo, Saved, Healed, Delivered: Advanced Manual*. Redding, CA: Sozo Ministry, 2011.

De Silva, Stephen K. *Prosperous Soul: Foundations Manual*. Redding, CA: Accent Digital Publishing, 2010.

Detwiler, Fritz. *Standing on the Premises of God: The Christian Right's Fight to Redefine America's Public Schools*. New York: New York University Press, 1999.

Diamond, Sara. *Not by Politics Alone: The Enduring Influence of the Christian Right*. New York: Guilford, 1998.

Diamond, Sara. *Spiritual Warfare: The Politics of the Christian Right*. Boston: South End Press, 1989.
"Divine Hiearchies: Class in America and Religious Studies by Sean Mccloud." University of North Carolina Press. Blurb. 2012. Web. 8 Mar 2014. http://uncpress.unc.edu/books/T-7875.html.
Doner, Colonel. *Christian Jihad: Neo-Fundamentalists and the Polarization of America*. Samizdat Creative, 2012. Kindle Edition.
Dorries, D.W. "New Apostolic Church." *The New International Dictionary of Petencostal and Charismatic Movements*. Revised and Expanded Edition. Ed. Stanley M. Burgess and Eduard M. Van Der Maas. Grand Rapids: Zondervan, 2002. 928–930. Print.
Dowden, Richard. "Inspiriation Behind the 'Terror Gang': The Acholi People of Uganda Trapped Between a Vicious Cult and a Vengeful National Army, Now See Only One Route to Peace." *The Guardian*. 1 Apr 2006. Web. 8 Mar 2013. http://www.theguardian.com/world/2006/apr/02/uganda.theobserver.
"Eagle's Wings Ministry: People." *Eagle's Wings Ministry*. N.D. Web. 8 Mar 2014. http://www.eagleswingsministry.com/people/.
Eberle, Harold. *The Complete Wineskin*. Yakima: Winepress Publishing, 1993.
Eckhardt, John. *God Still Speaks*. Lake Mary, FL: Charisma House, 2009.
Eckholm, Erik. "When Worship Never Pauses." *New York Times*. 9 July 2011. Web. 8 Mar 2014. http://www.nytimes.com/2011/07/10/us/10prayer.html?_r=1&.
Eim, Yeol Soo. "South Korea." *The New International Dictionary of Petencostal and Charismatic Movements*. Revised and Expanded Edition. Ed. Stanley M. Burgess and Eduard M. Van Der Maas. Grand Rapids: Zondervan, 2002. 239–246.
Eldred, Ken. *God Is at Work*. Montrose, Colorado: Manna Ventures, 2009. Kindle Edition.
Emerson, Michael, and Christian Smith. *Divided by Faith: Evangelical Religion and the Problem of Race in America*. New York: Oxford University Press, 2000.
"Endorsements." IHOPKC. 2014. Web. 8 Mar 2014. http://www.ihopkc.org/about/endorsements/.
Engle, Lou. *Digging the Wells of Revival*. Shippensburg, PA: Destiny Image, 1999.
Engle, Lou. "A Global Prayer Movement." *2012 Exodus Cry Abolition Summit*. Sermon. 2012 Exodus Cry Abolition Summit CD.
Engle, Lou. *Nazirite DNA*. 2010. Read by Lou Engle. MP3. The Call Inc.
Engle, Lou, and James Goll. *The Call of the Elijah Revolution*. Shippensburg, PA: Destiny Image, 2008.
Enlow, Johnny. *The Seven Mountains Prophecy: Unveiling the Coming Elijah Revolution*. Lake Mary, FL: Creation House, 2008.
Entwistle, David N. "Shedding Light on Theophostic Prayer Ministry 1: Practice Issues." *Journal of Psychology and Theology* 32.1 (2004): 26–34. Proquest. Web 10 Aug 2013.
Entwistle, David N. "Shedding Light on Theophostic Prayer Ministry 2: Ethical and Legal Issues." *Journal of Psychology and Theology* 32.1 (2004): 35–42. Proquest. Web. 8 Aug 2013.
Erickson, Paul A., and Liam D. Murphy. *A History of Anthropological Theory: Second Edition*. Orchard Park, NY: Broadview Press, 2003.
"Establishing an Institute for Research on Unlimited Love." *John Templeton Foundation*. Grant ID 2140. N.D. Web 6 May 2013. http://www.templeton.org/what-we-fund/grants/establishing-an-institute-for-research-on-unlimited-love.
"Exemplar Biosketches." *Flame of Love Project*. N.D. Web 6 May 2013 http://www3.uakron.edu/sociology/flameweb/research/exempbios.htm.
"FAQ Sozo: Questions and Answers." *Sozo the Foundations*. N.D. Web. 6 May 2013 http://www.sozothefoundations.com/faq/.
"FAQS: Mercy Ministries." *Mercy Ministries*. N.D. Web. 8 Aug 2013. http://www.mercyministries.org/who_we_are/about/faqs.html.

Filho, Elías Dantas. "Twentieth Century Mission Theology: Conciliar and Evangelical Streams in Conversation." Diss. Fuller Theological Seminary, 2005. Print.
Finto, Don. *Your People Shall Be My People*. Ventura, CA: Regal, 2001.
"The Flame of Love: Scientific Research on the Experience and Expression of Godly Love in the Pentecostal Tradition." Grant ID: 12490. N.D. Web. 6 May 2013. http://www.templeton.org/what-we-fund/grants/the-flame-of-love-scientific-research-on-the-experience-and-expression-of-godly-.
Fletcher, Jan. *Lying Spirits: A Christian Journalist's Report on Theophostic Ministry*. Columbia, KY: Jan Fletcher, 2005.
"Forerunner School of Ministry—Korean Program." *IHOPKC*. 2013. Web. 8 Mar 2014. http://www.ihopkc.org/ihopu/schools/fsm-korean/.
Franke-Ruta, Garance. "Bachmann Staffer Arrested for Terrorism in Uganda in 2006." *The Atlantic Monthly*. 17 Aug 2011. Web. 8 Mar 2014. http://www.theatlantic.com/politics/archive/2011/08/bachmann-staffer-arrested-for-terrorism-in-uganda-in-2006/243711/.
Fraser, Bob. *Marketplace Christianity*. Overland Park, KS: New Grid Publishing, 2006."
Fresh Fire Ministries. "Malawi-Report-Greater Battles, Greater Victories." *Fresh Fire Ministries*. 19 June 2003. Web. 13 May 2013 http://healing2thenations.net/news/03–06-19.htm.
Gaines, Adrienne. "Healing Rooms Movement Spreading Worldwide." *Charisma*. 21 Oct 2010. Web. 9 Sep 2013. http://www.charismamag.com/site-archives/570-news/featured-news/12034-healing-rooms-movement-spreading-worldwide.
Garzon, Fernado, and Margaret Poloma. "Theophostic Ministry: Preliminary Practitioner Survey." *Pastoral Psychology* 53.5 (May 2005): 387–396. Academic Search Premier. Web. 8 Aug 2013.
Gibson, David. "Looking for Catholic Art? Fundamentalist Bob Jones University Has It." *Christian Century*. 22 Nov 2011. Web. 8 Mar 2014. http://www.christiancentury.org/article/2011–11/looking-catholic-art-fundamentalist-bob-jones-university-has-it.
Gifford, Paul. *African Christianity: Its Public Role*. Bloomington: Indiana University Press, 1998.
Global Celebration. "Biography." *Global Celebration*. 2014. Web. 8 Mar 2014 http://www.globalcelebration.com/about-us/bio.
Global Celebration. "Georgian Banov & Bill Johnson on Economy Part 1." 11 Sep 2009. Web. 8 Mar 2014. https://www.youtube.com/watch?v=lnMHLGdE63I.
"Global School of Supernatural Ministry." *Global Awakening*. 2013. Web. 8 Mar 2014 http://globalawakening.com/schools/gssm.
Goff, James R. *Fields White Unto Harvest: Charles F. Parham and the Missionary Origins of Pentecostalism*. Fayetteville: University of Arkansas Press, 1988.
Gofman, Mikhail. Personal e-mail. May 18 2013.
Gohr, G.W. "Kansas City Prophets." In *The New International Dictionary of Petencostal and Charismatic Movements*. Revised and Expanded Edition. Ed. Stanley M. Burgess and Eduard M. Van Der Maas. Grand Rapids: Zondervan, 2002. 816–817.
Goldberg, Michelle. "The Uganda Anti-Gay Bill's U.S. Roots." *Daily Beast*. 11 Apr 2011. Web. 8 Mar 2014. http://www.thedailybeast.com/articles/2011/05/11/uganda-anti-homosexual-bill-inspired-by-american-evangelicals.html.
Greaves, Stuart. *False Justice: Unveiling the Truth About Social Justice*. Shippensburg, PA: Destiny Image, 2012.
Green, Arnold. "The Ways and Power of Love: Types, Factors and Techniques of Moral Transformation by Pitirim A. Sorokin." Review. *Journal of Sociology* 60, no. 6 (May 1955): 600.
Grimstead, Jay, ed. "A Manifesto for the Christian Church." Murphys, CA: Coalition on Revival, 1986. Ed. Jay Grimstead. *Christian Worldview Documents*. Coalition on Revival. Sunnyvale, CA: Coalition on Revival, 1989. http://www.reformation.net/COR_Docs/Christian_Manifesto_Worldview.pdf.
Gruen, Ernie (along with members of his staff). "Documentation of the Aberrant Practices

and Teachings of Kansas City Fellowship." 1990. Electronic Copy Prepared by Jon and Tricia Tillan, Banner Ministries. Derbyshire, England. http://www.banner.org.uk/kcp/Abberent%20Practises.pdf.

"Guatemala." *CIA World Factbook*. 2014. Web. 8 Mar 2014. https://www.cia.gov/library/publications/the-world-factbook/geos/gt.html.

"Guatemala." *Encyclopaedia Britannica. Encyclopaedia Britannica Online Academic Edition*. Encyclopaedia Britannica Inc., 2014. Web. 14 Mar. 2014. http://www.britannica.com/EBchecked/topic/701217/Guatemala.

Haggard, Ted. *Primary Purpose: Making It Hard for People to Go to Hell from Your City*. Lake Mary, FL: Charisma House, 1995.

Hague, Euan, Heidi Beirich and Edward H. Sebesta, eds. *Neo-Confederacy: A Critical Introduction*. Austin, TX: University of Texas Press, 2008.

Hague, Euan, and Edward H. Sebasta. "Neo-Confederacy and Its Conservative Ancestry." Ed. Euan Hague, Heidi Beirich and Edward H. Sebesta. *Neo-Confederacy: A Critical Introduction*. Austin: University of Texas Press, 2008.

Hall, Franklin. *Fasting: Atomic Power with God*. N.P: Wings of Healing, 1946. http://www.shiloahbooks.com/download/Atomic.pdf.

Hall, Franklin. *Glorified Fasting*. Revised Edition. Franklin Hall, 1973.

Hall, Franklin. *Subdue the Earth*. Franklin Hall, 1966.

Hammond, Frank, and Ida Mae. *Pigs in the Parlor: The Practical Guide to Deliverance*. Kirkwood, MO: Impact, 1973.

Hamon, Bill. *Apostles, Prophets and the Coming Moves of God*. Santa Rosa Beach, FL: Destiny Image, 1997.

Hamon, Bill. *The Day of the Saints: Equipping Believers for Their Revolutionary Role in Ministry*. Shippensburg, PA: Destiny Image, 2002.

Hamon, Bill. *The Eternal Church*. Shippensburg, PA: Destiny Image, 2003. Kindle Edition.

Hamon Bill. Foreword. *Restoring the Foundations*. 2nd Edition. By Chester and Betsy Kylstra. Hendersonville, NC: Proclaiming His Word Ministries, 2001. xiii.

Hamon, Bill. *Prophetic Scriptures Yet to Be Fullfilled: During the Third and Final Church Reformation*. Shippensburg, PA: Destiny Image, 2010.

Hankins, Barry. *Francis Schaeffer and the Shaping of Evangelical America*. Grand Rapids: Eerdmans, 2008.

Hannan, Caleb. "Jesus RX: The Untold Story Behind Mercy Ministries' One-Size-Fits-All Prescription for Recovery." *Nashville Scene*. 2 Oct 2008. Web. 8 Aug 2013. http://www.nashvillescene.com/nashville/jesus-rx/Content?oid=1198270.

Harmon, Cedric. "Can You Be Raped by the Devil? Can Demons Engage in Sexual Activity with Humans?" *Charisma*. 19 Nov 2012. Web. 8 Mar 2014. http://www.charismamag.com/spirit/spiritual-warfare/15889-can-you-be-raped-by-the-devil.

Harmon, Cedric. "God's Lightning Rod." *Charisma*. 31 Mar 2001. Web. 8 Mar 2014. http://www.charismamag.com/site-archives/156-features/issues-in-the-church/303-gods-lightning-rod.

Harrell, David Edwin, Jr. *All Things Are Possible: The Healing and Charismatic Revivals in Modern America*. Bloomington: Indiana University Press, 1975.

Hart, Carrie. "Global Day of Prayer Unites Millions." *CBN News*. 13 May 2008. Web. 8 Aug 2013. http://www.cbn.com/cbnnews/insideisrael/2008/May/Global-Day-of-Prayer-Unites-Millions-/.

Hatfield, Kezia. "The Journey of Restoration." *Exodus Cry*. Track 6. 2012 Exodus Cry Abolition Summit. Grandview, MO: Exodus Cry, N.D. (presumably 2012).

Hatfield, Kezia. Track 5. 2013 Exodus Cry Abolition Summit. Grandview, MO: Exodus Cry, 2013.

Hatfield, Kezia. (Twitter Inc). Twitter Account. N.D. Web. 8 Mar 2014. https://twitter.com/keziahatfield.

"Healing Room Testimonies." Healingrooms.com. Various dates. Web. 8 Aug 2013 http://healing

rooms.com/index.php?src=testimonies&page=1&perpage=50&startingpage=1&ending page=10&orderby=dateDesc&category_number=1272&l=&page_id=&testimonies= yes&view=global.
Hillborn, David. "A Chronicle of the Toronto Blessing." In *'Toronto' in Perspective: Papers on the New Charismatic Wave of the Mid-1990s*, ed. David Hillborn. Waynesboro, GA: Paternoster, 2001. 131–332.
Hillman, Os. *Change Agent: Engaging Your Passion to Be the One Who Makes the Difference.* Lake Mary, FL: Charisma House, 2011.
Hillman, Os. "Marketplace Meditations 10/5: Destroying High Places." N.D. Web. 8 Mar 2014. *Crosswalk*. N.D. 8 Mar 2014. http://www.crosswalk.com/devotionals/marketplace/ marketplace-meditations-10-or-5-547358.html.
"Hillsong Money Machine." *Current Affair*. 18 Feb. 2013. Web. 8 Aug 2014. https://www. youtube.com/watch?v=4TUT98mOwKs.
Hocken, P.D. "Alpha Course." *The New International Dictionary of Pentecostal and Charismatic Movements*. Revised and Expanded Edition. Ed. Stanley M. Burgess and Eduard M. Van Der Maas. Grand Rapids: Zondervan, 2002. 312.
Hocken, P.D. "Charismatic Movement." *The New International Dictionary of Pentecostal and Charismatic Movements*. Revised and Expanded Edition. Ed. Stanley M. Burgess and Eduard M. Van Der Maas. Grand Rapids: Zondervan, 2002. 477–519.
Hocken, P.D. "David Pytches." In *The New International Dictionary of Petencostal and Charismatic Movements*. Revised and Expanded Edition. Ed. Stanley M. Burgess and Eduard M. Van Der Maas. Grand Rapids: Zondervan, 2002. 1013.
Hocken, P.D. "House Church Movement." *The New International Dictionary of Pentecostal and Charismatic Movements*. Revised and Expanded Edition. Ed. Stanley M. Burgess and Eduard M. Van Der Maas. Grand Rapids: Zondervan, 2002. 773–774.
Holvast, Rene. *Spiritual Mapping in the United States and Argentina, 1989–2005: A Geography of Fear*. Boston: Brill, 2009.
Horrobin, Peter J. *Healing Through Deliverance: The Foundation and Practice of Deliverance Ministry*. Grand Rapids: Chosen, 2008.
Horrobin, Peter. "Sexual Sin: What It Is, What It Does and Finding the Way Out." In *How to Minister Freedom*, ed. Doris Wagner. Ventura, CA: Regal, 2005. 165–174. Print.
Horrobin, Peter. "Shedding Light on Soul Ties." In *How to Minister Freedom*, ed. Doris Wagner. Ventura, CA: Regal, 2005. 175–186.
Horton, Kenneth. "The Vineyard Movement and Eschatology: An Interpretation." Diss. Dallas Theological Seminary, 1999. Print.
Houreld, Katharine. "African Children Denounced as Witches by Christian Pastors." 18 Oct 2009. *Huffington Post*. 6 May 2013. http://www.huffingtonpost.com/2009/10/18/ african-children-denounce_n_324943.html.
Howard, Roland. *Charismania: When Christian Fundamentalism Goes Wrong*. London: Mowbray, 1997.
"Hrock SSM: School of Supernatural Ministry." *Harvest Rock School of Supernatural Ministry*. 2014. Web. 8 Sep 2014. http://www.hrockssm.com/.
Hunt, Stephen. *The Alpha Enterprise*. Aldershot: Ashgate, 2004.
Hunt, Stephen. *A History of the Charismatic Movement in Britain and the United States of America: The Pentecostal Transformation of Christianity*. 2 Volumes. Lewiston, NY: Edwin Mellen, 2009.
Hunt, Stephen, Malcolm Hamilton, and Tony Walter, eds. *Charismatic Christianity: Sociological Perspectives*. Basingstoke: Macmillan, 1997.
Hurst, Evan. "Jacksonville City Councilor Kimberly Daniels and Her Anti-Gay Word Salad." *Truth Wins Out*. 29 Sep 2011. Web. 8 Sep 2014. http://www.truthwinsout.org/press release/2011/09/19028/.
Hutchison, B. "Bentley Bends." *National Post*. 19 Aug 2008. Web. 6 May 2013. http://www.

nationalpost.com/story.html?id=848ee98d-daf2-41c0-b316-8bccfc0ad583&k=74884%20—age%2015%20convicted%20of%20sexually%20assaulting%20a%207-year-o.
"Inspire the Fire in Your Teen." *Teen Mania International*. N.D. Web. 2015.
"Instructors: Stephen Mory." N.D. Web. 7 May 2013. http://ga.us.churchinsight.com/PaymentGroup/Registration.aspx?group_id=1000031270.
"International Coalition of Apostles Membership Directory." *ICA*. 13 Jan 2010. Web. 8 Mar 2014. Available via https://drive.google.com/folderview?id=0By4yYtoydP-4ODU0NTIyYjEtMDBiYy00N2I5LThhOGYtNzNmZjQ3NjVjN2Qx&usp=drive_web&urp=http://www.talk2action.org/story/2011/9/3/9571/001&pli=1&hl=en_US (cached by Huffington Post writer Bruce Wilson).
International House of Prayer. "Loren Cunningham Is Speaking at Onething '09." 28 Dec 2009. Web. 8 Aug 2014. https://www.facebook.com/notes/international-house-of-prayer/loren-cunningham-is-speaking-at-onething09/226325034148.
Israel Today Staff. "Court Convicts Jewish Terrorist Who Bombed Messianic Youth." *Israel Today*. 17 Jan 2013. Web. 4 Mar 2014. http://www.israeltoday.co.il/NewsItem/tabid/178/nid/23625/Default.aspx?archive=article_title.
Izenberg, Dan. "Court Applies Law of Return to Messianic Jews Because of Fathers." *Jerusalem Post*. 22 Apr 2006. Web. 8 Mar 2014. http://www.jpost.com/Israel/Court-applies-Law-of-Return-to-Messianic-Jews-because-of-fathers.
Jackson, Bill. *The Quest for the Radical Middle: A History of the Vineyard*. Cape Town: Vineyard International Publishing, 2000.
Jacobs, Cindy. *The Reformation Manifesto*. Minneapolis: Bethany House, 2008.
Jaenen, Cornelius John. "The Pentecostal Movement." Masters Thesis. University of Manitoba, 1950.
"Jesus Camp." *Relevant Magazine*. N.D. Web. 8 Aug 2015.
"John Mulinde at IHOP KC 3-1-11." *Youtube*. 14 Nov 2011. Web. 8 Mar 2014. https://www.youtube.com/watch?v=NVtNfY3ebSc.
"John Templeton: Spiritually Rich and Passing It On." religionnewsblog.com. 20 Mar 2003. Web. 13 Apr 2013. http://www.religionnewsblog.com/2788/john-templeton-spiritually-rich-and-passing-it-on.
Johnson, Bill. "Creating a Supernatural Mindset." Interviewed by Day Spring Church. *Day SpringAu*. 4 May 2010. Web. 6 Mar 2014. https://www.youtube.com/watch?v=lWtzdsl2FsM.
Johnson, Bill. *When Heaven Invades Earth: A Practical Guide to a Life of Miracles*. Shippensburg, PA: Destiny Image, 2003.
Johnson, C. Neal. *Business as Mission: A Comprehensive Guide to Theory and Practice*. Downers Grove, IL: IVP Academic, 2009. Kindle Edition.
Johnson, Charles Neal. "God's Mission To, Within, and Through the Marketplace." Diss. Fuller Theological Seminary, 2004.
Johnson, Frecia. "Experiencing Jesus: Inner Healing Prayer for Personal Transformation, Church and Mission." Diss. Fuller Seminary, 2004. Proquest.
Johnston, Barry V. *Pitrim A. Sorokin: An Intellectual Biography*. Lawrence: University Press of Kansas, 1995.
Jones, Bob. "Visions and Revelations—Mike Bickle with Bob Jones [1]." 1988. Web. 8 Aug 2014. https://archive.org/details/VisionsAndRevelations-MikeBickleWithBobJones1988.
Joyner, Rick. *I See a New America*. Fort Mill, SC: Quest Ventures, 2011. Kindle Edition.
Joyner, Rick. "Rory and Wendy Alec Interview with Rick Joyner Concerning the Restoration of Todd Bentley." *God TV*. N.D. Web. 8 Mar 2014. http://www.god.tv/revivalalert/interview.
Joyner, Rick. "Volume 3, Number 2: Dear Oak Members." *The Oak Initiative*. 7 Mar 2011. Web. 8 Mar 2014. http://www.theoakinitiative.org/vol-3-no-2#.UyKjds6rMop.

"Justice for Ami Ortiz." *Maoz Israel*. 11 Apr 2013. Web. 8 Mar 2014. https://www.youtube.com/watch?v=JysQRYcMC44.
Kantel, Donald. "The 'Toronto Blessing' Revival and Its Continuing Impact on Mission in Mozambique." Diss. Regent University, 2007. Print.
Kaoma, Kapya, ed. "Colonizing African Values: How the U.S. Christian Right Is Transforming Sexual Politics in Africa." Somerville, MA: Political Research Associates, 2012.
Kaoma, Kapya. "Globalizing the Culture Wars." Somerville, Massachussets: Political Research Associates, 2009.
Kay, William. *Apostolic Networks in Britain: New Ways of Being Church*. Eugene, Oregon: Wipf and Stock, 2007.
Kemmelmeier, M. (2002). "True (Altruistic) Love Is Hard to Find." *Human Nature Review*. 2: 331–333. http://human-nature.com/nibbs/02/love.html.
Kidd, Thomas. *American Christians and Islam: Evangelical Culture and Muslims from the Colonial Period to the Age of Terrorism*. Princeton: Princeton University Press, 2009.
Kiley, Mike and Peter Doane. "The Christian Worldview of Making Disciples." Ed. Jay Grimstead. *Christian Worldview Documents*. Coalition on Revival. Sunnyvale, California: Coalition on Revival, 1989. http://www.reformation.net/COR_Docs/Christian_Worldview_Discipleship.pdf.
Kim, Ig-Jin. "History and Theology of Korean Pentecostalism: Sunbogeum (Pure Gospel) Pentecostalism." Diss. Uterecht University, 2003.
Kim, Won Ho. "A Strategy for Spiritual Warfare in Istanbul Turkey." Masters Thesis. Fuller Theological Seminary, 1999.
Kim, Wonho. "Spiritual Dynamics in Church Planting Among Turkish Folk Muslims." Diss. Fuller Theological Seminary, 2006.
"Kimon H. Sargeant." *John Templeton Foundation*. 2010. Web. 8 Aug 2014. http://www.templeton.org/who-we-are/our-team/staff/kimon-h-sargeant-phd.
Koop, C. Everett. "Corruption in Our Society: The Domino Effect." *New Wine Magazine* 12.7 (July/August 1980): 9–14, 16–17. Web. 8 Mar 2014. http://www.csmpublishing.org/res_newWine.php.
Koop, C. Everett. "Memorandum from C. Everett Koop to the Secretary of the Department of Health and Human Services [On the Preliminary Report on Grassroots Approach to the Discharge Petition]." Memorandum to the Secretary of the Department of Health and Human Services. 25 June 1981. Box 4, Folder 7. http://profiles.nlm.nih.gov/ps/retrieve/ResourceMetadata/QQBCCP.
"Korea." *Messianic Jewish Bible Institute*. 2014. Web. 8 Mar 2014. http://mjbi.org/Korea/.
Kraft, Charles. *Anthropology for Christian Witness*. Maryknoll, NY: Orbis Books, 1996.
Kraft, Charles. *Christianity in Culture*. Maryknoll, NY: Orbis Books, 1979.
Kraft, Charles. "Psychological Stress Factors Among Muslims." In *Media in Islamic Culture*. Wheaton, IL: Evangelical Literature Overseas, 1974. 137–144.
Kravitz, Rabbi Bentzion. "Messianic Truth in Advertising." *Jewish Journal*. 26 June 2008. Web. 8 Mar 2014. http://www.jewishjournal.com/opinion/item/messianic_truth_in_advertising_20080625.
Kron, Joshua. "In Uganda, Push to Curb Gays Draws U.S. Guest." *New York Times*. 2 May 2010. Web. 13 Mar 2013 http://www.nytimes.com/2010/05/03/world/africa/03uganda.html?ref=africa&_r=0;.
Kunsman, Cindy. "Coming to a Deeper Understanding of the Unwritten Rules of a Group: Oral Tradition, Oral Law, the 'Hidden Curriculum.'" *Under Much Grace*. 5 Feb 2012. Web. 8 Mar 2014. http://undermuchgrace.blogspot.com/2012/02/coming-to-deeper-understanding-of.html.
Kunsman, Cindy. "The Spiritual Eugenics of Multigenerational Faithfulness: More Social Darwinism." *Under Much Grace*. 11 Dec 2008. Web. 25 Aug 2013. http://undermuchgrace.blogspot.com/2008/12/spiritual-eugenics-of-multigenerational.html.

Kurtz, Nathan. "Huge Glory Cloud Bethel Church 11/13/11." 14 Nov 2011. Web. 8 Aug 2014. https://www.youtube.com/watch?v=y9eAgjH9cJQ.

Kylstra, Chester, and Betsy Kylstra. "About Us: History of Restoring the Foundations." *Restoring the Foundations*. N.D. Web. 8 Aug 2013. http://rtfi.org/?q=content/about-us.

Kylstra, Chester, and Betsy Kylstra. *Restoring the Foundations: An Integrated Approach to Healing Ministry*. 2nd Edition. Hendersonville, NC: Proclaiming His Word Publications, 2007.

Lambert, Steven. *Charismatic Captivation—Authoritarian Abuse & Psychological Enslavement in Neo-Pentecostal Churches*. Jupiter, FL: Real Truth Publications, 2003. Kindle Edition.

Langa, Stephen. "Resisting Sexual Colonialism: Africans Stand Against 21st Century Imperialists Wanting to Plant the Homosexual Flag." *Darrow Miller and Friends*. Unpublished paper. http://darrowmillerandfriends.com/wp-content/uploads/2011/06/resisting-sexual-colonialism.pdf.

Lawson, Leo. "The New Apostolic Paradigm and Morning Star International Churches." Masters Thesis. Fuller Theological Seminary School of World Missions, December 1997.

"Leadership." *Disciple Nations Alliance*. N.D. Web. 8 Mar 2014. http://www.disciplenations.org/leadership/.

Leclaire, Jennifer. "School Trains Christians in 'Prophetic Evangelism.'" *Charisma*. 30 Sep 2010. Web. 8 Aug 2014. http://www.charismamag.com/site-archives/570-news/featured-news/11771-training-a-new-kind-of-evangelist.

Lee, Matthew, and Margaret Poloma. *A Sociological Study of the Great Commandment in Pentecostalism*. Lewiston, NY: Edwin Mellen, 2009.

Lee, Matthew, Margaret Poloma, and Stephen G. Post. *The Heart of Religion: Spiritual Empowerment, Benevolence and the Experience of God's Love*. Oxford: Oxford University Press, 2013.

Lee, Matthew T., Margaret Poloma, and Stephen Post. "Introduction." In *The Science and Theology of Godly Love*, ed. Matthew T. Lee and Amos Yong. Dekalb: Northern Illinois University Press, 2012. 3–14.

Lee, Matthew T., and Amos Yong, eds. *Godly Love: Impediments and Possibilities*. New York: Lexington Books, 2012.

Lee, Matthew T., and Amos Yong, eds. "Preface." *Godly Love: Impediments and Possibilities*. New York: Lexington Books, 2012. ix-xi.

Lee, Matthew T., and Amos Yong, eds. *The Science and Theology of Godly Love*. Dekalb: Northern Illinois University Press, 2012.

Lennard, Natasha. "Maddow Discusses Rick Perry's Connections with a Christian Conspiracy Group." *Salon*. 11 Aug 2011. Web. 8 Mar 2014. http://www.salon.com/2011/08/11/maddow_on_perry_new_apostolic_reformation/.

Lepinski, Jon Paul. "Engaging Postmoderns in Worship: A Study of Effective Techniques and Methods Utilized by Two Growing Churches in Northern California." Diss. Liberty Baptist Theological Seminary, 2010. Print.

Levin, Tanya. "Why Mercy Ministries Was Godsent for Hillsong." *Sydney Morning Herald*. 18 Mar 2008. Web. 8 Aug 2013. http://www.smh.com.au/news/opinion/why-mercy-ministries-was-godsent-for-hillsong/2008/03/17/1205602284113.html.

Lewis, Tyson, and Richard Kahn. "The Reptoid Hypothesis: Utopian and Dystopian Representational Motifs in David Icke's Alien Conspiracy Theory." *Utopian Studies* 16.1 (2005): 45–74. JSTOR. Web. 13 Jul 2013.

Liebscher, Banning. *Jesus Culture: Living a Life That Transforms the World*. Shippensburg, PA: Destiny Image, 2009.

Lienesch, Michael. *Redeeming America: Piety and Politics in the New Christian Right*. Chapel Hill: University of North Carolina Press, 1993.

Lifton, Robert Jay. *Thought Reform and the Psychology of Totalism: A Study of "Brainwashing" in China*. Chapel Hill: University of North Carolina Press, 1989.

Lively, Scott. "Report from Uganda." *Defend the Family*. 17 Mar 2009. Web. 8 Mar 2014. http://www.defendthefamily.com/pfrc/archives.php?id=2345952.

Lobdell, William. "Evangelicals Praying for a Revolution." *Los Angeles Times*. 21 Feb 2003. Web. 8 Aug 2014. http://articles.latimes.com/2003/feb/21/local/me-revival21.

"Locations." *Mercy Ministries*. N.D. Web. 8 Aug 2013. http://www.mercyministries.org/who_we_are/about/locations.html.

"Lou Engle." *The Call*. 2012. Web. 8 Mar 2014. http://www.thecall.com/Articles/1000104027/TheCall/Who_We_Are/Lou_Engle.aspx.

Lybarger, Jeremy. "Foiled in the United States, Anti-Gay Evangelicals Spread Hate in Africa." *Mother Jones*. 9 July 2013. Web. 8 Mar 2014. http://www.motherjones.com/media/2013/07/evangelicals-gay-rights-ihop-god-loves-uganda-sundance.

Lyons, Mike. "Councilwoman Kimberly Daniels Goes on Rant About Human Rights." *First Coastal News*. 29 Sep 2011. Web. 8 Aug 2014. http://downtownjax.firstcoastnews.com/news/news/61507-councilwoman-kimberly-daniels-goes-rant-about-human-rights.

Macchia, F.D. "Theology, Pentecostal." In *The New International Dictionary of Pentecostal and Charismatic Movements*. Revised and Expanded Edition. Ed. Stanley M. Burgess and Eduard M. Van Der Maas. Grand Rapids: Zondervan, 2002. 1120–1141. Print.

MacCulloch, Diarmaid. *Christianity: The First Three Thousand Years*. New York: Viking, 2009.

Maddox, Marion. *God Under Howard: The Rise of the Religious Right in Australian Politics*. Crows Nest, NSW: Allen & Unwin, 2005.

"Manila Manifesto." *The Lausanne Movement*. 1989. Web. 8 Aug 2013. http://www.lausanne.org/en/documents/manila-manifesto.html.

Mansfield, Stephen. *Derek Prince: A Biography*. Lake Mary, FL: Charisma House, 2005.

Mantyla, Kyle. "Jacobs: Birds Are Dying Because of DADT Repeal." *Right Wing Watch*. 10 Jan 2011. Web. 8 Mar 2014. http://www.rightwingwatch.org/content/jacobs-birds-are-dying-because-dadt-repeal.

Mantyla, Kyle. "Jacobs: Our Prayers Stop Terrorism." *Right Wing Watch*. 29 Aug 2012. Web. 8 Mar 2014. http://www.rightwingwatch.org/content/jacobs-our-prayers-stop-terrorism.

Mantyla, Kyle. "Jacobs: Those with Native American/Indigenous Heritage Must Renounce and Repent for Their Ancestor's Sins." *Right Wing Watch*. 4 June 2013. Web 8 Mar 2014. http://www.rightwingwatch.org/content/jacobs-those-native-americanindigenous-heritage-must-renounce-and-repent-their-ancestors-sin.

Mantyla, Kyle. "'OWS Protests Driven by 'A Power of Darkness.'" *Right Wing Watch*. 20 Oct 2011. Web. 8 Mar 2014. http://www.rightwingwatch.org/content/jacobs-ows-protests-driven-power-darkness.

Mantyla, Kyle. "Prayer Warriors Descending on DC to Shift the Government and Claim the 7 Mountains." *Right Wing Watch*. 23 Sep 2010. Web. 8 Aug 2014. http://www.rightwingwatch.org/content/prayer-warriors-descending-dc-shift-government-and-claim-7-mountains.

Mantyla, Kyle. "The Religious Right's Organizing Philosophy: Victory Through Redundancy." *Right Wing Watch*. 9 May 2012. Web. 8 Mar 2014. http://www.rightwingwatch.org/content/religious-rights-organizing-philosophy-victory-through-redundancy.

Mantyla, Kyle. "Unity Through Redundancy." *Right Wing Watch*. 14 July 2009. Web. 8 Mar 2014. http://www.rightwingwatch.org/content/unity-through-redundancy.

Marsden, George. *Fundamentalism and American Culture*. New York: Oxford University Press, 2006.

Mash, Jerry. "Baal Divorce." *Heartland Apostolic Prayer Network*. N.D. Web. 8 Mar 2014. http://www.hapn.us/Websites/oapn/Images/Resource%20docs/baal%20divorce/Baal%20Divorce%20-%20Corporate%281-5-10%29.pdf.

Mason, Phil. *Quantum Glory: The Science of Heaven Invading Earth*. Maricopa, AZ: XP Publishing, 2010.

Martin, William. *With God on Our Side: The Rise of the Religious Right in America*. New York: Broadway Books, 1996.

"Matthew Barnett—the Dream Center." *Montana Christian Journal*. 1 Apr 2013. Web. 22 Aug 2014. http://www.mtcbd.org/2013/04/01/matthew-barnett-the-dream-center/.

Matthews, Carol Suzanne. "Taken: Constructions of 'Race,' 'Biology' and Colonialism Informing the Alien Abduction Narrative in the United States." Diss. University of Kansas, 2001. Print.
McBride, Dorothy. *Abortion in the United States: A Reference Handbook*. Santa Barbara: ABC-CLIO, 2007.
McCain, Danny. "The Metamorphosis of Nigerian Pentecostalism: From Signs and Wonders in the Church to Service and Influence in Society." In *Spirit and Power: The Growth and Global Impact of Pentecostalism*. Ed. Donald Miller, Kimon H. Sargeant, and Richard Flory. Oxford: Oxford University Press, 2013. Kindle.
McClymond, Michael J. "Agape, Self-Sacrifice, and Mutuality: An Exploration into the Thought of Jonathan Edwards and the Theme of Godly Love." In *The Science and Theology of Godly Love*. Dekalb: Northern Illinois University Press, 2012. Print. 33–55.
McDonald, Marci. *The Armageddon Factor: The Rise of Christian Nationalism in Canada*. Toronto: Random House of Canada, 2010. Kindle Edition.
McGavran, Donald. *Understanding Church Growth*. Grand Rapids: Eerdmans, 1970.
McGee, G.B. "Initial Evidence." In *The New International Dictionary of Pentecostal and Charismatic Movements*. Revised and Expanded Edition. Ed. Stanley M. Burgess and Eduard M. Van Der Maas. Grand Rapids: Zondervan, 2002.784–791. Print.
McKenna, Kathleen. "Jean Hardisty, 69; Founded Political Research Associates." *Boston Globe*. 9 Apr 2015. Web. 13 May 2015. https://www.bostonglobe.com/metro/obituaries/2015/04/09/jean-hardisty-wellesley-centers-for-women-senior-scholar-founded-political-research-associates/WRdUC4h7Kps759vb3XcqCL/story.html#.
McMichael, Richard, and Marie McMichael. *Sozo Training Manual*. Spokane: Healing Room Ministries Sozo Team, n.d.
McMullen, Cary. "Faith Healing 'Outpouring' Overflows Venue." *The Ledger*. 25 Apr 2008. Web. 8 Mar 2014. http://www.theledger.com/article/20080425/NEWS/804250386.
McVicar, Michael. "Reconstructing America: Religion, American Conservatism and the Political Theology of Rousas John Rushdoony." Diss. Ohio State University, 2010.
"Meet the JI Team." *Joseph International*. N.D. Web. 8 Mar 2014 http://www.josephinternational.org/Articles/1000103273/Joseph_International/About_Us/JI_Staff.aspx.
Mei, Yujun. "The Changing Discourse of International Humanitarian Charitable Relief NGOS." Diss. Arizona State University, 2003.
Menzie, Nicola. "Justin Bieber 'Breaks Down' During Pastor Carl Lentz's Hillsong NYC Sermon." *Christian Post*. 9 Sep 2013. Web. 8 Mar 2014. http://www.christianpost.com/news/justin-bieber-breaks-down-during-pastor-carl-lentzs-hillsong-nyc-sermon-104091/.
Menzie, Nicola. "Justin Bieber Tried to Get Baptized, 'Cleansed' at Hillsong NYC Church?" *Christian Post*. 4 Feb 2014. Web. 8 Mar 2014. http://www.christianpost.com/news/justin-bieber-tried-to-get-baptized-cleansed-at-hillsong-nyc-church-113961/.
Mercy Ministries. 2013. Web. 19 Aug 2013. http://www.mercyministries.org/.
"Mercy Ministries Celebrates 22 Baptisms." *Mercyministriesnews.Com*. 2 Sep 2010. Web 24 Aug 2013. http://www.mercyministriesnews.com/2010/09/mercy-ministries-celebrates-22-baptisms.html.
"Mercy Ministries Surprised with Prestigious Award." *Mercy Ministries*. 25 Oct 2011. Web. 26 Aug 2013. http://www.mercyministries.org/news/35/2011/10-25/mercy-ministries-surprised-with-prestigious-award.
Mercy Survivors. "Is Mercy Ministries a Cult?" *Mercy Survivors*. Apr 2012. Web 26 Aug 2013. http://mercysurvivors.com/2012/04/.
Meyer, Catherine. "Studying the Relationship Between Church and State: Practical Limits of Church, State, and Society Programs in Higher Education." M.A. Thesis. Baylor, 2005. Print.
Miller, Darrow. "The Development Ethic: The Meaning of Hope for a Culture of Poverty." FFH Position Paper, 1988.
Miller, Darrow. "Sexual Colonialism: The New Legacy of Western Elitism." *Darrow Miller and*

Friends. 24 June 2011. Web. 8 Mar 2014. http://darrowmillerandfriends.com/2011/06/24/sexual-colonialism-the-new-legacy-of-western-elitism/.
Miller, Darrow, Scott Allen and the African Working Group of Samaritan Strategy Africa. *Against All Hope: Hope for Africa.* Phoenix: Disciple Nations Alliance, 2005.
Miller, Darrow L. *Discipling Nations: The Power of Truth to Transform Cultures.* Seattle: YWAM Publishing, 2011. Kindle Edition.
Miller, Donald E., and Tetsunao Yamamori. *Global Pentecostalism: The New Face of Christian Social Engagement.* Berkeley: University of California Press, 2007. Kindle Edition.
Mleynek, Sherryl. "The Rhetoric of the 'Jewish Problem' in the *Left Behind* Novels." *Literature and Theology* 19.4 (November 2005): 367–383. Academic Search Premier.
Montgomery, Jim. "God's Hour for Guatemala." *Dawn Ministries.* San Jose, California, 1986 Report on Guatemala, Chapter 4.
Moore, S. David. *The Shepherding Movement.* London: T & T Clark, 2003.
Moriarty, Michael. *The New Charismatics: A Concerned Voice Responds to Dangerous New Trends.* Grand Rapids: Zondervan, 1992.
Morris, Linda. "Focus on Justice as Hillsong Changes Its Tune." *Sydney Morning Herald.* 3 July 2007. Web. 13 Aug 2013. http://www.smh.com.au/articles/2007/07/02/1183351125260.html.
Morrison, David "About Us: What's Happening at Iris Africa in Malawi." *Iris Global.* Feb 2011. Web. 8 Aug 2014. http://www.irisglobal.org/malawi/about.
Murphy, Ed. *The Handbook for Spiritual Warfare.* Nashville: Thomas Nelson, 1992.
Myers, P.Z. "Templeton Prayer Study Meets Expectations." *Pharyngula.* 4 Aug 2010. Web. 6 May 2013. http://scienceblogs.com/pharyngula/2010/08/04/templeton-prayer-study-meets-e/.
Myles, Francis. *The Order of Melchizedek.* Tulsa: Word & Spirit Resources, 2010.
Nathan, Debbie, and Michael Snedeker. *Satan's Silence: Ritual Abuse and the Making of a Modern American Witch Hunt.* New York: Basic Books, 1995.
"National COR Steering Committee." *Coalition on Revival.* 2008. Web. 8 Mar 2014 http://www.reformation.net/Pages/COR_Steering_Committee_Historic.htm.
New Wine Magazine. "Contributing Editors: October 1969." *New Wine Magazine* 1.2 (Oct 1969). Web. 8 Aug 2014. http://www.csmpublishing.org/res_newWine.php.
New Wine Magazine. "Contributing Editors: January 1971." *New Wine Magazine* 3.1 (Jan 1971). Web. 8 Mar 2014. http://www.csmpublishing.org/res_newWine.php.
Noll, Mark. *America's God: From Jonathan Edwards to Abraham Lincoln.* Oxford: Oxford University Press, 2002.
Nolot, Benjamin. "Restoring the Ancient Path of Abolition." 2012 Exodus Cry Abolition Summit, Track 8 2012 Exodus Cry Abolition Summit. Grandview, MO: Exodus Cry, N.D.
North, Gary. "An Economic Forecast for the Eighties." Interviewed by Dick Legatt. *New Wine Magazine* 11.11 (Dec 1979). Web. 8 Mar 2014. http://www.csmpublishing.org/res_newWine.php.
Oak Initiative. "'Marxism in America' by Lt. Gen (Ret) W.G. Boykin- OAK." *Oak Initiative.* 28 Oct 2010. Web. 8 Aug 2014. https://www.youtube.com/watch?v=Z7w3ZEbC09k.
Ochala-Lukwiya, Robert. "The Acholi Religious Leaders Peace Initiative: An Example of an Integral, Interculturated, and Ecumenical Approach to Pastoral Work in a War Situation." Thesis. University of Innsbruck, 2006.
Olasky, Marvin, ed. Freedom, *Justice and Hope: Toward a Strategy for the Poor and the Oppressed.* Westchester, IL: Crossway, 1988.
Oliver, Ansel. "Australian Coroner Rules Dingo Indeed Took Baby in 1980: Ruling Brings Relief to Chamberlains, Adventists Once Accused of Murder." *Adventist News Network.* 12 June 2012. Web. 8 Mar 2014. http://news.adventist.org/all-news/news/go/2012-06-12/australian-coroner-rules-dingo-indeed-took-baby-in-1980.
Olson, Walter. "Invitation to a Stoning: Getting Cozy with Theocrats." Reason.com. *Reason*

November 1998. Web. 8 Aug 2013. http://reason.com/archives/1998/11/01/invitation-to-a-stoning.
O'Neill, Kevin Lewis. *City of God: Christian Citizenship in Postwar Guatemala.* Berkley: University of California Press, 2010. Kindle Edition.
Ongere, George. "How Can the Concept of Humanism Solve Witchcraft Belief in Africa." *The Committee for Skeptical Inquiry.* 16 July 2009. Web. 18 Aug 2013. http://www.csicop.org/specialarticles/show/how_can_the_concept_of_humanism_solve_witchcraft_belief_in_africa.
Oord, Thomas Jay. "Testing Creaturely Love and God's Causal Role." In *The Science and Theology of Godly Love.* Ed. Matthew T. Lee and Amos Yong. Dekalb: Northern Illinois University Press, 2012. 94–118.
Oppenheimer, Mark. "On a Visit to the U.S, a Nigerian Witch Hunter Explains Herself." *New York Times.* 21 May 2010. Web. 6 May 2013. http://www.nytimes.com/2010/05/22/us/22beliefs.html?_r=0.
Orme, Brian. "The Hard Question of Religious Radicalism." *Relevant Magazine.* 16 Nov 2009. Web. 9 Sep 2015.
Osborne, Duncan. "A Ugandan Pastor with Global Reach." *Gay City News.* 15 Dec 2009. Web. 1 Jan 2013. (Note: The article in its original format is no longer available online).
Osborne, Duncan. "US Right Wing Charities Silent on Uganda Bill." *Gay City News.* 21 Dec 2009. Web. 8 Mar 2014. http://gaycitynews.com/us-right-wing-charities-silent-uganda-bill/.
Ostling, Richard N., and Joan K. *Mormon America: The Power and the Promise.* San Francisco: HarperCollins, 1999.
Otis, George, Jr. *Informed Intercession: Transforming Your Community Through Spiritual Mapping and Strategic Prayer.* Ventura, CA: Renew, 1999.
Otis, George, Jr. *The Last of the Giants.* Grand Rapids: Chosen Books, 1991.
Otis, George, Jr. *The Twilight Labryinth: Why Does Spiritual Darkness Linger Where It Does?.* Grand Rapids: Chosen Books, 1997.
"Our Board Members." *The Oak Initiative.* N.D. Web. 2015.
"Our Friends." *Catch the Fire.* 2011. Web. 8 Mar 2014. http://www.catchthefire.com/about/our-friends.
Overstreet, Jeffrey. "Is Jesus Camp Objective? Or Unfair?" *Christianity Today.* 29 Oct 2009. Web. 8 Aug 2015.
"Overview of GSSM." *Global School of Supernatural Ministry.* 2013. Web. 8 Mar 2014. http://gssm.globalawakening.com/about/overview.
Painter, Nell Irvin. *The History of White People.* New York: W.W. Nortion, 2010.
"Palin Pastor Prayed for Witchcraft Protection." *NBC News.* 25 Sep 2008. Web. 13 Aug 2013. http://www.nbcnews.com/id/26880901/ns/politics-decision_08/t/palin-pastor-prayed-witchcraft-protection/#.Uhj11dhLi3E.
Partners in Harvest "Who Is PIH?" *Partners in Harvest.* N.D. Web. 8 Mar 2014 http://partnersinharvest.org/media/resources/who-is-pih.pdf.
Patterson, Alice. *Bridging the Racial and Political Divide: How Godly Politics Can Transform a Nation.* San Jose: Transformational Publications, 2010. Kindle Edition.
Patterson, Steve. "Parvez Ahmed Faces New Criticism from Jacksonville City Council Member." *Florida Times Union.* 28 Sep 2011. Web. 8 Aug 2014. http://members.jacksonville.com/news/metro/2011-09-28/story/parvez-ahmed-faces-new-criticism-jacksonville-city-council-member.
Paulk, Earl. *Satan Unmasked: Exposing the Work of Satan in the World Today.* Atlanta: K Dimension Publishers, 1984.
"PCRI Staff." *Pentecostal and Charismatic Research Initiative.* N.D. Web. 9 Sep 2014. http://crcc.usc.edu/initiatives/pcri/pcri-staff.html.
"Pentecostalism and Changes in the Global Religious Economy." *USCC College.* Spirit in the

World Conference. 7 Oct 2006. Web. 8 Aug 2014. https://www.youtube.com/watch?v=Tc7-z8V8Hnk.

Petrie, Alistair. "Stewardship of God's Land." Diss. Fuller Theological Seminary, 1999.

Pierce, Cal. *Healing in the Kingdom: How the Power of God and Your Faith Can Heal the Sick.* Gospel Light, [2011]. Kindle Edition.

Pierce, Chuck, and C. Peter Wagner. "Chuck Pierce Florida Outpouring Receives Endorsements and Oversight—Includes Chuck Pierce, C. Peter Wagner and More." *Elijah List.* 2 July 2008. Web. 8 Mar 2014. http://www.elijahlist.com/words/display_word/6611.

Pollard, Ruth. "Ethics, Financial Probity for Review." *Sydney Morning Herald.* 18 Mar 2008. Web. 11 Aug 2013. http://www.smh.com.au/news/national/ethics-financial-probity-for-review/2008/03/17/1205602293119.html.

Pollard, Ruth. "God's Cure for Gays Lost in Sin." *Sydney Morning Herald.* 19 Mar 2008. Web. 8 Aug 2013. http://www.smh.com.au/news/national/gods-cure-for-gays-lost-in-sin/2008/03/18/1205602385236.html.

Pollard, Ruth. "Mercy Ministries Home to Close." *Sydney Morning Herald.* 28 Oct 2009. Web. 11 Aug 2013. http://www.smh.com.au/national/mercy-ministries-home-to-close-20091027-hj2k.html.

Pollard, Ruth. "They Prayed to Cast Satan from My Body." *Sydney Morning Herald.* 17 Mar 2008. Web. 11 Aug 2013. http://www.smh.com.au/news/national/they-prayed-to-cast-satan-from-my-body/2008/03/16/1205602195122.html.

Pollard, Ruth. "They Sought Help but Got Exorcism and the Bible." *Sydney Morning Herald.* Mar 2008. Web. 11 Aug 2013. http://www.smh.com.au/news/national/they-sought-help-but-got-exorcism-and-the-bible/2008/03/16/1205602195048.html.

Poloma, Margaret. *Main Street Mystics: The Toronto Blessing & Reviving Pentecostalism.* Walnut Creek, CA: Altamira Press, 2003.

Poloma, Margaret. "A Reconfiguration of Pentecostalism." In *"Toronto" in Perspective: Papers on the New Charismatic Wave of the Mid–1990s,* ed. David Hillborn. Waynesboro, GA: Paternoster, 2001. 99–130.

Poloma, Margaret. "Reviving Pentecostalism at the Millenium: The Harvest Rock Story." *Hartford Institute for Religious Research.* 9/10 Oct 1998. Web. 8 Mar. 2014. http://hirr.hartsem.edu/research/pentecostalism_polomaart4.html.

Poloma, Margaret. "The Spirit and the Bride: The Toronto Blessing and Church Structure." *Evangelical Studies Bulletin* 13.4. 1–5. Web. 6 May 2013. http://hirr.hartsem.edu/research/pentecostalism_polomaart6.html.

Poloma, Margaret. "Toronto Blessing." In *The New International Dictionary of Pentecostal and Charismatic Movements.* Revised and Expanded Edition. Ed. Stanley M. Burgess and Eduard M. Van Der Maas. Grand Rapids: Zondervan, 2002.1149–1152. Print.

Posner, Sarah. "Kosher Jesus: Messianic Jews in the Holy Land." *The Atlantic Monthly.* 29 Nov 2012. Web. 8 Mar 2014. http://www.theatlantic.com/international/archive/2012/11/kosher-jesus-messianic-jews-in-the-holy-land/265670/.

Post, Stephen G. *Altruism & Altruistic Love: Science, Philosophy & Religion in Dialogue.* Oxford: Oxford University Press, 2002.

Post, Stephen G. "Godly Love: Why We Cannot Endure Without It." *The Science and Theology of Godly Love.* Ed. Matthew T. Lee and Amos Yong. Dekalb: Northern Illinois University Press, 2012. 17–32.

Post, Stephen G. "Institute for Research on Unlimited Love 2007 Report—Funded Science Studies & Related Publications." *Institute for Research on Unlimited Love.* Apr 2007. Web. 6 May 2003. http://www.unlimitedloveinstitute.org/grant/pdf/complete_funding_overview.pdf.

Post, Stephen G., et al. "General Introduction." In *Altruism & Altruistic Love: Science, Philosophy & Religion in Dialogue.* Oxford: Oxford University Press, 2002. 3–14.

Priest, Robert J., and Esther E. Cordill. "Christian Communities and 'Recovered Memories' of Abuse." *Christian Scholar's Review* 41.4 (Summer 2012): 381–400.
"Profiles on the Right: Lou Engle." *Political Research Associates*. N.D. Web. 12 Mar 2014. http://www.politicalresearch.org/profiles-on-the-right-lou-engle/#.
"Programs." *IHOP KC*. 2014. Web. 8 Aug 2014. http://www.ihopkc.org/foundations/programs/.
"Project Co-Directors." *Flame of Love Project*. N.D. Web. 6 May 2013. http://www3.uakron.edu/sociology/flameweb/codirect.html.
Pytches, David. *Some Said It Thundered: A Personal Encounter with the Kansas City Prophets*. Nashville: Thomas Nelson, 1991.
Randles, Bill. *Weighed and Found Wanting: The Toronto Experience Examined in the Light of the Bible*. Cambridge: St. Matthew Publications, 1995.
Reed, Travis. "Florida Revival Drawing Criticism—And Thousands of Followers." *Pantagraph*. 28 July 2008. Web. 8 Mar 2014. http://www.pantagraph.com/lifestyles/faith-and-values/florida-revival-drawing-criticism-and-thousands-of-followers/article_0fe92491-afdd-51ee-9ccf-2f2d39d3b52a.html.
Reese, Andy. *Freedom Tools: For Overcoming Life's Tough Problems*. Grand Rapids: Chosen, 2008.
"Revival Alliance." *Revival Alliance*. N.D. Web. 6 May 2013. http://revivalalliance.com/.
Reynolds, Michael. "American Evangelicals in Kurdistan." *Investigative Fund*. 12 July 2010. Web. 8 Mar 2014. http://www.theinvestigativefund.org/investigations/1357/american_evangelicals_in_kurdistan.
Reynolds, Michael. "How American Right Wing Christians Are Waging Spiritual Warfare in Northern Iraq." *Alternet*. 12 July 2010. http://www.alternet.org/story/147513/how_american_right-wing_christians_are_waging_%27spiritual_warfare%27_in_northern_iraq.
"Rick Joyner Praying for Military Coup Over Obama." *The Lip TV*. 14 Oct 2013. Web. 8 Mar 2014. https://www.youtube.com/watch?v=eSBXR_PxPqM.
Riss, R.M. "John Arnott." In *The New International Dictionary of Petencostal and Charismatic Movements*. Revised and Expanded Edition. Ed. Stanley M. Burgess and Eduard M. Van Der Maas. Grand Rapids: Zondervan, 2002. 332. Print.
Riss, R.M. "Latter Rain Movement." In *The New International Dictionary of Pentecostal and Charismatic Movements*. Revised and Expanded Edition. Ed. Stanley M. Burgess and Eduard M. Van Der Maas. Grand Rapids: Zondervan, 2002. 830–832. Print.
Riss, R.M. "Mike Bickle." In *The New International Dictionary of Petencostal and Charismatic Movements*. Revised and Expanded Edition. Ed. Stanley M. Burgess and Eduard M. Van Der Maas. Grand Rapids: Zondervan, 2002. 417. Print.
Riss, Richard M. *Latter Rain: The Latter Rain Movement of 1948 and the Mid-Twentieth Century Evangelical Awakening*. Etobicoke, Ontario: Honeycomb Visual Productions, 1987.
Roach, Erin. "Israeli Supreme Court Sides with Messianic Jews." *Baptist Press*. 21 Apr 2008. Web. 8 Mar 2014. http://www.bpnews.net/printerfriendly.asp?ID=27874.
Robertson, Josh. "Hundreds Attend Faith Healing Schools Linked to Fundamentalist Bethal [Sic] Church." *Courier Mail*. 28 May 2011. Web. 6 May 2013. http://www.couriermail.com.au/news/queensland/hundreds-attend-faith-healing-schools-linked-to-fundamentalist-bethal-church/story-e6freoof-1226064378133.
Robins, R.G. *Pentecostalism in America*. Santa Barbara: Praeger, 2010.
Römer, Jürgen. "The Toronto Blessing." Diss. Abo Akademi University, 2002. Print.
"Rory and Wendy Alec: God TV." cbn.com. N.D. Web. 18 Aug 2013. http://www.cbn.com/700club/guests/bios/RW_Alec_052704.aspx.
Rosenberg, Paul. "America's Own Taliban: A Fast Growing Right-Wing Politico-Religious Presence Plans to Implement an End-Times, Christian Theocracy in the US." *Al Jazeera*. 28 July 2011. Web. 8 Mar 2014. http://www.aljazeera.com/indepth/opinion/2011/07/20117259426336524.html.

Works Cited

Rosenberg, Paul. "Rick Perry's Prayer-Rally Politics." *Reader Supported News*. 6 Aug 2011. Web. 7 Mar 2014. http://readersupportednews.org/opinion2/277-75/6923-rick-perrys-prayer-rally-politics.

Rubenberg, Cheryl. "Israel and Guatemala: Arms, Advice, and Counterinsurgency." Middle East Research and Information Project. *Middle East Report* May/June 1986. Web. 8 Mar 2014. http://www.merip.org/mer/mer140/israel-guatemala.

Sabalow, Ryan. "Ex Bethel Student Not at Fault in '08 Fall; Judge Says Woman Not Obligated to Act." *Redding Record Searchlight*. 13 Dec 2011. Web. 8 Jan 2014. https://www.redding.com/news/2011/dec/13/student-not-at-fault-in-08-fall/.

Sabalow, Ryan. "Faith Healing or Foul Play? 2008 Cliff Fall Victim Sues Bethel Students." *Redding Record Searchlight*. 21 Oct 2010. Web. 6 May 2013. http://www.redding.com/news/2010/oct/21/faith-healing-or-foul-play-on-cliff/.

Samarin, William J. *Tongues of Men and Angels: The Religious Language of Pentecostalism*. New York: Macmillan, 1972.

Sanchez, Casey. "Todd Bentley's Militant Joel's Army Gains Followers in Florida." *Intelligence Report* 131 (Fall 2008).Accessed 22 Mar 2013. http://www.splcenter.org/get-informed/intelligence-report/browse-all-issues/2008/fall/arming-for-armageddon.

Sanford, Victoria. "Violence and Genocide in Guatemala." Yale.edu. N.D. Web. 8 Mar 2014. http://www.yale.edu/gsp/guatemala/TextforDatabaseCharts.html.

Schaeffer, Edith. "Enduring as a Family: An Interview with Edith Schaeffer." Interview. *New Wine Magazine* 12.5 (May 1980): 3–6, 23–24. Web. 8 Mar 2014. http://www.csmpublishing.org/res_newWine.php.

Schaeffer, Francis. "The Decline of Twentieth Century Man." *New Wine Magazine* 11.2 (Feb 1979): 25–29. Web. 8 March 2014. Adapted from *How Should We Then Live*. http://www.csmpublishing.org/res_newWine.php.

"'School of Healing and Impartation: Spiritual and Medical Perspectives' West Haven Connecticut Sep 17–20." Elijah List. Advertisement. 14 Aug 2008. Web. 6 May 2013. https://www.elijahlist.com/words/display_word/6748.

Scotland, Nigel. *Charismatics and the New Millennium: The Impact of Charismatic Christianity from 1960 into the New Millennium*. Guildford, UK: Eagle, 2000.

"Sean Mcloud: Associate Professor and Director of Graduate Studies, Department of Religious Studies." *UNC Charlotte*. 8 Apr 2014. Web. 8 Sep 2014. https://clas-pages.uncc.edu/seanmccloud/.

"Senior Fellow Jeffrey P. Schloss." *Discovery Institute*. 2003. Web. 6 May 2013. http://web.archive.org/web/20030814073921/www.discovery.org/crsc/fellows/JeffreySchloss/index.html.

Sharlet, Jeff. *C Street: The Fundamentalist Threat to American Democracy*. New York: Little, Brown, 2010.

Sharlet, Jeff. *The Family*. New York: HarperCollins, 2008.

Sheets, Dutch. *Authority in Prayer*. Minneapolis: Bethany House, 2006.

Shultz, Steven. "2003 Word of the Lord—Apostolic Council of Prophetic Elders." *Elijah List*. 24 Feb 2003. Web. 8 Aug 2004. http://www.elijahlist.com/words/display_word.html?ID=1409.

Siew, Tye Yau. "Spiritual Territoriality as a Premise for the Modern Spiritual Mapping Movement." Diss. Fuller Theological Seminary, 1999.

Siker, Jeffrey. "African Traditional Religion." In *Homosexuality and Religion: An Encyclopedia*, ed. Jeffrey Siker. Westport, CT: Greenwood, 2007. 50–52.

Siker, Jeffrey. *Homosexuality and Religion: An Encyclopedia*. Ed. Jeffrey Siker. Westport, CT: Greenwood, 2007. 50–52.

Silk, Danny. *Culture of Honor: Sustaining a Supernatural Environment*. Shippensburg, PA: Destiny Image, 2009.

Silvoso, Ed. *Anointed for Business*. Ventura, CA: Regal, 2002.

Silvoso, Ed. "Redemption of the Marketplace." Sermon. Joseph Company Prophetic Summit. Spring 2004. 7 May 2004. Track 1. MP3. Private Collection.

Silvoso, Ed. *That None Should Perish: How to Reach Entire Cities for Christ Through Prayer Evangelism*. Regal, 1995. Kindle Edition.

Silvoso, Ed. *Transformation: Change the Marketplace and You Change the World*. Ventura, CA: Regal, 2007.

Sliker, David. Session 1. "Leadership Lessons from the Life of William Wilberforce." Exodus Cry Abolition Summit. Grandview, MO: Exodus Cry, N.D. 2013.

Smalley, William. "Language and Culture in the Development of Bible Society Translation Theory and Practice." *International Bulletin of Missionary Research* 19, no. 2.

Smith, Andrea. *Native Americans and the Christian Right: The Gendered Politics of Unlikely Alliances*. Durham: Duke University Press, 2008.

Smith, David. "Ugandan Group Sues Antigay Pastor in US." *The Guardian*. 15 Mar 2012. Web. 8 Apr 2014. http://www.theguardian.com/world/2012/mar/15/uganda-gay-group-sues-us-pastor.

Souders, Michael. "A God of Wealth: Religion, Modernity, and the Rhetoric of the Christian Prosperity Gospel." Diss. University of Kansas, 2011. Print.

"Sozo Basic Saved, Healed, and Delivered." 2013. *Ibethel.Org*. 6 May 2013. http://store.ibethel.org/p3343/sozo-basic-saved-healed-delivered.

"Sozo Overview." *Ibethel.Org*. 2013. Web. 6 May 2013. http://www.ibethel.org/sozo-overview.

Sparks, Evan. ""Great Men and Women: Hall of Fame, John Templeton." *Philanthropy Roundtable.Org*. N.D. Web. 6 May 2013 http://www.philanthropyroundtable.org/almanac/great_men_and_women/hall_of_fame/john_m._templeton.

"Spirit in the World: A Global Pentecostal Research Initiative." Grant ID 13839. Project Leader Donald Miller. https://www.templeton.org/what-we-fund/grants/spirit-in-the-world-a-global-pentecostal-research-initiative.

Spittler, R.P. "Glossolalia." In *The New International Dictionary of Pentecostal and Charismatic Movements*. Revised and Expanded Edition. Ed. Stanley M. Burgess and Eduard M. Van Der Maas. Grand Rapids: Zondervan, 2002. 670–676.

Sprague, Randy. "Cyrus Annointing: Part 1." Sermon. Joseph Company Prophetic Summit. Spring 2004. 8 May 2004. MP3. Private Collection.

Sprague, Randy. "Cyrus Annointing: Part 2." Sermon. Joseph Company Prophetic Summit. Spring 2004. 7 May 2004. MP3. Private Collection.

Springmeier, Fritz. "Fritz Springmeier—Author of the Bloodlines of the Illuminati- Alex Jones." Interview. Interview by Alex Jones. Infowars.com. 28 Jan 2012. Web. 8 Aug 2014. https://www.youtube.com/watch?v=gpGXD86-MMY.

Stafford, Tim. "Miracles in Mozambique: How Mama Heidi Reaches the Abandoned." *Christianity Today*. 18 May 2012. Web. 8 Mar 2014. http://www.christianitytoday.com/ct/2012/may/miracles-in-mozambique.html.

Stone, Perry. *Breaking the Jewish Code*. Lake Mary, FL: Charisma House, 2009.

"The Study of Godly Love." *Flame of Love Project*. N.D. Web. 2 May 2013. http://www3.uakron.edu/sociology/flameweb/.

Sweatte, Natahsa. "Mercy Ministries Offers Support to Sex Trafficking Victims." Kcbd.com. 26 Aug 2012. Web. 8 Sep 2013. http://www.kcbd.com/story/19380533/mercy-ministries-offers-support-to-sex-trafficking-victims.

Synan, Vinson. *The Century of the Holy Spirit: 100 Years of Pentecostal and Charismatic Renewal*. Nashville: Thomas Nelson, 2001.

Synan, Vinson. *An Eyewitness Remembers the Century of the Holy Spirit*. Grand Rapids: Chosen, 2010.

Tabachnick, Rachel. "Anti LGBTQ, Anti-Union 'Apostles' Fielding Another Democratic Candidate." *Political Research Associates*. 31 Oct 2013. Web. 8 Mar 2014. http://www.

politicalresearch.org/2013/10/31/anti-lgbtq-anti-union-apostles-fielding-another-democratic-candidate/.
Tabachnick, Rachel. "Christian Right Antigay PA. Gov. Candidate Launches Democratic Campaign at LGBT Center." *Political Research Associates*. 25 Mar 2013. Web. 6 May 2013 http://www.politicalresearch.org/tag/apostolic-network-of-global-awakening/.
Tabachnick, Rachel. "Col. Jim Ammerman, Apostle and New World Conspiracy Theorist." *Talk to Action*. 22 June 2009. Web. 8 Mar 2014. http://www.talk2action.org/story/2009/6/22/115820/165.
Tabachnick, Rachel. "Dominionism, Theocracy, New Apostolic Reformation, and Rick Perry." Interviewed by David Pakman. The David Pakman Show. 19 Dec 2011. Web. 8 Oct 2014. https://www.youtube.com/watch?v=x8j7CbB41sM.
Tabachnick, Rachel. "The Evangelicals Engaged in Spiritual Warfare." Interviewed by Terry Gross. *NPR*. 19 Aug 2011. Web. 13 Dec. 2013. http://www.npr.org/2011/08/24/139781021/the-evangelicals-engaged-in-spiritual-warfare.
Tabachnick, Rachel. "God's Plan for Israel: The End Times Prophecy Narrative of Christian Zionism." Presentation Document. N.D. Private Collection.
Tabachnick, Rachel. "Large RW Christian Group Plans Government Takeover." *The Young Turks*. Interviewed by Cenk Uygur. 2 Apr 2010. Web. 8 Mar 2014. https://www.youtube.com/watch?v=MgdZgBwMjIc.
Tabachnick, Rachel. "Max Myers and the Global School of Supernatural Ministry." *Political Research Associates*. N.D. Web. 8 Aug 2014. ttp://www.scribd.com/doc/131100746/Max-Myers-and-NAR.
Tabachnick, Rachel. "The New Christian Zionism and the Jews: A Love/Hate Relationship." *Public Eye* 24.4 (Winter 2009/Spring 2010): Online Edition. http://www.publiceye.org/magazine/v24n4/jews-new-christian-zionism.html.
Tabachnick, Rachel. "Part Two: The Prophecy/Conspiracy Genre." *Talk to Action*. 8 Dec 2010. Web. 8 Aug 2014. http://www.talk2action.org/story/2010/12/8/185728/155/Front_Page/Part_Two_The_Prophecy_Conspiracy_Genre.
Tabachnick, Rachel. "The Religious Right's Plot to Take Control of Public Schools." *Alternet*. 6 Mar 2012. Web. 8 Aug 2014 http://www.alternet.org/story/154435/the_religious_right%27s_plot_to_take_control_of_our_public_schools.
Tabachnick, Rachel. "Repent Amarillo's Spiritual Mapping and Vigilantism." *Talk to Action*. 6 Mar 2010. Web. 2 Sep 2014. http://www.talk2action.org/story/2010/3/6/95620/29842.
Tabachnick, Rachel. "Resource Directory for the New Apostolic Reformation." *Talk to Action*. 20 Jan 2010. Web. 8 Mar 2014. http://www.talk2action.org/story/2010/1/20/131544/037.
Tabachnick, Rachel. "Spiritual Warriors with an Antigay Mission: The New Apostolic Reformation." *Political Research Associates*. 22 Mar 2013. Web. 8 Aug 2014. http://www.politicalresearch.org/spiritual-warriors-with-an-antigay-mission/.
Tabachnick, Rachel. "Transcript of Gen. Boykin's 'Marxism in America.'" *Talk to Action*. 13 Jan 2011. Web. 8 Mar 2014. http://www.talk2action.org/story/2011/1/13/94755/8617.
Tabachnick, Rachel. "The 'Transformation' Movement." In *Colonizing African Values: How the U.S. Christian Right Is Transforming Sexual Politics in Africa*, ed. Kapya John Kaoma. Somerville, MA: Political Research Associates, 2012. 51–54.
Tallman, Matthew W. "Demos Shakarian: The Life, Legacy and Vision of a Full Gospel Business Man." Diss. Regent University, 2009. Print.
Tashman, Brian. "Ahn: America Needs to Confront Gay Marriage Like We Confronted Slavery." *Right Wing Watch*. 24 June 2011. Web. 8 Mar 2014 http://www.rightwingwatch.org/content/ahn-america-needs-confront-gay-marriage-we-confronted-slavery.
Tashman, Brian. "Barton: Demonic Powers Control Parts of the U.S. Government." *Right Wing Watch*. 8 Sep 2011. Web. 12 Mar 2014. http://www.rightwingwatch.org/content/barton-demonic-powers-control-parts-us-government.
Tashman, Brian. "'The Call: Detroit': Casting Demons Out of Mosques, Masonic Temples

and the State Senate." *Right Wing Watch*. 8 Nov 2011. Web. 8 Mar 2014. http://www.rightwingwatch.org/content/call-detroit-casting-demons-out-mosques-masonic-temples-and-state-senate.

Tashman, Brian. "'The Call' Whines About Right Wing Watch Exposing Their Anti-Muslim Rhetoric." *Right Wing Watch*. 22 Nov 2011. Web. 8 Mar 2014. http://www.rightwingwatch.org/content/call-whines-about-right-wing-watch-exposing-their-anti-muslim-rhetoric.

Tashman, Brian. "Engle, Joyner Come Together to Promote the Call." *Right Wing Watch*. 29 Aug 2011. Web. 8 Aug 2014. http://www.rightwingwatch.org/content/engle-joyner-come-together-promote-call.

Tashman, Brian. "Jacobs, Benefiel Meet with the Family Research Council to Plan for November Elections." *Right Wing Watch*. 23 Jan 2012. Web. 8 Mar 2014. http://www.rightwingwatch.org/content/jacobs-benefiel-meet-family-research-council-plan-november-elections.

Tashman, Brian. "Joyner: Obama Helping to Merge Christianity and Islam." *Right Wing Watch*. 31 Oct 2012. Web. 8 Mar 2014. http://www.rightwingwatch.org/content/joyner-obama-helping-merge-christianity-and-islam.

Tashman, Brian. "Joyner: 'The Lord Is Using Islam' to Punish America for 'Perversions' and 'Abortions.'" *Right Wing Watch*. 7 Sep 2011. Web. 8 Mar 2014. http://www.rightwingwatch.org/content/joyner-lord-using-islam-punish-america-perversions-and-abortions.

Tashman, Brian. "Newt Gingrich Names 'Apostle' Dutch Sheets to His Faith Leaders Coalition." *Right Wing Watch*. 26 Jan 2012. Web. 8 Mar 2014. http://www.rightwingwatch.org/content/newt-gingrich-names-apostle-dutch-sheets-his-faith-leaders-coalition.

Tashman, Brian. "Rick Perry Partner John Benefiel Claims Homosexuality Is an Illuminati Conspiracy." *Right Wing Watch*. 12 July 2011. Web. 8 Aug 2014. http://www.rightwingwatch.org/content/rick-perry-partner-john-benefiel-claims-homosexuality-illuminati-conspiracy.

Terry, Jonathan C., III. "A Liberationist Critique of the Church Growth Movement." Diss. Temple University. 1997. Print.

Thayer and Smith. "Greek Lexicon Entry for Sozo." *The NAS New Testament Greek Lexicon*. 1999. Web. 8 Aug 2013. http://www.biblestudytools.com/lexicons/greek/nas/sozo.html.

Tietz, Jeff. "Love and Death in the House of Prayer." *Rolling Stone*. 21 Jan 2014. Web. 8 Mar 2014. http://www.rollingstone.com/culture/news/love-and-death-in-the-house-of-prayer-20140121.

"Tikkun International Board." *Tikkun International*. N.D. Web. 8 Mar 2014. http://www.tikkunministries.org/board.php.

"Todd Bentley's Apostolic and Prophetic Commissioning 2/4." 28 Aug 2008. Web. 8 Mar 2014. https://www.youtube.com/watch?v=iVcXMkSrHEQ.

Tolkien, J.R.R. *The Lord of the Rings*. Boston: Houghton Mifflin, 1955.

Travis, John. "The C1 to C6 Spectrum: A Practical Tool for Defining Six Types of 'Christ-Centered Communities' ('C') Found in the Muslim Context." *EMQ* 34 (October 1998): 407–408.

Twiss, Richard. "Native Lead Contextualization Efforts in North America: 1989–2009." Diss. Asbury Theological Seminary, 2011. Print.

Twiss, Richard. *One Church, Many Tribes*. Ventura, CA: Regal, 2000.

"Undertaking to the Australian Competition and Consumer Commission Given for the Purpose of Section 87B." *Australian Competition and Consumer Commission*. 16 Dec 2009. Web. 6 May 2013. http://transition.accc.gov.au/content/item.phtml?itemId=906586&nodeId=3e5d2c62fdfda22b0c1c708fe24326ff&fn=Undertaking.pdf.

"Unforgettable Message of Hope from Marilyn Skinner." *Mercy Ministries*. 19 Oct 2011. Web. 8 Aug 2013. http://www.mercyministries.org/news/37/2011/10-19/unforgettable-message-of-hope-from-marilyn-skinner.

"University of Minnesota Morris: Biology Faculty." N.D. Web. 6 May 2013. http://www.morris.umn.edu/academics/biology/faculty/#myersp.

Vinzant, Don. "Historical Roots of the Discipling Movement Among Churches of Christ." *The Discipling Dilemma*, ed. Flavil Yeakley. Nashville: Gospel Advocate, 1988. 123–170.

Wagner, C. Peter. *Apostles Today*. Ventura, CA: Regal, 2006.

Wagner, C. Peter. *The Church in the Workplace: How God's People Can Transform Society*. Ventura, CA: Regal, 2006. Kindle Edition.

Wagner, C. Peter. *Churches That Pray*. Ventura, CA: Regal, 1993.

Wagner, C. Peter. *Churchquake!* Ventura, CA: Regal, 1999.

Wagner, C. Peter. *Confronting the Powers*. Ventura, CA: Regal, 1996.

Wagner, C. Peter. *Confronting the Queen of Heaven*. Colorado Springs: Wagner Institute for Practical Ministry, 1998.

Wagner, C. Peter. *Dominion! How Kingdom Action Can Change the World*. Grand Rapids: Chosen, 2008.

Wagner. C Peter. Foreword. *Apostles, Prophets and the Coming Moves of God*. Santa Rosa Beach, FL: Destiny Image, 1997.xxi-xxiii.

Wagner, C. Peter. Foreword. *Prophetic Scriptures Yet to Be Fullfilled: During the Third and Final Church Reformation*. By Bill Hamon. Shippensburg, PA: Destiny Image, 2010. 17–19.

Wagner, C. Peter. "How Deliverance Sustains Revival." In *How to Minister Freedom*, ed. Doris Wagner. Ventura, CA: Regal, 2005. 79–89. Print.

Wagner, C. Peter. "John Wimber." In *The New International Dictionary of Petencostal and Charismatic Movements*. Revised and Expanded Edition. Ed. Stanley M. Burgess and Eduard M. Van Der Maas. Grand Rapids: Zondervan, 2002. 1199–1200. Print.

Wagner, C. Peter. "New Apostolic Reformation." In *The New International Dictionary of Petencostal and Charismatic Movements*. Revised and Expanded Edition. Ed. Stanley M. Burgess and Eduard M. Van Der Maas. Grand Rapids: Zondervan, 2002. 930. Print.

Wagner, C. Peter. *On Earth as It Is in Heaven*. Ventura, CA: Regal, 2012. Kindle Edition.

Wagner, C. Peter. "Spiritual Warfare." In *Territorial Spirits*. Ed. C. Peter Wagner. Shippensburg, PA: Destiny Image, 2012. 33–54. Print.

Wagner, C. Peter, ed. *Territorial Spirits*. Shippensburg, PA: Destiny Image, 2012.

Wagner, C. Peter. "Third Wave." *The New International Dictionary of Pentecostal and Charismatic Movements*. Revised and Expanded Edition. Ed. Stanley M. Burgess and Eduard M. Van Der Maas. Grand Rapids: Zondervan, 2002. Print. 1141.

Wagner, C. Peter. *Warfare Prayer: How to Seek God's Power and Protection in the Battle to Build His Kingdom*. Ventura, CA: Regal, 1992.

Wagner, C. Peter. *Wrestling with Alligators*. Ventura, CA: Regal, 2010.

Wagner, C. Peter. *Your Church Can Grow: Seven Vital Signs of a Healthy Church*. Ventura, CA: Regal, 1976.

Wagner, Doris. "Forgiving the Unforgivable." In *How to Minister Freedom*. Ed. Doris Wagner. Ventura, CA: Regal, 2005. 91–101. Print.

Wagner, Doris, ed. *How to Minister Freedom*. Ventura, CA: Regal, 2005.

Walker, Andrew. "Thoroughly Modern: Sociological Reflections on the Charismatic Movement from the End of the Twentieth Century." In *Charismatic Christianity; Sociological Perspectives*. Ed. Stephen Hunt, Malcolm Hamilton, and Tony Walter. Basingstoke: Macmillan, 1997. 17–42.

Wallace, Alan. "Echoes of the Spirit." *New Wine Magazine* 9.6 (June 1977). Web. 8 Aug 2014. 10–11. http://www.csmpublishing.org/res_newWine.php.

Wallnau, Lance. Foreword. *Change Agent: Engaging Your Passion to Be the One Who Makes the Difference*. By Os Hillman. Lake Mary, FL: Charisma House, 2011. xi-xiii.

Wamutitu, Joseph Warui. "Economic Empowerment for Missions: Empowering the Church in Kenya for Holistic and Crosscultural Ministry." Diss. Fuller Theological Seminary, 2009.

Ware, S.L. "Resorationism in Classical Pentecostalism." In *The New International Dictionary of Pentecostal and Charismatic Movements*. Revised and Expanded Edition. Ed. Stanley M. Burgess and Eduard M. Van Der Maas. Grand Rapids: Zondervan, 2002. Print. 1019–1021.

Warnock, George H. *The Feast of the Tabernacles: The Hope of the Church*. Dallas: Bill Britton, 1951. http://ebookbrowse.com/feast-of-tabernacles-the-george-h-warnock-book-pdf-d255720380. Accessed 8 Mar 2013.

Warren, Rick. "New Churches for a New Generation, Church Planting to Reach Baby Boomers a Case Study: The Saddleback Valley Community Church." Diss. Fuller Seminary, 1993.

Weaver, C. Douglas. *The Healer Prophet: William Marion Branham, a Study of the Prophetic in American Pentecostalism*. Macon, GA: Mercer University Press, 2000.

Weaver, John. *Evangelicals and the Arts in Fiction: Portrayals of Tension in Non-Evangelical Works Since 1895*. Jefferson, NC: McFarland, 2013.

Weaver, John. "Jesus Freaks, Freaking Jesus: Evangelicalism and American Literature." Diss. State University of New York Binghamton, 2010. Print.

Weaver, John. "Unpardonable Sins: The Mentally Ill and Evangelicalism in America." *Journal of Religion and Popular Culture* 23.1 (2011): 65–81.

Weissman, Steve. "Indicting Reagan, Israel, and the God Squads in the Guatemalan Holocaust." *Reader Supported News*. 14 May 2013. Web. 8 Mar 2014. http://readersupportednews.org/opinion2/277-75/17431-indicting-reagan-israel-and-the-god-squads-in-the-guatemalan-holocaust.

Wells, G.A. *Cutting Jesus Down to Size*. Chicago: Open Court, 2009.

"Werner Swart." *Transform Our World*. 2014. Web. 11 Sep 2014. http://www.transformourworld.org/en/conference/global/international/faculty/details/werner-swart.

Wilder, Forrest. "Rick Perry's Army of God." *Texas Observer*. 3 Aug 2011. Web. 8 Mar 2014. http://www.texasobserver.org/rick-perrys-army-of-god/.

Wilkins, Steve and Doug Wilson. *Southern Slavery as It Was: A Monograph*. Moscow, ID: Canon Press, 1996. Digital Version in Private Collection.

Williams, Joseph. *Spirit Cure*. Oxford: Oxford University Press, 2011.

Wilson, Bruce. "Burning Buddhas, Books and Art: Meet the New Apostolic Reformation." *Talk to Action*. 14 Sep 2011. Web. 8 Aug 2014. http://www.talk2action.org/story/2011/9/14/192516/418.

Wilson, Bruce. "C. Peter Wagner Claims Margaret Poloma as His Own." https://www.youtube.com/watch?v=E7xetcrtP9M.

Wilson, Bruce. "Everything You Need to Know About the Speakers at This Weekend's Harvard Hate Conference." *Truth Wins Out*. 30 Mar 2011. Web. 8 Mar 2014. http://www.truthwinsout.org/pressrelease/2011/03/15753/.

Wilson, Bruce. "Kony 2012 Effort a Ministry in Antigay Evangelical Barnabas Group Reports LGBT Rights Nonprofit." *Huffington Post*. 10 Apr 2012. Web. 8 Mar 2014. http://www.huffingtonpost.com/bruce-wilson/kony-2012-effort-a-minist_b_1416371.html.

Wilson, Bruce. "Lance Wallnau Explains the Seven Mountains Mandate." 16 July 2009. Web. 8 Oct 2014. https://www.youtube.com/watch?v=qQbGnJd9poc.

Wilson, Bruce. "Palin Attended Church Event with Samurai Sword Ceremony." *Huffington Post*. 21 Sep 2010. Web. 14 Aug 2014.

Wilson, Bruce. Personal Email. 12 Nov 2013.

Wilson, Bruce. Personal Email. 21 Oct 2013.

Wilson, Bruce. "Sarah Palin Linked to Second Witch Hunter." *Huffington Post*. 24 Oct 2008. Web. 8 Aug 2014. http://www.huffingtonpost.com/bruce-wilson/sarah-palin-linked-to-sec_b_137532.html.

Wilson, Bruce. "Special Report: KONY 2012 Stealth Evangelism Exposed." *Truth Wins Out*. 21 Mar 2012. Web. 11 May 2014. http://www.truthwinsout.org/blog/2012/03/23536/.

Wilson, D.J. "William Marrion Branham." *The New International Dictionary of Pentecostal and*

Charismatic Movements. Revised and Expanded Edition. Ed. Stanley M. Burgess and Eduard M. Van Der Maas. Grand Rapids: Zondervan, 2002. 440–441. Print.

Wilson, David Sloan. *Evolution for Everyone: How Darwin's Theory Can Change the Way We Think About Our Lives.* New York: Delacorte Press, 2007.

Wimber, John, and Kevin Springer. *Power Evangelism: Signs and Wonders Today.* London: Hodder and Stoughton, 1985.

Winters, Amanda. "Bethel 'Signs and Wonders' Include Angel Feathers, Gold Dust, and Diamonds." *Redding Record Searchlight.* 19 Jan 2010. Web. 2 Sep 2013. http://www.redding.com/news/2010/jan/19/bethels-signs-and-wonders-include-angel-feathers/.

Winters, Amanda. "Faith Healings, Dead Raising Teams Part of Bethel Experience." *Redding Record Searchlight.* 18 Jan 2010. Web. 6 May 2013 http://www.redding.com/news/2010/jan/18/faith-healings-dead-raising-teams-part-of-bethel/.

Wolfe, J. Henry. "Insider Movements: An Assessment of the Viability of Retaining Socio-Religious Identity in High Religious Contexts." Diss. Southern Baptist Theological Seminary, 2011. Print.

Worthen, Molly. *Apostles of Reason: The Crisis of Authority in American Evangelicalism.* Oxford: Oxford University Press, 2014.

Worthen, Molly. "The Chalcedon Problem: Rousas John Rushdoony and the Origins of Christian Reconstructionism." *Church History* 77:2 (June 2008): 399–437. Web. Academic Search Premier.

Worthen, Molly. "Onward Christian Scholars." *New York Times.* 30 Sep 2007. Web. 8 Mar 2014. http://www.nytimes.com/2007/09/30/magazine/30Christian-t.html?pagewanted=all&_r=0.

Wright, Nigel. "The Nature and Variety of Restorationism and the 'House Church' Movement." *Charismatic Christianity; Sociological Perspectives.* Ed Stephen Hunt, Malcolm Hamilton, and Tony Walter. Basingstoke: Macmillan, 1997. 60–76.

Yamamori, Ted. Preface. *The Last of the Giants.* By George Otis Jr. Grand Rapids: Chosen Books, 1991.

Yanover, Yori. "GW Bush Fundraising for Proslytizers of Jews in America and Israel: The Messianic Jewish Bible Institute Mission Is to Train Leaders for Jewish Ministry Around the World." *The Jewish Press.* 8 Nov 2013. Web. 8 Mar 2014. http://www.jewishpress.com/news/breaking-news/gw-bush-fundraising-for-jewish-proselytizers-in-america-and-israel/2013/11/08/.

Yeakley, Flavil, ed. *The Discipling Dilemma.* Nashville: Gospel Advocate, 1988.

YWAM Publishing. "Darrow Miller." *YWAM Publishing.* 2012?. Web. 8 Mar 2014. http://www.ywampublishing.com/p-1216-darrow-miller.aspx.

Zeigler, J.R. "Full Gospel Business Men's Fellowship International (FGBMFI)." In *The New International Dictionary of Pentecostal and Charismatic Movements.* Revised and Expanded Edition. Ed. Stanley M. Burgess and Eduard M. Van Der Maas. Grand Rapids: Zondervan, 2002. 653–654. Print.

Zichterman, Joseph T. "The Distinctives of John Wimber's Theology and Practice Within the American Pentecostal-Charismatic Movement." Diss. Trinity Evangelical Divinity School, 2011. Print.

DVDs, Films and Documentaries

Architecture of Doom. 1989. Dir. Peter Cohen. Perf. Rolf Arsensius, Bruno Ganz, Sam Gray, Joseph Goebells, P.L. Troost. Sweden: First Run Features. 119 minutes.

Elmer Gantry. 1960. Dir. Richard Brooks. Perf. Burt Lancaster, Jean Simmons, Arthur Kennedy, Dean Jagger, Shirley Jones. USA: MGM, DVD.

Ewing, Heidi E., and Rachel Grady. *Jesus Camp.* Perf. Becky Fischer, Lou Engle, Levi O'Brien. Los Angeles: Magnolia Home Entertainment, 2006.

Hayes, Michael, and Melissa Saul. *My Town*. Perf. Doug Wilson, Joann Muneta, Paula Groves-Price. https://www.youtube.com/watch?v=4KolP1wMtfk.
Kim, Bradley. *Restoration*. 3 Nov 2010. Web. 8 Mar 2014. https://www.youtube.com/watch?v=XXWZpcdKC04.
Nolot, Benjamin. *Nefarious: Merchant of Souls*. Perf Dan Allender, Calev Myers, Don Brewster, Annie Lobert. USA: Exodus Cry, 2011.
Otis, George, Jr. *Let the Sea Resound*. Webvideo. USA. TransformNations Media, 2004.
Otis, George, Jr. *Transformations I: A Documentary*. Webvideo. Colorado Springs: Sentinel Group, 1999.
Otis, George, Jr. *Transformations II: The Glory Spreads*. Webvideo. Colorado Springs: Sentinel Group, 2001.
Otis, George, Jr. *Uganda: An Unconventional War*. Webvideo. Narrator Joe Michaels. The Sentinel Group, 2006.
Ronson, Jon. "Revelations: How to Find God." Channel 4 Documentary. 28 June 2009. Available via https://www.youtube.com/watch?v=Gug9QDm-_IM.
Williams, Roger Ross. *God Loves Uganda*. United States: Full Credit Productions, 2013.
Wilson, Bruce. *Transforming Uganda*. Documentary. Webvideo. Independently produced. https://www.youtube.com/watch?v=EOe_NA1d_E4. "Transforming in Uganda." Video. Harvest Evangelism.

Index

AD 2000 campaign 72–73, 79–80, 85–87, 90–91, 128, 207, 215, 241, 251
Africa 21, 100–105, 109, 131–132, 163, 189, 213, 248, 255; *see also* Kenya; Uganda
Ahn, Ché 14–15, 68–69, 95, 100, 103–106, 119–120, 158–159, 172, 176, 222–223, 270*ch*3*n*4, 272*ch*6*n*12
Aiona, Duke 132
Alcorn, Nancy 74, 124–128, 270*ch*3*n*5
Alec, Wendy 177–182
Allender, Dan 140–141
Alpha Course 242–244, 261
Ammerman, Jim 2, 269Pref*n*1
Anderson, Neil 108
Anglicanism 116, 232–233, 235, 237–243
Annacondia, Carlos 71, 107, 240–241, 270*ch*2*n*2
apostle 1, 2, 6–7, 9, 20, 29, 30–32, 45–46, 54–55, 65, 68–69, 88–92, 96, 100–101, 106, 112, 119, 126, 128, 142, 149, 153, 155–157, 173–174, 190, 197–201, 206, 214–216, 237, 246, 261, 264–265; horizontal apostles 115–116; vertical apostles 115–116; workplace apostles 149–152, 255
Apostolic Council for Prophetic Elders (ACPE) 88, 128
apostolic networks 3, 5, 7, 29, 45, 67–68, 74–79, 86, 88–143 *passim*, 165, 173, 223, 236–239, 244, 246, 256, 261, 264, 270*ch*3*n*3
Apostolic Roundtable for Deliverance Ministries (ARDM) 88, 125
Apostolic Transformation Network (ATN) 79
Argentina 67, 112–113, 115, 131–132, 174, 197, 219, 222, 240–241, 250–251, 270*ch*2*n*1; spiritual mapping 2–3, 70–74, 86
Arnold, Clinton 75, 270*ch*2*n*5
Arnott, Carol *see* Arnott, John
Arnott, John 2, 14, 67–68, 99–101, 105, 120, 135, 219, 221, 223
arts 110–111, 146, 150; *see also* music
Asia 79, 102, 105, 131–132, 189
Assemblies of God (AOG) 109, 111, 159, 245–247, 249
Atheism 84–85, 179–180
Australia 1, 101, 123–128, 231, 245–248, 252–253, 270*ch*3*n*5 Bachmann, Michelle 5, 232

Bahati, David 230
Baker, Heidi 68, 100–103, 132
Baker, Rolland *see* Baker, Heidi
Banov, Georgian 101–102, 119–120
Barrett, David 79
Basham, Don 12, 40–42, 46, 263, 267, 269*ch*1*n*4
Baxter, Ern 33, 41–42, 158, 236, 263
Beck, Glenn 216
Belmont Church *see* Mansfield, Stephen; Servant Group International
Benefiel, John 96, 129–131
Bentley, Todd 45, 96, 134, 221–224, 240, 264
Bethel Church 74, 101, 105, 108–115, 119–120
Beverly, James 30, 63, 67
biblical counseling movement 104, 158, 257–258
Bickle, Mike 2, 17, 25, 96, 130, 133–142, 165, 178, 264, 270*ch*1*n*16, 271*ch*3*n*11, 271*ch*4*n*8; economic thought 137–138, 141–142, 153; Forerunners 109–111, 136–137; intercessory activism 98, 130, 137–141; international activities 215–216, 233, 239–240, 242, 250, 255–256; Kansas City Prophets 34, 60–69, 128
Bieber, Justin 246
Birch, Bob 199, 218–219
Bob Jones University 118
Bottari, Pablo 71, 107, 112–113
Boykin (USA Ret), Lt. Gen William C. 133–134, 270*ch*3*n*8

302 Index

Branham, William 6, 25–28, 33–39, 63, 170–171, 177, 179, 217–218, 264, 267, 269*ch1n8*
Brazil 107–109
Bright, Bill 97, 267
British Israelism 20–21, 25–26, 213–214
Brown, Candy Gunther 3, 13, 15–16, 18, 102, 107–109, 256
Browne, Rodney-Howard 67
Buddhism 76, 78, 121, 130, 156, 213
Bulgaria 101
Bush, George W. 95, 144, 211–212, 216, 248
Bush, Luis 79, 85–86, 131, 207
Business as Mission (BAM) movement 7, 162, 165–169, 230, 232, 261 Caballeros, Harold 197–199

Cabrera, Omar 71–73
Cain, Paul 62–68, 128, 172, 264
Cali, Colombia 74, 185
Call, The 95–96, 106, 109–110, 127, 130–131, 133–135, 174–178, 216, 221, 233, 270*ch3n9*, 272*ch6n9*
Campbell, Stacey *see* Campbell, Wes
Campbell, Wes 221, 223
Canada 4, 8, 124, 199–201, 217–224; *see also* Arnott, John; Latter Rain Revival; Toronto Blessing
Catch the Fire 100–101, 105, 120, 219; *see also* Arnott, John; Partners in Harvest (PIH)
Catholicism 9, 36–37, 116, 195, 224; Charismatic Renewal 39, 42, 261–262
cell church system 41, 43–45, 159–160, 250
cessationism 6–7, 22, 50, 58, 92, 145
Charisma magazine 133, 139–140, 214
Charismatic Renewal 10–11, 16–17, 19, 27, 29, 33–34, 37–38, 39–47, 90–91, 159, 235–239, 261–262
Cho, David Yonggi 41, 249–251
Chosa, James 194, 200–202
Christian Broadcasting Network (CBN) 46, 195, 214, 216
Christian Healing Certification Program (CHCP) 108–109; *see also* Global Awakening
Christian Identity 25, 214, 269*ch1n7*
Clark, DeAnn *see* Clark, Randy
Clark, Randy 15–16, 67–68, 106–112, 135; *see also* Global Awakening
Clarkson, Frederick 4, 160, 263, 272*Concn1*
classical Pentecostalism 10–11, 22, 24, 26, 28–29, 38, 40
Coalition on Revival (COR) 104, 158–161, 232
Coates, Gerald 237, 240–241, 272*ch6n12*
Confucianism 121
Congo, Democratic Republic of 103, 229, 232

contextualization 189–193, 201, 204–205, 209, 272*ch6n2*
Córdoba, Argentina 71
covering 5–6, 45–46, 115–116, 261
Croatia 109
Cry, The 221; *see also* The Call
Cunningham, Loren 97, 195, 267, 271*ch4n8*; *see also* Youth With a Mission (YWAM)
Daniels, Kimberly 2, 116

Dawson, John 71, 73–74, 80, 82–84, 130, 185, 200–201, 215, 270*ch2n6*
Day, Stockwell 221
Dedmon, Theresa 110–111
Deep Healing Ministries 80, 165–166
Deere, Jack 64, 66, 68
Deiros, Pablo 73
deliverance ministries 1, 3, 11–12, 37–40, 71, 74, 101, 107–109, 112–115, 119–128 *passim*, 140–141, 262–263
Demian, David Mohsen 219–220
Dobson, James 116, 145, 160–161
dominionism 7, 61, 72, 97, 98, 101–102, 110, 131–132, 143
Doner, Colonel 160, 271*ch4n4*, 271*ch4n6*, 271*ch4n9*
DuPlessis, David 33, 37
Dupont, Marc 68, 103

Eastern Orthodox Church 32, 116, 272*ch5n12*
Eberle, Harold 92
Eckhardt, John 92, 121
education 47, 56, 97, 146, 150, 158, 247, 252, 257–258, 267; NAR educational views 105–106, 116–120; schools of supernatural ministry 101, 107, 109, 119–120
El Shaddai Church 197–199
Eldred, Ken 154–157, 168–169, 230, 232, 256, 268, 271*ch4n2*, 271*ch4n3*, 271*ch4n11*
Elías, Jorge Serrano 198
Ellel Ministries 242, 245
Engle, Lou 14, 25, 69, 84–85, 95–96, 104–106, 127, 134–135, 158–159, 174–177, 216, 221, 233
Enlow, Johnny 97, 161, 267
Escobar, Samuel 72–73
Europe 79, 101
Exodus Cry 138–141; *Nefarious* (film) 140, 217

Fiji 75, 185, 252
Finto, Don 214–216
Fischer, Becky 1, 95
fivefold gospel 1, 6, 26, 28, 32–33, 40–41, 46, 65, 90, 111, 135, 144, 237
Flame of Love Project 13–15, 252–253, 257
Food for the Hungry (FFH) 162–164, 232

Forerunners 22, 25–26, 63–64, 109–111, 135–137, 142; *see also* Joel's Army
Forster, Roger 240–241
Fort Lauderdale Five 16, 33, 41–43, 46, 88, 91, 236, 240, 263; *see also* Basham, Don; Baxter, Ern; Mumford, Bob; Prince, Derek; shepherding; Simpson, Charles
40/70 Window 79–89
Frangipane, Francis 178, 214–215, 219
Fraser, Bob 142
Full Gospel Business Men's Fellowship International (FGBMFI) 34, 37–38
Fuller Seminary 7, 49–51, 58–59, 70, 73, 86–87, 157–169, 206, 209, 250, 272*ch*6*n*16; *see also* church growth; spiritual mapping
fundamentalism 9, 22–24, 35, 40, 60, 65, 103, 118, 153, 159, 169, 228, 257, 263–264 Generals International *see* Generals of Intercession

Generals of Intercession 79–80, 219
generational curses 2, 12, 38–39, 125, 165, 170–174, 227, 263; *see also* identificational repentance
Gingrich, Newt 130
Glasser, Arthur 70
Global Awakening 15–16, 68–69, 106–109, 119–120, 135
Global Celebration 101–102
Global Consultation on World Evangelization II (GCOWE II) 87, 251
Global Harvest Ministries 79, 86, 94
Global Legacy 68, 100
Global Medical Research Institute 16
God Loves Uganda (film) 64, 233
God TV 178, 216, 221–222
Goll, James 69, 84–85, 182, 199, 214–215
Gospel Outreach 194–196
Grant, George 211–213, 232
Great Wealth Transfer 7, 149–152, 169, 255–256, 263
Greaves, Stuart 137–138, 153, 156
Greenwood, Rebecca 123
Grimstead, Jay 159–161
Gruen Report *see* Gruen, Ernie
Gruen, Ernie 61, 65–66, 239–240, 242
Guatemala 8, 74, 132, 159, 185, 194–199, 254
Gumbel, Nicky 242–244, 261 Haggard, Ted 94–95

Hall, Franklin 27–28, 174–175, 264, 270*ch*3*n*9
Hamon, Bill 31, 34, 36, 81, 84–85, 89–92, 199, 269*ch*1*n*5; Mercy Ministries 101, 123–128; racial theology 170, 172, 182–184, 190, 272*ch*5*n*11
Harper, Michael 235

Harper, Stephen 220–221
Harvest Evangelism 71, 79, 226
Harvest International Ministries (HIM) 68, 103–106, 135
Harvest Rock Church (HRC) 103–105, 119–120
Hatfield, Kezia 140–141
Hawaii 132, 159
Hayford, Jack 215, 242
Hetland, Leif 107
Hiebert, Paul 52, 192–193, 257
Hillman, Os 142, 146, 150, 153, 230
Hillsong 128, 23, 246–248
Hinduism 25, 76, 121, 188–189, 206–207, 213
Holy Spirit Movement 225, 228
Holy Trinity Brompton (HTB) 241–242, 261; *see also* Alpha Course
homogenous unit principle 41, 47–48, 192, 202, 243–244, 250, 257, 262; *see* McGavran, Donald
homosexuality 62, 83, 98, 106, 109, 130, 158, 176–177, 199, 218, 254, 266; Africa 15, 18, 63–64, 95, 127–128, 227, 230–233; deliverance 121, 124, 127–128
Horrobin, Peter 108–109, 121–122, 238, 245
human trafficking 125, 130, 138–141, 217, 248; *see also* sexual abuse
Hussein, Saddam 207, 211 Iceland 100

Icthus Fellowship 240–241
identificational repentance 76, 184–186, 188, 215, 218–220, 263
Illuminati 130, 180–181
Indonesia 119
Insider Movement (IM) 162, 188–189, 191–193, 202–206, 213–217
intercessory activism 98, 130, 135, 137–141, 152
International Coalition of Apostles\International Coalition of Apostolic Leaders (ICA\ICAL) 7, 88, 115–129 *passim*, 197, 215–216, 223, 270*ch*1*n*18, 270*ch*3*n*3, 270*ch*3*n*4
International House of Prayer (IHOP) 63–64, 66–67, 69, 96, 98, 133–142, 264; economic thought 135, 138, 141–142, 152–153, 165; intercessory activism 130, 135, 152–153; international activities 215–217, 221, 233, 250–252, 255–256; *see also* Bickle, Mike; Forerunners; Kansas City Fellowship; Kansas City Prophets
International Society of Deliverance Ministers (ISDM) 120–123, 245
Intrater, Asher 215–216
Iraq 206–208, 210–213
Iris Ministries 15, 68, 100–103, 105, 119–120

Index

Irving, Edward 20, 269Intron1
Islam 14, 76, 106–107, 116, 121, 130, 133–134, 156, 193, 206, 229; insider movement 188, 193, 203–206; NAR African activities 103, 229; NAR Middle Eastern activities 78, 206–213, 217
Israel 196, 202, 213–217, 220, 249, 255–256
Jackson, Bill 32, 62–64, 264, 270ch1n14

Jacobs, Cindy 2, 96, 98, 105, 121, 131, 182; economic thought 98, 144, 153, 161; international activities 73–74, 86, 199, 208–209, 219, 221, 240; prayer networks 80, 127–130, 219; spiritual mapping\prayerwalking 73–74, 79–80, 86
Japan 25, 200–201
Jesus Camp 1, 69, 95
Jesus Culture 109–110; *see also* Forerunners
Joel's Army 22–23, 25–26, 32, 62–66, 110–111, 136–137, 222, 240
Johnson, Bill 2, 68, 100–102, 108–115, 223, 252–253, 270ch3n2
Johnson, Charles Neil 165–166, 261, 271ch4n11
Johnson, Frecia 166
Jones, Alex 180
Jones, Bob 62–64, 68, 172, 270ch1n14
Jones, Bryn 236–237
Joseph Company 141–142
Joyner, Rick 2, 96, 100, 155, 199, 206, 219, 222–223, 270ch3n7; Morningstar 133–134
Judaism 2, 14, 25, 182, 188, 193, 202, 206, 208, 213–217, 220, 249, 255–256; *see also* Israel; Messianic movement
Juster, Daniel 215–216, 249 Kansas City Fellowship 17, 32, 34, 60, 61–69, 110–111, 128, 134–135, 240; *see also* International House of Prayer (IHOP)

Kansas City Prophets 7, 30, 32, 60, 61–69, 134–135, 151, 172; United Kingdom activities 239–240, 242
Kaoma, Kaypa 4, 226–227
Kelley, John 115
Kenya 74, 96, 109, 168–169, 185, 271ch4n10
Keswick Movement 20, 177, 234–235
kingdom now theology 59–61, 98, 211–212
kingdom theology 59–61
Kony, Joseph 225, 228–230, 232, 272ch6n10
Koop, C. Everett 145, 158
Kraft, Charles 39, 50–60 *passim*, 69, 74, 89, 91–92, 106, 120, 209–210, 257, 262; anthropological assumptions 47–48, 51–57, 70, 188–193, 201–206; healing ministry 80, 113, 121, 123, 166
Kryskow, Faytene 221

Ku Klux Klan (KKK) *see* Alice Patterson
Kunsman, Cindy 177
Kurdistan 210–213, 215, 272ch6n7
Kuyper, Abraham 98, 145, 164
Kylstra, Betsy *see* Kylstra, Chester
Kylstra, Chester 101, 107–108, 123–127, 170–171, 185 La Danse 219–220

Ladd, George Eldon 59–61
Lakeland Revival 45, 96, 221–224
Lakwena, Alice 225, 228
Lambert, Steven 17, 44
Langa, Stephen 231–232
Latin America 50–51, 58, 70–74, 101, 103, 107–108, 194–199, 255; *see also* Argentina; Brazil
Latter Rain revival 4, 6–7, 21–34 *passim*, 36–38, 44, 46–47, 60–63, 65, 69, 73, 81, 90–91, 98, 111, 126, 136, 151–152, 171, 173–175, 177, 182–183, 215, 217–219, 222–223, 235, 237, 254, 263–264, 267, 269ch1n5
Lausanne Movement 57–58, 72, 74, 86
Layton, Douglas *see* Servant Group International
Lively, Scott 230–231
Lobert, Annie 139
Lord's Resistance Army (LRA) 228–230
Lorenzo, Eduardo 71, 73 MacArthur, John 6, 17

Madava, Henry 107
mainline Protestantism 8–10, 39–40, 49, 244, 261–262, 264; *see also* Anglicanism
Mainse, David 220
Malawi 100–101, 103
Manifest Sons of God teaching 25, 27, 29–32, 34, 63–64, 98, 126, 151, 171–174, 177, 183, 264, 271ch5n2
Manila Manifesto 72–74
Mansfield, Stephen 212, 215
Maori *see* New Zealand
March for Jesus 240–241, 272ch6n13
Marxism\socialism 130, 134, 144, 154–157, 197, 206
Mayans 195, 197–199, 254
McCloud, Sean 3, 256
McDonald, Marci 4, 223
McGavran, Donald 47–51, 57, 70, 117, 188, 192, 202–204, 238, 250, 257, 262, 265, 269ch1n11; *see also* homogenous unit principle
Méndez, Ana 73, 94–95, 121
Mercy Ministries 1, 74, 108, 123–128, 231, 247, 270ch3n6
Messianic Movement 188, 202, 213–217, 249, 255–256

Mexico 109, 159; *see also* Méndez, Ana
Microenterprise development 167–169
Millar, Sandy 240, 242
Miller, Darrow 162–165, 167–168, 206, 212, 226, 231–232, 271*ch*4*n*8, 271*ch*4*n*9
Montt, Efrain Ríos 159, 194–197
Mormonism 78, 121, 184
Morningstar Network 7, 93, 100, 133–134, 223
Mozambique 102–103
Mumford, Bob 33, 41–42, 46, 158–159, 240, 263, 269*ch*1*n*4
Mumford, John 66, 238
Murphy, Ed 71, 73, 270*ch*2*n*3
Museveni, Yoweri 225–229, 233–234
music 30, 56–57, 91, 109–111, 204, 246–248; *see also* arts
Myers, Calev 216–217
Myles, Francis 174 Nashville, Tennessee 74, 124, 211

National Governmental Prayer Alliance (NGPA) 80, 129
National Resistance Army (NRA) 225, 229
Native Americans\First Nations peoples 25, 75–76, 131, 190, 192–202 *passim*, 206, 208, 213, 215, 219, 272*ch*6*n*1, 272*ch*6*n*5
New Age movement 31, 76, 110, 122, 199
New Apostolic Roundtable 88
New Atheists 84–85
New World Order 2
New Zealand 124, 200, 246, 252, 270*ch*2*n*6
Nicaragua 109, 159, 255
Nida, Eugene 51, 55
Nolot, Benjamin 138–140
North, Gary 144, 158
Norway 100, 107, 109 Oak Initiative 133–134

Obama, Barack 2, 133, 174, 181–182
Okia, Joseph 227, 233–234
Olasky, Marvin 165, 232
Operation Ice Castle 2, 94–95, 208–209; *see also* "Queen of Heaven"
Otis, Jr., George 74–82, 89–90, 96–98, 106, 120, 130–131, 182–183, 189, 199, 227–229, 231–232, 263; historiography 80–82; Islam 206–207, 209, 212, 229, 231; spiritual mapping 74–80, 86, 127, 130, 265; *Transformations* films 74–75, 96–97, 131, 185–186, 197, 201, 219, 227–229, 231–232; transformationalism 98, 131, 133; *see also Transformations* films
Oyet, Julius 230 Padilla, René 72

Palau, Luis 70–71, 242
Palin, Sarah 5, 95–96, 272*ch*5*n*13
Parham, Charles 6–7, 21–26

Parker, Fran *see* Parker, Rob
Parker, Rob 220–221
Partners in Harvest (PIH) 68, 99–101, 105
Patterson, Alice 83, 132
Paulk, Earl 31–32, 98
Peacocke, Dennis 159–160, 197
people movements 47, 192, 202–203, 262
People of Destiny International (PDI) 104–105, 158–159
Perry, Rick 5, 96, 130–132
Pierce, Cal 114
Pierce, Chuck 86, 121, 128–129, 182, 223
Plan Resistencia 72–74, 79, 115, 197–198, 227–228
Plan Rosario 71
Political Research Associates 4, 233–234
Poloma, Margaret 3, 11, 13–14, 18, 68–69, 102, 108, 252–253
prayer networks 79–80, 86, 94, 96, 128–130, 132
Prince, Derek 12, 41–42, 212, 245, 263, 267, 269*ch*1*n*4
prophecy 1–2, 6–7, 22, 26, 28–30, 32, 36–37, 41, 54–55, 59–60, 80, 85, 88, 92, 111, 112, 118–119, 128, 133, 135–137, 149, 151, 153, 200, 221, 236–240, 266; *see also* Kansas City Prophets
Purvis, Eldon 34
Pytches, David 239–241 Quebec 219–220; *see also* Canada

"Queen of Heaven" 2, 79, 94–95, 208–210; *see also* Operation Ice Castle race 7–8, 13, 25, 30, 34, 36, 76, 85, 126–127, 169–202 *passim*, 271*ch*5,n1, 271*ch*5*n*2, 271*ch*5*n*3

racial reconciliation 76, 80, 132, *188–202* passim, 220, 271*ch*5*n*2, 272*ch*6*n*1
Randles, Bill 17, 24, 63, 269*ch*1*n*1
Reconstructionism 7, 97–98, 104, 120, 143–144, 146, 157–165, 212, 232, 239–240, 262 263, 266
Reformed movement 4, 6–7, 9, 20–21, 36, 98, 106, 111, 116, 120, 143–145, 157–166 *passim*, 177, 257, 266; *see also Reconstructionism*
restorationism 1, 6, 20, 22–24, 26, 29, 40–41, 54, 81, 84–85, 89–90, 126–127, 157, 177, 266–267; British Restorationism 235–242, 269*ch*1*n*1
Restoring the Foundations 1, 101, 108, 124–127, 170–171, 185
Revival Alliance 7, 15, 68–69, 71, 95–96, 99–115 *passim*, 119–120, 135, 218, 223, 270*ch*3*n*4
Right Wing Watch (RWW) 17–18, 161
Robertson, Pat 39, 43–44, 195–197
Robison, James 64–65

Index

Rushdoony, R.J. 98, 144, 158–161, 164, 239–240
Russia 25, 30–31, 135

Sandford, Frank 20–21
Sandford, John 108–109, 121
Sandford, Loren *see* John Sandford
Satanic Ritual Abuse (SRA) 108, 140–141, 270*ch*2*n*5
Scandanavia 25, 199
Schaeffer, Edith 158, 165
Schaeffer, Francis 111, 158, 162–164
seeker-sensitive church 10, 267
Sentinel Group 78, 86–87, 90, 228, 241; see also *Transformations* films
serpent seed doctrine 26, 35–36, 63, 171, 177–182, 267
Servant Group International 210–212
Seven Mountains Campaign 7, 96–98, 132–133, 141–142, 150, 195, 263, 267; Revival Alliance 101–102, 110–111
sexual abuse 82–83, 104–105, 108, 122–123, 125, 140–141, 189, 245, 248; *see also* human trafficking
Seymour, William James 6, 21
Shakarian, Demos 37–38
Sheets, Dutch 80, 84, 128, 130, 174
shepherding movement 5–7, 16–17, 26, 28–30, 33–34, 36, 38–47 *passim*, 65, 85, 88, 90–91, 104–105, 142, 144, 158–161, 197, 212, 235–240, 244, 263, 266–267, 269*ch*1*n*4
Shintoism 121, 200–201
Silk, Danny 111–112
Silvoso, Ed 106, 115, 120, 141–142, 174, 182–183, 219, 244; spiritual mapping 70–74; transformationalism 79, 98, 131–133, 147–148, 150–154, 156, 167–168, 226–227, 233–234, 268, 271*ch*4*n*1; Ugandan activities 226–227, 233–234; *see also* transformationalism
Simpson, Charles 40–42, 158, 263, 269*ch*1*n*4
Singapore 115
Sithole, Surpresa 102–103
Sjöberg, Kjell 199–200, 219
Skinner, Gary 128, 226, 231
Smith, Chuck 44
Smith, Ed 108, 141
soul ties 82, 108, 122–123, 125, 139–140, 210, 245; *see also* identificational repentance; sexual abuse
South Africa 103, 255
South Korea 41, 106, 119, 248–252, 272*ch*6*n*16
Southern Poverty Law Center (SPLC) 68, 212
Sovereign Grace Ministries 104–105, 158–159
sozo healing model 71, 74, 108, 112–115, 140, 141, 272*ch*6*n*14
Speaking in tongues 10, 11, 20–22, 24, 39–40, 58, 103, 243, 262, 265
spiritual DNA 7–8, 170–174, 177–184, 186, 216, 272*ch*5*n*10; Nazarite DNA 25, 175–178
spiritual mapping 3, 7, 12, 49, 51–54, 57, 69–87 *passim*, 89, 91, 96, 107, 127, 129–130, 146, 184–185, 189, 191, 193–194, 197–202, 206–212, 227–228, 241, 250–251, 262, 265, 267–268, 270*ch*2*n*2
Ssempa, Martin 232–233
Stearns, Robert 214
"Strange Fire" conference 6
Strategic level spiritual warfare (SLSW) 2, 12, 39, 59, 70–76, 85–87, 127–128, 194, 199, 207–208, 210, 218–220, 227, 240–241, 265, 267–268
Sweden 25, 199–200
Syncretism 190, 193, 201, 206, 213

Tabachnick, Rachel 2–4, 17, 129–131, 214–216, 269Pref*n*1, 269*ch*1*n*1, 270*ch*3*n*8, 272Concn1
Talk to Action 17, 98, 269Pref*n*1
Tanzania 103, 225
Taoism 121
Templeton Foundation 13–15, 252–253, 257; *see also* Brown, Candy Gunther; Poloma, Margaret
10/40 Window 79, 94–95, 105, 189, 207–208, 211
Theophostic Prayer Ministry (TPM) 108, 140–141
Tikkun International 215–216
Tippett, Alan 50, 52, 192–193, 202–203
Tomczak, Larry 104, 158–159
Toronto Blessing 7, 14, 52, 67–69, 95, 99–100, 103, 105, 107, 134–135, 218, 223, 241–242
transformationalism 7, 79, 96–98, 131–133, 145–153, 164–165, 167–168, 212, 226–227, 230–233, 255–257, 267–268, 271*ch*4*n*1
Transformations films 74–75, 96–97, 131–132, 185–186, 197, 201, 219, 227–228, 230–231
Truth Wins Out 4, 17, 272*ch*6*n*10
Turkey 25, 208–210
Twiss, Richard 190–193, 201–202, 272*ch*6*n*2
Uganda 8, 15, 18, 63–64, 73–74, 95, 127–128, 176, 185, 224–234 *passim*, 254–255
Uganda: An Unconventional War 154, 228–233
Ukraine 107
Unitarianism 121
United Kingdom 89, 100, 106, 230, 234–245
Verbo Church 195–196

Vineyard movement 14, 17, 32, 52, 58–61, 64–69, 99, 105, 134–135, 238, 240, 242, 244

Virgo, Terry 237, 240 Wagner Leadership Institute 106, 116–120, 125, 270*ch*3*n*4

Wagner, Doris 50, 120–123, 128, 166, 222–223
Wagner, Peter 2, 3, 7, 10–11, 14, 34, 39, 47, 54, 58–59, 94, 96, 123, 128–129, 130–131, 141, 172–174, 182–183, 201–203, 214, 222–223, 233–234, 239–240, 244, 251–252, 269*ch*1*n*5, 270*ch*1*n*12, 270*ch*3*n*3; church growth 47–51, 74, 80, 192, 262; economic views 145–152, 161, 256; educational views 56–57, 106, 115–120, 257–258; spiritual mapping 70–75, 79, 85–88, 90–91, 94–95, 130, 197–198, 201, 208–210, 240–241, 270*ch*2*n*2, 272*ch*6*n*13; transformationalism 97–98, 130–131, 145–152; views on apostolic networking 45–46, 85–86, 87–91, 105, 115–117, 133, 245–246, 264–265
Waldron, Peter 212, 232
Wallis, Arthur 235, 237
Wallnau, Lance 97–98, 146–147, 150, 161, 267
Warnock, George 27–28, 30–31, 33
Warren, Rick 232–233

Watchmen for the Nations 218–221
Watoto Ministries 127–128, 231–232
Watson, David 235, 238
Weiner, Bob 158–159
White, John 71, 73
Whitehead, John 145
Wicca 76, 265
Wilson, Bruce 4, 17, 129, 165, 270*ch*3*n*7, 271*ch*4*n*7, 272*ch*6*n*10
Wimber, John 7, 14, 39, 51–52, 57–61, 64–67, 89–90, 106–107, 135, 192, 222, 238–240, 243, 257, 264, 266
Winter, Ralph 50, 70, 159
Woodley, Randy 190, 193, 272*ch*6*n*2
Word of Faith movement 10, 13, 17, 31–32, 37, 112, 147, 151–152, 227, 247, 251–252, 266, 267–269 Yamamori, Ted 163–164, 206, 231–232; *see also* Food for the Hungry (FFH); Miller, Darrow

Y

oido Full Gospel Church 41, 250–251
Youth with a Mission (YWAM) 71, 97, 165, 195, 271*ch*4*n*8 Zambia *see* Myles, Francis

www.ingramcontent.com/pod-product-compliance
Ingram Content Group UK Ltd.
Pitfield, Milton Keynes, MK11 3LW, UK
UKHW041925140426
5217IPUK00014B/318